OXFORD STUDIES IN LANGUAGE AND LAW

Oxford Studies in Language and Law includes scholarly analyses and descriptions of language evidence in civil and criminal law cases as well as language issues arising in the area of statutes, statutory interpretation, courtroom discourse, jury instructions, and historical changes in legal language.

The Legal Language of Scottish Burghs: Standardization and Lexical Bundles (1380–1560)
Joanna Kopaczyk

"I'm Sorry for What I've Done": The Language of Courtroom Apologies
M. Catherine Gruber

Dueling Discourses: The Construction of Reality in Closing Arguments
Laura Felton Rosulek

Entextualizing Domestic Violence: Language Ideology and Violence Against Women in the Anglo-American Hearsay Principle
Jennifer Andrus

Speak English or What?: Codeswitching and Interpreter Use in New York City Small Claims Court
Philipp Sebastian Angermeyer

Law at Work: Studies in Legal Ethnomethods
Edited by Baudouin Dupret, Michael Lynch, and Tim Berard

Speaking of Language and Law: Conversations on the Work of Peter Tiersma
Edited by Lawrence M. Solan, Janet Ainsworth, and Roger W. Shuy

Confronting the Death Penalty: How Language Influences Jurors in Capital Cases
Robin Conley

Discursive Constructions of Consent in the Legal Process
Edited by Susan Ehrlich, Diana Eades and Janet Ainsworth

From Truth to Technique at Trial: A Discursive History of Advocacy Advice Texts
Philip Gaines

Discourse, Identity, and Social Change in the Marriage Equality Debates
Karen Tracy

Translating the Social World for Law: Linguistic Tools for a New Legal Realism
Edited by Elizabeth Mertz, William K. Ford, and Gregory Matoesian

Conceptions in the Code: How Metaphors Explain Legal Challenges in Digital Times
Stefan Larsson

Deceptive Ambiguity by Police and Prosecutors
Roger W. Shuy

Legal Integration and Language Diversity: Rethinking Translation in EU Lawmaking
C.J.W. Baaij

Legal Translation Outsourced
Juliette R. Scott

Shallow Equality and Symbolic Jurisprudence
Janny H.C. Leung

Strategic Indeterminacy in the Law
David Lanius

Strategic Indeterminacy in the Law

David Lanius

OXFORD
UNIVERSITY PRESS

OXFORD
UNIVERSITY PRESS

Oxford University Press is a department of the University of Oxford. It furthers
the University's objective of excellence in research, scholarship, and education
by publishing worldwide. Oxford is a registered trade mark of Oxford University
Press in the UK and certain other countries.

Published in the United States of America by Oxford University Press
198 Madison Avenue, New York, NY 10016, United States of America.

Library of Congress Cataloging-in-Publication Data
Names: Lanius, David, author.
Title: Strategic indeterminacy in the law / David Lanius.
Description: New York : Oxford University Press, 2019. |
Includes bibliographical references and index.
Identifiers: LCCN 2018060077 (print) | LCCN 2018060217 (ebook) |
ISBN 9780190923709 (updf) | ISBN 9780190923716 (epub) |
ISBN 9780190923723 (Online Content) |
ISBN 9780190923693 (cloth : alk. paper)
Subjects: LCSH: Law–Language. | Indeterminacy (Linguistics). |
Semantics (Law). Classification: LCC K213 (ebook) |
LCC K213 .L37 2019 (print) | DDC 340/.14–dc23
LC record available at https://lccn.loc.gov/2018060077

9 8 7 6 5 4 3 2 1

Printed by Sheridan Books, Inc., United States of America

For my daughter Anouk

"If parliament does not mean what it says it must say so."
—Lord Mildew in *Uncommon Law*, by A. P. Herbert (1977, 313)

CONTENTS

FIGURES AND TABLES

DEFINITIONS

D21 An utterance u is CONTEXTUALLY INDETERMINATE 58
in context c iff it is unclear what is communicated by
u due to unclarity of c.

D22 The LEGAL CONTENT of some utterance u is u's 91
contribution to the legal obligations that obtain in a
legal system at a given time.

D23 A legal utterance u is LEGALLY INDETERMINATE in 96
the context of legal case c iff u's legal content in c is
unclear to a competent and well-informed lawyer.

D24 A speaker S CONVERSATIONALLY IMPLICATES that 154
q by uttering u in context c iff (1) S observes
the relevant conversational maxims in c, (2) the
assumption that S meant that q is required to make
sense of S's uttering u in c given the conversational
maxims, and (3) S believes that S's audience can
recognize condition (2) and can recognize that S
knows that.

D25 A SIGNALING GAME is a 2-agent-2-turn-game with 171
incomplete information such that the better-informed
agent S (the sender) observes state $\omega \in \Omega$ and sends
message $m \in M$, while the less-informed agent R (the
receiver) observes message m and chooses action
$a \in A$.

D26 A contract C is INCOMPLETE if C does not unequiv- 263
ocally determine for every contingency the (legal)
rights and duties of the contracting parties.

CASES

PREFACE

When as a student of philosophy I first read Tim Williamson's ingenious book "Vagueness", I was fascinated by the philosophical problems of vagueness—the paradox of the heap, the occurrence of borderline cases, and the threat to the logical principle of bivalence. Soon, my attention was drawn to the more practical problems of vagueness in the law, which as a practice—regulating human conduct in society—seemed to most paradigmatically strive for precision and, at the same time, to be most relevantly affected by borderline cases and Sorites reasoning.

After pondering the depths of vagueness for a while, I turned to the (surprisingly widespread) idea that there must also be something positive and valuable about it—why else should vagueness be so pervasive in legal language? So I began writing this book with the goal to identify the functions of vague language in the law. In the process, however, I became increasingly convinced that it was rarely (if ever) vagueness that was doing the trick. Instead, other forms of indeterminacy, or even entirely different properties of language, had the functions that I (and many others) had mistakenly attributed to vagueness.

Now that the book is written, its main thesis has turned to almost the opposite of the hypothesis with which I started writing it. Realizing the errors in my thinking, I differentiated between vagueness and related phenomena and broadened the scope of my argumentation—giving an account of strategic *indeterminacy* in the law. I had to categorize forms of indeterminacy that have not been explicitly discussed before in the literature and to argue against the main tenet in the debate. Probably more than anyone else, I was (and still am a little bit) surprised by the result: I don't think (anymore) that vagueness has *any* relevant function in the law.

In the great adventure of writing this book, many friends and colleagues have accompanied me in one way or another. First and foremost I would like to thank my doctoral supervisor Geert Keil from Humboldt University Berlin for his reliability and exemplary, competent, and always heartfelt support. My supervisor Ralf Poscher from the University of Freiburg invariably had helpful answers to my sometimes not so clever questions and set me on the right track for the whole project. In addition, my supervisor Andrei Marmor from the University of Southern

California kindly and fruitfully contributed to ensuring that this book would take its final form. Thanks to the constructive criticism of Andrei Marmor, I was able to put Ralf Poscher's advice into practice to comprehensively differentiate the various forms of indeterminacy.

Sebastian Bramorski, Kees van Deemter, Alexander Dinges, Daniel Gruschke, Timothy Endicott, Allen Frances, Lukas Grasskamp, Gillian Hadfield, James Hampton, Rico Hauswald, Matthias Kiesselbach, Beate Krickel, Jönne Kriener, Manfred Krifka, Martin Metz, Manfred Pinkal, Dennis Patterson, Diana Raffman, Bettina Rentsch, Robert van Rooij, Alex Sarch, Benedikt Schauberer, Scott Soames, Roy Sorensen, Andree Weber, Tim Wihl, and Robert Williams have helped me in different but always invaluable ways. I am infinitely thankful for the loving and selfless support I have received from Kathrin Kazmaier over the years. And, I am indebted to my grandmother Edith Pauckner—in more ways than I could possibly explicate.

I would also like to thank the German Academic Scholarship Foundation, which has made this book possible with its generous support, and the Volkswagen Foundation for the research project "Dealing Reasonably with Blurred Boundaries," with which I was associated. Furthermore, I want to express my gratitude to Hrafn Asgeirsson and Larry Solan for their counsel and to several anonymous referees for their generous comments and criticisms. And, finally, I'd like to thank Oxford University Press for its wonderful editorial support—and, in particular, Hannah Doyle, Hallie Stebbins, and Richa Jobin.

Throughout this book, I have tried to avoid as far as possible the use of gender pronouns to refer to persons whose gender is irrelevant or unknown. Whenever I use them, I systematically alternate between the male and female pronouns in an attempt to avoid gender bias—using "she" for any first occurrence of an agent whose gender is unknown (in most cases, the sender of a message, speaker, judge, or contract offeror) and "he" for any subsequent occurrence of an agent whose gender is unknown (in most cases, the receiver of a message, listener, defendant, or contract offeree). I hope that by doing so I did not replicate gender stereotypes, and I sincerely apologize if I inadvertently did anyway.

INTRODUCTION

The US Constitution states that freedom of speech shall not be abridged, but it does not tell us what kind of speech is protected. The German Basic Law states that human dignity shall be inviolable, but it does not tell us what kind of behavior would violate it. There have consistently been complaints that such constitutional provisions say nothing by themselves. Why are they phrased so broadly?

Statutory law is also often criticized for being too vague or ambiguous. For instance, the US Sherman Antitrust Act was openly attacked for its unclarity. Agencies and courts had to determine step by step what "restraint of trade" means for the purposes of the act. More recently, the German *Temporary Science Employment Law (WissZeitVG)* has come under criticism for the same reasons, and courts will presumably need to determine in due course what terms such as "reasonable limitation" mean for the purposes of the law. Is there a reason for enacting such indeterminate statutes?

While courts normally resolve indeterminacy in constitutional and statutory law, they can be a source of it, too. The European Court of Justice is said to generally fail giving clear directions. Its decision on Internet privacy in 2014 was criticized for being too broad and vague. Most famously perhaps, the US Supreme Court decided in 1955 that public schools should be desegregated "with all deliberate speed." The indeterminacy of this verdict was (and still is) criticized by both proponents and opponents of racial segregation. Should court decisions not be more definite?

Not even private law contracts are free of indeterminacy. After the financial crisis of 2007/2008, mergers and acquisitions contracts increasingly contain indeterminate *material adverse change* clauses, allowing the contracting parties more easily to withdraw from the deal. Also, insurance contracts, in particular, tend to be highly unspecific in what contingencies are excluded from coverage. Due to indeterminacy, it is sometimes even debatable whether a (legally enforceable) contract has been formed in the first place.

The pervasive indeterminacy in our legal texts cannot simply be the result of bad drafting or necessity. Laws, verdicts, and contracts are systematically and consistently indeterminate. There must be a reason why indeterminate legal terms and sweeping clauses have survived decades and centuries of legal practice. Do legislators, judges, and contract drafters use indeterminacy strategically for some positive function?

Legal theorists and practitioners seem to have a love-hate relationship with indeterminacy. On one hand, they hate indeterminacy because it threatens the *rule of law* and their very profession. It seems that only self-interested politicians, judges, and lawyers use indeterminate language to deceive honest citizens. As George Orwell (1946/1968, 137) famously said, the "great enemy of clear language is insincerity." According to this view, unclarity in the law results from the malevolence of some people, whose self-interest and hunger for power overshadow legal and political ideals—eroding the very core of the law. Indeterminacy jeopardizes the principle of legal certainty and the separation of powers by obstructing fair notice and giving unfettered discretion.

On the other hand, legal theorists and practitioners love indeterminacy. Legal language must be flexible and adjustable, they argue. Law cannot be rigid. It must adapt to the circumstances of individual cases and to changing social environments.[1] As George C. Christie (1964, 911) puts it, it gives law its "much needed flexibility."

Excessive determinacy, some claim, would dehumanize the law. As Arthur Kaufmann maintains, an adjudicating computer, which "is programmed *per saecula saeculorum* only once, would install fear into even the most imperturbable positivist."[2] They conclude that indeterminacy is required to encompass the various needs of the people and ensure the equity of the law. According to Richard B. Saphire (1978, 112), it allows one to build "play into the joints" and mend the content of the law. Indeterminacy may have undesirable consequences, but it is necessary for a functioning and equitable legal system. Benjamin N. Cardozo (1924, 68) says: "The curse of this fluidity, of an ever shifting approximation, is one that law must bear, or other curses yet more dreadful will be invited in exchange."

Unfortunately, nobody has ever made really explicit what this "flexibility" or "fluidity" of the law consists of. Where does it come from and why is it both curse and praise? While many have claimed that indeterminacy facilitates flexibility and can be used strategically, few have even recognized that there are more forms of

---

[1] As Chief Justice John Marshall famously phrases it in *McCulloch v. Maryland*, 17 U.S. 316, 415 (1819), with respect to the Constitution, it is "intended to endure for ages to come, and consequently, to be adapted to the various crises of human affairs."

[2] Kaufmann (1973, 371) literally writes that an adjudicating computer, which "nur ein einziges Mal per saecula saeculorum programmiert wird, [würde] auch den unerschütterlichsten Positivisten das Gruseln lehren."

indeterminacy than vagueness and ambiguity. This book is a contribution to solving the puzzle about the "flexibility" of legal language.

It is not a typical work in the philosophy of language or the philosophy of law, however. I do not argue for any particular account of indeterminacy or how we should deal with hard cases in the law. I explicitly do not discuss theories of vagueness and how they might successfully be applied to the legal domain. Instead, I use philosophical tools to analyze strategic language behavior in the law. In doing so, I hope to illuminate both legal theory, by providing it with sharpened conceptual distinctions, and the philosophical debate, by applying it to and testing it against the legal domain.

Legal language is particularly interesting for a philosophical analysis of strategic indeterminacy. Legal texts concern socially relevant issues, address heterogeneous audiences, and are applied in unforeseen circumstances. Legal decisions must be made due to the prohibition of denial of justice; they must be justified, documented, and published; and they usually precipitate an observable reaction. Due to conflicting interests and beliefs as well as the relevance of legal decisions, legal texts are generally phrased carefully. And, most importantly, indeterminacy is ubiquitous in the law—even despite the principles of the *rule of law* and the common perception that the "fluidity" of legal language is a curse.

In this book I give answers to three related questions:

(1) What are the sources of indeterminacy in the law?
(2) Which effects does indeterminacy have in the law?
(3) How can we strategically use indeterminacy in the law?

I first analyze in chapter 1 the various forms of linguistic indeterminacy from the perspective of the philosophy of language. After that, I demonstrate in chapter 2 that the importance of legal content changes the role that linguistic indeterminacy can play in the law. Based on the analysis in chapter 1 and the argument in chapter 2, I examine the relevance of the various forms of indeterminacy for the law in chapter 3. This examination provides an answer to both question (1) and question (2).

I then argue in chapter 4 that some forms of indeterminacy can be strategically used under certain circumstances, while others are less valuable. Finally, I show at full length in chapter 5 how the various forms of indeterminacy can be used specifically in laws, verdicts, and contracts. In combination, chapters 4 and 5 provide an answer to question (3).

1

Forms of Indeterminacy

In the infamous case *Papachristou v. City of Jacksonville* the Supreme Court of the United States struck down an ordinance of the Jacksonville vagrancy law that punished

> rogues and vagabonds, or dissolute persons who go about begging, common gamblers, persons who use juggling, or unlawful games or plays, common drunkards, common night walkers, ... persons wandering or strolling around from place to place without any lawful purpose or object, habitual loafers, disorderly persons.[1]

The Court unanimously found the ordinance *void for vagueness* because, as Justice William O. Douglas argued, it did not give fair notice to citizens and encouraged arbitrary and discriminatory arrests and convictions. The ordinance is an extreme example of indeterminacy. The elements of the crime are stated in a language so broad and widely interpretable that one can easily imagine circumstances under which the most innocuous and faultless behavior is punishable. What is it about the language of the ordinance that frustrates fair notice and encourages arbitrary law enforcement?

As we will see, the language of the ordinance is indeterminate in a number of different ways. The Justices of the Supreme Court did analyze its language, but they were not interested in the source of the ordinance's unclarity and did not differentiate between the different forms of its indeterminacy. While it is commonplace knowledge that lawyers need a good understanding of how language works, and legal language in particular, the specific effects of indeterminacy

---

[1] *Papachristou v. City of Jacksonville*, 405 U.S. 156 (1972); Jacksonville Ordinance Code § 26–57, cited in Ribeiro (2004, 78).

are, as I argue, systematically overlooked. Accordingly, the consequences of the ordinance on society—its particular way of guiding the citizens' and law enforcers' behavior—remains partly in the dark. Although the Court gave a sophisticated argument why the perceived effects of the ordinance were constitutionally undesirable, the Justices were rather unclear about how it might have caused these effects. Was it the generality and broadness of terms like "rogues and vagabonds" with which vagrancy is defined? Or was it the possibility that polysemous terms like "common drunkards" can be understood in different ways? Maybe it was the vagueness of terms like "disorderly persons," which does not clearly demarcate lawful from unlawful conduct; or were they pragmatic or even completely non-linguistic factors that brought about the unclarity, and ultimately the unconstitutionality, of the ordinance?

Neither in law nor in ordinary language do we usually differentiate between these different forms of indeterminacy. The terms "vague," "indefinite," "indeterminate," "ambiguous," "broad," and "unspecific" are almost synonymously used in everyday speech and even in many academic discussions. Few scholars pay attention to the differences between the various forms of indeterminacy. All too often, even linguists and philosophers lump them together and fail to distinguish semantic vagueness from polysemy, open texture, multi-dimensionality, or generality.

Surely, the Supreme Court cannot be expected to do in a single decision what philosophers and linguists have neglected to achieve in decades of research. However, in many legal decisions, indeterminacy is a decisive issue, and disagreement between judges is very often not simply due to political differences, but confusion about language and different opinions on how to understand and interpret it. Moreover, legal decisions impact on people's lives, and often quite drastically so.

Being an actual and socially pressing issue, linguistic indeterminacy has nevertheless been a minor topic in jurisprudence. Particularly, German legal scholars traditionally reject the notion of indeterminacy as something already resolved and overcome by legal theory. This professional disregard intensifies the widespread misunderstanding and confusion about indeterminacy. But, as John L. Austin (1957, 7) puts it, "words are our tools, and, as a minimum, we should use clean tools: we should know what we mean and what we do not."

We thus need an adequate conceptual toolbox to explain how indeterminacy is used in the law. A comprehensive account of (legal) indeterminacy is called for.[2]

---

[2] The account of indeterminacy I am going to give will neither be about semantic underdetermination nor radical legal indeterminacy. Underdetermination of lexical meaning is a practical issue only insofar as it actually leads to unclarity. This is rarely the case, however, because the context resolves most cases

In the following sections, I will give an analysis of the concept of linguistic indeterminacy. The analysis consists of a general definition of indeterminacy and a specification of its various forms. It lays the ground for the discussion of the use of indeterminacy in law in the subsequent chapters. First, I will provide a definition of indeterminacy based on the notion of unclarity with respect both to expressions and utterances (in section 1.1). Second, we will examine ambiguity as a form of indeterminacy, differentiating between lexical and syntactic ambiguity as well as, most notably, polysemy (in section 1.2). Third, it is necessary to clarify the notion of vagueness that the debate focuses on, which I call "semantic" vagueness (in section 1.3). There are three basic forms of semantic vagueness, namely, gradual vagueness, multi-dimensional vagueness, and open texture. Fourth, semantic vagueness must be distinguished from conversational vagueness, which typically results from generality (section 1.4).

A neglected but nonetheless important form of indeterminacy is pragmatic indeterminacy (section 1.5). There are at least four ways in which an utterance can be pragmatically indeterminate. It can be indeterminate with respect to what it implicates (implicature indeterminacy), what illocutionary force it has (speech act ambiguity), what it presupposes (presupposition indeterminacy), and what it implicites (impliciture indeterminacy). The most important form of impliciture indeterminacy is, finally, standard-relativity, which reveals the broader problem of context determination (section 1.6). After having analyzed indeterminacy in this way, I will clarify the relation between linguistic and legal content (in chapter 2) before we turn to an examination of the role of the various forms of indeterminacy in the law (in chapter 3).

1.1 Linguistic Indeterminacy and Unclarity

When we talk about indeterminacy of language, it seems natural to treat words or other expressions with semantic content as those linguistic entities that can be indeterminate in one way or other. This is the traditional view represented by the classical discussions of vagueness, ambiguity, and the like.

Expressions are words, sentences, or other linguistic entities that can be meaningfully used in oral or written utterances. Examples are single words like "heap,"

---

of semantic underdetermination. Even those who try to derive some form of radical indeterminacy from Wittgenstein's thoughts on rule-following (Wittgenstein, 1953/2009, §201) or Quine's under-determinacy thesis (Quine, 1960, 23–27) do allow for pragmatic and social constraints. The view that language is radically indeterminate only makes sense if we understand radical indeterminacy as radical semantic underdetermination. Then, however, the view is rather uncontroversial. Accordingly, I will assume a fairly commonsensical understanding of linguistic meaning in the sense that indeterminacy is (albeit mostly negatively connoted) part of our overall largely efficient language behavior. In other words, our use of indeterminate terms is embedded in a predominantly successful linguistic practice. See also section 2.3.4.

definite descriptions like "the tallest woman in California," predicate constructions like "is green," or sentences like "Human dignity shall be inviolable."[3] They certainly have meaning independently of the context in which they are used. This lexical meaning is described in dictionaries, and it is essential to the understanding and production of utterances.

Utterances, as acts of uttering expressions, are to be distinguished from expressions being uttered. Expressions have lexical, grammatical, and semantic properties, but only utterances have pragmatic ones. Only utterances have causal effects on us. Vague or ambiguous expressions are considered to be indeterminate because utterances can be unclear or reasonably understood in different ways due to the expressions' vagueness or ambiguity. Single expressions can thus be indeterminate, but only in virtue of being used in an utterance. In other words, the determinacy or indeterminacy of an expression depends on its use in an utterance.

In most cases of communication, we are not interested in the lexical meaning of an expression. We use it to determine what the speaker means by a particular utterance. Accordingly, we need to distinguish two notions of meaning. The *lexical meaning* is what an expression means independently of the context of utterance, while the *utterer's meaning* is what a speaker means in a particular situation when uttering an expression.[4] The latter is the one we are normally interested in when having a conversation. The utterer communicates the utterer's meaning by attaching content to the utterance.

There are several kinds of content that can be attached to an utterance. The *literal content* is what the utterance (literally) says or simply what is said.[5] It is what a competent speaker would assume an utterance to mean, knowing all relevant contextual background information. The literal content is thus derived from literal meaning, grammatical rules, and context of utterance alone.[6] There can be differences between what a speaker means by some utterance and what is (literally) said by it. We can criticize the speaker when the utterer's meaning and literal content diverge, for instance, when she misspoke or misunderstood the context.[7]

---

[3] Probably even grammatical expressions such as "because" or "and" can be reasonably understood in different ways and may thus be indeterminate. Since the focus of this book is the indeterminacy of utterances, the question of whether only content expressions (in contrast to grammatical ones) can be indeterminate need not be settled.

[4] See Grice (1968, 225–229).

[5] Compare Recanati (2001) on the notion of what is said. Although there are many differences between the philosophical accounts of what is said, the claims in this book about literal content should be largely uncontroversial.

[6] Context is here to be understood as *narrow context*, which is limited to basic facts about the utterance such as speaker, space, and time.

[7] As noted in the *Preface*, I have tried to avoid as far as possible the use of gender pronouns to refer to persons whose gender is irrelevant or unknown. Whenever I use them, I systematically alternate between

Normally we are even more interested in what is communicated than in what is said by an utterance. This *communicative content* can also be different from literal content.[8] Utterances are made in a social setting in which not only grammatical and semantic rules but also pragmatic maxims hold.[9] Consider the following example (E):

(E1) "You have to ask a doctor or a lawyer or someone like that."

What (E1) (in most contexts) says is merely that the hearer should ask someone like a doctor or lawyer. However, the utterer's meaning cannot always be identified with literal content. We often do not say directly what we mean, as this would be impolite or violate some other (social) convention.

If the speaker succeeds in articulating her (illocutionary) intentions, the utterer's meaning can be identified with communicative content. Speakers might communicate by (E1) that she does not want to be bothered with any questions. This would be the *implicated content* of her utterance. She would conversationally implicate that she does not want to be asked herself in addition to the literal content of her utterance. Because implicatures are ubiquitous in everyday conversations, most of them come so naturally to us that we process them completely unconsciously.[10]

Sometimes—in the extreme case of irony—what is communicated is the opposite of what is said. In this case, implicated content substitutes for literal content. The speaker might communicate that the hearer should never ask doctors or lawyers about a certain topic. Sometimes what is communicated is very similar to what is said. In that case, one speaks of *implicited content*. The speaker might, for example, communicate that the hearer should ask a doctor or lawyer in town.[11]

Figure 1 gives a general picture of these kinds of meaning and content.[12] There are four basic kinds of content, namely, what is said, what is implicated, what is

---

the male and female pronouns in an attempt to avoid gender bias—using "she" for any first occurrence of an agent whose gender is unknown (in most cases, the sender of a message, speaker, judge, or contract offeror) and "he" for any subsequent occurrence of an agent whose gender is unknown (in most cases, the receiver of a message, listener, defendant, or contract offeree). I hope that by doing so I did not replicate gender stereotypes, and I sincerely apologize if I inadvertently did anyway.

[8] Compare Saul (2002) on how speaker meaning, what is said, and what is implicated can fall apart.

[9] Compare Grice (1989a).

[10] In the famous example by Grice (1989b), the answer to the question "Do you know where I can get some gas?" is "There is a gas station around the corner." It implicates but does not say that the gas station is open and sells gas. This inference comes so naturally to us that we do not even notice that what is said is actually much less informative than what is implicated. It comes, in fact, so naturally that people cannot ignore implicatures even if they are asked to do so. See, for instance, the classical study by Glucksberg et al. (1982).

[11] Compare Bach (1994). See also our discussion of impliciture indeterminacy in section 1.5.

[12] This overview is inspired by Recanati (1989).

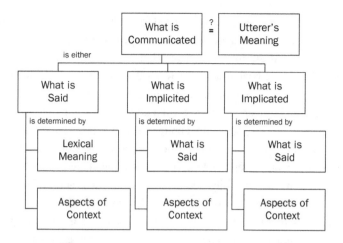

FIGURE 1 **Meaning and Content**

implicited, and what is communicated. What is said consists of the lexical meaning of the expressions used in the utterance and some minimal contextual information. The speaker can implicate something in addition to or in substitution of what is said, using further information from context. What is communicated can thus be what is said, what is implicated, or both. Additionally, there is the possibility that what is communicated is merely implicited.

Although there is some disagreement about the notion of communicative content, most philosophers of language take communicative content to be determined by the inferences that a competent and informed speaker is warranted in making about the utterance's intended content.[13] Thus, it may be identical to the utterer's meaning (in the case of communicative success), but it may also differ (e.g., in the case of malapropism). An utterance is indeterminate only if communicative content is unclear. Communicative content can be unclear either on the level of what is said, what is implicited, or what is implicated, or due to a discrepancy between utterer's meaning and communicative content.

The Jacksonville vagrancy ordinance is indeterminate partly because it is unclear which kind of behavior is ruled unlawful by it. There are different understandings of what the expressions "rogues and vagabonds" or "disorderly persons" in the context of the ordinance mean. It is unclear what is said. Nobody, not even the best trained lawyers in US constitutional law and Florida state law, could have

---

[13] A noteworthy exception is Neale (2005), who argues that communicative content is simply the content intended by the speaker. See also section 2.4.1 for a discussion of different notions of linguistic content with respect to the law.

known that one can be arrested and convicted for such a trifle as waiting around in a car near a used-car lot. This is precisely what happened in *Papachristou*. The police officers who detained the four defendants claimed that the arrest had no relation to their racially mixed background but was solely due to the committed offense of "prowling by auto." The ordinance was indeterminate in what it communicated both to citizens and officers. Moreover, even after the first conviction, it remained unclear whether the ordinance really applied to such a case. This was only finally decided by the Supreme Court. But how does the Supreme Court decide such hard cases? How does it understand and interpret indeterminate legal texts?

These questions will be fully addressed in chapters 2 and 3. First, we need to identify the source of the ordinance's indeterminacy. One way to explicate indeterminacy is to say that an indeterminate utterance is one that is unclear because of the ambiguity, vagueness, generality, etc. of the expressions used in it. Something like this is implicitly assumed by most participants in the debate on vagueness in law. However, such an explication is not particularly useful because it does not explain what the various forms of indeterminacy have in common. I will, in contrast, try to give a comprehensive definition of indeterminacy by linking it to the concept of unclarity in this section.

Neither philosophers, psychologists, nor linguists have spilled a lot of ink over the concept of unclarity. In the philosophical debate on vagueness, unclarity is commonly seen as a basic concept that does not demand explanation.[14] It is also fundamental to the game theoretic concept of *uncertainty*, which will be discussed in chapter 4. My basic assumption is that unclarity is the constitutive effect of indeterminacy.

In some conversations, it remains unclear to the hearer what the speaker wanted to tell her or what she should do when following the speaker's advice. A natural reaction to such an utterance is to ask:

(E2) "What do you mean by this?"

Of course, whether an utterance is unclear or not depends entirely on the context in which it was made. In fact, an utterance is only clear or unclear in a particular context and to somebody. We can, for instance, imagine a context in which (E1) is completely clear to the person addressed because there is enough common knowledge between the speaker and hearer such that both know the utterance is simply meant as a request to not ask the speaker herself.[15] But this is not always

---

[14] See, for instance, Williamson (1994), Égré and Bonnay (2010), or Bobzien (2010).

[15] In section 1.5 on pragmatic indeterminacy we will see that there can be also unclarity with respect to what kind of speech act was made. Also, (E1) is a case of pragmatic vagueness, which will be discussed in section 1.4 in some detail.

the case. Sometimes an utterance such as (E1) results in hesitation, (the expression of) doubt, further queries or questions, disagreement, or confusion.

Unclarity of an utterance seems, at first glance, to entail that one does not quite know what is communicated. This ignorance can, of course, be caused by shortcomings of one's cognitive capacities; by limited access to the utterance or its context; or by lack of linguistic competence. However, we can also be ignorant because of the utterance itself—because of what it says, implicates, or implicates. Unclarity is closely connected to the question of what knowledge is required to understand an utterance. This includes knowledge about the lexical meaning of the expressions used, about the context of the utterance, about pragmatic conventions, and about general facts of the world. If some state of affairs is unclear to you, you lack (exact) beliefs or knowledge about it.

An utterance is thus unclear if it causes particular cognitive states such as, for example, confusion. At the same time, it fails to create certain cognitive states that one would usually be expected to have when hearing some utterance, such as beliefs about the speaker's intentions or about what is said. The unclarity of an utterance can be due to ignorance and thus be identified with either *epistemic uncertainty* or *risk* as used in game theory.[16] An indeterminate utterance has the effect that one does not quite know its content.

While unclarity is an epistemic or psychological phenomenon, indeterminacy, in contrast, is a primarily linguistic one. Thus, we might tentatively say that an utterance is indeterminate in some context if it is unclear to somebody in that context, while this unclarity does not arise from any ignorance of the facts. In other words, an utterance is indeterminate if it is unclear to a well-informed person who knows everything about the relevant contextual facts.

However, the person might not be proficient in the language in which the utterance is made or she might be cognitively impaired. The indeterminacy of an utterance does not simply depend on the cognitive state of some speaker or other. That is why the unclarity of utterances must be relative to a competent language user.[17] Traditionally, a competent language user is considered to be a person who knows the

> language perfectly and is unaffected by such grammatically irrelevant conditions as memory limitations, distractions, shifts of attention and interest, and errors (random or characteristic) in applying his knowledge of this language. (Chomsky, 1965, 3)

---

[16] I will spell out the game theoretic understanding of uncertainty and risk in the discussion of indeterminacy in signaling games in section 4.5.

[17] An utterance can be unclear not only to individuals but also when competent speakers disagree about what is communicated and there is no straightforward way to resolve the disagreement. The language community as a whole might be unclear about the truth or felicity of an utterance, and this is possible even if each individual is free of psychological or epistemic uncertainty.

This idealized notion of linguistic competence might seem problematic, but it ensures that the unclarity of the utterance is not caused by insufficient competence in language or cognitive limitations. It is irrelevant for present purposes what precisely this competence consists of or how we can recognize it. All we need is some form of convergent language behavior, that is, some form of convention in David Lewis's sense.[18]

Based on these considerations, let us now define (D) indeterminacy such that:

(D1) An utterance *u* is (linguistically) INDETERMINATE in context *c* iff it is unclear to a competent and well-informed language user what is communicated by *u* in *c*.

This definition of indeterminacy of utterances allows us to derivatively ascribe indeterminacy also to individual linguistic expressions:

(D2) An expression *e* is (potentially) INDETERMINATE iff there possibly is an utterance *u* such that *u* is indeterminate in some context *c* because of *e*.

According to this definition, virtually all natural language expressions are indeterminate. This is because expressions are generally called ambiguous or vague if they just possibly lead to unclarity. An utterance containing an ambiguous or vague expression does not need to be indeterminate. We thus have to distinguish between potential and actual indeterminacy. Definition (D2) refers to potential indeterminacy. The notion of an expression's indeterminacy that is more interesting for our purposes is the following one:

(D3) An expression *e* is ACTUALLY INDETERMINATE in context *c* iff *e* is in fact used in an utterance *u* such that *u* is indeterminate in *c* because of *e*.

Expressions can thus be potentially or actually indeterminate. They are only actually indeterminate if they in fact result in an utterance's being indeterminate. In contrast, an utterance's indeterminacy is by the very nature of utterances always relative to some context. Vagueness and ambiguity are, hence, *forms* of (potential) indeterminacy and *sources* of actual indeterminacy.[19]

The (communicative) content of an utterance is determined by semantic and pragmatic factors. What is communicated can be (literally) said or pragmatically conveyed (e.g., implicited or implicated). Based on these kinds of content, we can distinguish between semantic and pragmatic indeterminacy:

---

[18] See Lewis (1969).

[19] Compare the definition by Pinkal (1995, 15) of "semantic indefiniteness," which addresses actual indeterminacy: "A sentence is semantically indefinite if and only if in certain situations, despite sufficient knowledge of the relevant facts, neither 'true' nor 'false' can be clearly assigned as its truth value." Since Pinkal is concerned only with ambiguity and vagueness in declarative sentences, his definition is too narrow for our purposes.

(D4)   An utterance *u* is SEMANTICALLY INDETERMINATE if it is unclear to a competent language user what is said by *u* in some context *c*.[20]

(D5)   An utterance *u* is PRAGMATICALLY INDETERMINATE if it is unclear to a competent language user what is pragmatically conveyed by *u* in some context *c*.[21]

Semantic indeterminacy includes unclarity due to an expression's ambiguity or vagueness, while pragmatic indeterminacy comprises unclarity on the level of implicatures, presuppositions, implicitures, and illocutionary force.[22]

Discussions of indeterminacy in law focus on semantic indeterminacy. At best, scholars draw a distinction between vagueness, ambiguity, and generality.[23] These phenomena are prominently discussed in both the philosophical and linguistic literature. However, the trichotomy of vagueness, ambiguity, and generality is misleading for two reasons. First, if we are concerned with actual cases in the law, we should not focus on expressions but utterances because only utterances, which are located in time and space, have effects on other people. Second, there are forms of indeterminacy on the level of communicative content that are missed if we confine ourselves to semantic indeterminacy. As I will argue, pragmatic indeterminacy is highly relevant to actual conversation, including the use of legal language.

In the following sections, I will thus differentiate between ambiguity and semantic vagueness, on one hand, and conversational vagueness and pragmatic indeterminacy on the other hand. It should be noted that this taxonomy of indeterminacy is anything but exhaustive. I discuss those forms of indeterminacy that either are continuously being discussed in the literature or that most frequently lead to actual indeterminacy in the law.

1.2 Ambiguity

Utterances can be misunderstood or remain unclear for many reasons. A very prominent source of unclarity is ambiguity. As Victor Raskin (1984) points out,

---

[20] There might be rare cases in which it is clear to a competent language user what is communicated, even though it is unclear to her what is said. Normally, however, grasping the literal content is a prerequisite for grasping the communicative one, even when they differ or contradict each other.

[21] In the literature there is no theoretical agreement about whether one should strictly differentiate between semantics and pragmatics and, if so, where to draw the line. This is an important issue. However, for my account of indeterminacy, it suffices that we can roughly differentiate between what is said and what is merely pragmatically conveyed, and that there are clear cases of both kinds of content.

[22] See sections 1.2 and 1.3 for a discussion of ambiguity and vagueness and sections 1.5 and 1.6 for pragmatic indeterminacy and the context determination respectively.

[23] See, for instance, Poscher (2012).

the capability of ambiguous terms to create misunderstandings is exploited in jokes such as the following:

(E3) "One morning I shot an elephant in my pajamas. How he got into my pajamas I'll never know."

(E4) "How do you make a turtle fast? Take away his food."

In (E4), the term "fast" is ambiguous, since it can mean *quick* (which is primed by the expression "turtle") or *to abstain from food* (which is the only viable understanding in the light of the second sentence).

In (E3) the phrase "I shot an elephant in my pajamas" is ambiguous because the expression "in my pajamas" could modify either "I shot" (which is the more natural assumption) or "an elephant" (which must be the correct understanding once the second sentence is uttered). In general, an ambiguous expression can reasonably be understood in two or more different ways because of its syntactical or semantic properties.

Even though many utterances contain ambiguous expressions, they are not necessarily indeterminate. Ambiguity and unclarity are logically independent. Context can fail or succeed to disambiguate an ambiguous expression. Only if it fails to do so, the utterance is indeterminate.

Context is usually sufficiently clear, and we rarely consider other potential meanings of an ambiguous expression. For instance, when we read the joke in (E4), we do not think for a moment of the expression "fast" meaning *firmly fixed*—as in the sentence "The roots are fast in the ground." Even if there is no explicit context, there are always background assumptions about the nature of the world that guide our understanding of what is said. The jokes are funny precisely because the added context disambiguates the ambiguous expression in an unexpected way.

A third form of ambiguity can be illustrated by the term "make" in (E4). It can mean *to cause to be in a certain way*, as it is understood in the example; but, related to that, it can also mean *to produce*, *to prepare*, or *to compose*. There are, thus, three primary forms of ambiguity. The jokes in (E3) and (E4) exemplify syntactic and lexical ambiguity, respectively, while the term "make" is an example of polysemy.

1.2.1 SYNTACTIC AMBIGUITY

Not only jokes, but also many utterances in everyday conversations are ambiguous because they are made up of expressions whose logical or grammatical structure is unclear:

(D6)   An expression *e* is SYNTACTICALLY AMBIGUOUS iff *e* has two or more possible logical structures.[24]

Note that syntactically ambiguous expressions, according to this definition, are only potentially indeterminate. Only used in an utterance in which the context does not disambiguate, the expression is also actually indeterminate according to (D3). Probably the most famous example for a syntactic ambiguity is the sentence "Flying planes can be dangerous," mentioned by Chomsky (1965, 21). The sentence is syntactically ambiguous because it is unclear whether it says that it can be dangerous to fly planes or whether planes that are flying can be dangerous. The logical structure of the sentence allows for two different interpretations of what is said.

Some referential ambiguities can be seen as a subclass of syntactic ambiguities:

(E5)   "John waved to Peter. He smiled."

The pronoun "he" can refer to either John or Peter; and without further contextual information, we simply do not know what is said due to the ambiguity of the utterance.[25]

There are also non-syntactic forms of referential ambiguity, since the act of reference can be unclear too. If someone says "She did it" while pointing to a group of women, it is unclarity in the ostension that makes the utterance indeterminate. Again, the context is not sufficiently clear to provide for one salient interpretation. Although this is generally regarded to be a kind of ambiguity, such utterances are indeterminate ultimately due to underdetermination of the context.[26]

Another subclass of syntactic ambiguities are elliptical utterances such as "I love you, too", or "John loves his mother and Fred does, too."[27] There are several potential candidates for completing the ellipsis. "I love you, too" (L) can mean either:

(L1)   "I love you (just like you love me)."
(L2)   "I love you (just like someone else does)."
(L3)   "I love you (and I love someone else)."
(L4)   "I love you (as well as liking you)."

It is feasible (and sometimes more reasonable) to treat such cases as instances of pragmatic indeterminacy. More precisely, (L1) to (L4) would count as instances of

---

[24] Syntactic ambiguity is sometimes also called "amphiboly."

[25] Compare Pinkal (1995, 69–70).

[26] Compare section 1.6 on the problem of context determination. (E5) might thus also be seen as an instance of pragmatic indeterminacy.

[27] See Bach (1982) for a discussion of these cases.

impliciture indeterminacy, as defined in section 1.5.4.[28] We will revisit this issue there.

Yet another subclass of syntactic ambiguities are relational ambiguities as in the expression "the love of God," which is ambiguous between meaning *the love God has for one* and *the love one has for God*.[29] Again, it usually goes without noticing that there is an ambiguity here at all because even when the context is minimally informative, there is a salient understanding of the phrase that trumps any other. If not otherwise indicated, we tend to understand the expression "the love of God" such that it means *the love God has for one*.

The reason lies in our general background knowledge of the world and pragmatic rules. Analogously to conversational implicatures, the speaker can always cancel the salient content of an ambiguous utterance.[30] In (E3), for instance, the salient content that the speaker, while wearing pajamas, shot a naked elephant is canceled by the second sentence.

Any fairly complex sentence can theoretically be understood in more than one way. Only the richness of context in everyday conversation combined with the speakers' general background knowledge of the world and their proficient use of conversational maxims ensure a smooth understanding of them. For example, even purely pragmatic aspects such as intonation can disambiguate syntactic ambiguities. This is why computerized language processing, which cannot as easily as human speakers deal with pragmatic rules and contextual data, still poses such a problem. Human speakers are directed to the salient understanding of most utterances right away.[31]

Despite this prompting of salience, syntactically ambiguous utterances do sometimes give rise to unclarity due to equally plausible readings of their logical structure. Because the context of utterance and the context in which the utterance is interpreted are distinct, this is more often the case in written utterances such as laws, verdicts, or contracts than in oral conversations. In section 3.1, we will evaluate the relevance of syntactic ambiguity to the law.

1.2.2 LEXICAL AMBIGUITY

Not only in jokes as in (E4) but also in normal conversations do we sometimes encounter utterances that are unclear because they can be understood in two or more very different ways. An utterance that contains the lexically ambiguous

---

[28] Bach (1994) coined the term *structural underdetermination* for this and similar cases.

[29] This is the terminology of Partee (1984). Lyons (2005) calls this form of ambiguity transformational.

[30] Compare Levinson (2000); originally in Grice (1989a). See also our discussion in section 3.4 about the use of implicatures in the law.

[31] It has been reliably shown that we are trying to make sense of a text without entertaining all possible interpretations. As a result, ambiguities are rarely recognized. Compare Gilbert (1991).

expression "right" can turn out to be indeterminate, as in the famous taxi driver example.

Theoretically, it can be confusing, when a taxi driver asks, "Shall I turn left?" and gets the answer "Right!" Because the utterance of the expression "right" can be understood as either *correct* or *located on the right hand side*, the taxi driver might end up in a situation in which she does not know whether she should turn *right* or whether it is *right* to turn left. Such situations are on the verge of situational comedy, since—as in the case of syntactic ambiguity—there are pragmatic rules, context, and general background knowledge that guide our understanding in a rather straightforward way. Even if the cab client used the ambiguous expression "right" in such a situation, one would expect him to indicate what he meant by further verbal or non-verbal means of expression.

In general, one can say that lexical ambiguity is the property of an expression to have multiple, typically unrelated meanings:

(D7) An expression *e* is LEXICALLY AMBIGUOUS iff *e* has two or more (unrelated) lexical meanings.[32]

This definition entails that lexically ambiguous expressions are only potentially indeterminate. Only when used in an utterance in which the context does not disambiguate, the expression is also actually indeterminate according to (D3).

(D7) also entails that a lexically ambiguous expression is a single expression with multiple meanings. It should be kept in mind, however, that this is purely conventional, since "right" can with equally good reasons be considered to be two expressions that just look and sound the same instead of a single one having two meanings.[33] We will use definition (D7) because it captures the more common and less controversial notion of lexical ambiguity.

An expression such as "peep" is lexically ambiguous because it can mean the act of *making a shrill sound* or the very different one of *looking furtively*—they are completely unrelated and just happen to look and sound alike. However, most lexically ambiguous expressions like the term "right" haven't always been used with two so different meanings, as both meanings are etymologically related. As a consequence, there are borderline cases of lexically ambiguous and (what we will see, are) polysemous expressions.[34]

---

[32] For a discussion of different ways to define (lexical) ambiguity, see Gillon (1990, 393-406).

[33] Linguists also distinguish between homography and homophony. Homography is the phenomenon that two expressions are written the same, while homophony is the phenomenon that two expressions sound the same. Moreover, two expressions are homonymous if both spelling and sound are identical, that is, if the expressions are both homographic and homophonic—as, for instance, in the taxi driver case.

[34] For further arguments on this claim, see Tuggy (1993).

1.2.3 POLYSEMY

One could argue that the expression "peep" meaning *the act of making a shrill sound* is a distinct expression from the one meaning *the act of looking furtively*. In contrast, the expression "school" does sometimes mean *the school building* and sometimes *the school as an institution*, but it is one and the same expression. One cannot reasonably say as in the case of lexical ambiguity—that there are two expressions that just happen to look and sound the same.

Nevertheless, we can use this expression to refer to the concrete place as in

(E6) "She's been at school all day."

or to the abstract institution as in

(E7) "She'll start school next year."

This can generate indeterminacy in utterances in just the same way as lexical and syntactic ambiguity do.[35] Depending on the context of utterance, a polysemous expression can be used to express different, though related, meanings. In other words:

(D8) An expression *e* is POLYSEMOUS iff *e* has two or more (related) senses of one lexical meaning.

If there are multiple related meanings of an expression, we will call them senses and subsume them under one lexical meaning. The relevant difference between polysemy and lexical ambiguity is the relatedness of its meanings. Relatedness of meaning is a rather vague condition, however. It thus comes as no surprise that there is a continuum between the two.

It seems that the vast majority of our natural language expressions is polysemous. For instance, consider Aristotle's discussion of the expression "healthy."[36] One can predicate healthiness to a person such as Socrates (S), but also to very different objects:

(S1) "Socrates is healthy."
(S2) "Socrates' complexion is healthy."
(S3) "Socrates' exercise regimen is healthy."

In these examples, the senses of "healthy" are related, but different. While (S2) and (S3) mean something like *is indicative of health* and *promotes health*,

---

[35] Because one could say that polysemous expressions have only one lexical meaning, and it is only the extension that the context divides in different sub-extensions, some linguists and philosophers do not consider polysemy as a form of ambiguity at all, but as a form of context-dependency—a phenomenon that will be discussed in section 1.6. Carston (2002), for instance, argues for this view. Luckily, it makes no difference in the argument for the strategic use of indeterminacy whether we treat polysemy as a form of ambiguity or pragmatic indeterminacy, as we will see in sections 3.4 and 4.4.

[36] Aristotle discusses the different uses of "good" and "health" in his "Nicomachean Ethics," 1096a28.

respectively, (S1) means something more fundamental: perhaps *is functioning well*. (S2) and (S3) appeal to health in the primary sense of (S1).

However, they are not borderline cases. Both (S2) and (S3) are as clear cases of health as (S1). The same holds, as we saw, for the term "school," which can be used to refer to the institution in its primary sense and the building in its secondary sense.

Many terms seem to have an indefinite amount of secondary senses. Consider the polysemous term "to have" (H), which can be used in the following utterances with varying senses:[37]

(H1) "I have a pen." (holding a possession or carrying)

(H2) "We have civil rights." (holding an entitlement)

(H3) "She has a house." (owning)

(H4) "September has 30 days." (containing as part or whole)

(H5) "He has seven children." (standing in a certain relationship)

(H6) "They are having dinner." (partaking of)

The list could go on and on.[38] This openness in the use of polysemous expressions stems from the fact that polysemy and the figurative use of an expression are not clearly separable. Andrei Marmor (2014, 122) illustrates the point with the use of the expression "man" (M) in the following utterances:

(M1) "Socrates is a man and therefore mortal." (species)

(M2) "Marriage is a contract between a man and a woman." (gender)

(M3) "Jo finally behaved like a man." (stereotype)

These examples are usually presumed to be instances of polysemy. However, as Marmor points out, the use of the expression "man" to stand for a stereotype can be seen as quasi-figurative, one that goes well beyond the lexical meaning of the word. There is hence no clear-cut boundary between the literal and figurative, or even metaphoric, use of an expression.

This is also evident from the fact that expressions that have been used metaphorically for some time tend to integrate the metaphoric meaning into their lexical meaning. Arguably, most expressions in modern English have been used

---

[37] Searle (1983, 145) makes a similar point with the different senses of "to open."

[38] Similarly, the expression "window" can be used to refer to the glass, the inner frame, or the outer frame of the window as in the examples by Marmor (2014, 121):"I broke the window," "I opened the window," and "I entered through the window." But again, depending on the context, the expression can be used with numerous other senses as well, as in the utterance "the address must show through the window in the envelope"—up to quasi-metaphorical ones as in the utterance "a window opened in the fog and revealed a castle in the distance."

to such an extent metaphorically in the past that the former merely metaphoric meaning is now part of their present lexical meaning.[39] Because this is a continuous process, there are borderline cases between the figurative and lexical meaning of an expression. It thus can be unclear whether an utterance is indeterminate due to an expression's polysemy or some form of pragmatic indeterminacy.[40]

This openness to figurative use is characteristic of polysemy and differentiates it from lexical ambiguity, even though they cannot be sharply separated either.[41] Most polysemous expressions are also very general, that is, they can be used to apply to many cases indiscriminately.[42] Polysemous expressions are often used to apply to only a subset of those cases. This is vertical polysemy, since there is a more general or *broader* sense of the expression that includes the more specific or *narrower* one:

(D9) An expression *e* is VERTICALLY POLYSEMOUS iff *e* has at least two (related) senses such that *e*'s extension in its narrower sense is a subset of *e*'s extension in its broader sense.

Consider the expressions "intelligent" and "stubborn." Normally, when saying that somebody is intelligent, we mean that he is intelligent in a specific aspect. For instance, we might qualify statements about IQ tests by saying that they measure intelligence only in a technical sense. The expression "stubborn" is generally used to designate either a good or bad character trait. It has been shown that both expressions when used in the description of a person were interpreted strikingly differently depending on the order of their occurrence—making a different, specific, sense salient.[43]

A phenomenon that seems to be related to polysemy are *cluster terms*. These are expressions like "religion" or "game," which are sometimes called *family resemblance* terms following Ludwig Wittgenstein's terminology. A cluster term's meaning lacks a single defining feature. It is characterized by a semantic cluster of loosely interconnected properties.

---

[39] The reason for this is supposedly a gap in the vocabulary. An interesting example is the expression "to understand," which like its counterparts in other Indo-European languages like Greek or German has its etymological roots in the concept of standing. The process has been called *catachresis* by Black (1954, 280). A similar process is the grammaticalization of expressions that used to represent actions or objects: as, for instance, "through," which has the same etymological roots as "door."

[40] Compare section 1.5 on pragmatic indeterminacy.

[41] For this reason, there is a variety of tests to distinguish them. See Zwicky and Sadock (1975), Bosch (1979), or Gillon (1990).

[42] Compare section 1.4 on generality.

[43] See Asch (1946). For example, if the expression "intelligent" was mentioned first, the expression "stubborn" was interpreted positively.

These properties can be identified with the different dimensions of a multi-dimensional term.[44] By using the term "game" in a particular context, a speaker can pick certain dimensions from the shared pool of characteristics of games in general. Talking about ring-a-ring-a-roses, for instance, she picks the dimension of doing something for fun, while leaving others (such as the goal to win) aside. The context of utterance in effect narrows the extension of the term "game."

Cluster terms can thus be seen as a subclass of polysemous expressions: namely, they are extremely polysemous expressions whose senses are related because in each sense they have some dimensions present that are also present in another sense, even though they do not share a single commonality.[45] In contrast to vertically polysemous terms, they do not have a single, general, core meaning but multiple ones. I will thus treat cluster terms as a special class of polysemous terms.[46]

In contrast to lexical ambiguity, polysemous expressions—and, especially, cluster terms—are highly context-sensitive. Presumably, because of the fuzziness between literal and non-literal uses and the resulting openness in the determination of what is said, polysemy is also sometimes confused with the phenomenon of semantic vagueness.

1.3 Semantic Vagueness

It has been notoriously and ironically difficult to define vagueness. Usually, philosophers of language introduce the notion by simply listing examples of vague expressions like "heap," "tall," or "red," and go on to explain the Sorites paradox. There is no consensus on what vagueness is or how the paradox should be solved. For present purposes, suffice it to say that whatever the philosophical account, vagueness has certain effects on how we use language, how we reason with it, and how we understand it. I will analyze vagueness purely on this linguistic level, without assuming anything about its underlying properties. That is, I do not want to take a stance on the question of whether vagueness is best described by a supervaluationist, epistemicist, contextualist, or multi-valued account.[47]

---

[44] A multi-dimensional term has multiple dimensions of meaning. For instance, a system of beliefs and practices can be more or less *religionlike* on different dimensions such as belief in supernatural beings or practice of sacred rituals. I will discuss the multi-dimensionality and contestedness of terms like "religion" in detail in the next section on semantic vagueness (in particular, section 1.3.2).

[45] Compare Wittgenstein (1953/2009, §66).

[46] More precisely, they are a form of multi-dimensionally polysemous terms, as I will define them in (D15) on page 34 in section 1.3.2.

[47] See Williamson (1994) or Keefe (2000) for profound discussions of this question in general. See Soames (2012) or Gruschke (2014) for discussions of the question of which theory best describes vagueness in law.

There are three basic criteria for vagueness. According to Rosanna Keefe (2000, 6–7), vague expressions are commonly understood to (1) be susceptible to the Sorites paradox, (2) lack sharp boundaries, and (3) admit borderline cases. These three criteria are, however, rarely accepted as individually necessary and collectively sufficient conditions for vagueness. More often, they are treated as symptoms or signs of vagueness.

Consequently, there is no commonly accepted definition of vagueness. An influential way to understand vagueness has been put forward by H. Paul Grice, however:

> To say that an expression is vague … is … to say that there are cases (actual or possible) in which one does not know whether to apply the expression or to withhold it, and one's not knowing is not due to ignorance of the facts. (Grice, 1989b, 177)

Cases in which an expression does neither clearly apply nor clearly not apply, and the reason for this unclarity is not ignorance of the facts, are called "borderline cases." Following Grice, we can then say that vagueness is the property of expressions to allow for borderline cases.[48] In short

(D10) An expression *e* is (semantically) VAGUE iff *e* allows for borderline cases.[49]

The notion of a *competent language user* is implicit in this definition, since it makes use of the notion of borderline case, which in turn is based on the notion of clarity. For that reason, utterances containing vague expressions are potentially indeterminate in the sense of our definition (D1). The following utterance will typically be indeterminate if Peter is of medium height:

(E8) "Peter is tall."

Peter is neither clearly tall nor clearly not tall. He is a borderline case of tallness. For that reason, an utterance such as (E8) is neither clearly true nor clearly false. With respect to borderline cases, we do not know what is said by (E8). That is why vagueness is a form of indeterminacy.[50]

---

[48] A very concise characterization of vagueness in these terms can be found in Williamson (2001, 61).

[49] An expression is precise iff it is not vague. In this book, I will omit the specifications "semantically" and "semantic" if the reference is clear.

[50] Note that one can also differentiate between vagueness of application and individuation—a distinction made by Alston (1967, 219). The debate on vagueness in law focuses on vagueness of application (i.e., semantic vagueness). Vagueness of individuation is basically the phenomenon underlying the *Problem of the Many*: Clouds, tables, and tigers—anything with fuzzy boundaries—seem to be individual objects, but are—at closer look—many, very similar, objects in the same places. Since there are thousands of water droplets at any cloud's edge that are neither clearly part of the cloud nor clearly outside it, we are forced

There are ambiguous precise and unambiguous vague terms, that is, ambiguity and vagueness are logically independent. For instance, the term "function" is ambiguous. In its mathematical meaning it is completely precise, since every mathematical object is either a function or not.[51] In its ordinary language meaning, it is vague since there are things that neither clearly have a function nor clearly do not have a function.

The characteristic feature of vague expressions is that they allow for borderline cases. The most consequential effect of borderline cases is that there are multiple, equally permissible, ways to apply the expression. In that sense, is it true when Raffman (2014, 106) claims that "vagueness is a form of arbitrariness." In borderline cases, we can usually decide either way.[52] To adequately describe these cases in the law, the distinction between *core of meaning* ("Bedeutungskern") and *corona of meaning* ("Bedeutungshof") was introduced by Philipp Heck (1914). It is comparable with what H. L. A. Hart (1958, 607) famously called "core of settled meaning" and "penumbra of debatable cases."

Borderline cases, in which we can apply the expression either way, are necessarily rare. Our language use is, for the most part, not arbitrary. Most everyday applications of vague expressions are clear cases; many are even *very* clear cases such as prototypes and paradigmatic examples of the expression. Otherwise, we could not communicate with each other as efficiently as we do. Part of the reason is that we, as language users, acquire concepts and learn language by clear examples. Once learned, we use those concepts which best fit our experience to understand the world around us.[53]

When language is used as a means to exchange information, this is best accomplished by employing expressions that clearly convey that information. In this case, we have an incentive to avoid applying vague expressions to borderline cases. Instead we opt for slightly different expressions that clearly apply. For instance, instead of calling borderline tall Peter tall such as in (E8), one might say:

(E9) "Peter is of medium height."

That is why our utterances are not indeterminate all the time, even though "virtually all our words and concepts are vague."[54] Hence, utterances containing

---

to say that every combination of droplets that contains the core droplets of the cloud and some number of the droplets at its edge is a cloud, too, and thus that there are millions of clouds where it seemed like there was only one. This problem belongs to metaphysics, and is, arguably, as such largely irrelevant to the use of indeterminacy in the law.

[51] It is or is not a function, depending on the formal definition: A function f from X to Y is a subset of the Cartesian product $X \times Y$ subject to the following condition: Every element of X is the first component of one and only one ordered pair in the subset.

[52] See Ripley (2011) for empirical evidence on how people react to borderline cases.

[53] Compare Rosch, Mervis, Gray, Johnson, & Boyes-Braem (1976).

[54] See Graff Fara and Williamson (2002, xii).

vague expressions are not necessarily indeterminate or unclear. Unclarity and vagueness are logically independent.

One way to illustrate this independence between clarity and precision is the distinction drawn by Roy A. Sorensen (2004, 21–39) between *relative* and *absolute* borderline cases. Relative borderline cases are cases in which we can gain knowledge in principle if we gather more evidence.[55] For instance, we can decide for some numbers rather quickly whether they are prime or not. Three, five, and seven are clear cases of prime numbers. Four, six, and eight are clear cases of non-prime numbers. However, there are numbers like 743,377, of which we do not know right away whether they are prime. But even for those numbers, we can eventually find out. They are borderline only relative to our knowledge, that is, they are unclear to us because of our ignorance.

There are also relative borderline cases when it comes to determining whether a number is large or not. Maybe we do not know right away whether a number is large in a particular context; but after considering the context, we can find out that, let's say, 50 is a large number and thus merely a relative borderline case. However, some numbers will resist categorization. Some numbers below 50 are neither clearly large nor clearly not large, even if we know everything knowable about mathematics, language, and the context of utterance. These are absolute borderline cases. They are due to the vagueness of the expression "large."

This distinction illustrates that sometimes it is not easy to tell apart ignorance of the facts from indeterminacy of the utterance. The more complex the expressions and the context of utterance are, the more difficult it can become to tell which borderline cases are relative and which ones are absolute. This difficulty matters when interpreting legal texts.[56] It can be unclear whether sufficient evidence has been gathered, whether something counts as relevant evidence, or whether something is evidence at all and not part of the law. Initially, seemingly hard cases can turn out to be just relative borderline cases. Sometimes, *prima facie* linguistic indeterminacy is nothing else but plain epistemic unclarity.

Another way to illustrate the independence between clarity and precision is the traditional interest of philosophers in the mere possibility of borderline cases. An expression is called vague if some case is conceivable in which it neither clearly applies nor clearly does not apply. In both actual conversation and the law, we generally want to minimize the occurrence of *actual* borderline cases, however. All vague expressions admit indefinitely many possible borderline cases, but they

---

[55] Strictly speaking, then, relative borderline cases are not borderline cases at all, since the unclarity is actually due to ignorance of the fact. Relative borderline cases only seem to be—that is, can be confused with—real (absolute) borderline cases.

[56] We will revisit this issue in section 2.3 on legal interpretation.

differ considerably with respect to the number of actual borderline cases, that is, with respect to real cases that in fact (in the actual world) are unclear. For that reason, an expression can be more or less vague only with respect to the number of actual borderline cases but not with respect to the number of possible borderline cases.

This difference is reflected by Rudolf Carnap's distinction between intensional and extensional vagueness:

(D11)   An expression *e* is INTENSIONALLY VAGUE iff *e* allows for possible borderline cases.

(D12)   An expression *e* is EXTENSIONALLY VAGUE iff *e* allows for actual borderline cases.[57]

Our original definition (D10) is ambiguous between the two readings.[58] By definition, every extensionally vague expression is intensionally vague.

Carnap's distinction is itself ambiguous between a time-relative and a time-independent reading of intension and extension. Both intension and extension can change over time. The lexical meaning of a term evolves due to changes in language use. This is a problem when time of utterance and time of application come apart—when we read historical texts such as, for example, the Constitution of the United States. An expression like "cruel and unusual punishment" as used then has changed in meaning today.

But even if the intension of the term remains stable, its extension can vary from context to context. Classically, a term's extension is the set of objects to which it lexically applies. In this sense, extension is as stable as intension. For instance, the term "human being" is extensionally vague only to a low degree because there are no borderline cases now, and in history, there have been only a few (due to the gradual evolution from other life forms).[59]

Arguably, the term "human being" has a precise extension when applied today. However, the term was highly extensionally vague at some point in history when there were a lot of borderline cases of Homo sapiens and Homo erectus around. Analogously, the future might bring new borderline cases of "human being'—for instance, when medical robotics advances.

Of course, one can also easily imagine a series of gradually less and less human-like creatures—up to a point where we would hesitate to call them human

---

[57] Compare Carnap (1955, 39).

[58] This distinction is made in a similar fashion by Fine (1975, 266) and Rolf (1980, 319). Intensional vagueness is what is called "open texture" by Hart (1961/1994), borrowing the term from Waismann (1945). Compare section 1.3.3.

[59] As Carnap (1955, 36) puts it, for some terms such as "human being," the actual borderline area "is relatively very small; the degree of their extensional vagueness is low."

beings anymore. This is due to the intensional vagueness of "human being." One can evaluate the responses of competent speakers to "descriptions of strange kinds of animals, say intermediate between man and dog, man and lion, man and hawk, etc."[60] One could ask these speakers whether they would apply the term "human being" to such animals. Presumably most speakers would not know how to use the term in such situations. Luckily, "this lack of clarity does not bother [us] much because it holds only for aspects which have very little practical importance," as Carnap (1955, 39) claims.

However, in another sense, the extension of a term can be narrowed by its use in context (e.g., due to its vertical polysemy). Its intension determines its lexical extension, but there is also a context-specific extension, which is determined by its lexical extension combined with contextual factors. This context-specific extension can thus vary from context to context, even if intension and lexical extension are fixed.

The context-specific extension is especially relevant for legal utterances for which the lawmaker wants to regulate future behavior. If we are concerned with actual unclear cases in the law (and other areas of human life), neither intensional nor lexically extensional vagueness seem to matter much. What matters are borderline cases in the extension relative to the context of utterance.

We tend to recognize vagueness only when we actually come across borderline cases. Friedrich Tezner (1892, 335), for instance, argues that even though there is no sharp cut-off point between "alley" and "street," we do not realize it until we actually encounter a borderline case between alley and street. Since actual borderline cases, and not possible ones, lead to unclarity about the application of terms, intensional vagueness is rarely more than a theoretical problem.[61] However, possible borderline cases could be transformed into actual ones by changes of context, for example, when context of utterance and context of application fall apart.[62] Contrary to Carnap's claim, it is thus by no means evident that intensional vagueness does not sometimes affect aspects of practical importance, as it could well be for indeterminacy in the law.

Hence, when the extension can change over time, the lack of clarity in intension might bother us after all. In particular, when future behavior is to be regulated by legal utterances, intensional vagueness may indeed be of practical importance because it could always turn extensional.

---

[60] See Carnap (1955, 39).

[61] But a theoretical problem it is—for the bivalence of classical logic as for the *rule of law*. Compare Endicott (2000) or Culver (2004) for discussions of this problem. See also section 1.3.1 on gradual vagueness and section 5.2.2 on Sorites reasoning in verdicts.

[62] A problem that will come up again and again is the potential discrepancy between context of utterance and context of application. I will discuss it in detail with respect to legal language in sections 2.1 and 2.3.

However, not even extensionally vague terms necessarily make an utterance indeterminate since the context can be sufficiently clear such that no unclarity with respect to application or content of the utterance arises. Consider a situation in which Peter is the only person of medium height out of a group of very tall people. If the speaker utters (E8) in this situation, it is perfectly clear what is said by (E8). The term "tall" is extensionally vague, but only with respect to its lexical extension. Peter clearly falls within the context-specific extension of "tall." It is thus a question of context whether even extensional vagueness leads to actual indeterminacy.

Actual borderline cases do give rise to unclarity and disagreement. However, borderline cases are not the only characteristic of vagueness. We can neither draw a line between a vague term's extension and anti-extension nor between its clear and its borderline cases. We have to deal with the logical and, more importantly, practical consequences of the Sorites paradox due to the fuzziness of vague terms. Vague terms are Soritical by nature. Many philosophers emphasize that the crucial feature of vague terms is in fact their Sorites susceptibility. I think that this is true for the special case of gradually vague terms.

1.3.1 GRADUAL VAGUENESS

At first glance, our definition (D10) of semantic vagueness overgeneralizes, since there might be borderline cases that do not occur on a continuum. For instance, the term's application may be unclear because its application conditions are incommensurable or the circumstances of application are highly unusual.[63] That is why R. Mark Sainsbury argues that the essence of vagueness does not lie in borderline cases, but in the fuzziness of the terms' application.

Sainsbury (1997, 251) claims that vague terms have no boundaries at all, by which he means the following:

> A vague concept is boundaryless in that no boundary marks the things which fall under it from the things which do not, and no boundary marks the things which definitely fall under it from those which do not definitely do so; and so on. (Sainsbury, 1997, 257)

---

[63] The definition by Peirce (1902, 748) suffers from the same apparent overgeneralization: "A proposition is vague when there are possible states of things concerning which it is *intrinsically uncertain* whether, had they been contemplated by the speaker, he would have regarded them as excluded or allowed by the proposition. By intrinsically uncertain we mean not uncertain in consequence of any ignorance of the interpreter, but because the speaker's habits of language were indeterminate." We will discuss other types of borderline cases in the following sections on multi-dimensional vagueness and open texture.

This boundarylessness seems to be the source of the Soriticality of vague terms. It is the reason why the Sorites paradox (or paradox of the heap) arises.[64] Competent language users of English agree that a nanosecond does not make a difference in whether a person is counted as young. This seems to be part of the meaning of the term "young." It lacks (sharp) boundaries. The following principle, usually called "tolerance principle," seems to be true:

(T) If x is young, and y is only a nanosecond older than x, then y is also young.

The trivial premise that there is a young person together with repeated applications of principle (T) leads to the valid conclusion that every person is young—which is clearly false. Why is principle (T) so compelling? Why do extensions of vague terms lack boundaries?

The reason seems to be based on the way we think about the world. Concepts are learned by grouping similar cases (objects or events) together, and every new case is then judged with respect to its similarity to these initial prototypical cases. If it is similar enough, we can apply the term that corresponds to the concept. Similarity is intrinsically a matter of degree. For that reason, borderline cases are not simply cases in which we do not know whether to apply a term. They are cases that are neither sufficiently similar nor sufficiently dissimilar to prototypical applications such that it remains unclear whether the term can be applied or not.[65]

If we think of furniture, we tend to have tables, bookshelves, and sofas in mind. The question whether a piano is a piece of furniture leads us to compare it with paradigmatic types of furniture. The comparison has the (unsatisfactory) result that (to most people) it is simply not clear whether pianos are sufficiently similar to those pieces of furniture.[66] Of course, the question whether something is similar to something else necessarily depends on some aspect of similarity. For instance, whether a piano should be counted as a piece of furniture depends on its similarity in function, appearance, material, and so forth. The fuzziness of similarity persists on all these different dimensions of lexical meaning, and it can be hard or impossible to compare these dimensions.[67] The gradual nature of similarity seems to be the underlying reason for the boundarylessness of vague terms.[68]

---

[64] See Moline (1969) or Burnyeat (1982) for details on the origins of the paradox, which dates back to Eubulides of Miletus.

[65] Compare Rosch (1973).

[66] Compare Rosch et al. (1976).

[67] We already touched the issues of multi-dimensionality and incommensurability. Compare section 1.3.2 on multi-dimensional vagueness for a detailed discussion. Compare also section 1.6 on the problem of context determination.

[68] The boundarylessness seems to be responsible, in turn, for the phenomenon of higher-order vagueness, which consists in there being not only borderline cases, but also borderline cases of borderline

The gradual nature of similarity also seems to be the source for the *tolerance* of vague terms. As Crispin Wright points out, vague terms are tolerant to small changes: "What is involved ... is a certain tolerance ..., a notion of a degree of change too small to make any difference, as it were."[69]

Boundarylessness and tolerance are semantic notions, even though they concern practical aspects of language application. The extensions of vague terms are not well-defined, that is, there are objects that neither clearly fall nor clearly do not fall within the predicate's extension. As a consequence, vagueness is a phenomenon that will persist even if the context is fixed.[70] Even after the context is completely determined, the utterance containing the vague term will remain indeterminate if applied to a borderline case.

Based on the notion of tolerance, we can define gradual vagueness:

(D13) An expression *e* is GRADUALLY VAGUE iff *e* allows for borderline cases due to *e*'s tolerance.[71]

Gradually vague terms lead to inconsistencies when used in a certain, *prima facie* innocuous, way. From apparently true premises by logically valid reasoning we can derive contradictions. Because of the tolerance of the term "young" (and the relative precision of the term "year") we cannot reasonably say that there is a last day of one's being young, even though we can say that there is a last day of the year.[72] Of course, we can go through a Sorites series step by step. We can ask, Is a person of 10 years young? Is a person of 10 years and one nanosecond young? And so on.[73]

Such questions effectively touch moral and legal issues when it comes, for instance, to questions of accountability or diminished responsibility. The problem

---

cases, and so on. See, for instance, Williamson (1999). This poses an insurmountable problem for every theory that relies on subcategories or additional truth values, as Williamson (1994, 111–141) showed. However, this is not totally uncontroversial. On one hand, proponents of three-valued logics like Tye (1997) do try to accommodate higher-order vagueness. On the other hand, Wright (2010), for instance, argues that higher-order vagueness is merely an illusion. But, most vagueness theorists take vagueness to be essentially higher-order, and, more importantly to us, they take tolerance to be an essential feature of vague terms. See, for instance, Raffman (1994, 41).

[69] See Wright (1997, 156).

[70] Compare Åkerman and Greenough (2010).

[71] Gradual vagueness is also called Soritical vagueness, quantitative vagueness, or vagueness of degree. Alston (1964, 87) defines it prominently in a slightly different way as "the lack of a precise cut-off point along some dimension."

[72] This holds equally for constructions like "the oldest adolescent" or "the smallest heap." Wittgenstein (1953, § 240) calls questions asking for the smallest heap simply "nonsense." Note that the gradability of many natural language terms is not to be confused with gradual vagueness. For instance, the term "dangerous" is gradable, since some *x* can be more or less dangerous. It seems that all gradable terms are vague because if *x* can be more or less *F*, *x* can also be (theoretically) in such a state that it is neither clearly *F* nor clearly ¬*F*. However, the converse does not hold. There are vague non-gradable terms (such as "car").

[73] See Raffman (1994), Graff Fara (2000), or Shapiro (2006) for discussions of the "forced march" through the Sorites series.

appears thus to have a special bearing on the law. Timothy A. O. Endicott (2000, 57) gives an illustration of Soriticality in the prohibition of raves in the English county of Shropshire by the *Criminal Justice and Public Order Act*:

> Imagine one million rave organizers charged with disobeying a police order to shut down their music. All appear in the same court one after the other. The first defendant tormented most of Shropshire by emitting a succession of repetitive beats at a deafening volume, and he is convicted. All the defendants played the same music in the same way under the same conditions, except that each successive rave organizer played the music at an imperceptibly lower volume—until the one millionth rave organizer played it at a hush that undeniably caused no distress to anyone. He will be acquitted. But if the decrement in volume in each case is trivial, it seems that no particular conviction ought to be the last. Between any two successive defendants in the series, there is no difference that the inhabitants of the locality can perceive. Finding the organizer guilty in one case and not in the next case seems arbitrary, if there is no sharp boundary to the application of the term "serious distress." A court should be able to justify its decisions, and how can a trivial change in the music justify the difference between conviction and acquittal? If like cases should be treated alike, then the legal treatment of two cases should not be materially different when there is no material difference between them.

This "scenario of the million raves," as Endicott calls it, shows that there is a deep problem about the Soriticality of vague terms. It highlights the "ineliminable arbitrariness," which Diana Raffman (2014, 106) attributes to vagueness. Every cut-off point the court could draw is inextricably arbitrary—at least from a linguistic point of view. This arbitrariness poses a challenge to some of our most valued legal principles.[74] It may, however, also be used for certain strategies.

For instance, many small decisions that are individually perceived to be immaterial may cumulatively result in a qualitative difference. Alfred E. Kahn (1966) calls this strategy the *tyranny of small decisions*.[75] The reason for this is the tolerance for small changes in our assessment of the decision's impact.

It has been argued that the tolerance of our natural language terms also allows for the gradual shifts of meaning over time.[76] For example, the term *"Gewalt"* ("violence") in German criminal law means something quite different today than

---

[74] Compare section 5.1 for a discussion of various forms of arbitrariness in the law.

[75] The tyranny of small decisions is a type of the *tragedy of the commons*, introduced by Hardin (1968), which is itself an application of the prisoner's dilemma.

[76] In linguistics, this phenomenon is also called "meaning drift," which leads to a broadening or narrowing of the lexical meaning of a term. Compare section 4.3.2 for the role of semantic vagueness in language change.

fifty years ago. Multiple judicial decisions and a continuous legal discussion shifted, that is, broadened, its meaning to include instances of mobbing and all sorts of mental violence.[77]

The decisions that German courts made with regard to the legal concept of *Gewalt* exhibit the pattern of the tyranny of small decisions. Even though they presumably tracked merely the gradual change of our general concept of violence, a supporting factor that allowed for better public acceptability was arguably their step-by-step nature. This reasoning is based on the (sometimes fallacious) *argument from gradualism* that each step is acceptable and, thus, that the outcome is acceptable, too.[78]

A possible answer to this type of argumentative strategy is the *slippery slope argument*.[79] Typical slippery slope arguments claim that a comparatively small first step leads to a chain of further steps, culminating in some bad effect. This first step is, so the argument goes, like a small kick given to an object that pushes it over the edge of a slope sliding all the way down to the bottom, as in the following:

(E10) "We must stop the government from banning pornography. Once they started to ban one form of literature, there is no stopping them. Next thing you know, they will be burning books!"

This kind of reasoning is very often combined with causal claims about the effect of precedent and how one small step can cause the next one, and so on. For instance, a primarily causal variant of the argument is the infamous *domino theory*, warning against the fall of South Vietnam during the Cold War. Some have argued that many slippery slope arguments gain their support from the Soriticality of vague terms. If these arguments are additionally backed up by causal evidence, they are not only logically valid (as the Sorites paradox), but also quite convincing. Volokh (2003) shows, for example, that judiciary decisions can facilitate—by setting legal precedent—more and more decisions in the same direction, leading to eventually unintended and unwanted consequences.[80]

Soritical arguments are naturally blocked by realization gaps. As we have seen, terms can be more or less vague with respect to actual borderline cases. There are often natural gaps between clear positive and negative cases, on one hand, and borderline cases, on the other. Then, the reasoning of the argument can be

---

[77] A similar example is the broadening of the meaning of "illness" due to changes in the *The Diagnostic and Statistical Manual of Mental Disorders* (DSM), which allows for more and more people to be called ill. Compare Frances (2013).

[78] Perelman and Olbrechts-Tyteca (1969) call this argumentative strategy the *device of the stages*.

[79] Compare Walton (1992, 21).

[80] We will revisit the role of gradual vagueness in slippery slope arguments in section 5.2.2 in a discussion on step-by-step verdicts by German courts, which gradually widened the extension of the German word for "violence."

stopped by drawing a non-arbitrary boundary. For instance, natural kind terms are only intensionally vague, but not extensionally—due to wide realization gaps.[81] Even most extensionally vague terms are used in a way such that they apply to mainly clear cases, as we saw in section 1.3. For efficient communication, however, it is essential that when uttered in some context, there are such gaps in the context-specific extension of the vague terms used. The context makes their extension more precise—it *precisifies* it, by picking a subset, usually by means of an impliciture.[82]

Whether Soriticality is a problem or not, depends on realization gaps. In natural language as well as in law, there are ways to react to the occurrence or even likelihood of borderline cases. By re-defining terms, we can shift realization gaps and minimize actual borderline cases, which is daily routine in the sciences. Biologists discuss again and again the correct categorization of life forms, thereby adjusting our biological vocabulary in such a way as to reduce actual borderline cases. Something similar is done in law with respect to the correct interpretation of legal terms such as "violence." But even if an immediate decision is required, there is usually some room to interpret a legal term in such a way that no actual borderline case occurs. This is due to the discretion given to the interpreter by a combination of different (semantic and pragmatic) forms of indeterminacy.[83]

1.3.2 MULTI-DIMENSIONAL VAGUENESS

A distinction can be made between *transparently*, *ordinarily*, and *extravagantly* vague terms.[84] Transparently vague terms are, for example, "rich," "tall," or "heap." They are commonly used as illustrative examples in the philosophical debate on vagueness because they are vague with respect to one salient dimension. Someone is poor depending on one's wealth. Something is a sand heap depending on its number of sand grains. In contrast, ordinarily and extravagantly vague terms have more than one salient dimension. Examples for ordinarily vague terms, on one hand, are "house," "vehicle," and "window." Examples for extravagantly vague terms, on the other hand, are "neglect," "intelligent," or "reasonable."

While transparently vague terms are usually avoided in legal texts, ordinarily and extravagantly vague terms are not. The reason is, according to Marmor (2014, 87), that it is comparatively easy to replace them with precise terms. It is easy to draw a boundary, since there is only one clearly relevant dimension. One can stipulate that someone is poor for some particular purpose or conversation if, for example, her income falls below $1.90 a day, as the World Bank does for the

---

[81] Compare Pinkal (1995, 105–109) and Hauswald (2014, section 3.1–3.4)

[82] See sections 1.5.4 and 1.6.

[83] This claim will be substantiated in sections 3.2, 4.3, and 5.1.

[84] The distinction is due to Endicott (2011b, 24–25).

concept of absolute poverty.[85] Such (legal) definitions do not necessarily replace a vague term with a precise homonymic (legal) one; but it can, instead, merely shift the borderline area in a way such that realization gaps emerge. Both techniques to reduce actual borderline cases are easily available for transparently vague terms because of their one-dimensionality.

It is thus not gradual vagueness that differentiates transparently from ordinarily and extravagantly vague terms. Ordinarily and extravagantly vague terms are different from transparently vague ones because they are multi-dimensional.[86] Terms like "house" or "intelligent" have multiple constitutive dimensions that determine their application. The term "intelligent," for instance, has a number of dimensions with respect to which someone can be more or less intelligent.[87] Whether one is intelligent or not depends on one's capacity for memory, abstract thought, self-awareness, communication, learning, emotional knowledge, creativity, and problem-solving. This list is, of course, expandable. The term "intelligent" is gradually vague with respect to each dimension, that is, a person is borderline intelligent if she scores neither clearly low nor clearly high in all of these dimensions. But it can also be unclear whether someone is intelligent due to the multi-dimensionality of the term.

On one hand, it can be unclear how the dimensions of intelligence are to be weighted against each other in cases of conflict or doubt. How do we decide whether someone's capacity for communication weighs more than her capacity for memory or creativity? And even if we could decide it, how much more would it weigh? Is somebody intelligent who scores high in problem-solving but lacks abstract thought or emotional knowledge? What would be the case if she scored slightly less in problem-solving or slightly more in abstract thought?

Some borderline cases arise because some dimensions are instantiated to a high degree and others to a low degree. Someone who can learn a language within a few months, but cannot solve a simple mathematical equation is, arguably, a borderline case of intelligent. Even though sometimes dimensions literally cancel each other out, the basic problem is that they cannot even properly be compared.[88] They are incommensurable. There is no measure to weigh the dimensions to ensure a

---

[85] See Cruz, Foster, Quillin, and Schellekens (2015, 3).

[86] See also Marmor (2014, 89), who makes basically the same point.

[87] Of course, the application of most vague terms depends on more than one dimension; also, the supposedly one-dimensional, transparently vague terms are only idealized fictions. The term "heap" does in fact depend not only on the number of grains of sand but also on their arrangement, their size, their environment, and so forth. But there is at least one *salient* dimension on which a line can be drawn.

[88] One could argue that multi-dimensional vagueness is the property of expressions to allow for borderline cases due to strict conflict between their dimensions. Then, however, multi-dimensional vagueness would be even less interesting than gradual vagueness.

correct decision for all cases.[89] The incommensurability of dimensions triggers *multi-dimensional* vagueness. Following Burks (1946, 481), we can say that

(D14)   An expression *e* is MULTI-DIMENSIONALLY VAGUE iff *e* allows for borderline cases due to incommensurability between *e*'s dimensions.

Multi-dimensional vagueness is, however, only one form of indeterminacy that can result from an expression's multi-dimensionality. The other form is sometimes confused with multi-dimensional vagueness or missed altogether.

The term "intelligent" is potentially indeterminate also because it can be unclear which dimension or which combination of dimensions must be instantiated for being intelligent. In cases of conflict or doubt, some but not sufficiently many dimensions are instantiated. Most speakers of English would call somebody intelligent if she had all the previously mentioned capacities. However, the list is clearly not exhaustive. It seems that extravagantly vague terms like "intelligent," "nice," or "reasonable"—and even ordinarily vague terms like "house," "vehicle" or "chair"—have indefinitely many dimensions.[90] More importantly, competent language users can reasonably disagree about whether some dimensions are even part of what it means for someone to be intelligent or for something to be a house. This results in a fundamentally different form of indeterminacy, which stems from unclarity or disagreement about which features are intrinsic to the concepts of *intelligence* or *house*. It is thus not a question of the terms' borderline application (as in cases of semantic vagueness), but the involved indeterminacy concerns their very meaning.

Sometimes, it makes sense to say that an expression has one meaning that is unclear or contested. The meaning of "intelligent" is contested because it is unclear which dimensions must be instantiated in someone to count as intelligent. Sometimes, it makes more sense to say that "intelligent" has multiple meanings or senses that stand for how different people understand intelligence. In other words, they stand for the various conceptions that people have of the concept of *intelligence*. We can call this form of indeterminacy "multi-dimensional polysemy":

(D15)   An expression *e* is MULTI-DIMENSIONALLY POLYSEMOUS iff it is unclear which dimensions are part of *e*'s lexical meaning such that *e* has two or more (related) senses.

Multi-dimensional vagueness, in contrast, concerns cases in which different dimensions are instantiated to different degrees such that the expression neither

---

[89] As Marmor (2014, 89) puts it, "no common denominator would allow a quantitative comparison of the various constitutive elements on a single evaluative scale."

[90] Compare Black (1937, 433–434) on the museum of chairs.

clearly applies nor clearly does not apply. It is thus not to be confused with so called "qualitative" or "combinatorial vagueness," which, according to Alston (1964, 87), "stems from an indeterminacy as to just what combination of conditions is sufficient or necessary for the application of the term." Consequently, "combinatorial vagueness" includes both multi-dimensional vagueness and multi-dimensional polysemy.[91]

Recall cluster terms. The term "religion" has numerous dimensions that can be evaluated in different ways. Dominic Hyde (2008, 16) explicates some of them:

> If we consider clear cases of religions, such as Roman Catholicism and Orthodox Judaism, we find that they exhibit certain striking features, each of which seems to have something to do with making them religious. These include: (1) Beliefs in supernatural beings (gods). (2) The demarcation of certain objects as sacred. (3) Ritual acts focused around sacred objects. (4) A moral code believed to be sanctioned by the gods. (5) Characteristic feeling, such as awe and a sense of mystery, which tend to be aroused in the presence of sacred objects and which are associated with the gods. (6) Prayer and other forms of communication with the gods. (7) A world view, that is, a general picture of the world as a whole, including a specification of its over-all significance, and a picture of the place of the individual in the world. (8) The individual's more or less total organisation of his life based on the world view. (9) A social organisation bound together by the preceding characteristics.

The term "religion" is gradually and multi-dimensionally vague as well as (multi-dimensionally) polysemous. There is neither consensus on the relevant features themselves nor on their relevance for its correct application. In part for this reason, "religion" is also called an *essentially contested concept* term. Other examples of essentially contested concept terms are "democracy," "human dignity," or "art."[92]

Essentially contested concepts are characterized by general agreement on their essence, but deep, almost inextricable, disagreement on their realization. However, they are not merely *hotly* disputed. They are *essentially contested* because it is disputed what exactly the concept essentially is.[93] People have essentially different conceptions of them. As such, essentially contested concept terms are paradigmatic examples of multi-dimensional polysemy as defined in (D15).[94]

---

[91] Compare also Alston (1967, 219). Haack (1996, 111), too, classifies one-dimensional and multi-dimensional vagueness as well as multi-dimensional polysemy as three kinds of "vagueness."

[92] See Gallie (1956) and Hurley (1989).

[93] Compare also Waldron (2002).

[94] Such terms are sometimes also described as *essentially ambiguous* because they are polysemous between a practical and a theoretical sense. Van der Burg (2009) argues, for example, that the expression

The main difference to other multi-dimensional terms lies in the multi-dimensional polysemy of essentially contested concept terms. Because of it, they are more likely to lead to disputes over their meaning. They function as keywords in political, philosophical, moral, or legal debates.[95] Disagreements can be attached to them. This has a particular bearing on legal and wider philosophical questions, as will become evident in chapter 5 on strategic indeterminacy in the law.[96]

Let us return to the distinction between transparent, ordinary, and extravagant vagueness from the beginning of this section. The distinguishing feature between transparently vague terms, on one hand, and non-transparently vague terms, on the other hand, is that transparently vague terms have one salient dimension, while non-transparently vague terms are multi-dimensional. As a consequence, while "heap" is only gradually vague, "house" and "intelligent" are both gradually and multi-dimensionally vague.

Moreover, what distinguishes ordinarily and extravagantly vague terms is entirely unrelated to vagueness. Extravagantly vague terms are more likely to create unclarity in utterances because they are multi-dimensionally polysemous—in addition to being semantically vague.[97] In fact, they are indeterminate in various ways at once. Some extravagantly vague terms such as "neglect" are essentially contested concept terms; others, such as "reasonable," are highly general and standard-relative.[98]

In general, multi-dimensional vagueness seems to have more impact on the indeterminacy of utterances than gradual vagueness.[99] If borderline cases actually become an issue, they usually are cases of multi-dimensional vagueness. Many examples of indeterminacy, however, draw on neither gradual nor multi-dimensional vagueness but multi-dimensional polysemy. Is a glass brick element of a facade a window? Is a boot a dangerous weapon when kicked at someone's head? Is the Missouri river a tributary of the Mississippi or the other way round?[100]

These questions depend on a borderline application neither with respect to only one of the term's dimensions nor due to unclarity in their weighting. The

---

"my religion" is inherently ambiguous between the speaker's religious doctrine and her religious way of life. Strikingly, the same seems to hold for the expression "law," which can be used to refer to legal practice, legal theory, or the results of legal practice.

[95] Compare Rodgers (1998, 6) for a similar, more specific, claim with respect to American political debates.

[96] See also my discussion of interpretive concept terms in section 2.3.3.

[97] A similar objection to Endicott's categorization is made by Soames (2012).

[98] Compare section 1.4 on generality and conversational vagueness and section 1.6 on standard-relativity.

[99] Compare Endicott (2000, 41–48).

[100] The examples are from Quine (1960, 128) and Poscher (2012, 132).

indeterminacy in those cases stems from unclarity or disagreement in the terms' having or not having a particular dimension. Does "window" require the possibility of opening and closing? Does "weapon" include tools that are not designed as weapons? Does "tributary" depend on the length or the volume of the river? Semantic vagueness increases the problem because it is additionally unclear how each of these, possibly borderline instantiated, dimensions is to be balanced against other salient dimensions. But the basic problem is multi-dimensional polysemy. The basic problem is that it is unclear which dimensions are part of the meaning of "window," "weapon," and "tributary."

This raises doubt on whether semantic vagueness can be strategically used since we might be confusing it with multi-dimensional polysemy. As we saw in section 1.2.3, polysemous terms seem to have an important function in communication, and extravagantly vague terms are useful possibly only because they are polysemous.[101]

1.3.3 OPEN TEXTURE

In the previous two sections, we differentiated various kinds of semantic vagueness. Especially in the philosophy of law, a form of indeterminacy is often discussed that sometimes is classified as yet another kind of semantic vagueness. This is the porosity or *open texture* of language.

The following statement by Friedrich Waismann (1945, 123) suggests that "open texture" is simply a different expression for intensional vagueness: "Open texture, then, is something like *possibility of vagueness*."

This statement is presumably the reason why Hart (1961/1994)—and after him so many others—understood "open texture" and "intensional vagueness" synonymously. However, the examples Waismann uses to explain open texture point to a similar, but different, phenomenon. He describes a creature as having all the usual properties of a cat, but

> what, for instance, should I say when that creature ... grew to a giant size? Or if it showed some queer behaviour usually not be found with cats, say, if under certain conditions, it could be revived from death whereas normal cats could not? Shall I, in such a case say that a new species has come into being? Or that it was a cat with extraordinary properties? (Waismann, 1945, 121–122)

Such a creature is neither clearly a cat nor clearly not a cat. But are such cases borderline cases? According to Waismann, even scientific expressions such as the natural kind term "gold" allow for such wild scenarios, and presumably

---

[101] I think that they are in fact useful for a number of very different reasons. See, in particular, section 3.2.2 on extravagant vagueness in the law and chapter 5 for a full argument with respect to their use in laws, verdicts, and contracts.

all linguistic expressions are open textured in this sense. In contrast to gradual vagueness, open texture does not entail boundarylessness, though. There is no continuum on which cases of open texture could be ordered. Instead, an entirely new dimension is introduced that is not clearly part of the expression's meaning. By considering such wild scenarios, new aspects come into play that have not been relevant for the expression's application before.[102]

Just as with gradual and multi-dimensional vagueness, open texture is a form of semantic vagueness because it is characterized by the existence of borderline cases. In short, open texture is the possibility of strange and unforeseen cases in which a competent and well-informed language user has doubts about the application of the term—something similar to, but not the same as, intensional vagueness.

In general, all types of semantic vagueness can create indeterminacy, and they all do so in the same way—by allowing for borderline cases:

(D16) An utterance u is SEMANTICALLY VAGUE in context c iff u is a borderline application of some expression e in c.

Similarly to ambiguous expressions, vague terms do not necessarily make an utterance indeterminate. Whether something is a borderline case and whether the existence of a borderline case leads to unclarity depends on the context of utterance.

First, whether the use of the term "tall" allows for borderline cases depends on its context-specific extension. The extension might consist only of clear tall and clear non-tall people. There is then no indeterminacy because there are no borderline cases.

Second, even if there are borderline cases, context can resolve the unclarity about them. Recall the use of the term "tall" in (E8) when applied to borderline tall Peter. If there is nobody that is smaller and everybody else is considerably taller than Peter, there is no actual indeterminacy in the utterance. Despite the gradual vagueness on the level of pragmatics, the utterance is clear and determinate.

In the next section, we turn to a type of vagueness that is rarely discussed and entirely on the level of pragmatics.

1.4 Conversational Vagueness

Generality is often seen as a form of indeterminacy—contrasted with ambiguity and semantic vagueness. And, indeed, general expressions are used in indeterminate utterances. In particular, they can be used in utterances that are intended

---

[102] Of course, on most new dimensions, there is a continuum on which the expression can be more or less applicable. For instance, we can let Waismann's creature grow more or less or revive it under more or less weird circumstances. This is, however, simply gradual vagueness, which exists in addition to open texture.

to mislead or to avoid answering a question. Consider the following telephone conversation, taken from Eric Dickey's *Milk in My Coffee*:

(E11) PETER: "Where are you?"   KIMBERLY: "East Coast."[103]

In *Milk in My Coffee*, Kimberly considers it none of Peter's business where she is. Peter, however, expects to receive more specific information about Kimberly's location and in reply to her evidently unsatisfactory answer he complains:

(E12) "Could you be a little more vague? The East Coast spreads from Canada to Florida."[104]

What Peter means by "vague" clearly is not semantic vagueness. He is not complaining about there being borderline cases of "East Coast."[105] When considering literal content, it might seem puzzling why there should be indeterminacy in Kimberly's utterance at all. There is nothing unclear about what is said, and it might even be completely clear what is implicated. In the context of their conversation, Kimberly tries to convey that she thinks that her location is none of Peter's business, and Peter might easily grasp it.

I claim that the generality of "East Coast" is the source of indeterminacy, even though it is not itself a form of indeterminacy. Let me explain. A general, but otherwise determinate, utterance doesn't leave any semantic questions open. There are neither borderline cases nor multiple admissible interpretations as for semantically vague or ambiguous expressions, respectively. There is no unclarity about what is said. For instance, the utterance

(E13) "It was someone between 18 and 40 years of age."

is semantically almost completely determinate. Pragmatically, however, it can lead to unclarity, since the general expression "someone between 18 and 40 years of age" might potentially refer to a wide range of persons. As a consequence, the utterance will be true for many states of affairs and contexts, and the audience receives very little information. Technically speaking, the expression has a large extension and a small intension.

There are two basic ways to make the utterance more determinate. First, one can add information regarding the person's age and, thus, decrease the age range. The expression is general because the interval between 18 and 40 is

---

[103] Compare Dickey (1999, 137).

[104] See Dickey (1999, 137).

[105] Names such as "East Coast" might exhibit vagueness of individuation. If names can be vague, the name "East Coast" is relatively precise, however. It contains the US federal states Maine, New Hampshire, Massachusetts, Rhode Island, Connecticut, New York, New Jersey, Delaware, Maryland, Virginia, North Carolina, South Carolina, Georgia, and Florida. Be this as it may, borderline cases are not the problem here.

relatively large—relative to a conversation's purposes. Second, one can bring in new information regarding other personal traits, decreasing the range of potential referents in that way. (E13) does not tell us anything apart from the fact that the person is neither very young nor very old. For most conversations, this is too unspecific to be of much use. Many questions are left open such as "Was the person male or female?" or "What profession did she or he have?" To Peter, it is not clear whether Kimberly is in the Canada-part or Florida-part or anywhere in-between on the East Coast. This loose, and often uninformative, use of language is caused by some expression's generality:

(D17) An expression e is GENERAL iff e can be used to refer to a wide range of cases indiscriminately.[106]

There is an apparent problem with this definition of generality. Namely, it involves the semantically vague term "wide range." How many cases are a wide range of cases? Does it depend on the context whether an expression is general or is generality a purely semantic property that merely causes indeterminacy on the level of pragmatics?

There are expressions like "object," "person," "vehicle," or "tool" that have small intensions and large (lexical) extensions. Because of this, they can generally be used to refer to many things in the world indiscriminately. However, whether a general expression causes indeterminacy depends on its informativeness in the context of use. Kimberly's utterance can be informative enough or totally uninformative—depending on the context, background knowledge, shared assumptions, and purposes of the conversation. If I utter (E13) when you ask me who came by yesterday, I say almost certainly something true, while being rather uninformative at the same time. But one can imagine situations in which it counts as a relevant and informative contribution to the conversation. Imagine that the goal is to find a fugitive whose identity lies completely in the dark until a witness utters (E13). Maybe the witness knows only that the person is neither very young nor very old—which might be just enough to narrow down the search.

At best, we can say that, ceteris paribus, the more specific an expression is, the more informative the utterance becomes. Or, conversely, ceteris paribus, the more general the expression is, the less informative the utterance becomes. Instead of (E13), I could utter

(E14) "It was a 31-year-old woman in an elegant white dress with a wide-brimmed hat called 'Catherine',"

---

[106] An expression is specific iff it is not general.

which is true only under very particular circumstances. The expressions used are more specific; and, as a consequence, the utterance is more informative.

If general expressions are semantically determinate, what then is the indeterminacy in (E11)? Particular information relevant to the conversation is left unclear. Indeterminacy due to generality is thus a phenomenon on the level of pragmatics. Following Marmor (2014, 91), we will say that Kimberly's answer is *conversationally vague*. Kimberly's utterance is only borderline relevant to the conversation. It is too general to answer Peter's question clearly, that is, it is not specific enough for the purposes of this conversation. Often when politicians are criticized for being too vague, their utterances are conversationally vague in this sense. They might be evading answering a question by using general expressions such that no (or very little) information can be deduced.

The expressions "East Coast" and "someone between 18 and 40 years of age" are fairly unambiguous and precise. There is one salient way to understand them and there are no (actual) borderline cases. The indeterminacy arises because the expressions fail to specify some important information.[107] In this way, generality is fundamentally different from ambiguity and semantic vagueness. While ambiguity and semantic vagueness are phenomena on the level of what is said, the indeterminacy due to generality concerns the relevance of the utterance itself.

There are general expressions that are precise as well as specific expressions that are semantically vague. In other words, semantic vagueness and generality are logically independent. There are also general expressions that are unambiguous as well as specific expressions that are ambiguous. In other words, ambiguity and generality are logically independent. However, as Geeraerts (1993) points out, there is no sharp distinction between generality and polysemy. The related senses of a polysemous expression are sometimes so similar that they can reasonably be subsumed under the single meaning of a general term. Sometimes, a general expression has such a diverse extension that it makes sense to speak of its having multiple senses. The transition is fluent between the figurative use of a general expression and the already established lexical sense of a polysemous one.[108] Quine (1960, 130) uses as an example for this fluidity between both phenomena the expression "hard," which is neither clearly one or the other: When talking about *hard cases* and *hard chairs* it can be *hard* to decide whether the expression "hard" is

---

[107] Alternatively, we could define generality such that a linguistic expression *e* is GENERAL iff *e* does not discriminate between objects with relevantly different characteristics. This, however, would preclude the talk of general statements being used in a perfectly determinate way—for instance, if knowing that Kimberley is at the East Coast is all the information that is required for the purposes of the conversation.

[108] See our discussion of figurative use in section 1.2.3 on polysemy. See also the next section 1.5.1 on impliciture indeterminacy.

general, polysemous, or even lexically ambiguous. In section 1.2 on ambiguity, we found that there are borderline cases between lexically ambiguous or polysemous expressions. There is thus a continuity between generality, polysemy, and lexical ambiguity.[109]

Even though generality is not to be confused with polysemy, it is important to keep in mind that one reason for the indeterminacy of utterances in which general expressions occur (besides conversational vagueness) is the fact that there are pragmatically often different ways to specify them. This can result in either vertical polysemy or impliciture indeterminacy.[110]

We tentatively said that utterances are conversationally vague if they are indeterminate because of generality. Unclarity arises not because of the semantic properties of the expressions used but because of indeterminacy in the context. The utterance is indeterminate because it is borderline relevant to the purposes of the conversation, or in Marmor's words, "conversational vagueness is typically a function of the relevance of the speaker's contribution to the conversation in question."[111]

Conversational vagueness, thus, touches the conversational Maxim of Relation.[112] However, not only the Maxim of Relation can be borderline satisfied but other conversational maxims, too. In the context of *Milk in My Coffee*, (E11) also fails to clearly satisfy the Maxim of Quantity.[113] It is neither clearly informative nor clearly uninformative.

Conversational vagueness should consequently be defined thus:

(D18) An utterance u is CONVERSATIONALLY VAGUE in context c iff u borderline satisfies some Gricean maxim m in c.

Generality is certainly the most prominent and most discussed source of conversational vagueness. Recall our very first example from section 1.1:

(E1) "You have to ask a doctor or a lawyer or someone like that."

The expression "a doctor or a lawyer or someone like that" is general because in many contexts, it will not be sufficiently relevant or informative or clear for the purposes of the conversation. Besides generality, however, there are many other ways in which utterances can be conversationally vague. For instance, a political

---

[109] Compare Moore (1981, 182), who makes the same claim.

[110] Compare section 1.2.3 on vertical polysemy and section 1.5.4 on impliciture indeterminacy. For its legal ramifications, see section 3.3 on conversational vagueness in the law.

[111] See Marmor (2014, 91).

[112] It simply says, "Be relevant" (Grice, 1989a, 27)

[113] The Maxim of Quantity says, "Make your contribution as informative as is required. Do not make your contribution more informative than is required." (Grice, 1989a, 26–27)

candidate P can react to the suspicion that another person X channeled funds to P indirectly by publicly stating

(E15) "I did not receive a single dollar from X."[114]

P's utterance is conversationally vague since it is not clearly relevant to the point. The question is not whether X directly transferred money to P, which is what P can claim to have meant by her utterance. P evades the question at hand by answering a similar, but uninteresting, question. P's answer borderline satisfies the Maxim of Relation.

However, if P would have said explicitly that no money was handed over to her directly, her utterance would have been fairly clearly irrelevant to the question. What makes P's utterance in (E15) astute is an underlying semantic indeterminacy. The expression "receive" is polysemous because it can mean that one is given something directly or that one comes into its possession indirectly. By exploiting this polysemy, the political candidate P can say something that is neither clearly relevant nor clearly irrelevant to the question.

Another special case of conversational vagueness is the borderline application of semantically vague expressions. The utterance of the sentence "Peter is tall" in (E8) only borderline satisfies the Maxim of Quality, since it is neither clearly true nor clearly false.[115] At the same time, it fails to satisfy the Maxim of Manner, since the utterer does not avoid obscurity.[116] All cases of indeterminacy are *by definition* failures to satisfy the Maxim of Manner.

The notion of conversational vagueness should not be confused with what Endicott (2000, 50–54) calls "pragmatic vagueness." He differentiates between vagueness on the level of what is said and on the level of what is communicated. Consider the following utterance:

(E16) "At 5pm."

On the level of what is said, (E16) is perfectly precise. However, utterances such as (E16) can and often are interpreted loosely. On the level of what is communicated, they often are vague, allowing a margin of some minutes before or after 5pm sharp.

In contrast, the utterance

(E17) "At about 5pm"

is semantically vague. It allows for borderline cases on the level of what is said. However, (E17) can be uttered in a context in which the expression "about" is

---

[114] The example is due to Marmor (2014, 91).

[115] The Maxim of Quality says "Try to make your contribution one that is true" (Grice, 1989a, 27).

[116] The Maxim of Manner says "Avoid obscurity of expression." See Grice (1989a, 26–27).

added merely because of conventional politeness. What might be communicated is that one should be there at 5pm sharp. As a consequence, there are no actual borderline cases on the level of communicative content.[117]

Pragmatic vagueness leads to unclarity much in the same way as semantic vagueness does, the only difference being that pragmatic vagueness is on the level of pragmatics and not semantics. Pragmatic vagueness is a special case of a phenomenon that I call *pragmatic indeterminacy* in the next section.

1.5 Pragmatic Indeterminacy

Indeterminacy is primarily "a contextual matter," as Soames (2011, 32) claims. The indeterminacy of an utterance depends on its context. Context quite successfully dissolves the vast majority of potentially indeterminate cases. Sometimes context fails to do so as in cases of actually ambiguous utterances or actual borderline cases. In yet other cases context generates indeterminacy rather than dissolving it. Some utterances are pragmatically indeterminate.

The existence of pragmatic indeterminacy shows that semantic underdetermination is of little significance when it comes to unclarity in actual utterances. The fact that many utterances are semantically underdetermined does not entail their indeterminacy. Utterances of sentences such as

(E18) "It rains."

or

(E19) "She has taken enough from you."

are semantically underdetermined—to the effect that they require contextual ingredients to express a full proposition.[118] What is said is, so to say, incomplete.

Context often determines what is communicated, even when literal content fails to produce a meaningful proposition, as in the case of category mistakes or presupposition failures.[119] We can see this in the following example, in which the speaker is clearly pointing to somebody who is drinking water and not a martini:

(E20) "Who is the man drinking a martini?"[120]

---

[117] Of course, there are always possible borderline cases in any application of language to the world—even if some of these borderline cases are due to (unavoidable) imprecision in measurement. Compare section 4.3.2 on the value (and necessity) of semantic vagueness.

[118] Compare Bach (1994, 125–134). Some say that such utterances need to be "enriched" by the context of the utterance. This is called "pragmatic enrichment." I do not want to take a stance on the precise nature of this process. For our purposes, it suffices to clearly see the difference between indeterminacy and semantic underdetermination.

[119] Some philosophers even go so far to say that semantics does not play any decisive role in determining what is communicated. See, for instance, Recanati (2001).

[120] This is the famous example by Donnellan (1966, 287) distinguishing between speaker's reference and semantic reference. See also Kripke (1977, 256).

Is this utterance meaningless? No, the question can be completely clear and comprehensible, even though the speaker does not succeed *semantically* to refer to anybody. It can be completely clear what is communicated, while something is funny on the level of what is said.[121]

Conversely, even if what is said is perfectly clear, what is communicated can be obscured by pragmatic factors. Context can clarify the communicative content of utterances with category mistakes or presupposition failures such as in (E20). Context can disambiguate an ambiguous expression or dissolve the unclarity around a borderline application of a vague expression. But context can also make things less clear than they would have been from a purely semantic point of view.

One source of such pragmatic indeterminacy can be found in the just mentioned referential-attributive distinction. The expression "the man drinking a martini" is pragmatically ambiguous between a referential and an attributive reading. It can be used to refer to the man who the speaker in (E20) points to. In this case, she would refer to the man who in fact drinks water. Or, it can be used to refer to the man who, as a matter of fact, drinks a martini. In that case, she would refer to someone other than she thought. Context will usually determine which reading is salient, but not always.

In the following, four interconnected ways in which language can be pragmatically indeterminate will be discussed. There are probably more distinctions to be made, and these four ways are by no means an exhaustive—or even comprehensive—account of pragmatic indeterminacy. I hope, however, to show that indeterminacy—when found in actual activities such as the law—is a phenomenon with a much more diverse nature than commonly recognized and that pragmatics is not only a means to resolve indeterminacy but a source of it, too.

1.5.1 IMPLICATURE INDETERMINACY

What is communicated by an utterance can be unclear if it is unclear what is implicated by it. There are two basic ways in which this can be the case: (1) it may be unclear whether an implicature is made in the first place, or (2) the content of the implicature may be unclear. The implicated content can be unclear because (2a) there are two or more ways to understand what is implicated, or (2b) there is a borderline application in the implicated content. In other words, there are forms of ambiguity and vagueness on the level of implicated content as well.

---

[121] Luckily, in most situations, we can simply ask what the speaker wanted to say. We can ask whether she has this or some other man in mind drinking something that looks like a martini. We can point out to the speaker that she is apparently making a false assumption. This is, however, rarely possible for written utterances, and thus, for most utterances in the law. The implications of the characteristics of legal language will concern us in chapter 2 in more detail.

We will call this phenomenon *implicature indeterminacy* and define it in the following way:

(D19)   An utterance u is IMPLICATURE-INDETERMINATE in context c iff it is unclear what is implicated by u in c.

Consider the following example:

(E21)   "Peter and Kimberly went to Paris."

Its most natural reading is that Peter and Kimberly went to Paris together. This is not what is said by (E21), but it will usually be implicated. However, if the speaker and hearer know that Peter and Kimberly are not on speaking terms for a while, it can be unclear whether it is actually implicated that they went together. It is then unclear whether one or the other implicature is made—or any implicature at all.

Also, the content of the implicature may be unclear. The speaker might (more or less clearly) implicate with (E21) that Peter and Kimberly are on speaking terms again. There might be vagueness with respect to the degree to which they speak again. There might also be ambiguity within the implicature as, for instance, in (E20). It is ambiguous whether the expression "the man drinking a martini" is referentially or attributively used.[122]

In figurative and metaphorical utterances, implicatures play an important role. It is thus not surprising that what is implicated is more frequently unclear when figurative phrases or metaphors are used. What is said and what is communicated is quite different in these cases, and context is even more important to figure out what is meant by the speaker. More precisely, it is generally the case that the more similar communicative and literal content are, the less context is required to determine them. In metaphorical utterances, both kinds of contents are particularly far apart, as in the following example:

(E22)   "You're the icing on my cake."

Such an utterance can implicate many different things depending on the context. We know that the speaker does not mean what is said, but that she is implicating something.[123] This openness to interpretation is precisely what makes figurative speech so powerful. Now we know the source of this openness to interpretation—it is due to implicature indeterminacy.

---

[122] Implicature indeterminacy is rarely recognized as a form of indeterminacy. Exceptions are, for instance, Grice (1989b), Gazdar (1979), and Horn (1985). However, they focus on pragmatic ambiguities as in (E20). So far there is no comprehensive analysis or account of implicature indeterminacy.

[123] Note that many other implicatures do not substitute literal content with implicated content, but merely add to it. Accordingly, we can distinguish between substitutional and additive implicatures, following Meibauer (2009, 374). Compare also section 1.1.

Implicature-indeterminate utterances can additionally happen to be borderline relevant to the conversation because it might be relevant on one interpretation and irrelevant on the other. Implicature indeterminacy is also a source of conversational vagueness. Consider the following example, in which a Frenchman replies to the question whether he can cook:

(E23) "I am French."

This is not a lie, since he is in fact French. If he cannot cook, however, his utterance is at least misleading, since he implies that he can cook by saying that he is French.[124] (E23), if understood literally, is clearly irrelevant to the question. (E23), if understood figuratively, is clearly relevant to the question. If (E23) is implicature-indeterminate, however, it is neither clearly relevant nor clearly irrelevant to the question. It is thus conversationally vague.

1.5.2 SPEECH ACT AMBIGUITY

Utterances are usually used to produce some effect in people's behavior. However, instead of simply issuing commands, it is generally more productive to be a bit more subtle. Very often we do not make speech acts directly. We normally do not, for instance, command to be given the salt at the dinner table. Rather, we ask whether somebody can pass the salt or mention that we might need it. These are indirect speech acts—they are still, even though indirectly, requests to be given the salt.

This indirectness is a matter of degree, and the balancing of it can result in unclarity. The implicature of an utterance might be ambiguous between two or more possibilities; or, as Austin (1962, 115) puts it, "ambiguity of meaning or reference is perhaps as common as deliberate or unintentional failure to make plain 'how our words are to be taken' (in the illocutionary sense)."

When the speaker deliberately or unintentionally fails to make plain how her words are to be taken, the utterance exhibits, how I call it, *speech act ambiguity*. It is unclear what kind of speech act is performed. To put it more precisely, it is unclear what illocutionary force the speech act has.[125] Speech act ambiguity is an important form of pragmatic indeterminacy.

---

[124] See Saul (2012) for the difference between lying and misleading. Other interesting cases in which one can deliberately mislead are out of context quotations, the exploitation of mishearing, or the use of implicatures when being polite or tactful.

[125] The illocutionary force of an utterance is either the basic intention in or actual action performed by making it. See Searle and Vanderveke (1985) for the former view and Bach and Harnish (1979) for the latter view.

The utterance

(E24) "Could you pass me the salt?"

is grammatically a question, but it usually is used as a straightforward request to actually pass on the salt to the speaker. Pragmatic rules and social conventions make it clear that (E24) is not meant as a question.

However, sometimes, we are at a loss with respect to the question of what function a particular utterance has. An utterance might not clearly count as any particular speech act. It can be unclear whether the utterance

(E25) "Could you finish this report by 5pm?"

is a genuine question or actually a command. It might be a more polite way to make a request that leaves it unclear whether it is made with the authority of a command or the politeness of a question.

Sometimes, speech act ambiguity is unintentionally or at least unconsciously used, but it can also be very deliberate. Imagine that Peter wants to bribe a police officer, and he does not know how the officer will react to his attempt at bribery. In this situation, Peter has an incentive not to be too explicit about the function of his utterance. He might want to implicate that he is willing to bribe the officer, but only indeterminately so—with the possibility to deny any unwanted implications. He might want to leave it open whether he was, for instance, just speculating on ways to make some extra money.[126]

1.5.3 PRESUPPOSITION INDETERMINACY
Presuppositions are implicit assumptions whose truth is taken for granted. Consider the following utterance:

(E26) "Peter no longer takes drugs."

In most contexts, (E26) clearly presupposes that Peter once took drugs. Sometimes, however, it is indeterminate whether a presupposition actually is made or what its content is.

If Peter has settled down from his drug-free, but wild youth, the utterance can simply be meant to comment on this change by way of figurative speech. If it is indeterminate whether (E26) is to be understood literally or figuratively, it will also be unclear whether Peter actually took drugs before.

The form of pragmatic indeterminacy in

(E20) "Who is the man drinking a martini?"

---

[126] Compare section 4.4.4 on strategies of pragmatic indeterminacy.

can also be analyzed as a presupposition indeterminacy. (E20) presupposes that there is a man drinking a martini. The audience can normally take this presupposition for granted and read (E20) referentially. Sometimes, however, there are reasons to assume that this is not what the speaker means.[127]

(E20) is indeterminate if the speaker pragmatically refers to someone not drinking a martini, but there is in fact another person to whom "the man drinking a martini" semantically refers. It is then indeterminate what is presupposed by (E20). In that case, the audience could also take the speaker to merely attribute to the contextually salient referent the property of drinking a martini.

1.5.4 IMPLICITURE INDETERMINACY

Many utterances convey content in ways even more subtle than in (E22), (E23), or (E24). Consider the classic example by Kent Bach (1994, 136):

(E27) "You're not going to die."

If a mother utters (E27) to her crying son upset about a cut finger, she clearly does not mean that he is immortal. Rather, she means that he is not going to die *from that particular cut.*

Another example by Bach is the following utterance:

(E28) "Sorry, you must be 21 years old."

If a barkeeper utters (E28) to a youngster who has asked for a drink, the barkeeper clearly does not mean that the youngster must be exactly 21 years old. Rather, she means that the youngster must be *at least* 21 years of age.[128]

In both cases, the speaker does not mean what is (literally) said by the utterances. Instead, they convey *implicitures* that expand on their literal content.[129] (E27) and (E28) involve so called expansion implicitures. Bach (1994) distinguishes them from *completion implicitures* such as

(E29) "I am ready."

---

[127] Some philosophers of language have discussed this form of indeterminacy as "pragmatic ambiguity." Here, the truth value of a sentence hinges on listener presupposition or speaker intent. Stalnaker (1970, 281–287), for instance, illustrates pragmatic ambiguity with this example: "The man with the purple turtleneck shirt is tall." This utterance can be ambiguous between the referential and the attributive use of "the man with the purple turtleneck shirt." It can carry the presupposition of who the man is and attribute the property of having a purple turtleneck shirt of him, or it can simply refer to whoever the man with the purple turtleneck shirt is. Rather technically, Stalnaker (1970, 286) defines pragmatic ambiguity such that "a sentence has the potential for pragmatic ambiguity if some rule involved in the interpretation of that sentence may be applied either to the context or to the possible world."

[128] Compare Soames (2008a) and Marmor (2008) for a discussion of this impliciture with respect to possible legal ramifications.

[129] Sperber and Wilson (2001) and Carston (2002) use the concept of *explicature*. According to Bach (2010), the notions of impliciture and explicature are largely synonymous. For convenience, we will follow Bach's terminology. Compare Recanati (2014) on pragmatic enrichment in general.

Without additional contextual information, we do not quite know what is (literally) said by (E29). The expression "ready" in (E29) is too general for just about any purpose. What is the speaker ready for? On its own, (E29) is not even truth-evaluable. Something is missing that must be provided by the context to make the utterance felicitous.[130] There is usually no doubt that the utterance does not communicate what is (literally) said since what is said is, in some sense, incomplete.

The "collective-distributive ambiguity" is another case of impliciture indeterminacy. Consider the following example:

(E30) "The boys came."

Does this utterance convey that the boys came together or separately? (E30) allows for a collective or distributive reading. Neither reading is part of the literal content of the utterance. Without more contextual information, (E30) does not express a full proposition: It requires a completion impliciture. However, it may be indeterminate whether (E30) implicites the collective or distributive reading. Sometimes, context does not tell.

In the case of expansion implicitures, on the other hand, it can be indeterminate whether communicative content is an impliciture or just what is said. The following is an example by Marmor (2008):

(E31) "Have you eaten blackberries?"

If Marmor utters (E31) to his wife, he can sensibly mean to ask her either (1) whether she had blackberries on the day of his utterance or (2) whether she has ever had blackberries before. She might reasonably ask him for clarification of his question in return.

Expansion implicitures also figure in generic statements such as the following:

(E32) "Birds fly."

At first glance, generics might appear to be related to generality. Generics are sentences in which often general expressions are used in a loose way. What (E32) literally says is that all birds fly. But (E32) is rarely used to communicate that each and every bird flies at the moment of utterance. Under most circumstances, the expression "fly" can correctly be applied to birds but not to all subgroups of birds. For instance, even if we accept that birds fly and that penguins are birds, we do not

---

[130] It might be argued that examples of ellipsis such as "I love you, too," which we treated as syntactic ambiguity, also require completion. It probably turns on the exact nature of the example. In written utterances, the analysis as syntactic ambiguity makes more sense, since the different possibilities of grammatical structure are given by the co-text. In oral utterances, the non-linguistic context must provide the missing information, which is more clearly a pragmatic process.

need to accept that penguins fly, too.[131] Most generalizations such as (E32) are true only if we interpret them generically. They are prone to have counterexamples or exceptions, and that is why they are defeasible.

(E32) is defeasible not because it is general, semantically vague, or polysemous (which it also is) but because it carries an impliciture that changes its communicated content such that *most* or *normal* birds *can* fly. However, it is not always clear how exactly the context changes the content of an utterance such as (E32). In some cases (e.g., in scientific discourse), we do not know whether the speaker does not in fact want to make the stronger, non-generic, claim. Thus, (E32) can carry an indeterminate expansion impliciture, leaving it open whether it is supposed to be read as a more or less generic (or even non-generic) statement.

In the case of both expansion and completion implicitures, it can be indeterminate what the content of the impliciture is. If you utter (E29) when getting dressed for a party, you might mean that you are ready *to leave the house*, that you are ready *to go to the party*, that you are ready *to party all night*, and so forth. There are, presumably, indefinitely many possibilities of what exactly is communicated by (E29). And, it is usually not determinate exactly which proposition is expressed. For most purposes, a more or less indeterminate impliciture is sufficient.

Sometimes, there is not even a clear way to distinguish between what semantics and what pragmatics contribute to the content of utterance. In what way can the speaker be ready such that (E29) comes out true? Must she be ready for a specific purpose? Or could she be ready for just anything? Is (E29) true if she is only ready to blink or shake her head?

The differences in content can be explained either by reference to expansion implicitures such as in (E29) or the polysemy of "ready"—its having multiple senses as discussed in section 1.2.3.[132] The most general sense of "ready" is narrowed by context to a more specific sense, which can provide sufficient content for (E29) to be truth-evaluable. Which explanation we favor depends on where we want to draw the line between semantics and pragmatics—a project I cannot undertake here.

The kind of impliciture most important for our purposes is standard-relativity, which we will discuss in section 1.6 in relation to the problem of context determination. It is a kind of completion impliciture, which is latently present in many terms—usually when their usage depends on a comparison class of some sort.

In sum, indeterminacy on the level of pragmatics can occur at least in two basic forms—as conversational vagueness and pragmatic indeterminacy. Generality

---

[131] Such reasoning is called non-monotonic. See Carlson and Pelletier (1995) for an overview of genericity.

[132] This will become crucial in our discussion of the case *Smith v. United States*, 508 U.S. 223 (1993) in section 3.4 with respect to the meaning of "to use a firearm."

is the most prominent form of conversational vagueness, whereas impliciture indeterminacy is the most prominent form of pragmatic indeterminacy. We will now turn not to another form of indeterminacy but to a fundamental problem present in all forms of indeterminacy.

1.6 Context Determination and Standard-Relativity

Williamson (1994, 281) claims that vagueness can be "reduced but not eliminated by context." In contrast, ambiguity can—in many cases—be completely resolved. But both ambiguous and vague expressions are context-dependent, that is, their extension can vary from context to context. Semantically underdetermined expressions are generally context-dependent.[133] However, context-dependence is a phenomenon quite distinct from ambiguity and vagueness, or semantic underdetermination in general.[134]

Sentences in which context-dependent expressions are used must be placed in some context of utterance to determine their literal content. What is said—and thus the truth of an utterance—depends on (at least) three factors. It depends (1) on the world in which the utterance is made and (2) on the meaning of the expressions used in the utterance.[135] Due to semantic underdetermination, (3) context is generally required, too.[136]

However, context – normally the best warranty for determinacy – can itself be unclear. Endicott (2000, 132) even maintains that "contexts are typically *unspecific*." And, in fact, what counts as the relevant context anyway? There is not even theoretical consensus on the question of what the context of an utterance is.[137] Every utterance has a context that we need to know in order to determine what is communicated. An utterance can be indeterminate because its context is not sufficiently clear. But it does not only depend on context whether some utterance is indeterminate or not; it can also be difficult to determine what the relevant context is in the first place. The potential underdetermination of context is probably the most intractable form of indeterminacy because it plays a role in all other forms of indeterminacy that we analyzed so far.

In principle, an utterance can be indeterminate "either because some particular aspect of the contextual background happens not to be sufficiently clear, or because

---

[133] Compare Bach (2012).

[134] Compare Williamson (1994, 215).

[135] Compare Austin, Strawson, and Cousin (1950, 124).

[136] Compare Kaplan (1978), distinguishing between character and content with respect to demonstratives.

[137] Compare Finkbeiner et al. (2012).

in spite of the shared contextual background some aspect of content conveyed remains unclear."[138]

So far we examined different ways in which "some aspect of content conveyed remains unclear." We examined utterances that are indeterminate due to some form of linguistic indeterminacy. In this section, we turn to the case of when "some particular aspect of the contextual background happens not to be sufficiently clear."

Context is the framework or setting in which an oral or written utterance is made and is required to fully understand it. Only some aspects of the setting are relevant for the understanding of an utterance. Classically, these aspects are seen as variables in the determination of the truth-value of the utterance of a semantically underdetermined sentence. Even though the context is not part of the utterance, it essentially determines the form, content, and relation of the expressions used in it. Aspects of context are, for instance, the time and place of the utterance, the speaker, the hearer, the respect in which the utterance is made, and contrastive categories and comparison classes of concepts used by the speaker.[139] They can also include personal or social relations between speaker and hearer as well as other utterances made prior to or even after the utterance.[140]

Context is, prima facie, an epistemic notion. If there is unclarity in context, it must be uncertainty with respect to the knowledge we have about it and about other people's beliefs. However, besides this epistemic uncertainty of what the relevant contextual factors are, there are normative questions concerning the relevance of these factors as well as indeterminacy in the metalinguistic principles of interpretation and the description of context. This unclarity in context is potentially due to a fundamental problem in the process of context determination. It is a normative question whether some aspect of context ought to be considered relevant or not. There may not always be clear and unequivocal rules of interpretation to be followed. Also, there may be unclarity about how to weigh different aspects of context against each other.

The list of relevant aspects of context is (potentially) open-ended, and there is probably no way to determine these aspects theoretically:

> It seems to me impossible to lay down in advance what sort of thing is going to count as a context of use. ... The moral here seems to be that there is no way of specifying a finite list of contextual coordinates. (Cresswell, 1979, 138)

---

[138] See Marmor (2011b, 140).

[139] There is a narrow and broad notion of context. The narrow context is required to determine what is said and, classically, includes only time, place, and speaker. The broad context is required to determine what is pragmatically conveyed. It concerns the pragmatic aspects of language. Compare Bach (2012) for a discussion of the two notions of context.

[140] See Eikmeyer and Rieser (1983) for a discussion of the social aspects of the context.

The hearer has to fill the "gappy" lexical meaning of context-dependent expressions by means of such contextual variables. The most obvious examples are indexicals such as "I," "here," or "today." But also all the previously discussed (potentially) indeterminate expressions seem generally to be context-dependent.[141]

Context-dependency is an essential feature of ambiguity. Only context can tell whether an ambiguous expression has one or the other meaning. Context-dependent expressions are also almost always vague, and vice versa. As Hans Kamp puts it:

> [I]t is typical of a vague predicate that what objects it is true of depends on the context in which it is used. There are certain adjectives in particular—such as e.g. large, or soft, or clever—about whose extensions we can hardly say anything in abstraction from any contextual setting; it is only with respect to a given context of use that we can meaningfully ask whether a certain object is large, and there are very few, if any, objects of which it is clear absolutely whether or not they are clever or soft. Different contexts resolve these questions in different ways; the same object may count as definitely clever in one context and yet as definitely not in another. (Kamp, 2013, 281)

Expressions such as "large," "soft," and "clever" are certainly gradually and multi-dimensionally vague. Whether their vagueness leads to actual indeterminacy or not is a contextual matter, however. It depends on the context whether an actual borderline case occurs, even though (potentially) vague expressions are vague independently of context.

The reason why we cannot say much about the applicability of these expressions in abstraction from a contextual setting lies in their relativity to context. What is soft for a surface in one context can be hard for the same surface in another context. And even a small elephant is still a large animal. The expression "fast" in (E4) about the turtle is context-relative in precisely this way. An utterance in which it occurs can vary in content depending on the comparison class against which it is interpreted. A fast turtle is slower than even the slowest racing car.

If we talk about the ship *Santa Maria* with which Columbus discovered America, it is certainly false to say that it was a fast ship—compared to modern ships. If we compare it with the ships of its time, however, then the statement could easily be true. The context-specific meaning of such terms might even depend on the purposes of the participants of the conversation. For instance, a house can be big or small—depending on whether it is for a family with two or six children.[142]

The comparison class—as part of the context—usually resolves this kind of indeterminacy. Without a comparison class, it is not even possible to determine what the expression "fast" means in any relevant detail. This context-relativity,

---

[141] Compare Pinkal (1995, 71) on the relation between indefiniteness and context.

[142] Compare Raffman (1996).

which is inherent to such relational expressions, facilitates different understandings of the expression "fast" depending on the context in which it is used.[143] This includes the possibility of understanding the expression to mean *actually fast* in contrast to *potentially fast* because a ship can be slow in the sense of having a certain speed at the moment of utterance, while at the same time being fast in the sense of being able to reach a certain—much higher—speed in theory.

These forms of context-relativity are instances of implicitures. Utterances such as

(E33) "Santa Maria was a fast ship."

or

(E34) "The house is big."

usually carry completion implicitures of the sort that *Santa Maria* was a fast ship *compared to other ships of its time* or that the house is big *for a family with two children*. Without such implicitures, it is impossible to say whether the utterances are true or what is communicated by them.

The kind of impliciture most important for our purposes is standard-relativity.[144] Recall the following utterance:

(E8) "Peter is tall."

(E8) implicites that Peter is tall *relative to a contextually valued standard*. Instead of contextually valued standards, one can also (more specifically) speak of comparison classes, which are needed to determine what is said.[145] Standard-relativity can be defined in the following way:

(D20) An expression *e* is STANDARD-RELATIVE iff *e* is relative to a contextually valued standard.

In contrast to (E8), utterances such as

(E35) "Peter is taller than John."

or

(E36) "Peter is as tall as John."

---

[143] Because they have no definite meaning by themselves and independently of context, expressions such as "large," "soft," or "fast" are sometimes also called "syncategorematic." Compare Endicott (2000, 131).

[144] Compare Rett (2014), who calls standard-relativity "evaluativity."

[145] Compare Ludlow (1989).

are not standard-relative because one does not need to know anything about the standard of tallness given to know their truth or falsity. Neither utterance requires judgment about or comparison to some standard.

Just as with other implicitures, it can be unclear what standard or comparison class is implicited. Sometimes, we do not know what the relevant standard is, or context does not provide an appropriate comparison class. This form of indeterminacy is neither polysemy nor multi-dimensional vagueness, but another, pragmatic, way in which context can fail to determine what is communicated. When using terms such as "fast," "big," or "tall," we rely, more or less implicitly, on some standard or comparison class. However, the notion of a comparison class or standard is not much clearer than the one of context. In fact, the discretion that seems to be present when determining the relevant aspects of context appears to be equally present when determining what the comparison class or standard is:

> To judge what comes within the comparison class is not to answer a question of fact whose precise answer is unknowable, but to make an evaluative judgment concerning what *matters* for the purpose in question. This fact ties the unspecificity of context dependence to the vagueness of evaluation. (Endicott, 2000, 133)

This evaluative judgment is called for in many instances in which we have to decide what the relevant aspects of context are. Usually these factors are salient; even for general terms such as "ready" or "tasty" in which the audience needs to know a lot about speaker and context to figure out their context-specific extension. Extravagantly vague terms such as "substantial," "material," or "reasonable" are (potentially) indeterminate primarily because we do not quite know what they mean without a standard relative to which they can be understood.

Other extravagantly vague terms such as "neglect," "kindness," or "cruel and unusual punishment" are not only relative to some contextually valued standard but they involve an additional impliciture—they involve a genuine value judgment. They are *evaluative* terms and express what Williams (1985) calls *thick concepts*.[146]

Williams's examples of thick concept terms include "economy," "prudence," "coward," and "exploited." All these terms are equally polysemous and multi-dimensionally vague. In addition, they are evaluatively loaded, that is, they are generally used to express a pro-attitude. As a consequence, the utterance

(E37) "She is very kind."

---

[146] See also Eklund (2011) for a thorough discussion on thick concepts.

can equally inform about the person referred to and the speaker herself.[147] Thick concept terms are "thick" because they have both descriptive and prescriptive elements. They can be used to describe something and, at the same time, to make a value judgment.

Because these terms are evaluatively loaded, it can be difficult to tell whether utterances in which they occur are true or false. It can be relatively easy to determine whether the utterance

(E38) "This is an oil painting."

is true if in fact the painting is painted in tempera. It cannot be as easily resolved, however, whether the utterance

(E39) "This is a piece of art."

is true or not. There can be substantial disagreement, even if all relevant facts are known to the disputants. The polysemy of the term "art" facilitates this disagreement as well as resolutions of it, while its semantic vagueness may additionally aggravate the disagreement. The real difficulty lies, however, in the *thickness* of the term. It involves an impliciture that makes reference to a truly evaluative standard. This explains the extravagance about extravagantly vague terms. They are extravagantly indeterminate partly because they are multi-dimensionally polysemous and contested and partly because they are thick and evaluatively loaded.

In cases of thickness and standard-relativity, it can clearly be seen that the determination of context is not merely an epistemic matter, but comprises normative and evaluative aspects. However, in all cases of indeterminacy, we have to determine what the content of the utterance is in a balanced act between factual and normative questions. We have to answer both questions simultaneously because there are multiple ways to determine what is communicated and the relevant aspects of context, and the answer to each question depends on the other one.

The context—including, for instance, evidence in law—is required for the interpretation at the same time as the interpretation of the utterance is required to determine what the relevant context is. Interpretation involves an act of evaluation.[148] Potential indeterminacy created by vague or ambiguous expressions will be resolved by *constructing* a precisifying or disambiguating context. When interpretation is called for, we have to actively evaluate the context and decide which aspects of it are relevant for the determination of the content of the utterance.

Additionally, the context is usually stated in the same indeterminacy-prone language as the utterances to be interpreted. This is especially a problem in law

---

[147] Of course, one can also always use such utterances in a detached way. Compare section 2.1 on the normativity of legal language.

[148] Compare section 2.3 for an argument of this claim.

in which the case at hand (the context) as well as interpretation principles and other laws are stated in the same language. Once there is unclarity on the level of content, the context cannot be assumed to be given. It must be evaluated and, as a consequence, there can be substantial disagreement about its relevant aspects.

The problem of context determination is also known as the "frame problem."[149] In addition to linguistic indeterminacy, there is unclarity about the correct framing of the context. The frame problem aggravates all forms of linguistic indeterminacy.

For legal utterances, it is particularly difficult to frame the context because they are written. Accordingly, the context of utterance and the context of application can come apart. Consider, for example, the indexical "today" in the sentence

(E40) "I promise to take out the trash today."

scribbled on a note. Does it mean that the author will take out the trash on the day when she wrote the note, when the note is supposed to be read, or when it is actually read? This is not only a problem for utterances with indexicals but also for standard-relative expressions such as "tall" since they require a contextually valued standard that might be different for the contexts of utterance and application.

Hence, there are at least three ways in which the context itself can be unclear. First, there is *epistemic unclarity* when we do not know some relevant aspect of context or even what is relevant at all. Second, there is *normative unclarity* concerning the relevance of contextual aspects and interpretation principles when there is substantial disagreement on the relevance of certain aspects of context or the application of interpretation principles. Third, there is *metalinguistic unclarity* concerning the description of the context when there are semantic and pragmatic forms of indeterminacy on the level of the description of the relevant contextual aspects.

Even though the relevant aspects of context are usually salient enough to facilitate direct understanding, we cannot really specify them in any precise way: "More often than not, the context features that are relevant to the assignment of a sense to an expression cannot be clearly identified at all."[150] We normally understand an utterance even if we are not able to determine its context precisely. But sometimes we do not. When this is the case, we will say that utterances are unclear because of context indeterminacy—in addition to the forms of linguistic indeterminacy we analyzed so far:

(D21) An utterance u is CONTEXTUALLY INDETERMINATE in context c iff it is unclear what is communicated by u due to unclarity of c.

Context indeterminacy stems from the (just mentioned) fundamental unclarity in context determination and its evaluative and normative character. Note that

---

[149] Originally, this is a problem in artificial intelligence concerning adequate sets of axioms for a viable description of a robot environment. Compare McCarthy and Hayes (1969).

[150] See Pinkal (1995, 65).

also context indeterminacy—as the forms of linguistic indeterminacy discussed so far—is relative to a competent and well-informed language user. An utterance is not contextually indeterminate simply if anyone finds it unclear due to unclarity of context.

Usually, we do not even want the context to be too specific. For instance, the degree of granularity of an expression will be coarse- or fine-grained for the purposes of many conversations. As we saw in section 1.4 on generality, a general expression like "East Coast" can be perfectly determinate if uttered in a context in which the degree of granularity is coarse-grained.[151] It will typically be unnecessary to rely on a highly specific comparison class and to fix the context precisely:

> Suppose that we confront "France is hexagonal" with the facts, in this case, I suppose, with France, is it true or false? Well, if you like, up to a point; of course I can see what you mean by saying that it is true for certain intents and purposes. It is good enough for a top-ranking general, perhaps, but not for a geographer." (Austin, 1962, 143)

It can even be obstructive for an understanding of the utterance to set the degree of granularity too finely. Under most circumstances, when the speaker utters

(E34) "The house is big,"

the hearer does not have to know which specific comparison class of "big" the speaker has in mind to understand what she means. Under most circumstances, the hearer will not have any specific comparison class in mind. Usually, we make more or less specific and more or less precise statements, and the context gives us the comparison class in a correspondingly more or less coarse-grained way.

In sum, neither theoretically nor practically is there a way to determine the context at any level of specificity or precision. There is no theoretical consensus on the question of what context is. In practice, too, there is much too often substantial disagreement about what aspects of context are relevant for the interpretation of a particular utterance. As Endicott (2000, 132) puts it, ordinarily "nothing will count as fixing the context precisely."

1.7 Summary

In this chapter, we analyzed the concept of linguistic indeterminacy. We defined it in general terms with reference to unclarity in content and discussed its various forms in detail.

---

[151] Compare Keil (2006, 99–106). See also Keil (2010, chapter 7) on the degree of resolution ("Auflösungsgrad") of predicates. The degree of resolution determines the standard on which an utterance's truth will be measured. The degree of granularity in utterances can also be analyzed as expansion implicitures. Compare Bach (1994, 134) for a short discussion.

We first differentiated between three forms of ambiguity. While cases of lexical ambiguity can normally be resolved, indeterminacy due to syntactic ambiguity is harder to avoid. We found that polysemy plays an essential role in actual conversation since it cannot be avoided and has several effects that make it prone to strategic use.

We also discussed three forms of semantic vagueness. Gradual vagueness captures the boundarylessness of expressions. It can be problematic when leading to the Sorites paradox. Multi-dimensional vagueness enables interpretative discretion when incommensurable dimensions of the term conflict, but it must not be confused with (multi-dimensionally) polysemous or evaluative terms. Open texture concerns the occurrence of wild cases and is, thus, neither avoidable nor useful.

Pragmatic forms of indeterminacy are particularly interesting. Conversational vagueness, which is the borderline application of conversational maxims, causes utterances to be indeterminate due to irrelevance or non-informativeness. Its most common form is generality. Implicature indeterminacy raises interpretive questions when the implicated content of an utterance is unclear. Speech act ambiguity, presupposition indeterminacy, and impliciture indeterminacy obscure what the utterance's illocutionary force is, what it presupposes, and what it implicites, respectively. Impliciture indeterminacy is most relevant when a contextually valued standard is implicited, that is, in the form of standard-relativity.

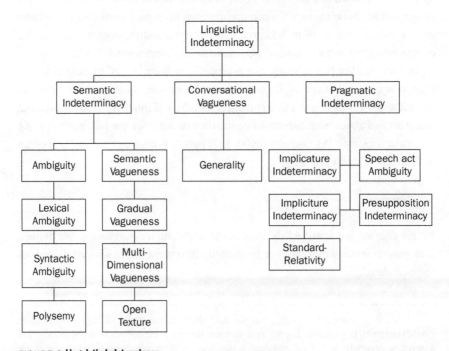

FIGURE 2 **Linguistic Indeterminacy**

Context indeterminacy accompanies all forms of linguistic indeterminacy. There is no direct way to use it, but some forms of indeterminacy can be used in combination with context indeterminacy to resolve other forms of indeterminacy.

Figure 2 shows, in summary, the three main forms of linguistic indeterminacy. Ambiguity and semantic vagueness are forms of semantic indeterminacy, on one hand. Implicature, impliciture, and presupposition indeterminacy and speech act ambiguity are forms of pragmatic indeterminacy, on the other hand. Generality is a form of conversational vagueness, which, albeit on the level of pragmatics, is a special form of indeterminacy because it obscures neither what is said nor what is communicated.

In chapter 2, we will first look at the characteristics of legal language and interpretation. We will review the *communication theory of law* on which most participants in the debate on vagueness in the law (explicitly or implicitly) rely. After that, we will analyze in chapter 3 what role the different forms of linguistic indeterminacy have in the law.

2

Language and the Law

Language is essential to the law. This is evident in all its forms and areas: when the Justices of the US Supreme Court argue about the correct understanding of the Constitutional text; when lobbying groups spend time and money in trying to influence the phrasing of a European Union directive; when parliament, committees, and experts collaborate to formulate a new national statute; when agencies transform statutory law into detailed regulations; when contracting parties send drafts back and forth with ever so slight changes to a merger agreement. Judges, lobbying groups, legislators, agencies, and companies—they all wield the language of the law.

Because it matters. Returning a verdict; enacting a directive, law, or regulation; or forming a contract directly affects those addressed. A person might or might not be forced to go to jail. A building company might or might not be allowed to construct a park. A sale might or might not be closed. These things are made possible by words.[1] But how do mere words facilitate such changes in the world? Or, to put it more precisely, what is the relation between the linguistic utterance and its legal effect?

A position in legal philosophy re-emerged in recent years, stating that law is basically a form of communication. Legal philosophers such as Stanley Fish (2005) or Andrei Marmor (2011b) claim that the content of a law is identical to or determined by its linguistic content. Following Mark Greenberg (2011a), I will call this position the *communication theory of law* (CTL). Most participants in the debate on vagueness in law either implicitly or explicitly accept some version of

---

[1] Many of the examples Austin (1962) originally gives for speech acts pertain to the legal domain. I take it to be uncontroversial that (at least most) legal norms are created by legal speech acts. Langton (1993), for instance, even claims that political power can be measured by the ability to perform certain speech acts.

it.[2] CTL entails that utterances in the law can be understood and interpreted more or less like utterances in everyday life. This, in turn, entails that vagueness and all other forms of linguistic indeterminacy discussed in chapter 1 have very much the same effect to the law as they have to communication in everyday life.

Surely in the law wording matters more than almost anywhere else. But does it follow that law is nothing but communication? If it does not, what does this mean for the role of linguistic indeterminacy in the law? It might well be the case that legal content can be determined independently from linguistic content. As a result, indeterminacy in linguistic content would be far less relevant than proponents of CTL assume it to be.

As a matter of fact, there are highly influential positions in the philosophy of law—such as Ronald M. Dworkin's interpretivism or John Finnis's natural law theory—which directly contradict the main tenet of CTL.[3] The relation between linguistic content and legal content draws on important questions in the debate on the nature of law. I will not go into this debate here.[4] Instead, I will give a constructive analysis of legal speech acts and legal interpretation based on mostly uncontroversial assumptions about the law.[5]

First, in section 2.1, I examine features that are specific to the law and potentially relevant to the (strategic) use of indeterminacy. Second, in section 2.2, I give a positive account of three prototypical kinds of legal speech acts, that is, I will analyze the enactment of laws, rendering of verdicts, and formation of contracts as legal performatives.[6]

Third, we will inquire into the characteristics of interpretation in the law in section 2.3. Legal interpretation differs from interpretation in everyday communication in several respects. Most importantly, legal interpretation consists of a linguistic and a specifically legal part. While linguistic interpretation yields linguistic content, legal construction is needed to determine legal content. Both can, and often do, fall together, but only if CTL is correct, they always do so. In other words, if CTL is correct, legal construction is nothing more than the linguistic interpretation of legal text.

---

[2] See, for instance, Endicott (2000), Solan (2005), Soames (2012), Asgeirsson (2012b), or Marmor (2014).

[3] See Dworkin (1986) and Finnis (1980), respectively.

[4] A discussion of the debate would go far beyond the scope of this book.

[5] I expect that my conclusions about the role of language in the law are compatible with most theories of the nature of law, even though it is probably the case that positivist theories can accommodate them more easily.

[6] I will not explicitly discuss constitutional law, supranational law, or agency regulations. However, I will sometimes clarify whether and to what degree my conclusions can be generalized to other kinds of legal performatives.

Finally, in section 2.4, I discuss whether CTL can be correct in the form presupposed by the participants in the debate on vagueness in law. Even if we accept that linguistic content is more than just what is said, there seem to be some cases in which legal content and linguistic content come apart or in which there is at least consistent theoretical disagreement about the grounds of law. If this is true, then linguistic indeterminacy, and in particular semantic vagueness, is potentially less relevant in law than in ordinary communication.

2.1 Legal Language

Let us first examine those features of legal language that differentiate it from ordinary language and impact the potential strategic use of linguistic indeterminacy. While there are many linguistic differences, only some are relevant to the phenomenon of indeterminacy in the law.[7] In short, there are two basic differences between legal language and ordinary language that bear on our discussion of indeterminacy. First, legal language can appear especially unclear and indeterminate because of its technical jargon and complexity. Second, legal speech acts have a number of characteristics setting them apart from other speech acts occurring in ordinary language.

Legal language is often perceived to be cumbersome, antiquated, or cluttered—and as a result, not easily comprehensible by the layperson.[8] While ordinary language is grammatically and lexically heterogeneous, legal language has a very particular technical style and jargon. Ordinary language expressions, once used in the dialect of legalese, acquire new meanings that take on a linguistic life of their own. Ralf Poscher (2009) metaphorically compares the law with the Hand of Midas; every ordinary language expression it touches transforms into a legal one. For instance, the innocuous seeming expression "night" has a different, though related, meaning from its ordinary language counterpart— in fact, it has multiple meanings varying with the area of law in which it is used.

The law certainly aims at precisifying the meaning of its linguistic expressions. It has three basic tools of precisification. First, it can in fact establish legal definitions that precisify and disambiguate otherwise potentially indeterminate expressions. The lawmakers and courts can authoritatively change and decide what some legal expression means and how it should be applied. For ordinary language,

---

[7] See Danet (1980), Kurzon (1997), Tiersma (1999), and Fiorito (2006) for comprehensive linguistic comparisons between ordinary and legal language. Evidently, there are also many differences between the various legal languages within and across legal systems just as there are between legal systems themselves. In this book, I will focus on the similarities, as my arguments do not depend on distinctive features of, for instance, German or US law or legal language. See also section 2.3 on legal interpretation.

[8] See Enquist and Oates (2013, 127).

no comparable authority exists. Such changes and determinations of meaning are brought about not only by explicit definitions and stipulations, as Karl Larenz and Claus-Wilhelm Canaris emphasize, but by their use in legal contexts.[9] Legal academics, lawyers, and legal institutions change the meaning of legal expressions by arguing about them, proposing new interpretations, and by simply using them in converging ways. Thus, second, the law adapts its language to its tasks by legal theory, continuing practice, and interaction between theory and practice. In the United States, for instance, there is the American Law Institute that continuously gives recommendations to lawyers and lawmakers alike. Finally, the meaning of legal expressions can be precisified by precedent since a Supreme Court's (or other final) decision in an indeterminate case can determine an expression's extension for future cases similar to the one decided.

The practice of law can be understood as a special language game with specific rules.[10] As such, it differs from ordinary language "not just in vocabulary, but also in morphology ..., syntax ..., semantics ..., and other linguistic features," as Richard C. Wydick (2005, 10) points out.[11] The rules of legal language vary according to the institutional practices of the interpreting community.[12]

These differences are important. However, I am not concerned with unclarity in the law due to its technicality or complexity but with the forms of linguistic indeterminacy outlined in chapter 1. Their use does not depend on linguistic or non-linguistic differences in legal areas but on the kind of speech act in which they are used. There are three paradigmatic types of legal speech acts, namely, the enactment of laws, rendering of verdicts, and formation of contracts.[13] These

---

[9] See Larenz and Canaris (1995, 24), who claim: "normative expressions have a much more precise meaning in the language of jurisprudence than they have in general everyday language. This meaning, however, arises again and foremost not from a definition, but from its role, its function in the context of meaning of the normative sphere of law" ("Ausdrücke, die Normatives besagen, erhalten in der Sprache der Jurisprudenz zwar eine sehr viel präzisere Bedeutung, als sie in der allgemeinen Alltagssprache haben. Diese Bedeutung ergibt sich aber wiederum und in erster Linie nicht aus einer Definition, sondern aus ihrer Rolle, ihrer Funktion im Sinnzusammenhang der normativen Sphäre des Rechts")

[10] There is ongoing controversy between linguists about the specificity of legal language and whether it should be treated as a sub-language, register, dialect, idiolect, or domain of natural language. Compare Tiersma (1999), arguing for legal language as a sub-language, or Trosborg (1995), arguing for legal language as a special domain.

[11] See also Podlech (1976), who argues that legal language cannot be translated into ordinary language without loss in content.

[12] See Fish (1980, 116). Not only can the practice of legal language as a whole be seen as a language game distinctive from other uses of language such as business slang or teenage talk, but within the law there are several different (sub-)games, which have their own vocabulary and rules. A conveyancer will, for example, use a different idiom of legalese than a government expert in immigration laws.

[13] Legal analysis in the form of, for instance, client letters or motions is another form of legal speech that shares many of the special features of legalese. It is a different type of speech act, however. For reasons of conciseness, I limit my discussion to laws, verdicts, and contracts. When I use the expressions "legal

legal speech acts share a number of features that are relevant to our discussion of indeterminacy. They are typically (1) normative, (2) directed toward future events, (3) addressed to heterogeneous audiences, and (4) applied in a wide variety of circumstances. Let us discuss each feature in turn.

First, legal speech acts are typically normative. There is a significant overlap between law and morality. For instance, there is not only the legal obligation to refrain from killing or stealing but also a moral obligation to do so. Criminal law accommodates many paradigmatic moral norms, and also constitutional law strongly relies on issues of morality. Consider the interpretation of the evaluative term "human dignity" in many European legal systems or the term "cruel and unusual punishment" in the US Bill of Rights. The interpretation of these expressions invokes moral considerations.

More importantly yet, laws, verdicts, and contracts determine what *ought* to be done. Enactments of laws, renderings of verdicts, and formations of contracts positively create legal obligations.[14] They change the rights and duties of those involved. Legal utterances are thus normative also in a weaker sense: They create and express legal norms.

Such normative utterances require what H. L. A. Hart calls social rules, which are regular patterns of conduct accompanied by a "distinctive normative attitude." According to Hart (1961, 255), this attitude "consists in the standing disposition of individuals to take such patterns of conduct both as guides to their own future and as standards of criticism." However, normative utterances can also be made without committing oneself to the rule stated. As Joseph Raz (1990, 171–177) points out, they can be made in a detached way.[15]

The rule of recognition, being a social rule, validates other—legal—rules. Without a rule of recognition, no legal speech act could constitute a valid norm. There would not be any *legal* speech acts. In this sense, legal speech acts are institutional. Legal systems require institutions and processes for their creation and interpretation. It is institutions, not individuals, which are given the authority to bring about new law and decide disputes about the application of an already existing one. The enactment of laws, rendering of verdicts, and formation of contracts are institutionalized, that is, verdicts can only be rendered by the proper court, laws only enacted by the legislature, and contracts only formed by natural or

---

utterance" or "legal speech act," I thus generally refer to instances of legal drafting, leaving aside other forms of legal speech.

[14] As Brian Bix (2012a, 145) claims, law "is guidance through language, whether the language of statutes, judicial decisions, constitutional provisions, contracts, or wills."

[15] Raz distinguishes between committed and detached statements about the law. According to Raz (2009a, 153), someone making a committed statement expresses acceptance of the rule, while a detached statement does not. It adopts another perspective from which the rule is considered legitimate.

legal persons. This has to be done in a particular manner, without which these acts would be infelicitous, failing to create legally binding norms.[16]

Second, legal speech acts are typically directed toward the future. Laws, in particular, neither describe matters of fact nor refer to particular objects or events. They tell us what is going to happen if we fail to comply with the legal norm. Verdicts and contracts also prescribe some course of action. Verdicts pronounce a ruling that must be complied with. Contracts determine which objects or services must be exchanged.

Many legal speech acts are written. Laws are almost universally enacted in writing, and even spoken language in judicial proceedings (such as verdicts) usually has legal effect only once it is put down in written protocol. Although many everyday transactions are concluded orally, most of them are complemented by (written) standard business conditions. Moreover, due to non-repudiation, contracting parties also almost universally resort to writing if stakes are high.

In law it is thus primarily written speech acts that change individuals' rights and duties. This circumstance considerably changes their pragmatic effects because they can be made in one context and applied in quite another.[17] As a result, context of utterance and context of application are separated in time and space and sometimes even culturally and linguistically.[18] While in most conversations we naturally take into account the relevant aspects of context, it is far more difficult to ascertain what the context of a written utterance even is. Our grasp of an expression's comparison class or standard, or any other aspect of context, is thus structurally hindered when compared to spoken language.[19]

Third, legal speech acts are typically addressed to heterogeneous audiences. Laws are read by lawyers, officials, politicians, and citizens. They aim to regulate

---

[16] Müller-Mall (2012, 221) argues, for instance, that it can only be determined ex post whether a speech act has created a legal norm if it has been used and applied by other institutions. This, however, depends on whether these institutions recognize the legal speech act as felicitous. As Thomale (2013) objects, it cannot be the iterated use and application that validates legal norms because judges must decide the first case based on the law. They cannot wait for other legal institutions to react to its enactment. Be this as it may, speech acts must satisfy some basic conditions to successfully create legal norms. But if they satisfy them, the legal norms are thereby created—even if this can only be determined in due time.

[17] This has also a significant impact on the form of law. Spoken language is less grammatically complex because one must rely on the working memory of one's audience. In contrast, written language can be read again and again at one's own pace. As a result, sentences in legal texts are significantly longer and contain more subordinate and passive clauses than sentences in ordinary spoken language. See Tiersma (1999, 56–59) and Tiersma (2015). It also accounts for the fact that legal language appears antiquated and old-fashioned because written language typically changes considerably slower than spoken one.

[18] See sections 1.3 and 1.6 for discussions of this problem. Compare also section 2.4.2 on the *Argument from Divergence*.

[19] This is one reason why context-dependent expressions are less frequently used in legal utterances. Whereas indexicals are almost never found in laws, even many standard-relative expressions such as "rich" are either precisely defined or altogether omitted.

human behavior in society and must be understood by those affected (ultimately at least). Verdicts are communicated to the involved lawyers, executing authorities, plaintiffs, defendants, and even present and future judges and legislators. Contracts must be understood by the contracting parties, their lawyers, and potentially the judges who will decide in the case of disagreement and conflict. This heterogeneity might require the use of indeterminacy if beliefs and interests of those addressed are deemed irreconcilable.[20]

Fourth, legal speech acts must be applied in a wide variety of circumstances. Laws are applied not only in courtrooms but within the administration, in the lawmaking process itself, and in everyday human life. Also contracts must potentially be applied in diverse contexts. Unforeseen and substantially different events can occur in which they obligate the contracting parties to potentially undesirable acts. Even verdicts, which normally treat individual cases, must allow for eventualities, especially if they are rendered by supreme courts and likely to be used as precedents.

While contracts and verdicts can at least in principle be fairly concrete and specific, laws must be sufficiently abstract and general to be applicable to a complex and possibly unforeseeable world. As we have seen in chapter 1, the abstractness and generality of linguistic terms are not by themselves forms of indeterminacy. It has been argued, however, that this requirement of the law necessitates legal indeterminacy.[21]

Thus, legal speech acts create or express legal norms for heterogeneous audiences in various future circumstances. In law, there are essentially four types of norms.[22] First, *regulatory laws* are norms that are enacted by or result, in some other form, from legislation. This includes both statutory and constitutional law, as well as administrative regulations. An example is the Jacksonville vagrancy ordinance discussed in chapter 1. Second, *judicial decisions* are norms that become valid through adjudication. An example is the decision in *Miranda v. Arizona*, which constituted the right to remain silent.[23] Third, *contract clauses* are norms that describe legal transactions. An example are the standard business conditions of many companies. Fourth, *legal principles* are norms generated by jurisprudence or legal practice. An example is the principle of presumption of innocence, which is acknowledged in most legal systems including the United States and Germany. In section 2.2, we will discuss the legal speech acts that create or express regulatory

---

[20] See chapter 5, in particular, section 5.1.4, on double-talk in laws.

[21] See Hart (1961), for instance. See section 3.3 on conversational vagueness in the law for a detailed discussion of Hart's argument.

[22] See Vesting (2007, 17).

[23] *Miranda v. Arizona*, 384 U.S. 436 (1966).

laws, judicial decisions, and contract clauses. After that, we will turn to legal principles in section 2.3 on interpretation in the law.

2.2 Legal Performatives

In law, just as in everyday life, we do things with language. We use language to curse, dismiss, or convict others. A judge's sentence changes the defendant's legal status by pronouncing her guilty. Concluding a contract, the offeree's acceptance commits the contracting parties to the terms of the contract. The enactment of a statutory ordinance orders a public authority to execute it.

Most legal acts are speech acts. In courts of justice, locutionary, illocutionary, and perlocutionary acts are performed on a daily basis. There are locutionary acts such as reading the minutes, illocutionary acts such as finding someone guilty, and perlocutionary acts such as convincing the jury or intimidating a witness. Such speech acts can be unclear due to indeterminacy on the level of linguistic content if a term used is, for example, ambiguous or vague. But speech acts can also be unclear due to indeterminacy on the level of illocutionary force. For instance, the utterance (from chapter 1)

(E25) "Could you finish this report by 5pm?"

can be a question or a command depending on its illocutionary force. If it is unclear which illocutionary force is used, the source of unclarity is speech act ambiguity.[24]

Classically, five kinds of speech acts are distinguished.[25] Speech acts that are true or false are *representative*, as, for example, statements or descriptions. Somebody who states or describes something, also commits herself to the truth of the expressed proposition.[26] Non-representative speech acts such as

(E40) "I promise to take out the trash today."

or

(E41) "Drive me to the airport!"

can be felicitous or infelicitous—they can fail or succeed but hardly be true or false. Some such utterances merely express some attitude or feeling. Utterances such as "I am sorry," or "I wish you a happy birthday!" are *expressive* speech acts.

---

[24] See section 1.5.2 for an introduction of the notion of speech act ambiguity.

[25] This categorization is due to Searle (1976). There are some problems with it, but so far there is no alternative that is more intuitive and does not face similar problems. Alternatives are, among others, Fraser (1974), Katz (1977), Bach and Harnish (1979), Ballmer and Brennenstuhl (1981), Croft (1994), as well as Austin's original one (Austin, 1962). For this reason and because Searle's categorization is the most widely accepted one, we will use it as the basis for the following investigation of legal speech acts.

[26] See Ernst (2002, 102).

Apart from representative and expressive speech acts, there are directive, declarative, and commissive ones. *Directive* speech acts are, for instance, commands, requests, and advices. By illocutionary force, the speaker makes the hearer perform or refrain from some future action. *Declarative* speech acts are, for instance, christenings, appointments, and legal findings. The speaker changes by its illocutionary force the state of the object which she refers to in her utterance. *Commissive* speech acts are, for instance, promises, oaths, and threats. By its illocutionary force, the speaker commits herself to perform or refrain from some future action.

Statutory laws are classically considered to be directives, verdicts to be declarations, and contracts to be commissives. Many legal speech acts create, change, or end by their successful performance the rights and duties of individuals and institutions.

Often, the illocutionary force of a legal utterance is specified at the beginning of the legal document. Legal utterances are, hence, typically explicit performatives in Austin's sense.[27] The explicit performative verb can be found in the beginning of many statutes, which is called the enacting formula. For instance, the enacting formula in most US laws is the following:

> Be it enacted by the Senate and the House of Representatives of the United States of America in Congress assembled, That ...

The enacting formula is phrased in the passive voice of the imperative mood.[28] Of course, this does not mean that its illocutionary force is directive. It sounds very natural to say that Congress *declares* a new statute to be enacted. But does it for this reason have the illocutionary force of a declaration? Arguably, different parts of a statute have different illocutionary forces and thus count as different types of speech acts.[29]

A speech act's function is, however, not limited to its illocutionary effect. Frequently, even the intended perlocutionary effect is documented in some form to facilitate interpretation. Preambles of many statutes contain statements of policy or purpose. A good example is UCC (Uniform Commercial Code) § 1-103 (a):

> The Uniform Commercial Code must be liberally construed and applied to promote its underlying purposes and policies, which are ...

---

[27] In ordinary language, of course, we tend to be less explicit and say, instead of "I promise that I will be there tomorrow," simply "I will be there tomorrow." with the same illocutionary force. In law, the illocutionary force is often stated in the preamble or some clause before the material part of the statute or contract.

[28] This is remarkable, as the passive voice of the imperative mood is rarely used even in legal English. See Kurzon (1986, 10).

[29] Compare Fotion (1971) for a study on the hierarchical structure of speech acts.

The intended perlocutionary effect of legal utterances is not always stated sincerely. When negotiating, contracting parties are, for obvious reasons, not always interested in revealing the ultimate goals of their contract offers. Public knowledge of further objectives—as a buyout in the long term, for example—can be disadvantageous. In contrast, the illocutionary force must usually be clearly recognizable for the speech act to count as, for instance, a contract offer in the first place.

The strategic use of (indeterminate) legal utterances depends on the agents' objectives. Thus, in later chapters, we will broaden our discussion to include both illocutionary and perlocutionary effects.[30] In the following sections, we limit it to the question of what illocutionary acts are performed in laws (section 2.2.1), verdicts (section 2.2.2), and contracts (section 2.2.3).

2.2.1 LAWS

Regulatory laws are, classically, taken to be directive speech acts. Many statutes resemble commands of the lawmaker to the citizenry to perform or refrain from some action. Commands are a subclass of directives that require sanctions (of some sort) for non-compliance. Consider the following example:

(E41) "Drive me to the airport!"

(E41) is an illocutionary act that is used by the speaker to bring about some action of the hearer, namely, to drive her to the airport. Analogously, the lawmaker can be seen as using laws to bring about certain actions by citizens. It was assumed at some point that laws generally are commands—as did Jeremy Bentham (1776) and John Austin (1832/1999).[31] While this view is in its traditional formulation universally rejected, one can still plausibly analyze laws as directives more generally. Many laws clearly have the form of permissions or prohibitions, for instance.[32]

First and foremost, in criminal law, there are good candidates for directives. Criminal laws aim typically to suppress certain actions, as for example, 190a of the Californian Penal Code (PC):

> Every person guilty of murder in the first degree shall be punished by death, imprisonment in the state prison for life without the possibility of parole, or imprisonment in the state prison for a term of 25 years to life.

---

[30] In chapters 4 and 5, we tackle from different angles the question of what impact indeterminacy has on a speech act's illocutionary and perlocutionary effect.

[31] Bentham and Austin analyzed laws explicitly as utterances in the form of commands. However, many legal scholars such as, for instance, Posner (1993, 265), still speak of laws as commands at least metaphorically.

[32] See Kurzon (1986).

The enactment of PC 190a can be seen as a directive in the sense that it prohibits murder. By its illocutionary force it obliges the citizens to refrain from murder, and it specifies sanctions in the case of non-compliance.

However, PC 190a might also be seen as merely informing about the legal consequences of murder in California. Laws typically have the logical structure of conditionals, with the facts of the case in the antecedence and the legal consequences in the consequence, as PC 190a has, too. It does not say anywhere in the California Penal Code explicitly that murder is unlawful or prohibited. Statutory laws usually do not state literally what one should and should not do. They state legal consequences of generally described acts. The normative vocabulary that is used typically concerns the actions that legal institutions or other authorities are prescribed to take if a generally described offense has been committed.[33]

A speech act is a representative or directive depending on its illocutionary force—whether it is visible at the grammatical level or not. It is quite natural to say that what is communicated by PC 190a is that murder is unlawful. Arguably, the effect of its enactment was the prohibition of murder by law. And even the fact that the explicit aims of some law can diverge from or even be in conflict with its actual ones does not undermine the claim that its illocutionary force is directive. Maybe some laws do completely lack the *aim* to promote or inhibit certain kinds of behavior, when in fact they *do* have that function.

But do they always have this function? Some law and economics scholars argue that many statutes of criminal law should instead be seen as having the illocutionary force of commissives. They should be analyzed as promising or threatening citizens that they will be punished if they murder someone. I take it that laws sometimes have both functions at once. They can prohibit a certain kind of behavior and at the same time threaten with legal repercussions in the event of non-compliance.

Laws are not only addressed to the general public. PC 190a might prohibit murder or incentivize to refrain from murder by specifying a sentence for it. But it also orders the appropriate authorities to prosecute persons who commit murder and to hand out certain punishments to them, such as death or imprisonment. According to Bentham (1776, 430), there are two important rules in each law:

> A law confining itself to the creation of an offence, and a law commanding a punishment to be administered in case of the commission of such an offence, are two distinct laws; not parts of one and the same law. The acts they command are altogether different; the persons they are addressed to are altogether

---

[33] For that reason, Kelsen (1945/2007) treats laws as directives to authorities in general. However, as Hart (1961/1994) points out, this would make it impossible to account for the difference between taxes and fines. Moreover, there are, as a matter of fact, laws that do explicitly prohibit certain actions. The Code of Ordinances of Manitou Springs, Colorado, 1697 § 1, states, for example, that it "is unlawful for any person to shoplift or steal goods."

different. Instance, *Let no man steal*; and, *Let the judge cause whoever is convicted of stealing to be hanged.*

While there is disagreement whether there is such a rule as "Let no man steal" addressed to the general public, I take it to be uncontroversial that most law enactments in some way or other command courts or agencies to enforce the legal consequences established by them, as "Let the judge cause whoever is convicted of stealing to be hanged" does. Meir Dan-Cohen (1983) calls the first rule a "conduct rule" because it aims at guiding the conduct of the general public; and the instruction to the authorities a "decision rule" because it directs their decisions in applying conduct rules.[34] PC 190a undeniably has directive force with respect to its decision rule: It orders the appropriate authorities to prosecute murderers.

There are some laws, however, which can hardly be seen as directives in any plausible way. Power-conferring rules—as Hart (1961/1994) calls them—do not aim to bring about someone's action. They do not even change anybody's obligation to do anything. They change what certain individuals or institutions are allowed to do. For example, UCC § 2-204 empowers people to create their own rules of conduct. It states how a sales contract can be formed:

> A contract for sale of goods may be made in any manner sufficient to show agreement, including offer and acceptance, conduct by both parties which recognizes the existence of a contract, the interaction of electronic agents, and the interaction of an electronic agent and an individual.

The enactment of UCC § 2-204 can be seen as a declaration that changed the status of potential contracting parties. Its enactment enabled them to form (legally enforceable) contracts. They can now become contracting parties for the purposes of the UCC.

Similarly, there are laws that are *expository* (in Austin's sense). They determine the meaning of some legal term or identify the national anthem, for example. They, too, are declarations. For instance, UCC § 1-201 (12) defines the term "contract" in the following way:

> "Contract" ... means the total legal obligation that results from the parties' agreement as determined by the Uniform Commercial Code as supplemented by any other applicable laws.

It appears that neither the enactment of UCC § 2-204 nor UCC § 1-201 (12) can reasonably be seen as directives. According to Dick W. P. Ruiter (1993), most laws are declarations, some of which have additional commissive or directive elements.

---

[34] See also section 5.1.4.

Laws are enacted, and by their enactment their content becomes *the law*. From this perspective, law enactments are declarations because they change the law in accord with the content of the legal text.

Certainly, laws can be generally described as declarations, but even law enactments such as UCC § 2-204 or UCC § 1-201 (12) have directive elements. Even they tell people how to perform certain actions. As Marmor (2011b, 60–61) emphasizes, all "legal norms are basically directives or instructions issued by an authority aiming to guide the conduct of others."[35] What matters ultimately is the law's effect on people, and this is typically achieved by legal instruction.

Even though enactments of laws are not generally commands, there is a fruitful insight in Austin's command theory: most laws are normative, that is, they prescribe a certain kind of behavior. From this viewpoint, it makes perfect sense to say that they have the illocutionary force of directives.[36] The enactments of UCC § 2-204 and UCC § 1-201 (12) are directives because, in the context of the UCC as whole, they tell citizens, agencies, and courts what must be done to form a (legally enforceable) contract.

Enactments of laws are, of course, complex speech acts. Parts of them have different illocutionary forces. However, there typically is one main aspect.[37] Some legal provisions explicitly determine which kinds of behavior are permitted or prohibited. These are created by enactments with the force of directives. Some legal provisions constitute new kinds of behavior or in some other way complement those laws that instruct people to show or omit certain kinds of behavior. These are created by enactments with the force of declarations.[38] However, the main aspect of most laws in which either kind of legal provisions occur is directive, that is, they are created to prescribe some kind of behavior.

Law enactments do not only have different effects depending on their illocutionary force, but they also affect citizens, judges, and authorities in different ways. Some effects are illocutionary, such as the directive to an authority; some are perlocutionary, such as the actual reduction of crime in society. Lawmakers bring about some of these effects strategically. They need to address audiences with different beliefs, interests, and abilities. The ordinary citizen will understand and react to a new law differently than a Supreme Court Justice. The heterogeneity of the audience must be taken into account when drafting a new law. Also, different beliefs and interests within the legislature itself has an impact on its phrasing.

---

[35] See also Raz (1994).

[36] See also Raz (2009a). and Marmor (2011a).

[37] Cf. Fotion (1971) on master speech acts.

[38] Habermas (1995), for instance, captures this difference by distinguishing between constative and regulative speech acts.

Before a law can be enacted, it must be agreed on by the legislators representing the population or at least a large part thereof.

The lawmaking process itself can thus be divided into at least two stages. There is, first, a conversation among the legislators themselves. Compromises have to be found. The individual politicians constituting the legislature are often asymmetrically informed, have diverging interests, and have conflicting ideologies and beliefs. At the end of this internal negotiation, at best a common position is reached. Its result is a collective speech act addressed to the subjects of the law, agencies, and courts.

In this second conversation, the legislature might want to convey different messages to courts and the population in general. Different groups within the legislature might even aim for different effects to different audiences. This complexity in the lawmaking process hints at a potential need for linguistic indeterminacy. In fact, as I will argue in section 5.1, the indeterminacy of legal language is a pivotal factor when it comes to collective speech acts of heterogeneous groups addressed to heterogeneous audiences.

2.2.2 VERDICTS

At first glance, verdicts are paradigm cases of declarative speech acts: "Declarations bring about some alteration in the status or condition of the referred-to object or objects solely in virtue of the fact that the declaration has been successfully performed."[39] A verdict creates or changes a state of affairs. The judge or jury, by uttering the verdict, finds someone guilty or not guilty. By doing so, the individual acquires a new legal property. Her (legal) status has changed through the speech act. Merely the (successful) utterance of

(E42) "We find the defendant guilty as charged."

brings about that the defendant is, in fact, legally guilty. However, in contrast to other declarative speech acts such as appointments or war declarations, verdicts do not only have the illocutionary force of a declaration: They also seem to ascertain facts. The defendant might not in fact have committed the crime she is found guilty of. Although factual innocence does not change anything about the legal status created by (E42), there is still a sense in which the judge or jury got it wrong.

As John R. Searle (1976) describes them, there is an overlap between declarations with representatives. They have two illocutionary forces at the same time. Courts of justice try to get it right, but their job is done even if they got it wrong. Verdicts are authoritative:

> The argument must eventually come to an end and issue in a decision, and it is for this reason that we have judges .... [They] make factual claims [such as]

---

[39] See Searle (1976, 14).

'you are guilty.' ... But at the same time, [they] have the force of declarations. ... Some institutions require representative claims to be issued with the force of declarations in order that the argument over the truth of the claim can come to an end somewhere and the next institutional steps which wait on the settling of the factual issue can proceed: the prisoner is released or sent to jail. (Searle, 1976, 15)

Because of this dual character, verdicts can be called representative declarations. Even though they change some state of affairs if performed felicitously, verdicts can be criticized for being incorrect or insincere. Searle (1976, 15) even maintains that "judge[s] ... can, logically speaking, lie."

However, it seems that someone can lie only when saying something that can theoretically be true or false.[40] But this is not so clear for verdicts. It is even questionable whether verdicts (or legal processes generally) are primarily designed for ascertaining the truth.[41]

This structural unclarity about verdicts is important since it helps judges to maintain and fulfill their distinctive role in society. They can claim to apply the law and ascertain facts in a way reproducible by legal experts, while at the same time issue authoritative and final decisions. Due to this structural indeterminacy in the speech act itself, judges can satisfy two conflicting legal principles. They are required to deliver judgments that are both in accordance with the legal facts and can be relied on as binding for the present and future. The *principle of legal certainty*, which postulates that legal decisions must be (reasonably) predictable, is sometimes in conflict with the *prohibition of denial of justice*, which postulates that legal decisions must (at some point) be made.[42] The source of this conflict is indeterminacy in the law.[43] Its remedy is the structural speech act ambiguity of verdicts.[44]

Verdicts typically have the illocutionary force of both representations and declarations. But higher courts, for instance, when issuing court orders to lower courts or agencies, also perform directive speech acts. This is particularly true

---

[40] While virtually all definitions of lying require truth-aptness, most require the speech act to be representative; the classical definition takes "a lie to be an assertion, the content of which the speaker believes to be false, which is made with the intention to deceive the hearer with respect to that content" (Williams, 2002, 96).

[41] See Danet (1980, 461).

[42] The principle of legal certainty is a central requirement for the *rule of law*. See Koch and Rüßmann (1982) and Christensen and Kudlich (2008) for the German perspective and Fuller (1969) for the Anglo-Saxon point of view. The prohibition of denial of justice is the requirement to universally provide legal protection. See Schumann (1968) and Rüthers (2008) for its discussion in German jurisprudence and Endicott (2011a) for its discussion in Anglo-Saxon jurisprudence.

[43] See section 2.3.4 for a discussion of indeterminacy in legal content.

[44] Recall section 1.5.2 on speech act ambiguity.

for supreme courts, deciding cases relevant to large parts of society, as when the US Supreme Court ruled the segregation of schools unconstitutional in *Brown v. Board of Education of Topeka*.[45] But even verdicts by lower courts are to some degree directive in illocutionary force. For instance, the conviction of a murderer will involve some sort of pronouncement of legal consequences, for example, that the murderer be sent to jail. This pronouncement can be understood as a command or request to an agency to enforce the verdict.

Verdicts do not consist of a conviction alone. They are complex speech acts that not only involve a conviction and pronouncement of legal consequences but also an opinion. The opinion of the court typically has the form of an argument why the verdict is justified, that is, why the verdict made is the (legally) correct one.

In general, arguments can be described as a set of representative speech acts. The premises in legal arguments, however, are rarely purely representative. Statements about the applicable law and facts of the case involve declarative elements. There is a qualitative difference between the interpretation of a statute by a law professor and the judge deciding the case in question.[46] The interpretation by the judge brings about a change in the applicable law (at least for the case at hand), whereas the interpretation by the law professor does not—it is merely a commentary or advice. The judge's mere consideration of the fact of the case changes its state—as a legal case. Thus, the interpretation of the statute as well as the assertion of some state of affairs, if made by a judge in a court hearing, create institutional (legal) facts.

Furthermore, verdicts sometimes involve elements of expressive speech acts, for example, when used to morally condemn the accused. Hock L. Ho (2006) claims that the speech act of the verdict is to create a sense of shame or remorse. Such moral condemnation can function as deterrence, in addition to the actual sentence.

Judges can use these illocutionary functions. They can mention some legal facts in their arguments but not others, making only the former legally relevant. They can put pressure on the jury by morally condemning the offense. They can hand out the maximum penalty to make a political statement. And, they can do it in more or less determinate language.

Indeterminacy is, as we saw, structurally relevant to the institution of verdicts itself. It might be used in the representative part of the speech act to allow for deniability or in the declarative part to smooth its application to the case at hand or future cases when used as precedent. Indeterminacy also may be called for when

---

[45] *Brown v. Board of Education of Topeka*, 347 U.S. 483 (1954).
[46] See Bernal (2007, 8).

the issue is a socially or legally controversial one—potentially due to linguistic indeterminacy on the level of the application of law.[47]

2.2.3 CONTRACTS

Contracts consist of at least two separate speech acts by at least two different (natural or legal) persons. One person makes an offer, which the other person accepts. In traditional contract theory, both offer and acceptance are considered to be promises or some other form of commissive.[48]

By a commissive speech act, the speaker commits herself to perform or refrain from some future action. The utterance

(E40) "I promise to take out the trash today."

is a speech act that (if felicitously performed) commits a speaker to take out the trash on the day of the utterance. In contrast to a mere statement of one's intent, which reflects only a speaker's momentary state of mind, a commissive commits the speaker—independently of her actual intent and even if she changes her mind later on.[49] Such understood, offer and acceptance cannot be mere *expressions* or *manifestations* of intent.[50]

In general, while the performative verb can help to make explicit that one is making a promise, it is clearly not necessary to use it. I can make the same promise as in (E40) by simply uttering "I will take out the trash today." Similarly, it is neither necessary nor sufficient that the terms "offer" or "acceptance" are used.[51] For instance, uttering "I offer to take out the trash today" is typically not an offer or promise, but a proposal. Conversely, one can form a contract without uttering anything by simply acting in a certain way as in the case of supermarket purchases. Thus, literal content does not determine whether the (speech) act forms a legally binding offer or acceptance. Its illocutionary force is what matters.[52]

As we saw in section 1.5.1, there can be indeterminacy not only in the content of the utterance but also with regard to its force. Often, the problem for courts is to

---

[47] These remarks will be substantiated in section 5.2 on strategic indeterminacy in verdicts.

[48] Compare Fried (1981), Tiersma (1986), or, more recently, Bix (2012b). Classically, in German law, contracts are based on declarations of intention ("Willenserklärungen"), which are a particular kind of commissive speech act. Compare Richter (2009, 37–39).

[49] As Austin (1946, 171) notes, ""when I say 'I promise,' a new plunge is taken: ... I have bound myself to others, and staked my reputation, in a new way."

[50] This is in apparent conflict with some other non-traditional theories of contract formation. See Shiffrin (2012) for a discussion of such non-traditional views.

[51] See Tiersma (1986, 191–193).

[52] I take it that also non-linguistic utterances—in Grice's (1968) sense—have illocutionary force, or, at the very least, acts such as offers made tacitly (e.g., at the supermarket counter), which are in principle expressible or reconstructible as explicit performatives. However, since my focus is on written utterances, nothing hinges on this assumption.

figure out whether an act constituted an offer or acceptance in the first place, that is, whether a contract was formed. This is a prototypical case of speech act ambiguity. In normal conversation, such speech act ambiguities can easily be resolved by asking a clarifying question. Often, though not always, it suffices to add the explicit performative phrase "I offer" or "I accept" to render the utterance's illocutionary force explicit.

However, the illocutionary force of the utterance is only part of the requirements for a (legally enforceable) contract. The contract commits the contracting parties to perform or refrain from actions on which they have agreed. Structurally, the contracting parties make a promise to each other when contracting. But not just any promise amounts to an offer or acceptance.[53]

To see this, let us distinguish between autonomous and cooperative speech acts.[54] For instance, by uttering

(E43) "You are fired!"

an employer may dismiss her employee. Dismissals are *autonomous* speech acts since they require no reaction by the hearer.

In contrast, making a bet requires acceptance because the hearer must react in some affirmative manner, for instance, by uttering

(E44) "You are on."

There is a bet only if both speaker and hearer performed the appropriate speech acts. Accordingly, betting is a *cooperative* speech act. It is infelicitous if the required reaction is missing.

Ordinary promises are autonomous speech acts since—just as with dismissals—one can make them without cooperation by the hearer. A daughter can promise to take out the trash on her own account. What is required for it being a promise rather than a threat is that what is promised is (at least) intended to be beneficial. But her audience does not need to react in any particular way to make her utterance succeed as a promise.

Are offers conditional promises then? Of course, the daughter can say:

(E45) "I promise to take out the trash if you (promise to) give me cookies."

The utterance in (E45) might indeed constitute an offer. However, the utterance

(E46) "I promise to take out the trash if it doesn't rain."

---

[53] Some say that contracts do not consists of promises at all but of purely legal acts. See, for instance, Atiyah (1986). However, this does not entail that contracts are not speech acts. They might be special legal speech acts that are not conceivable without the law.

[54] See Schane (2012) for this distinction.

is also a conditional promise, but hardly an offer. It does not require acceptance by the hearer.

Maybe offers are promises conditional on a promise or act by the hearer then? For (E45) to constitute an offer, the daughter must additionally accept the promise or act by her parents in return. As Tiersma (1986, 197) explicates, an offer "commits the speaker not only to his own promise, but also to accepting a specific promise or act in exchange."

In US contract law this is called the requirement of consideration (or sometimes mutuality or simply exchange), but it exists also in German contract law in which it is called synallagmatic relation. Thus, only such mutual promises are candidates for offer and acceptance.[55]

In contrast to ordinary promises, however, one can form a contract only because there are laws that constitute the institution of contracts.[56] This differentiates the speech acts involved in contracting also from other speech acts with legal consequences such as defaming or bribing. The law makes it possible for us to form contracts. If and only if one adheres to the rules laid down in the UCC and common law doctrine does one form a binding sales contract according to US law.

In some sense, the contracting parties can determine on their own authority what counts as "true or false" between them; they can create their own rights and duties for each other.[57] In this sense they are like private laws.[58] Analogously to statutes, for example, contracts often contain stipulative definitions, which have the illocutionary force of declarations.

In conclusion, the formation of a contract consists of two primarily commissive speech acts: an offer and an acceptance. An offeror proposes to do something in exchange for something being done (or promised) by an offeree. In response to the offeror's conditional proposal, the offeree can accept, reject, or make a counteroffer. Only if she accepts is a contract formed.[59]

---

[55] In German contract law, the offer is more binding than in US contract law. According to § 145 BGB ("Bürgerliches Gesetzbuch," or German Code of Civil Law), a revocation of the offer is ineffective after a reasonable period. See also § 146 and § 147 BGB. Under US common law, in contrast, there must generally be *consideration* to form a (legally enforceable) contract. What ought to be done or promised by the offeree must be of value to the offeror to constitute consideration. Mutuality is thus comparatively more important in US contract law.

[56] This is what makes Atiyah (1986) claim that contract law is not about promises.

[57] See Bassenge and Palandt (2013, § 145).

[58] In German law, the freedom of contract has been asserted by the Federal Constitutional Court based on the general freedom of action given in art. 2(1) GG ("Grundgesetz," or German Basic Law). Cf. BVerfGE ("Entscheidungen des Bundesverfassungsgerichts," or Decisions of the German Federal Constitutional Court) 8, 274 and BVerfGE 95, 267.

[59] There are, of course, additional legal requirements, some of which are in dispute or different depending on the legal system. An uncontroversial example for such a requirement is *consideration* in US contract law.

The offer determines the content of the contract. Indeterminacy can occur when it is unclear whether a contract has been formed in the first place because of speech act ambiguity or because the respective contract laws are not perfectly adhered to or themselves indeterminate. Indeterminacy can also occur when the subject matter of the contract is unclear due to some form of linguistic indeterminacy in the offer's content. If the content of the offer is indeterminate, the obligations of the contracting parties to each other might become unclear. This unclarity can lead to disagreement and conflict between the parties, in which case a court may need to resolve the indeterminacy. If the content is too indeterminate, the court might even declare the contract void.

2.3 Interpretation and the Law

In section 2.2.2 I analyzed three kinds of legal speech acts. Renderings of verdicts are primarily representative declarations, enactments of laws are primarily directives, and formations of contracts are primarily commissives. They correspond roughly to the three types of legal norms introduced in section 2.1. Laws are norms that result from legislation. Verdicts are norms that result from adjudication. Contract clauses are norms that result from contract formation. In chapters 3 and 5, I will investigate which forms of indeterminacy occur in these kinds of speech acts and for what reasons. Let us now turn to the fourth type of norms in the law—legal principles, that is, norms that result from jurisprudence or legal practice.

Legal principles are, for the most part, developed to guide judges in interpreting other legal norms. Statutes, precedents, and contract clauses are continuously applied to new cases, and it must be decided whether the case at hand fall under the rule established by a statute, precedent, or contract clause. This involves interpretation if unclarity about its application arises.

Recall our discussion of the case *Papachristou* (1972) from the beginning of chapter 1. The Jacksonville Ordinance Code is indeterminate in a number of ways. There is (at least a preliminary) unclarity about the elements of the crime, that is, whether the defendants were correctly charged with vagrancy as "prowlers," "loiterers," and "vagabonds," since none of these polysemous, vague, highly general, and standard-relative terms were in any way defined or precisified. As a result, the courts needed to interpret the ordinance.

But what is interpretation? Timothy A. O. Endicott (2000, 159) says that interpretation is an answer to the question "What do you make of this?" A bit more concisely, Marmor (2011b, 99) clarifies: "Interpretation is typically an attempt to understand what something means." In Raz's words, interpretation is "an explanation ... of its object" and "it explains [it] by making plain its meaning."[60]

---

[60] See Raz (2009b, 301).

In ordinary conversation, interpretation is thus usually an attempt to understand or explain what a speaker means by her utterance.

This is one sense of "interpretation." In this sense, "interpretation" is synonymous with "explanation," "theorizing," or "understanding." However, the term "interpretation" is polysemous; and this broad sense is not very illuminating for the purposes of legal interpretation.[61] For that reason, Marmor (2005, 9) identifies a narrow, more interesting, sense of "interpretation." He claims

> When judges interpret the law, they do not purport to explain it. Similarly, musicians debating the appropriate way to perform a Mozart sonata would not be described as arguing about the explanation of the sonata, or Mozart, or whatever; their argument is … a distinctly interpretative one.

Referring to interpretation in this narrow sense, Endicott (2012, 109) specifies: "Interpretation is a creative reasoning process of finding grounds for answering a question as to the meaning of some object." As such, it is not necessarily an attempt to understand what the author actually meant. As Marmor (2011b, 99) remarks, "even if we know what the author meant, some interpretive questions may remain open. Or we might not be particularly interested in the author's intention; or there might not even be an author."

What then does interpretation aim at? One way of answering this question is to say—as Dworkin (1986, 52) does—that interpretation is "a matter of imposing purpose on an object or practice." This answer highlights two aspects. First, interpretation, and in particular, legal interpretation, seems to rely on questions of purpose. We care about the aims of a statute, its underlying rationale, and broader ramifications. Second, it is a matter of imposing something on its object. There are interpretations that are innovative in the sense that "the meaning they explain is not one the object had independently of them."[62]

We can then say that legal interpretation is the reasoning process that aims at finding the correct (or at least a justified) decision in a legal case. This may include considerations of language, intention, and purpose. Interpretation, in this narrow sense, is essential to legal decision-making in general and dealing with legal indeterminacy in particular.[63]

---

[61] Unfortunately, many legal scholars use "interpretation" in this broad sense. When Scalia and Garner (2012, 53), for instance, claim that "[e]very application of a text to particular circumstances entails interpretation," they refer to the broad definition of "interpretation" by Tiffany (1900, 2).

[62] See Raz (2009b, 301).

[63] See Patterson (1990, 940, my emphasis) for an account of "law as an *interpretive* enterprise whose participants engage in the production of, and debate about, explanatory narratives—narratives that account for the history of the practice and are produced in the service of argumentation about *how to resolve legal problems.*"

The object of literary interpretation is literature. But what is the object of legal interpretation? Is it the legal text, the legal utterance, or something more abstract? Are all interpretations innovative? What is the relation between language, intention, and purpose?

In the following sections, I first characterize legal interpretation in comparison to other forms of interpretation (section 2.3.1) and then highlight the distinction between linguistic content and legal content by differentiating between linguistic interpretation and legal construction (section 2.3.3) in preparation for our investigation of CTL.

A short explanatory note is in order before we can move on. Some have said that legal interpretation is much less important than the literature on it suggests.[64] The reason supposedly lies in law's function to guide future conduct. Legal interpretation, however, decides facts already happened. Interpretation thus concerns events in the past, which are not the primary object of law. Moreover, legal interpretation might be especially insignificant for the purposes of this book. After all, the strategic use of indeterminacy concerns the reasons and effects of legal utterances, not their interpretation.

However, the opposite is the case. How an utterance is understood or interpreted will be anticipated by the strategically minded speaker. Her message will be understood or interpreted in a particular (not always intended) way, and the effect her message has depends on the way in which it is understood or interpreted. The speaker must know how her utterance will (likely) be understood or interpreted to communicate strategically. In law, interpretation is thus not only crucial with respect to judicial decision-making but also for the process of lawmaking and contract formation. Legislators and contract drafters use their knowledge about interpretative practices to better achieve their goals, that is, to write better laws and contracts. Especially if they deliberately use indeterminacy, legal interpretation is paramount. Without taking into account the methods of interpretation, one cannot strategically use indeterminate language.[65]

2.3.1 THREE CHOICES

The interpretation of (written) utterances involves a number of interpretive choices. The following three choices are particularly relevant for the discussion of strategic indeterminacy in the law.[66]

First, there is the choice between *subjective interpretation versus objective interpretation*. Should the interpreter try to find out how the actual utterer meant her utterance or should she try to establish how a reasonable language user would

---

[64] See Finnis (1987), for instance.

[65] This is even more so the case if CTL is incorrect, and linguistic indeterminacy is relatively less relevant in the law.

[66] See Greenawalt (2011, 6–8), who lists seven "dimensions" of choice.

understand it? When we interpret an utterance, it is natural to assume that it was made by someone with an intention. Language is typically a means to communicate this intention. By way of linguistic utterances, the speaker tries to get the intention across, and the hearer uses them to figure it out. For written utterances such as statutes it is, however, often not easily answerable who the speaker is. Moreover, even in ordinary conversation, we might want to criticize someone if they express themselves unclearly. This requires a distinction between what is (objectively) communicated and what the utterer (subjectively) meant to communicate, that is, between communicative content and the utterer's meaning.[67]

More importantly still is the question whether, or to what degree, the intention of the lawmaker should count. After all, enactments of law are not utterances like any other. They are collective speech acts made by an institution designed to fulfill a particular role in society. This role might entail that laws are to be interpreted with a disregard of their makers' actual intention. Law is not just about communicating what someone (even if it is an elected representative of the people) intends, but, arguably, about regulating society. It might be desirable that a reasonable person can figure out what the law is by trying to understand legal texts without recourse to the history of the legislative process. Interpretation in law could thus aim for either (1) the actual intention of the legislature or (2) the intention that a competent, reasonable, and informed language user would be warranted in ascribing to it.

Second, there is the *perspective of interpretation*. Should the interpreter take up the perspective of the utterer, the audience, or a combination of both? If an ordinance is to be applied, its readers are typically agencies or courts. If the actual intention of the legislature is given priority (subjective interpretation), agencies and courts need to rely on the (historical) context of utterance to determine it. If, however, the intention that a competent, reasonable, and informed language user would be warranted in ascribing to the lawmaker is deemed more important (objective interpretation), another choice must be made. Should the interpreter focus more on the context of utterance or the context of application? Each choice yields potentially different legal outcomes, since what is communicated, as well as the relevant legal and moral norms and values, might alternate with the context. Moreover, there are different, equally good, candidates for the context of application. Legal speech acts are, as we saw, typically addressed to heterogeneous audiences. What is the audience of a law enactment? Is it the general public? The relevant authorities? Maybe the legally trained? Or all of them at once? How do we determine the context of application if we do not know the utterance's audience?

---

[67] See section 1.1.

Third, there is *abstract versus contextual interpretation*. To what extent should the interpreter take the context into account at all? We know that context is decisive to understand or interpret an utterance. Without context, we cannot even determine what is said since the (context-specific) extension of many terms such as ambiguous ones or indexicals depends on it. The interpreter could focus on the term's lexical meaning or instead figure out the term's context-dependent sense. She could focus on what is said, focusing on minimal aspects of context. Alternatively, she could focus on what is communicated more generally, also taking into account implications and other pragmatically conveyed content.[68] Finally, she could focus on factors that are not clearly aspects of context at all, such as social, political, or moral considerations.

There is, arguably, a difference between those aspects of context that are *legally* relevant to the case at hand and those that are not. After all, judges do not only want to understand what is communicated by the law; they also need to apply it to a particular case. They need to determine its legal content and the legal effect to that case. They need to provide a rule of application.[69] Assumptions about the context in which, and the background against which, the utterance is made can lead to different results. It can be contested to what degree social, political, and moral considerations matter. It may be controversial what social, political, and moral considerations are correct or relevant to the case at hand. Even the principles of legal interpretation themselves might or might not be considered relevant to the case at hand. There are choices to be made about the particular framing of the case in terms of context, background assumptions, and legal ideology.

Whether the interpreter is oriented more toward abstract or contextual interpretation, she thus has to figure out what is part of the context (even if it is just the minimal context to establish what is said). How far outside the textual evidence can judges go? Does the legislative history matter when interpreting a controversial constitutional concept? Can oral communications be relevant when interpreting a written contract? And, taking into account general objectives, public policies, ideas of justice, and social desirability—should the interpreter promote the literal meaning, the specific aims of a text, or the general objectives of society, including moral and ethical considerations?

The fact that many legal utterances are directed toward future contexts poses a particular problem for legal interpretation.[70] While many contexts can be anticipated, the legislature does not—and maybe cannot—know beforehand all contexts in which a law will be applied. How do we know what the legal text means

---

[68] See, for instance, the discussions of *Church of the Holy Trinity v. United States*, 143 U.S. 457 (1892), or *Smith v. United States*, 508 U.S. 223 (1993) in section 3.4.

[69] See Endicott (2012, 111).

[70] See also section 1.6 on context indeterminacy.

in a particular situation when the lawmakers themselves could not have known it? In law, in contrast to ordinary language, we can rarely ask the utterer what she meant. Usually, we cannot even reconstruct what she must have meant because we are partly ignorant about the context of utterance due to a systematic lack of empirical data, but also due to the fact that the utterance was made by a complex institution. Furthermore, the meaning of a law might not even depend on what the lawmaker intended it to mean, as this depends on a theoretical choice between subjective versus objective interpretation.

In law—much more than in everyday life—it is often rather unclear what would count as the relevant context to determine what is said or communicated by an utterance. This unclarity is problematic, especially since the consequences of legal interpretation have such a large impact. A judge's interpretation dictates whether people will thrive or prosper, and in some cases, whether they will live or die. This requires the interpreter to produce strong arguments for her interpretation and the legislature, court, and contract drafters to carefully and strategically use their language (including the opinion and interpretation itself).

Fortunately, the context does usually not need to be completely determined, and the three choices of interpretation often lead to the same conclusions. If the legal text is clear and determinate, what is communicated expresses the intention of the lawmaker and conforms to the law's purpose; the contexts of utterance and application are in their relevant aspects the same; and what is communicated can be easily and uncontroversially derived from the expressions' lexical meanings, contextual data, background assumptions, and conversational maxims. But if indeterminacy occurs at the level of the law's language, context determination tends to become a problem as do the outcomes of the interpretive choices that tend to come apart.

The choices of legal interpretation are comparable for all kinds of legal interpreters and all objects of legal interpretation. Laws and contracts are not only interpreted by judges. US presidents claim continuously to have their own right to interpret the Constitution. Agencies must understand and interpret legal texts if they want to apply them. Even citizens must in some way or other understand their legal obligations. The legislature must have in mind the various kinds of interpreters and the choices that they can make if it wants to strategically legislate.

2.3.2 THEORIES OF LEGAL INTERPRETATION

Judges, and interpreters generally, have to (at least implicitly) address these interpretive choices. Different schools of legal interpretation and different practical approaches give different answers and decide cases differently. Code-based legal systems as in Germany, on one hand, traditionally appear to focus on literal meaning and are sometimes seen as clinging to formalism. However, the majority position in German statutory interpretation is the *objective theory* favoring the "objective" purpose of the law as interpretive criterion—in contrast to the less adhered to *subjective theory*, which gives priority to the "subjective" intention of the lawmaker.[71]

Common law systems as in the United States, on the other hand, historically rely heavier on the authority of custom and precedent. However, due to the advancing codification of common law, many of the same questions have to be answered by US legal theory. This is happening in the debate between textualists and purposivists.[72]

Despite these differences, there are basically three types of theories of legal interpretation both in Germany and the United States. There are those who argue that the purpose of a law should take priority over other considerations when interpreting the legal text.[73] There are those who argue that the historical intent of the lawmaker should play the crucial role for the interpretation of laws.[74] Finally, there are those who argue that the legal text itself should be interpreted first and foremost linguistically and other considerations be subordinated.[75]

These differences in legal theory and methodology of interpretation are rather a matter of degree than categorical disagreement.[76] In fact, neither in Germany nor in the United States are there judges who consistently take into account only the broader goal of the statute while ignoring the legislature's intent or literal meaning. Nor are there judges who confine themselves to solely the written text or the historical intention. The ranking of the interpretative methods, so often demanded in Germany, is equally illusory.[77] The relative importance of the method depends on the circumstances of the case and the purpose the interpreter imposes on the text. Interpretation is, as we noted, innovative in the sense that it adds something to its object. As a result, there cannot be a definite theory of legal interpretation in the form of a ranking of its methods—at least none with any ramifications for

---

[71] See Larenz and Canaris (1995). This represents cum grano salis the interpretative choice between subjective versus objective interpretation in section 2.3.1.

[72] See Gluck (2010, 1762–1764). There is a similar debate with respect to constitutional law between originalists and living constitutionalists. Cf. Bennett and Solum (2011, 67).

[73] See Breyer (2005) for the US legal system and Larenz and Canaris (1995) for the German legal system.

[74] See Bierling (1905) for the German legal system.

[75] See Scalia (1997) for the United States and Koch and Rüßmann (1982) for Germany.

[76] See Solan (2010). Most famously, Driedger (1983, 87) states, "today there is only one principle or approach, namely, the words of an Act are to be read in their entire context and in their grammatical and ordinary sense harmoniously with the scheme of the Act, the object of the Act, and the intention of Parliament."

[77] See Savigny et al. (1976, 14–26) for a comprehensive survey of the various proposals to rank the methods.

legal practice.[78] Eventually, it comes down to a balancing of the methods. When interpreting a statute, the judge will try to produce a verdict that takes into account language, intent, and broader goals of the legislation.[79]

Even ardent textual originalists such as Antonin Scalia and Bryan A. Garner (2012, xxvii), who want judges to

> "look for meaning in the governing text, ascribe to that text the meaning that it has borne from its inception, and reject judicial speculation about both the drafters' extra-textually derived purposes and the desirability of the fair reading's anticipated consequences,"

allow for interpretational discretion in a large number of cases. When absurd or unjust consequences were to follow, Scalia and Garner, too, would dismiss the literal meaning of the text. In their book *Reading Law*, they offer a bouquet of interpretation principles that are anything but purely textual or originalist.[80]

Because of this balancing of interpretation principles, there is indeterminacy not only on the level of application, but also on the level of theory. It might be unclear what the law requires in a particular case because the assumed purpose of the law contravenes the linguistic content or assumed intention of the lawmaker. But even if there were agreement between legal experts on the level of theory, that is, if they would agree on a set of interpretation principles and how to weigh them, not all indeterminacy could be resolved, since interpretation principles need to be interpreted in cases of (higher-order) unclarity as well. For instance, the *Rule of Lenity* is an interpretation principle to decide ambiguous criminal law cases. It says, "[A]mbiguity should be resolved in favor of lenity."[81]

However, the principle is silent with respect to which cases are ambiguous and which are not. There are borderline cases between ambiguous and unambiguous

---

[78] See Raz (2009b, 118), who writes that "innovation defies generalization." But even Larenz (1991, 334), who tries to establish a ranking, acknowledges that there is "no definite ranking" ("kein festes Rangverhältnis").

[79] These methods of legal interpretation correspond to the grammatical, historical, and teleological canon in German legal theory, respectively, as they are presented, for instance, by Wank (2011, 39–53). German legal interpretation traditionally involves a fourth canon. The so called systematic method is, however, not a method of interpretation. Instead, the principle that a statute must be interpreted such that it fits its (legal) context and does not lead to contradiction is a general requirement for interpretation.

[80] For instance, most of the "Expected-Meaning Canons" in Scalia and Garner (2012, 247–251) are principles relying on normative questions as the value of constitutionality.

[81] See *Bell v. United States*, 349 U.S. 81 (1955); reaffirmed in *United States v. Bass*, 404 U.S. 336 (1971).

cases. It remains unclear whether the Rule of Lenity can be applied to them or not.[82]

Consequently, interpretation principles can only reduce linguistic indeterminacy. They cannot eliminate it. But does this mean that there can never be a strict formal subsumption of a case under a norm, as described by textualists such as Hans-Joachim Koch and Helmut Rüßmann (1982)? As Karl Larenz and Claus-Wilhelm Canaris (1995, 25, my translation) in their classical German textbook on legal interpretation claim: "The conclusion [of the interpreter] is not a logically compulsory conclusion, but a choice motivated by adequate reasons between different possibilities of interpretation."

In one sense, they are clearly right when they say that no application of the law is logically compulsory. There is no logically compulsory application of a rule or norm to any real case because logical inferences operate between linguistic entities only. In another sense, however, it is clearly possible to give logically compelling arguments for a legal conclusion—simply by adding new premises. It thus depends on the defensibility of the premises used in the argument. That is why Robert Alexy (1995, 78) claims that legal interpretation is always argumentation. As Dennis M. Patterson (2005) puts it, the methods of interpretation are "forms of argument" judges can use when justifying their decisions. When these forms of argument diverge, unclarity results.

This is the case also when interpreting contracts or verdicts. Contracts are, as we saw, commissive speech acts, that is, they establish rights and duties between individuals. As such, they have no validity for other people. In contract interpretation, there are two extreme views. According to the subjective view, the legal content of a contract is primarily based on the actual intent of the parties; whereas, according to the objective view, it is primarily based on its expression. This corresponds to the interpretative choice between subjective versus objective interpretation discussed previously.

The case for the subjective view with respect to contract interpretation is, at first glance, stronger since contracts are about the obligations one intends to assume.[83] However, the actual intention is not always recognizable by the other party. For reasons of reliability, it has thus been argued that the expression of intent should trump the actual intention of the drafter.[84] There is no need to argue for either

---

[82] This does not mean that the principle is useless. Far from it, as there are countless cases in which there is no higher-order unclarity and it helps to disambiguate the case.

[83] The primary goal of contract interpretation, according to US contract law, is to determine and enforce the intent of the parties. Compare *Turner v. Alpha Phi Sorority House*, 276 N.W.2d 63, 66 (1979).

[84] For instance, it is widely held that some form of linguistic indeterminacy must be found before the intention of the contracting parties is admitted as evidence. See Burton (2009, 63–70) for a discussion of the ramifications of the parol evidence rule. Note that Corbin (1965), Farnsworth (1967), the Restatement (Second) of the Law of Contracts, as well as the UCC oppose this view.

position here as long as we keep in mind that neither the actual intention nor the expressed intent will be consistently and reliably embraced by the courts in cases of disagreement.

There are three main differences between statutory and contract interpretation that are relevant for our purposes. They are rooted in (1) the act of the utterance, (2) the style of drafting, and (3) the resolution of indeterminacy. First, while it is in most cases uncontroversial whether an utterance of parliament is an enactment of law, there are a significant number of cases in which there is considerable and justified doubt about whether an agreement between two parties constitutes a (legally enforceable) contract. As a result, the (logically) first step when interpreting a contract must be to answer the question whether some behavior has been a legal transaction. Only then can the judge determine its content.

Second, while "words are chosen and interpreted with unusual care" when it comes to statutes and verdicts, "elsewhere, the law must interpret utterances of a more spontaneous sort, where the actual meaning of a word or phrase is not always found in a standard dictionary and a grammar text."[85] This is the case for the drafting and interpretation of contracts. Consequently, what an expression means in the context of the contract depends not only on its usage in ordinary discourse, but it is from time to time idiosyncratic to the drafter's idiolect and the context of drafting. The interpreter must make allowance for this by taking into account this form of polysemy.

Third, because of such "more spontaneous" utterances, contracts produce different forms of indeterminacy than statutes. Pragmatic indeterminacy plays a greater role there than in statutory interpretation. But also semantic forms of indeterminacy are resolved differently. For instance, there is the principle of contract interpretation that (usually in form of a statute as, for instance, § 305c BGB) says that indeterminacy must be resolved in favor of the weaker contracting party—the one that has not formulated the terms of contract.

Just as with statutory interpretation, contract interpretation aims at legal content. However, a contract's legal content is the contribution that it makes to the legal obligations of the contracting parties. It thus does not affect the legal system as a whole but only some of its members.

While some verdicts (by the Supreme Court, for instance) change the legal obligations that obtain in a legal system in a wider sense, most of them affect only those directly involved in the trial—most notably the defendant. However, all verdicts must be understood and interpreted by agencies and future courts—be it

---

[85] See Tiersma (1986, 189).

that the verdict is executed by the authority carrying out the sentence, appealed by a higher court, or used as a precedent in the verdict of a later case.

There is a theoretical dispute on the interpretation of verdicts between the traditional theory of the ratio decidendi and the predictive theory that sanctions legislative holdings.[86] The ratio decidendi is a legal rule derived from the legal reasoning that has led to the decision of the court. It is limited by the legally salient facts of the case that is decided. In contrast, a legislative holding by a court "states a broad rule that decides the case at hand but may go far beyond its facts."[87] A new case before the court might thus involve conversational vagueness with respect to the relevance of a precedent, which not only might (or might not) be sufficiently similar, but also might (or might not) be legally binding.

In sum, the interpretation of statutes, verdicts, and contracts depends on interpretive choices made by different schools of legal theory. In essence, the focus can be on either the language of the legal text, the intention of the author, or the purpose of the utterance. In section 2.3.3 I examine how the interpretive choices lead to different constructions of legal content.

2.3.3 INTERPRETATION AND CONSTRUCTION

The interpreters' primary access to a law is its written form. It appears that the object of interpretation is and can only be the legal text. However, as we saw in section 2.2, it is the speech act that changes legal obligations; and it is these changes interpreters are normally interested in. The text is only the manifestation or testimony of the utterance. Because both utterance and text must be interpreted, I will say that the primary object of interpretation is the text because that is what the interpreter actually deals with; and its secondary object is the utterance, which is what interpretation is ultimately about.

While the objects of legal interpretation are texts and utterances, its aim is their meaning or content. Even linguistically, however, there are different kinds of contents. In chapter 1, we distinguished between what is said, what is implicated, what is implicited, and what is communicated. In law, there is yet another kind of content, namely, legal content. Following Greenberg (2011a, 219), we can define legal content in the following way:

(D22) The LEGAL CONTENT of some utterance u is u's contribution to the legal obligations that obtain in a legal system at a given time.

Many legal utterances change in some way or other the set of legal rights and duties of a legal system. This change is their legal content, and it is the ultimate

---

[86] See Solum (2006, 188–201). This is only seriously debated in the United States due to the comparative insignificance of precedent in the German legal system.

[87] See Solum (2006, 188).

aim of legal interpretation. Although the forms of indeterminacy discussed in chapter 1 are entirely on the level of linguistic content, what lawmakers, judges, and contracting parties are ultimately interested in is the legal effect of their utterances. For that reason, if we want to examine the use of linguistic indeterminacy in the law, we need to understand how legal and linguistic content are related, since it is legal content that determines legal effects. Lawrence B. Solum (2010b) offers the distinction between (linguistic) interpretation and (legal) construction: while interpretation provides linguistic content, legal content is construed.

As we saw, legal interpretation is the reasoning process that aims at finding the correct (or at least a justified) answer to a legal question. This reasoning process, we can call it "legal reasoning," can be divided into a linguistic and a specifically legal part. A judge confronted with a legal case must first identify the applicable law in the form of legal texts such as statutes or precedents. If the text is clear and determinate, it can be *understood* without (linguistic) interpretation. If not, it must be *interpreted*.[88] In both cases, however, before the legal text can be applied to the case, its legal content must be *construed*. If the legal content is changed in the process of adjudication (in contrast to purely applying it), the law is *revised*. Understanding and interpretation thus concern linguistic (e.g., literal or pragmatically conveyed) content, while construction and revision concern legal content. Interpretation, in particular, is the activity of discerning the communicative content of an utterance, while construction is the activity of determining its legal effect.[89]

In practice, a judge will rarely carve up activities like this. She will neither linguistically try to understand the text independently of legal considerations nor construe its legal content without recourse to the text. But even from a theoretical perspective, the lines are blurred. There are borderline cases both between understanding and interpretation and between construction and revision. The fuzziness between understanding and interpretation highlights the higher-order indeterminacy of language since sometimes it is indeterminate whether an utterance is indeterminate. As a result, some cases of indeterminacy cannot be resolved within the limits of language.

---

[88] The essential difference between understanding and interpretation is that interpretation, in contrast to understanding, implies that there is more than one plausible interpretation of the utterance. Interpretation is required to determine the content of an utterance if it is unclear. If it is clear, however, it can be directly understood without any creative or innovative reasoning. Whether there is direct understanding in the law is a controversial issue. See, for instance, Fuller (1958), Moore (1981), Dworkin (1982), Larenz and Canaris (1995), Golanski (2002), or Solum (2013) for the claim that all judicial decisions involve (legal) interpretation. See, for instance, Schauer (1985), Marmor (2005), or Patterson (2005) for the claim that only judicial decisions in hard cases involve (legal) interpretation. We will tangentially touch this issue in section 2.4.

[89] See Solum (2010b, 96).

It is an important jurisprudential question whether a legal decision is a construction or revision. There are principles in the law that set legal decisions apart from other decisions. Revision is potentially in conflict with the principles of legal certainty, fair notice, and equality. In a certain sense, it is arbitrary to revise the law.[90] Revision creates uncertainty about the application of the law and may even result in discrimination and corruption.[91] However, the principle of equity and the prohibition of denial of justice might positively necessitate revision. Absurdity or injustice might result from a direct, "mindless," application of the legal text or legal indeterminacy may even preclude direct application altogether. Precisely when the law is still construed or already revised depends on the relation between linguistic and legal content. Linguistic indeterminacy in the law might or might not result in revision.

This jurisprudential question is also relevant for the purposes of this book insofar as different reactions are expected when the judicial decision is considered to go beyond what the courts are allowed to do. Judges generally have an incentive to make their decisions look like instances of mere linguistic interpretation.[92] As Richard A. Posner (2012) argues:

> Judges tend to deny the creative—the legislative—dimension of judging, important as it is in our system, because they do not want to give the impression that they are competing with legislators, or engaged in anything but the politically unthreatening activity of objective, literal-minded interpretation, using arcane tools of legal analysis. The fact that loose constructionists sometimes publicly endorse textualism is evidence only that judges are, for strategic reasons, often not candid.

Judges do not want to arouse the suspicion of making new law, as this might be considered going beyond their responsibility. If suspicion is imminent, however, the judge is particularly likely to use indeterminate language in both verdict and opinion to avoid its reversal.[93]

Legal interpretation comprises thus both the reasoning process (R1) to establish the linguistic content of a legal utterance (linguistic interpretation) and the reasoning process (R2) to establish the legal content from its linguistic content and potentially other variables (legal construction).[94] Legal construction is, however, itself ambiguous between (at least) two kinds of reasoning, namely, the reasoning

---

[90] Compare section 5.1.3 for a discussion of different forms of arbitrariness in the law.

[91] Recall, for example, the case *Papachristou* that we discussed in chapter 1.

[92] See Marmor (2011b, 90).

[93] See section 5.2.3 on the strategic use of indeterminacy in verdicts for this purpose.

[94] See Köpcke Tinturé (2010) for a discussion of the differences between legal and other types of reasoning.

process (R2a) to establish the legal content for the case at hand and the reasoning process (R2b) from legal content to a decision of the case at hand.

Establishing the legal content is, as we saw in section 2.3.1, establishing a rule of application. The legal content of a legal text can be identified without making it bear on the case, even though it provides the rule that is applied to the case. The decision of the case at hand requires a second reasoning process, which results in the actual application of the rule and determination of its legal effects. There are different ways in which linguistic content, legal content, and the application of legal content to the case at hand can be indeterminate.

This demonstrates how "law does things differently," as Frederick F. Schauer (2009, 211) emphasizes. Not even positivists want to find the correct answer to a legal question only in terms of the linguistically correct application of a legal text or expression to the case at hand. Nor does anybody want to find the correct answer to a legal question in terms of justice and morality only. Lawyers (whether positivists or not) want to find the *legally correct* answer. The question consists thus in how the legally correct answer is determined. Can linguistic content do all the work, or do we need to rely on an array of doctrinal, formalistic, and perhaps political or moral considerations? Do we also have to differentiate between indeterminacy in linguistic and in legal content? And, can there be indeterminacy on the level of legal content irrespective of linguistic indeterminacy?

2.3.4 LEGAL INDETERMINACY

When legal scholars or philosophers of law use the term "legal indeterminacy," they usually refer to a long-standing debate between legal realists, positivists, natural law theorists, and interpretivists.[95] Legal realists often claim that all legal questions are indeterminate, that is, legal content does not determine the outcome of particular legal disputes. Legal decisions depend solely on what the court thinks fit, since law is nothing but window dressing that clever lawyers and judges can use to justify any decision they please. This is what supposedly some Critical Legal Studies (CLS) scholars argue for and what has been coined the *radical indeterminacy thesis* by Endicott (2000).[96] The opposite of this thesis is Dworkin's legal interpretivism, which claims that legal content does determine every legal

---

[95] See, for instance, Dworkin (1977), Solum (1987), and Kress (1989) for this use of the term "legal indeterminacy."

[96] Solum (2010a), among others, calls it simply the *indeterminacy thesis*. This position is a variant of legal realism. Its most prominent advocate is Holmes (1882/2009). Other proponents are, among others, Oliphant (1928), Frank and Gray (1930), Radin (1940/2000), Cohen (1959), and Llewellyn (1962). See also Peller (1985), Kennedy (1986), Horwitz (1992), and Peller and Tushnet (2004). According to Tushnet (1993, 340), however, most CLS scholars who defend the indeterminacy thesis actually understand it as questioning a "connection between determinacy and legitimacy in the lived experience of actors in the United States political and legal system."

question. In other words, every legal decision has a single right answer. We can call this view the *radical determinacy thesis*.

Neither radical thesis has truly been refuted, and there are powerful arguments for and against both of them.[97] Nevertheless, the majority position is—as so often—a moderate one. There are determinate and indeterminate questions of law.

In this book, I am not concerned with any radical claims about indeterminacy. Even if all legal questions were radically determinate or indeterminate, there are easy cases because legal experts generally agree on their interpretation, and there are hard cases because they generally disagree.[98] Claims of radical determinacy or indeterminacy are usually understood as claims about the *metaphysical* nature of law. For instance, Dworkin's single right answer thesis entails that all legal questions have true or false answers in some fundamental sense, but is silent about whether actual judges can arrive at the right answer in any given case.[99] For the purposes of this book "what matters is what happens in law as practiced," as Tushnet (1993, 342) puts it. And, in practice, there is a lot of agreement about many legal questions. In the words of Leiter (2009, 1227), it is a fact that

> *most* cases that are presented to lawyers never go any further than the lawyer's office; that *most* cases that lawyers take do not result in litigation; that *most* cases that result in litigation settle by the end of discovery; that *most* cases that go to trial and verdict do not get appealed; that *most* cases that get appealed do not get appealed to the highest court...: there is massive and pervasive agreement about the law throughout the system.

Whether the actual agreement or disagreement in the practice of law is undermined by an underlying radical determinacy or indeterminacy is irrelevant to the purposes of this book. I am concerned with legal cases that are indeterminate in the sense that it is *unclear* to a competent and well-informed lawyer what their legal consequences are—analogously to the linguistic indeterminacy defined in (D1) on page 12.[100] We can thus define legal indeterminacy in the following way:

---

[97] Dworkin's arguments for legal interpretivism have been developed over a long series of publications, but most notably in Dworkin (1978). Holmes (1897) offers the classical argument for legal realism. Endicott (2000, 11—29) gives forceful arguments against the plausibility of the radical indeterminacy thesis, while striking arguments against Dworkin's theory are collected in Guest (2009). For a short survey of the Hart–Dworkin debate, see Shapiro (2007).

[98] I will use the terms "easy case" and "hard case" as a shorthand for "legally determinate case" and "legally indeterminate case," respectively. Compare Bix (2003, 63), who claims that easy cases concern "legal questions that seem so obvious that there is no question as to what their proper resolution should be." See also (D23) of legal indeterminacy.

[99] This can be seen most plainly in Dworkin's earlier work as, for instance, Dworkin (1975).

[100] Moreover, claims of radical determinacy or indeterminacy are anything but uncontroversial. If Endicott (2000) is right, there really are no proponents of the radical indeterminacy claim. If Solum (2010a) is right, there are (almost) no proponents of the radical determinacy claim either.

(D23)   A legal utterance *u* is LEGALLY INDETERMINATE in the context of legal case *c* iff *u*'s legal content in *c* is unclear to a competent and well-informed lawyer.

Also, a proponent of CTL can maintain that there is legal indeterminacy that does not have its source in language.[101] As we saw, there are many ways in which an utterance can be linguistically indeterminate. But the law is not merely a set of statements—it is a system of rules that are stated in language.[102] These rules can be indeterminate because they are stated in indeterminate language. They can be indeterminate also because of other, more specifically legal, reasons.

Indeterminacy on Different Levels

In general, there can be legal indeterminacy on three different levels. First, on the most fundamental level, there can be indeterminacy with respect to legal ideologies and meta-interpretation.[103] Second, on the level of legal theory, there can be indeterminacy with respect to the sources of law (what are the relevant texts or conventions), the authority of law (who is to decide), and the interpretative principles (the methodology of law). Third, on the level of application, there can be indeterminacy with respect to the particular case—what are the norms relevant to the case at hand? This involves two steps. The first step is to determine what the norms are given the legal text—that is, legal reasoning in the sense of (R1). The second step is to apply them to the case given the sources, the authority and the methodology of law—that is, legal reasoning in the sense of (R2).

On the level of application, there are—apart from the linguistic forms of indeterminacy analyzed in chapter 1—two basic forms of *non-linguistic* indeterminacy in the law.[104] First, it sometimes happens that a case comes up before the court for which the judge cannot find any applicable statute. Prima facie, the law contains a gap in this case, since it does not give an answer for this legal question. This situation is called a non liquet. An example is *Marbury v. Madison*, 5 U.S. 137 (1803), in which the court established the principle of judicial review about which

---

[101] Recall that CTL entails only that linguistic content determines legal content.

[102] Hart (1961/1994, 79ff.), classically, defines law as the "union of primary and secondary rules." In contrast, the law can also be seen as the "prophecies of what the courts will do," advocated by Holmes (1897, 460f.). However, even for a full-blown legal realist such as Holmes, the law can be described as a system of rules stated in language that (more or less reliably) tell us how the courts will decide.

[103] See Shapiro (2011) for the distinction between interpretation and meta-interpretation. According to Shapiro (2011, 305), a theory of meta-interpretation "does not set out a specific methodology for interpreting legal texts, but rather a methodology for determining which specific method is proper." See also Pino (2013) for a discussion of Shapiro's distinction with regard to theoretical disagreement.

[104] Endicott (1996, 667) seems to think that there are countless forms of non-linguistic indeterminacy. He discusses conflicts between norms, doubts about lawmaking powers, unclarity about admissible evidence, conflicts with equity considerations, unclarity of limits of discretion, and even unclarity about "whether a witness will make it to court."

the Constitution is completely silent.[105] In such a case, the law is indeterminate because it does not provide a rule on how to decide the case.

Second, it sometimes happens that the law gives multiple answers for a legal question that contradict each other. Confronted with a new case, the judge finds two conflicting, but equally applicable, statutes. Prima facie, the law contains a contradiction here. An example is *Wertz v. Grubbs* in which the tolling provisions of the *Medical Malpractice Act* and limitation periods imposed under the *Wrongful Death Act* conflicted.[106] In such a case, the law is indeterminate because it provides (or seems to provide) no single rule on how to decide the case.

The law might also contain contradictions between different types of legal norms. A statute can be in conflict with a legal principle, which might or might not be constitutionally laid down. This includes cases of "absurdity" in which the indeterminacy is due to neither contradicting statutes nor gaps in the law. In such a case, there is a clearly applicable statute, but it results in blatant injustice or plainly contradicts its stated purpose. The judge can then reason that this injustice or policy miscarriage cannot possibly be what the lawmaker had in mind or what is good for society. However, it will not always be clear whether the judge is entitled to override the "plain meaning" of the statute even in those cases—in particular, when the resulting injustice or policy miscarriage is contested or only marginal.[107]

Such cases can also be considered as conflicts between legal principles contradicting each other directly, including principles of legal interpretation.[108] In the classic case *Riggs v. Palmer*, the plaintiffs sought to invalidate the will of their recently deceased father.[109] The will gave the bigger part of the bequest to his grandson—the defendant, who murdered him, fearing that his grandfather might change the will. While there was a statute for punishing the defendant for murder, there was none that invalidated the will based on his murdering the testator.

---

[105] Naturally, a legal interpretivist would analyze the case differently. Adversaries of most stripes of interpretivism would deny that there are any gaps in the law at all. However, interpretivists would presumably concede that there is unclarity and disagreement in the legal community in such cases.

[106] *Wertz v. Grubbs*, 245 Va. 67 (1993).

[107] For instance, see the opinion in *Abley v. Dale*, 11 C.B. 378 (1851): "If the precise words used are plain and unambiguous in our judgment, we are bound to construe them in their ordinary sense, even though it lead, in our view of the case, to an absurdity or manifest injustice."

[108] Legal interpretivists might argue that there is no such thing as contradiction between principles. The reason is that principles are unlike statutes, which indeed can contradict each other. Principles can only be in tension with each other, but ultimately one trumps the other. However, this form of legal indeterminacy is—just as the linguistic forms of indeterminacy—based on unclarity of and disagreement between competent and well-informed lawyers. Even if Dworkin's fictitious omniscient "Judge Hercules" may be able to find the single right answer, most judges and lawyers face unclarity and disagreement in cases of competing principles, and so do we—primarily with respect to the linguistic manifestations of legal principles, which are themselves susceptible to all forms of (linguistic) indeterminacy.

[109] *Riggs v. Palmer*, 115 N.Y. 506 (1889). The case was made famous by Dworkin (1978, 23). See also Dworkin (1986, 15–20) for a discussion of this case as "Elmer's Case" with a rather different focus.

In this case, there are two legal principles in clear conflict with each other. On the one hand, the generally valid *supremacy-of-text principle* states that if what is said by an applicable statute is clear and determinate, then this is its legal content.[110] On the other hand, the moral principle, which the court relied on in its decision, states that no person should profit from her own wrong. In the opinion of the court, it says literally:

> No one shall be permitted to profit by his own fraud, or to take advantage of his own wrong, or to found any claim upon his own iniquity, or to acquire property by his own crime. These maxims are dictated by public policy, have their foundation in universal law administered in all civilized countries, and have nowhere been superseded by statutes.[111]

Even though, today, it is fairly uncontroversial that the principle that no person should profit from her own wrong generally overrules the supremacy-of-text principle, at its time, *Riggs v. Palmer* was not uncontroversially resolved.[112]

Practically more relevant is the conflict between principles or provisions that express policy goals. Because of the general validity of the supremacy-of-text principle, this conflict usually becomes apparent only when the statute in question is already linguistically indeterminate. Linguistically indeterminate legal cases will presumably be decided on the basis of which purpose or policy the judge assumes the statute to accomplish. Consider the famous vehicle in the park example.[113] The fictitious statute says that no vehicles are allowed in the park. Borderline cases of "vehicle" include, arguably, mopeds, roller-skates, and segways. If the judge determines that the purpose of the statute is to ensure the tranquility of the park rather than to prevent dangerous collisions, she ought to decide for segways differently than for mopeds. The overall goal of having the park is, let's say, to provide space for recreation to the general public. This can be enhanced or diminished by permitting some borderline cases of "vehicle" to be in the park.

---

[110] See Scalia and Garner (2012, 56) for this principle.

[111] See *Riggs v. Palmer*, 115 N.Y. 506, 511–512 (1889).

[112] See Schauer (1988, 515ff.) for a discussion of how to choose between different applicable legal principles. He claims that *Riggs v. Palmer* is actually an easy case, since the moral principle that no person should profit from her own wrong supersedes what the statute literally means. However, at the time of decision, it was by no means clear which principle should be given priority. Judge Gray in his dissent argued that the court was not permitted to add further punishment without a written statute. Only in hindsight can we say that such principles usually trump the literal meaning of the text if otherwise absurdity would result—a statement that even new textualists such as Scalia accept, as his dissent in *United States v. X-Citement Video*, 513 U.S. 64 (1994) shows. There are many cases in which the supremacy-of-text principle in fact overrules other legal and moral principles. Ex ante, we frequently do not know which principle trumps another.

[113] The original example is given in Hart (1958) with the influential response from Fuller (1958). Schauer (2008) provides a short overview over the Hart–Fuller debate.

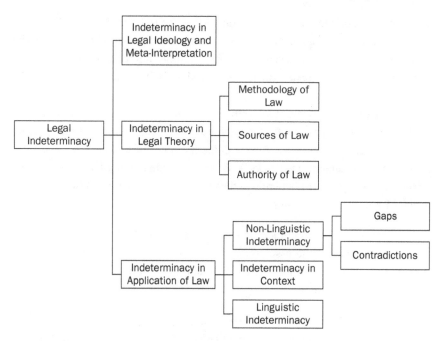

FIGURE 3 **Legal Indeterminacy**

Thus, the judge has to balance various potentially conflicting policy goals when deciding whether, for instance, segways ought to be allowed into it.

As can be seen in Figure 3 at a glance, unclarity in legal questions can thus be due to indeterminacy on all levels some of which is linguistic, some not. Most theories of legal interpretation aim to provide guidance in dealing with indeterminacy on the level of theory and application.

A judge might wonder whether a particular law is semantically vague or ambiguous or whether a law is applicable to the case at hand. In doing so, she might also be confronted with second-order indeterminacy concerning interpretation principles or sources of law, or even third-order indeterminacy concerning underlying legal ideologies. Legal indeterminacy on the level of theory and meta-theory is not linguistic, even though principles of interpretation as well as statements about the sources, authority, and ideology of the law are stated in language, too—which can, of course, be linguistically indeterminate. The linguistic indeterminacy most relevant to the purposes of this book is, however, on the level of application.

The Problem of Context Determination Revisited

There is another form of indeterminacy that is not directly linguistic and that can give a clever lawyer the possibility of raising doubt even about otherwise clear cases. It is trivially true that one can understand and interpret an utterance only within its context. Moreover, one can only know the (relevant aspects of) context once one has a fairly good grasp on the utterance's content. This is a potential source for indeterminacy because there are multiple interpretations possible for different aspects of contexts, which in turn lead to different understandings of the utterance.

This is particularly relevant to normative utterances such as laws. Karl Engisch (1943, 14f.) famously illustrates the interdependence between the normative legal text and the description of the case with his metaphor of looking back and forth ("Hin- und Herwandern des Blicks"): When confronted with a legal dispute, one starts with the legal norms and moves then to the relevant matters of fact, and back again. Martin Kriele explicates:

> From the infinite amplitude of events in the stream of life a "case" is set apart only due to the assumption that certain facts be "legally relevant." A thousand details of who, where, when and how can be omitted, only certain circumstances matter.[114]

This is the problem of context determination discussed in section 1.6. However, context determination gains a new, qualitatively different, dimension in law. Not only does one have to determine context and content at the same time, one also needs to take into account that the legal content might be very dissimilar to the linguistic content of the legal utterance.[115] Thus, considerations about legal principles, other relevant laws, questions of equity and morality, and the legal effects of one's interpretation become relevant in the process of legal reasoning.

Interpretive Concepts

There might be yet another form of legal indeterminacy stemming from the paradox that competent speakers of English share knowledge about the meaning of an expression such as "vagabond" but disagree sincerely and constantly over how to use it in many cases. This is closely related to *Dworkin's Semantic Sting*. Dworkin criticizes the misconception that the language of law can be meaningful only if lawyers share uncontroversial tests for the truth of the propositions of law provided by the conventional meaning of the word "law." CTL and other

---

[114] "Aus der unendlichen Fülle der Ereignisse im Strom des Lebens hebt sich ein 'Fall' überhaupt nur durch die Annahme heraus, daß gewisse Tatsachen ... 'juristisch relevant' seien. Tausend Einzelheiten des wer, wo, wann und wie kann man weglassen, nur auf gewisse Umstände kommt es an." (Kriele, 1976, 199, my translation).

[115] This interdependence should not be confused with claims, for instance, by Fish (1989, 302ff.) about the necessity of interpretation in all matters of understanding. As Christensen (1989, 221f.) shows, the interdependence is not a logical, but a hermeneutic circle. Preceding all normative considerations, there is an everyday understanding that can be improved on each time one goes through the steps.

[s]emantic theories suppose that lawyers and judges use mainly the same criteria (though these are hidden and unrecognized) in deciding when propositions of law are true or false; they suppose that lawyers actually agree about the grounds of law.[116]

While there is a lot to be said against Dworkin's criticism of semantic theories,[117] for our purposes there is an important lesson here. Dworkin claims that many legal terms including the term "law" itself express *interpretive concepts*. The correct application of such a term is not determined by defining criteria, but by the theory which gives the best interpretation of the practice in which the concept is used.[118]

Dworkin's notion of interpretive concepts is problematic because it rests, as David Plunkett and Timothy Sundell (2013b, 246) argue, on the flawed premise that

> the best way to explain how an exchange between two speakers serves to express a genuine disagreement is, in almost all circumstances, to suppose that those speakers mean the same thing—that is, express the same concepts—with the words they use in that exchange.

According to Plunkett and Sundell, speakers use the same terms to express different concepts. Interpretive concept terms are multi-dimensionally polysemous. However, like essentially contested concept terms, their indeterminacy cannot be resolved through context because it rests on different views about how such concepts should be used. It rests on different answers to normative questions. Speakers not only use the same terms differently, they also disagree that concepts should be expressed by them. They conduct *metalinguistic negotiations*.[119]

While most forms of linguistic indeterminacy may or may not result in legal indeterminacy, this form of indeterminacy is more fundamental. There is often not

---

[116] See Dworkin (1986, 33). The basic structure of Dworkin's argument did not change over time, even though the focus is different in his more recent thinking; Dworkin (2006, 225f.) criticizes the mistaken "assumption that all concepts depend on a convergent linguistic practice, ... a practice that marks out the concept's extension either through shared criteria of application or by attaching the concept to a distinct natural kind. The infection of the semantic sting, I shall now say, is the assumption that all concepts of law ... depend on a convergent practice in one of those two ways. The pathology of the semantic sting remains the same. Lawyers who are stung will suppose that an analysis of the concept of law must fit—and only fit—what lawyers mainly agree is law."

[117] As, for instance, that most of them do not actually claim that such tests need to be complete and uncontroversial. See Marmor (2005) for a direct reply to Dworkin on this matter.

[118] See Dworkin (2011, 244). He distinguishes interpretive concepts from *natural kind concepts*, which refer to natural kinds, and *criterial concepts*, the application of which is determined by defining criteria.

[119] Such metalinguistic negotiations seem to warrant the view that interpretation is the exercise of authority, which Venzke (2012, 11) defends for the case of international law. The struggle over law is thus a struggle for interpretive dominance—a view already put forward by Jhering (1872).

only disagreement about the application of some legal text independently of other questions of law, but also disagreement on the second level, that is, on the level of theory. Participants in such metalinguistic negotiations argue for the view or interpretation on the second level, which, following Dworkin, best fits or justifies the object of interpretation on the first one.[120] Following Plunkett and Sundell, they argue for the view or interpretation that is based on the concept they deem better. It is important to keep in mind that in neither case do they merely verbally disagree, even if their disagreement is in some way about the use of words. It is a fundamental disagreement about how certain multi-dimensionally polysemous expressions such as "law" *should* be understood.[121]

In sum, there are forms of indeterminacy entirely on the level of legal content such as gaps or contradictions. Legal content must, even if it is determined by it, be differentiated from linguistic content. The central goal in the remainder of this chapter is to examine whether linguistic indeterminacy can be treated in law as in ordinary communication. It might turn out that linguistic indeterminacy—and, in particular, semantic vagueness—is less consequential than most participants in the debate on vagueness in law suggest. In the section 2.4, I will try to establish whether there are easy cases in spite of linguistic indeterminacy, that is, whether CTL can be defended.

2.4 The Content of the Law

It is uncontroversial that constitutions, statutes, contracts, and verdicts are made and communicated by means of language. It is also uncontroversial that legal content depends at least to some degree on the linguistic content of legal utterances. But while laws are expressed with words and can be created by speech acts, they are not (mere) linguistic entities. There is a difference between the utterance, its linguistic content, and its legal content. In section 2.3. I introduced Solum's notion of legal construction: while linguistic content can be understood or interpreted, legal content must be construed.

Lawyers are generally not interested in the linguistic content of legal utterances. They care about the legal effect given by their legal content. Most participants in the debate on vagueness in law rely either implicitly or explicitly on some version of CTL, which entails that legal content is identical to or determined by linguistic content.[122] But CTL is anything but trivial.

---

[120] Contrary to Dworkin, I think that there is also indeterminacy on the third level, that is, on the level of meta-theory, but I will not argue for this claim here.

[121] See Waldron (1999), Besson (2005), or Poscher (2013) for more comprehensive discussions of disagreement in the law.

[122] See also the beginning of this chapter.

2.4.1 LINGUISTIC CONTENT

The importance of linguistic content is uncontroversial both in the German and Anglo-Saxon legal debate. Its determination of and impact on legal content, however, is theoretically and practically contested.[123] There are those who say that linguistic content marks the divide between interpretation and revision of the law.[124] In German legal theory, this is the majority position. Then, there are those who say that linguistic content does not and maybe even cannot in principle do.[125]

The main argument against those who say that linguistic content marks the divide between interpretation and revision of the law (including the proponents of CTL) is that linguistic content is too underdetermined to determine legal content in actually easy cases. As Greenberg (2011a, 220) puts is, CTL "lacks the resources to say what any statute's [legal content] is." Often, however, this argument is based on a confusion over what linguistic content is. As our discussion in chapter 1 showed, one can distinguish between different linguistic contents an utterance can have.[126]

First, *literal meaning* of an utterance is what the expressions used literally mean.[127] One can distinguish the literal meaning at the time of utterance and the time of application. The expressions used in a statute might mean something different now than what they used to mean at the time of enactment. This can lead to different assessments in the determination of literal meaning. Moreover, there are different ways to establish what the literal meaning of an utterance is. For instance, dictionaries may yield different results from linguistic corpus studies. However, there rarely is a compelling reason to take any method to be the one that indubitably gives the correct literal meaning.

Second, *utterer's meaning* is what is meant by the speaker. The legislature usually intends enacted laws to be understood in a certain way. Firstly, we can distinguish between different speakers to whom legislative intent can be attributed. On one hand, there are the intentions of the legislators. They frequently pursue very different goals when legislating. On the other hand, there is the intention of the legislature as an institution. Second, we can distinguish between different intentions attributable to the speaker. Speakers have perlocutionary and illocutionary intentions. Perlocutionary intentions are not part of utterer's meaning, since they go beyond language. In contrast, a speaker illocutionarily intends what her speech act is meant to communicate. In the case of the

---

[123] See Christensen (1989).

[124] See, for instance, Alexy (1980), Koch and Rüßmann (1982), Neumann (1986), Bydlinski (1991), Pawlowski (1991), Larenz and Canaris (1995), Klatt (2005), Zippelius (2006), Marmor (2008), Raz (2009a), or Wank (2011). Note that these authors are not all proponents of CTL.

[125] See, for instance, Finnis (1980), Teubner (1995), Moore (2002), Müller and Christensen (2004), Christensen and Kudlich (2008), or Greenberg (2011a).

[126] See section 1.1, in particular.

[127] See Recanati (2004).

law, the legislature illocutionarily intends what the legal content of the enacted law should be. Such an intention can be called legal intention, following Rosen (2011). Fish (2005), for instance, claims that illocutionary intention is identical to legal content, as do proponents of the legal theory of *original intent* generally.[128]

As we saw in section 2.3.1, there is yet another distinction relevant to legal interpretation, which is mirrored by one in the philosophy of language. Strawson (1964), Grice (1989b), and Neale (2005) argue, on one hand, that the content of an utterance is identical to the speaker's actual intention. Soames (2011) and Marmor (2014) argue, on the other hand, that the content of an utterance is the intention that a competent, reasonable, and informed language user would be warranted in ascribing to the speaker.[129]

Third, *what is said* is literal meaning plus those aspects of context that are required to express a proposition—in short, the literal content.[130] There are different theories of what is said ranging from the contextualism by Recanati (2001) to the minimalism by Cappelen and Lepore (2005). The issue is how much contextual information is included in what is said. In a minimal theory, what is said is tightly connected to the sentence uttered, up to the point where literal content collapses into literal meaning.[131] Less constrained theories not only include contextual information for indexicals and ambiguities, but also the determination of implicitures. Recanati (2001), for instance, sees what is said primarily determined by pragmatic factors.[132] Furthermore, also with respect to what is said, there is practical and theoretical disagreement about the determination of context. Proponents of textual originalism, for example, focus on the context of the utterance, while proponents of other stripes of textualism also take the context of application into account.

Fourth, *what is implicated* is linguistic content that is pragmatically conveyed in addition to or instead of what is said. Again, there are different theories of implicatures such as the Neo-Gricean account by Horn (1984) or relevance theory as developed by Sperber and Wilson (2001). There is also disagreement about what forms of implicatures there are and how they are made, that is, what conversational

---

[128] The legal theory of original intent or intentionalism is a form of *originalism*. See Bennett and Solum (2011). It is comparable to the subjective theory in German jurisprudence. See also section 2.3.2.

[129] See section 2.3.1 for a discussion of the interpretive choice between subjective and objective interpretation.

[130] See also section 1.1.

[131] Such minimal understandings of what is said include the notions of "semantic content" by Cappelen and Lepore (2005) or Soames (2010).

[132] In-between are constrained theories by, for instance, Bach (1994), Stanley and Szabó (2000), Sperber and Wilson (2001), and Stainton (2006).

maxims can be used or must be flouted to implicate something.[133] Moreover, it is controversial whether implicitures are part of what is said, what is implicated, or something different altogether.

Fifth, *what is communicated* can be identical to what is said, what is implicited, or what is implicated. In ordinary conversation, following the Neo-Gricean theory, what is communicated is to be identified with the utterer's meaning. We usually want to know what the speaker means by her utterance. Sometimes, however, it is controversial whether we really want to identify the utterer's meaning. For instance, when the speaker misspeaks or misses a relevant aspect of context, what is said or implicated may differ from what is illocutionarily intended. In such cases, the utterer's meaning differs from the intention a competent, reasonable, and informed language user would be warranted in ascribing. The content of the latter but not the former intention is what is communicated. In law, as we saw, it is controversial whether interpretation should even generally aim for the utterer's meaning. Marmor (2008), for instance, claims that legal content is identical to what is communicated—irrespective of the speaker's actual intentions.[134]

Finally, *legal content* is what an utterance contributes to the legal obligations that obtain in a legal system at a given time. As we saw in section 2.3, there are different theories of legal interpretation that give different answers to the question of how legal content is determined. It is thus a real possibility that legal content is neither identical to nor determined by linguistic content. CTL cannot be assumed without argument.

However, the relevance and potential strategic use of linguistic indeterminacy in the law depends on how legal content is determined. There are basically two possibilities that would undermine the relevance of linguistic indeterminacy. It might be possible that (1) a case is easy because legal content is determined by extralinguistic principles, even though linguistic content is indeterminate; and (2) a case is hard because linguistic content contradicts some extralinguistic principle, even though it is itself determinate.[135]

---

[133] Any form of comprehensive application of pragmatic theories to the law is in its fledgling stages. Pioneers are Marmor (2008) and Carston (2013).

[134] If not indicated otherwise, I use "communicative content" to refer to the content of the intentions a competent, reasonable, and informed language user would be warranted in ascribing to the speaker and not to the content of her actual illocutionary intentions. Linguistic indeterminacy, as we defined it in (D1), is on the level of communicative content in this objective sense. Also, the subjective theory in the law is really a minority position. See Hurd (1990), for instance, who argues against CTL based on any subjective notion of communicative content.

[135] There are many legal scholars who claim that both questions must be answered positively. See Stoljar (2001, 448), for example, who says that the "existence of semantic or logical gaps does not imply that there are legal gaps, and the existence of legal gaps does not imply that there are semantic or logical gaps."

In section 2.3, we already established that there can be hard cases despite linguistic determinacy. If CTL is correct, however, (1) cannot be possible. There cannot be easy cases if linguistic content is indeterminate. How then do linguistic and legal content relate? Is legal content identical to or determined by linguistic content, as CTL maintains?

The Argument from Semantics

The bad reputation that CTL enjoys in some circles is partially due to a misunderstanding about linguistic content. Contrary to what many lawyers seem to think, what the law says is not identical to its literal meaning. At least in Germany, this misconception is, to some extent, rooted in the legal tradition to discern between interpretation and revision by what is called *"Wortlautgrenze."*[136] This is, according to Matthias Klatt (2005, 344), a misnomer since it concerns neither words nor sounds.[137] A legal decision is interpretation of the law if it is determined by linguistic content. If it is determined by other factors, the legal decision is construction of the law. An utterance's linguistic content is, however, not the same as words or sounds, although it is constituted partially by the literal meaning expressed by words or sounds.[138]

Once the confusion between literal meaning and linguistic content is resolved, a number of problems for CTL vanish into thin air. For instance, intent and purpose might be required as variables to determine the linguistic content of a legal utterance—as in ordinary speech, when we figure out what the speaker means by presupposing that her utterance is made with a particular intention and for a particular purpose. We typically need to know the basic intentions of the speaker and the general purpose of the conversation to determine what is communicated by an utterance. Intentions and purpose are thus usually relevant aspects of context or part of the background assumptions.

This claim is something altogether different from the one that legal content is determined by something other than linguistic content. A statute can be indeterminate, for instance, because it is unclear whether an implicature is made in its enactment. This unclarity can arise out of the fact that the statute's purpose is not sufficiently clear. However, this does not entail that intention or purpose overrule linguistic content. Rather, linguistic content is indeterminate precisely because intention and purpose are not sufficiently recognizable or in conflict with it or each other. In other words, linguistic content is indeterminate due to context indeterminacy.

---

[136] It literally means *boundary of the word's sound.*

[137] Klatt criticizes also the expression "Grenze" ("boundary"), which misleadingly suggests that there is a sharp demarcation between interpretation and revision. See also Larenz (1973) for a similar point.

[138] See Kiesselbach (2012) for a general critique of this view in the legal domain.

But even then there may be easy cases, even though the relevant legal utterances are linguistically indeterminate. Sometimes, it is obvious that the law must be understood in a way that contradicts its *"Wortlaut."*[139] Does this entail that legal content is determined by something else than linguistic content?

This is precisely the mistake a thorough analysis of linguistic content can avoid. Linguistic content is not identical with the literal meaning of the words used in the legal utterance. If it can only be understood in a way that contradicts its literal meaning, then this is nothing else than the application of a conversational maxim. What the legal utterance communicates is an implicature that happens to contradict its literal meaning. If there is doubt, the communicative content is either itself indeterminate or perhaps not what the interpreter wants the law to be. In either case, the legal decision cannot be justified by legal content, but must be accepted to be a revision of the law.[140]

There could also be hard cases because intention and purpose contradict the determinate linguistic content. Linguistically it may be clear what the law means, but there are extralinguistic reasons to interpret the law *contra legem*. However, it is perfectly consistent with CTL to say that literal meaning contradicts the intent or purpose of the law. All too often, what the law communicates is not its literal meaning or even what is said. The content of the law may be what is pragmatically conveyed by the relevant legal utterances. Sometimes, the legislature makes mistakes. Just as one can misspeak, the legislature can enact a law with unintended consequences or in unwanted conflict with some higher purpose. The case might then seem to be hard because it feels "hard" to reach the legally determinate, but morally or socially undesirable, conclusion. It seems hard because we want to ignore the legal content and revise the law. This is sometimes entirely justifiable (on moral, or other non-legal, grounds). However, it is not interpretation of the law, but revision—the creation of something new.

While there certainly are cases in which the courts decide against the linguistic content of the relevant legal utterances by consulting legal principles, they refer to legal principles most of the time if there is some form of indeterminacy based on linguistic content already. Of course, it is not always clear whether there in fact is linguistic indeterminacy, and judges sometimes argue for its existence to justify their verdict. But this is only evidence that judges know that they cannot overrule linguistic content without good reason.

---

[139] The German term "Wortlaut" is part of the composite term "Wortlautgrenze" and means something like "wording." See also above.

[140] There is a structural incentive to pretend to interpret the law rather than to revise it. This is itself a strategic use of indeterminacy with regard to interpretation itself. It is useful for judges troubled with cases of injustice and absurdity or other cases to their dislike to cloak their decisions in (alleged) indeterminacy. See section 5.2.3 on deniability in verdicts.

The distinction between literal meaning and linguistic content also clarifies that CTL does not entail textualism about legal interpretation. One can consistently accept CTL and reject textualism, as do Soames and Marmor, for instance. A proponent of CTL can use all methods of interpretation. Asgeirsson (2012b, 174–214), for instance, argues for some version of legal *intentionalism* based on CTL. Textualists, intentionalists, and purposivists tend to overlook that also in ordinary conversation literal meaning, intention, and purpose are factors that determine the communicative content of an utterance. None of them has strict priority. Why would any canon of interpretation be strictly dominant when it comes to legal utterances?

The Argument from Pragmatics

Other forms of linguistic content—apart from literal meaning—can only be relevant in the law if certain assumption hold in the legal domain as well as in ordinary conversation. According to Greenberg (2011a), Marmor (2008) and Soames (2008b) mistakenly assume that law is basically a form of cooperative information exchange susceptible to conversational maxims. But if conversational maxims are to be applied in the law, there must be a minimum level of cooperation. Otherwise, the Cooperative Principle would not hold.[141] So if law is not a cooperative form of communication, the Cooperative Principle is not valid and, hence, there are no implicatures or other forms of pragmatically conveyed content. As a consequence, the only linguistic content relevant to law is either literal meaning or what is said—neither of which can sufficiently determine legal content.

As a matter of fact, Marmor explicitly argues that law is a strategic enterprise.[142] There are conflicting interests in society and law is the arena in which many of them are fought out. Marmor (2014, 7) recognizes that "the strategic nature of legal communication calls into question the reliability of implicated content in the law." According to Greenberg (2010), the cross-purposes and lack of cooperation within the legislature and between it and various parts of the audience make it difficult to see how the Cooperative Principle could hold in the law.

Marmor (2014, 52) argues that implicated content in the law is potentially unreliable for three reasons rooted in context indeterminacy.[143] First, there is indeterminacy about who counts as a relevant party to the conversation. Second, there is inherent uncertainty about what counts as a relevant contribution to the conversation that the parties are allowed to make. And, third, there

---

[141] The Cooperative Principle says that people make their contributions "such as is required, at the stage at which it occurs, by the accepted purpose or direction of the talk exchange in which [they] are engaged" (Grice, 1989a, 26).

[142] See Marmor (2011b, 136–159), Marmor (2008, 429), and Marmor (2014, 35–60).

[143] See section 1.6.

is indeterminacy about which aspects of the legislative process are relevant to determine implicated content. Thus, according to Marmor (2014, 53), the applicability of the conversational maxims "partly depends on the normative—that is, moral-political, understanding of the role of legislation in a legal system—and partly on the interpretative practices that courts actually follow."

There indeed is theoretical and sometimes practical unclarity about who the legislature is, what should count as its speech act, and how language, intention, and purpose must be balanced to determine the content of the law.[144] But does this mean that the Cooperative Principle cannot hold?

The conversational maxims hold in conversations in which there is cooperation between the participants. In such contexts it is reasonable to use language as clearly, unambiguously, and informatively as possible—at least as long it is required for successful communication. Of course, deliberate violations of conversational maxims are possible and, in fact, necessary to use conversational implicatures. However, they have to hold and to be known to hold in the first place.

At closer inspection, however, neither legislation nor adjudication lack cooperation in the required sense. As Endicott (2014, 47) argues, "it is a fundamental necessity of legal order that the institutions of a legal system communicate on a cooperative basis that sustains legal analogues of the standard conversational maxims."

After all, there are countless principles of legal interpretation and construction. Marmor (2014, 54) concedes that over "time, the norms of statutory interpretation that are actually followed by the courts may partly determine some conversational maxims of legislation." Although skeptical about the legislative procedure because "staffers, lobbyists, and professional drafters write laws rather than elected representatives," Victoria A. Nourse and Jane Schacter (2002, 575) acknowledge that such "drafters are generally familiar with judicial rules of construction." That is, both legislators and interpreters can assume the conversational maxims in the form of principles of interpretation and construction to hold.

Not only is legislation and adjudication more cooperative than Greenberg suggests, but also ordinary conversation is far less cooperative than often assumed.[145] Even Grice is rather cautious when formulating the Cooperative Principle:

> Our talk exchanges ... are characteristically, *to some degree at least*, cooperative efforts; and each participant recognizes in them, *to some extent*, a common purpose or set of purposes, or *at least a mutually accepted direction*. (Grice, 1989a, 26, my emphasis)

---

[144] See section 2.3.

[145] See, for instance, Arielli (2005) who argues that cooperation is less frequent in everyday communication than Grice suggests.

Grice notes that there is a great deal of uncertainty and tolerance about the extent to which there is a common purpose or mutually accepted direction of our everyday conversations. Many conversations are clearly not entirely cooperative. As Marmor (2014, 44) himself points out,

> It would be terribly naïve, for example, to assume that a car dealer trying to sell you a used car is going to adhere to the maxims of quantity, not telling you too little or too much.

There are many different ordinary conversations, some of which are highly strategic, while others do not even have a clear purpose altogether:

> There is nothing out of the ordinary about a conversation in which the participants have very different purposes that include being generous, sounding clever, making a good impression, encouraging someone, embarrassing someone else, causing confusion, being economical with the truth, etc. etc. All that unlimited plethora of purposes, of course, is compatible with what Grice says about conversational maxims. (Endicott, 2014, 53–54)

Quite often speakers pursue various perlocutionary intentions at the same time and with the same illocutionary act. Unlike legislation, an ordinary conversation's general purpose is usually not agreed on in any definite way, nor must there necessarily be a common purpose in the first place.[146]

Thus, we can conclude with Endicott (2014, 53) that "[t]here is no general basis for saying that ordinary conversation involves cooperation in a way that legislation does not." We can maintain with Marmor, however, that implicatures in legal utterances exhibit a certain kind of uncertainty due to the mentioned disagreement in the methodology of legal interpretation. According to Marmor (2014, 55), "inconsistent and less-than-fully-predictable application of conversational norms by the courts (acquiesced by the legislature), is probably the main mechanism that allows this uncertainty to be continuously maintained."

Despite this uncertainty, legal content includes not only what the legislature asserts, but also the implicated content that courts have reason to ascribe to legal utterances. Legal utterances may be more complex and "rife with the ignoring of implicatures," as Endicott (2014, 53) claims, but this does not imply that they do not possess pragmatically conveyed content. It might in fact be the case that pragmatic indeterminacy is actually rather widespread in the law.[147]

---

[146] According to Endicott (2014, 53), "the open-ended nature of conversation means that the purposes potentially under pursuit are much, much more various and undefined than the purposes of legislation."

[147] See section 3.4 on pragmatic indeterminacy in the law.

2.4.2 CTL ON TRIAL

The following three arguments against CTL are based on cases in which even communicative content fails to determine legal content. In some way or other, legal practice indicates a "gap" between what the relevant legal utterances communicate and what the law is.[148] The first argument concerns the sources of legal indeterminacy. The second one concerns differences between linguistic and legal content due to changes in the law. The third one concerns customary law for which there appears to be no linguistic content at all.

The Argument from Indeterminacy

A striking case in which communicative content fails to determine legal content seems to be legal indeterminacy in general. Consider the forms of linguistic indeterminacy discussed in chapter 1 and legal indeterminacy discussed in section 2.3.4. According to Solum (2013, 509f.), each of them is a reason why legal content must differ from linguistic content.

First, some legal utterances are semantically vague. The law supplements semantically vague utterances with legal doctrines that eliminate or reduce border-line cases. Second, some legal utterances are irreducibly ambiguous. Sometimes, context is insufficient to disambiguate the utterance. This can be an epistemic problem or related to the problem of context determination discussed in section 1.6. The problem is especially vivid when ambiguity is strategically employed. Third, some legal utterances are pragmatically indeterminate. Again, some recourse to legal doctrine, natural law, or other means to tip the scales is necessary to resolve the indeterminacy. Fourth, the relevant legal utterances combined provide a set of norms that contain a gap. In this case, some legal decision-maker needs to employ a default norm or create new law to cover it. Fifth, the relevant legal utterances combined have linguistic content that is contradictory. Since legal effects cannot be contradictory, legal content must be construed such that contradiction is avoided.

The existence of such indeterminacy shows that CTL must be false, does it not? Solum's argument can be reconstructed as follows:

(P1) Linguistic content is sometimes indeterminate.
(P2) If linguistic content is indeterminate, other means to determine legal content are necessary.
(C) Legal content is sometimes determined by something other than linguistic content.

Is indeterminacy really a reason why legal content cannot be determined by linguistic content? Solum's argument is based on (P2), which presupposes that legal content cannot ever be indeterminate. Surely, legal decision-makers must make

---

[148] This is why Asgeirsson (2016) calls this also the "Gappiness Problem."

tough calls. Judges often have to give legal effect to some norm even though the case is linguistically indeterminate and no salient means of tipping the scales is available.

One could in principle call the legal decision reached by the judge in such a case "legal interpretation" or "construction." One could say that the legal provisions used in her argument have whatever legal content she ascribes to them. However, this is not what these provisions contribute to the legal obligations in a legal system—at least not before the decision is made. This "legal content" is not based on any rule of application. It would not be based on anything anybody would recognize as law. As such, it is rather revision of the law than application of it.

The proponents of CTL actively maintain that vagueness, ambiguity, gaps, and contradictions in the law leave legal content indeterminate. They positively accept that legal content is indeterminate precisely because linguistic content does not determine it. By taking (P2) for granted, Solum is begging the question against CTL.

The Argument from Divergence

There appear to be cases in which the communicative content of a legal utterance differs from its legal content because of changes in legal practice. Consider the First Amendment of the US Constitution:

> Congress shall make no law respecting an establishment of religion, or prohibiting the free exercise thereof; or abridging the freedom of speech, or of the press; or the right of the people peaceably to assemble, and to petition the Government for a redress of grievances.

As Solum (2013, 480) points out, the expression "Congress" in the First Amendment is usually understood to refer to the Congress of the United States, consisting of the House of Representatives and the Senate. It refers to Congress by means of its communicative content. However, its legal content goes beyond anything that can be provided for by mere linguistic interpretation. As a matter of fact, the freedom of the press applies equally to judicially created defamation law. Thus, the legal content of the First Amendment not only entails that Congress shall make no law abridging the freedom of press but also that the Supreme Court and other legal authorities are not allowed to do so. Similarly, the constitutional provisions associated with the freedom of speech have legal content that is much richer than their respective communicative content. An example by Solum (2013, 501) is the free speech doctrine that contains rules concerning prior restraint, which cannot be part of the Constitution's communicative content.

There are similar cases at the statutory level. Greenberg (2011b), for instance, points out that the requirement of mens rea is presumed to be part of most criminal laws, even if they do not explicitly mention it. According to common law tradition, criminal liability usually depends on whether one has committed the crime (actus reus) and intended to commit the crime (mens rea). The common law test for guilt or innocence is captured by the Latin saying "*actus reus non facit reum nisi mens sit rea*" ("the act is not culpable unless the mind is guilty"). This requirement is, however, not stated in any statute, and "[i]t would be strain to argue that *mens rea* requirements are somehow part of the linguistic content of criminal statutes, whatever their wording and whatever the circumstances of their enactment."[149] According to Greenberg, the common law requirement of mens rea modifies the legal content of such statutes without thereby changing their communicative content.

Moreover, legal and communicative content seem to systematically come apart in contract clauses. Most contracts leave some questions open that are settled by contract law. According to Solum (2013, 494), the contract's communicative content cannot be identical to its legal content, since most of its legal content is determined by contract law, which is not part of the contract. The communicative content of the utterances of offer and acceptance does not fully determine the legal obligations to which offeror and offeree commit themselves by forming the contract. Contract law generally enriches contracts by adding and changing its legal content. Thus, a contract's legal content is *typically* different from its communicative content.

Do such cases constitute a knock-down argument for CTL? Presumably not. There are at least two possible replies by the proponent of CTL. First, she can argue that such changes in legal practice are changes in context. One can simply include the relevant legal practice as aspects of context that would affect the legal utterance's communicative content even after it is made. The communicative content of the First Amendment differs with new legal constructions of the Constitution. A new decision by the Supreme Court literally changes what is communicated by the Constitution because it changes its context. Analogously, what is communicated by a statute or contract depends on their legal context, namely, on other legal utterances such as precedents and the statutes of contract law.

A possible rejoinder by Solum and Greenberg could be that context is arbitrarily and unduly expanded. Such inclusion of other legal utterances is at best an ad hoc explanation. While one might make a case for the claim that the mens rea requirement is contextually implied in many criminal statutes, it would be absurd to say that what is communicated by the First Amendment is also that the judicial branch must not render verdicts that abridge the freedom of speech. The notion of context would be overstretched to include legal practice established decades and centuries after the framing of the Constitution.

---

[149] See Greenberg (2011b, 76).

The plausibility of this reply depends on the particular notion of communicative content. If communicative content is identified with an utterer's meaning or illocutionary intention, it is indeed absurd to stretch context this far. However, if communicative content is identified with what the intention a competent, reasonable, and informed language user would be warranted in ascribing to the speaker, the relevant context could be the context of the utterance, the context of application, or a combination of both. In other words, one has the choice of the perspective of interpretation.[150] In fact, communicative content in this objective sense can change after an utterance has been made also in ordinary conversation. What a competent, reasonable, and informed language user is warranted in ascribing to the speaker changes when facts change. Consider speaker S who says in front of her friends to hearer R

(E22) "You're the icing on my cake."

In the context of utterance, a competent, reasonable, and informed language user might be truly warranted in ascribing to S the intention of telling R that R is really wonderful. However, after a few days, it might become clear that S is in fact increasingly antipathetic to R, and this becomes commonly known to their friends—so much so that everybody is now warranted in ascribing to S the intention of telling R by (E22) that R is just the opposite of really wonderful. Evidently, S must have meant (E22) ironically.

This example shows that communicative content (if understood in the objective sense) can indeed change over time. If this is true, the same explanation would not be ad hoc for legal utterances and changes in legal practice.

A second possible reply for the proponent of CTL is to argue that the communicative content of other legal utterances can change the First Amendment's legal content without changing its communicative content. There might be a misconception because legal utterances are unrealistically limited to statutory and constitutional provisions. But also common law principles, precedents, and principles of interpretation used in precedents are expressed in legal utterances. They, too, can change by their communicative content the legal content of former legal utterances.

It can be argued that the legal content of the First Amendment is broader than its communicative content because other legal utterances changed it—just as utterances in ordinary conversation can change how a former utterance must be understood, even though at the time of the utterance, its communicative content required a different understanding. CTL could be defended, albeit in a modified version. It is not the case that the communicative content of an individual legal utterance is identical to or determines its legal content, but the communicative

---

[150] See section 2.3.1.

contents of all relevant legal utterances determine the legal content of any individual legal utterance.

However, even such a holistic approach would fail if there are legal norms that, even though expressible in language, are established by non-linguistic social practices. There might be legally valid norms established by custom; they would have legal content without linguistic content.

The Argument from Custom

In every legal system, there are some laws that were established by custom. Some statutory laws make reference to customary law such as the German § 242 BGB, for instance; but courts can also directly determine the content of customs.[151] Customary law comprises social practices observed and considered to be law by the relevant actors. This subjective element of custom as a source of law is *opinio juris*.

In the United Kingdom, for example, if a custom is clear, consistent, and practiced for "Time Immemorial," it can be recognized as customary law. Consider the custom to moor a vessel. If a group of houseboats on a mooring has been in continuous use for the last 25 years, the mooring may continue to be used by houseboats. Such a law clearly has legal content, but there is no utterance to which communicative content could be ascribed. Hence, there appear to be cases in which communicative content and legal content come apart.

A possible objection by the proponent of CTL is that customary laws only obtain legal content when they are either acknowledged by a court or codified by the legislature. Before that, they are not legal norms, but merely social ones. According to Max Weber (1967, 337), it is judges who ultimately decide when a custom becomes legally valid. Thus, customary law is judge made law and, as such, based on verdicts, that is, legal utterances that do have communicative content.

While this might be convincing for some cases of customary laws in which there is some residual uncertainty with respect to their legal validity, other customary laws do not need to be legally recognized to be valid. It is their continuous general practice, their *longa consuetudo*, which makes them legally valid. There might be no doubt at all that a court would enforce them if challenged. Such clear instances of customary law do seem to constitute legal norms without linguistic content.

2.4.3 THEORETICAL DISAGREEMENT IN PRACTICE

The *Argument from Divergence* and the *Argument from Custom* are powerful arguments. However, they concern only marginal cases. Most legal norms are, arguably, affected by neither of them. Moreover, CTL might, as we saw, be amended to deal with them in some manner.

---

[151] In Germany, the authorization to do so is given by § 293 ZPO.

Unfortunately, there is a more fundamental problem to all CTL-based accounts of indeterminacy in the law. If we are interested in the value, function, or strategic use of linguistic indeterminacy, it does not matter what the content of the law according to some theory is but how legal practitioners actually determine it. Authors of legal utterances must take into account how their audience will understand and interpret them. However, if interpreters adhere to and put into practice different theories of legal interpretation, legal content is in fact determined in these different ways. The fundamental problem for CTL is the persistent theoretical disagreement about legal interpretation in actual legal practice.

The problem consists of two parts. First, the fact that there is a multitude of possible notions of linguistic content undermines the basic idea of CTL. As we saw, there are several theories of literal meaning, utterer's meaning, what is said, what is implicated, and communicative content. There is theoretical disagreement about how to demarcate semantics and pragmatics. As Greenberg (2011a) argues, CTL does not have the resources to single out the notion of linguistic content relevant to law. Moreover, there might not even be a fact of the matter what *the* linguistic content is that we should attribute to utterances in general and legal utterances in particular, since there are, arguably, different notions of linguistic content that serve different explanatory purposes.

Second, there is also a multitude of possible theories of legal interpretation and legal ideologies. As indicated in section 2.3, lawyers have to make at least three choices of interpretation. First, there is the choice between subjective and objective interpretation. Should the interpreter try to find out how the actual utterer meant her utterance or should she try to establish how a reasonable language user would understand it? Second, there is the choice of the perspective of interpretation. Should the interpreter take up the perspective of the utterer, the audience, or a combination of both? Thirdly, there is the choice of abstract versus contextual interpretation. To what extent should the interpreter take the context into account at all? The answer to each question does not only depend on facts about language and communication.

According to Greenberg (2011a, 244), proponents of CTL have nothing to say about why legal content is to be identified with some type of linguistic content rather than another. Neither philosophy of language nor linguistics can directly address a legal utterance's contribution to the legal obligations in a legal system. There is a fundamental difference between legislation and communication in ordinary discourse in this respect. Legislation has a number of goals, which are, even though hotly debated, specific to the law. Goals such as promoting justice, fostering the moral legitimacy of a legal system, or realizing the interests of the groups represented in parliament are not necessarily most effectively advanced if a statute's legal content is identified with its linguistic content. There are many goals of a legal system that may be better served if CTL is rejected. Legal experts can reasonably disagree about these goals and how to advance them.[152]

As I argued in sections 1.6 and 2.3, the determination of context in indeterminate cases involves normative questions. Especially in the law, there is not always a matter of fact of what is relevant to the case at hand or what is a legal utterance's exact purpose or goal. This is reflected in the different and conflicting theories of legal interpretation we discussed in section 2.3.1. There is not even agreement about the criteria of what makes a good legal theory.[153]

Rubin (2010, 548) claims that "legal scholarship ... experiences basic problems with its core identity." It oscillates between a descriptive and prescriptive approach. Legal experts substantially and continuously disagree on the grounds of law.[154] There is, as we saw in section 2.3.1, no agreement on the principles of legal interpretation. Both in Germany and the United States, many different forms of legal arguments are used and advocated.[155]

According to Shapiro (2007), Dworkin's Semantic Sting can be generalized to an *Argument from Theoretical Disagreement*. This generalized argument can be stated as follows:

(P1) If legal experts agree on all empirical facts relevant to a legal question but still disagree about its answer, they either disagree about the grounds of law or talk past each other.

(P2) If CTL is true, they cannot disagree about the grounds of law.

(P3) CTL is true.

(C) Thus, in cases of continuing disagreement, legal experts talk past each other.

Since (C) is plainly absurd, the argument must be unsound. Since the argument is valid, one premise must be false. According to Dworkin, (P3) is the most promising candidate to drop. His argument—in this general form—poses not only a threat to legal positivism, as Smith (2010) emphasizes, but to all kinds of "plain fact theories" such as CTL. While CTL can account for disagreement over

---

[152] The fact that lawyers massively and pervasively agree on the level of application does not entail that they do not disagree on the level of theory. Conflicting theories of legal interpretation can and usually do result in convergent rulings of most cases. Often, it is occurrences of linguistic indeterminacy that unveil theoretical disagreement. See chapter 3 for a discussion of this claim. See, in particular, section 3.3.

[153] See Rubin (1992).

[154] Grounds of law are propositions in virtue of which propositions about law are true and false. See Dworkin (1986, 4). According to Leiter (2009, 1216), grounds of law are the criteria of legal validity, that is, the criteria some norm must satisfy to count as "legally valid."

[155] See Savigny et al. (1976, 14–26) for the German legal system and Bobbitt (1982, 93–94) for the US legal system.

empirical facts and linguistic misunderstanding, it cannot account for theoretical disagreement.

Dworkin uses this argument to defend his claim that the concept of law is "interpretive."[156] It implies that if one shares the same concept of law, one accepts the same legal paradigms. According to Endicott (1998, 293), one adopts an interpretive attitude that regards legal practice as having a purpose or value.[157] It also implies that identifying the law is an act of interpretation, grounded in convictions about the point of legal practice as a whole.[158]

Disagreement might not be as essential to law as Dworkin suggests. There is widespread agreement on many legal questions among legal experts.[159] However, widespread agreement does not itself answer the challenge of theoretical disagreement. It would still be a troublesome consequence if the remaining legal disagreements were merely verbal, especially if such disagreements do not only concern cases of indeterminacy, but also "pivotal cases," which are at the core of law.[160] It would be especially troublesome for CTL-based accounts of indeterminacy because they cannot accommodate the fact that legal texts are interpreted according to substantially different legal theories of interpretation and meta-interpretation.

The classical answer to Dworkin's Argument from Theoretical Disagreement is some adjustment to one's theory of legal positivism along the lines of Hart (1961/1994), Kramer (1999), Coleman (2001), Raz (2009b), or Shapiro (2011). By doing so, one might save legal positivism—however, at the expense of CTL.[161]

Hart's proposal is probably the least drastic. According to him, there are secondary rules in any legal system such as the Rule of Recognition, which is constituted by the actual practice of officials deciding questions about the grounds of law. Just as with the Rule of Recognition, many secondary rules are social rules. But social rules do not have linguistic content, since they emerge from the actual practice of convergent behavior. Then, however, not all legal content is identical to or determined by linguistic content.

There are two further possible replies suggested by Leiter (2009). First, a proponent of CTL can cast doubt on (P1). Besides talking past each other, there are two other possibilities to explain apparent disagreement in the law. Besides merely verbal disagreements, legal disagreements may be either disingenuous or mistaken. Leiter denies thus the existence of genuine theoretical disagreements. Legal experts

---

[156] See our discussion of interpretive concepts in section 2.3.3.

[157] See also Dworkin (1986, 47).

[158] See Dworkin (1986, 87–88).

[159] See section 2.3.4.

[160] See Dworkin (1986, 41–43).

[161] In fact, all proposals here mentioned give up on CTL eventually.

are not really disagreeing about preexisting law or the criteria for identifying it but just pretend to do so for political reasons. They are, consciously or unconsciously, trying to change it.

In other instances, they honestly think that there is a fact of the matter about the grounds of law. But they err because there is no convergent practice of behavior among the officials on this point, resulting in legal indeterminacy. The occurrence of misunderstanding, disingenuousness, and error can easily explain, according to Leiter, why we think that there is genuine disagreement about the grounds of law, even though in fact there is none.

However, one would expect participants in legal debates to criticize others for such behavior. But, as Shapiro (2011, 290f.) points out, such criticism is notably absent. Is it really plausible that the vast majority of legal experts do not realize the degree of misunderstanding, disingenuousness, and error in legal interpretation?

Second, a proponent of CTL could simply bite the bullet. The Argument from Theoretical Disagreement does not do much, if anything, to undermine CTL. Dworkin would need to show also that theoretical disagreement is an essential feature of law. There does not seem to be widespread disagreement in the application of many legal norms. Maybe there are no genuine disagreements about the grounds of law. So what? Let us call this reply the *"so what" response*, following Levenbook (2015, 5).

Neither reply by Leiter is tempting. However, one might be able to strengthen the "so what" response by pointing out that verbal disagreements are not always misunderstandings. They are sometimes part of meta-linguistic negotiations, as Plunkett and Sundell (2013b) call them.[162] When we disagree about what "law" means, we do not only have different understandings of the expression "law" but make normative claims of how one should use it—which understanding is the better one. In this case, accepting (C) would be fine because the conclusion is only absurd at first glance.

Unfortunately, this is not possible for the proponent of CTL because verbal disagreements in meta-linguistic negotiations are disagreements about the grounds of law just the same. One would inadvertently deny (P2), which is not an option since CTL entails that the grounds of law are fixed in a particular way. Disagreeing about them would be tacitly rejecting CTL.

It is crucial to note that theoretical disagreement is not only disagreement between textualism, intentionalism, and purposivism, or, to speak in terms of German legal theory, between the grammatical, historical, and objective method. It also encompasses disagreement between different conceptions of linguistic content, different ways to determine (counterfactual) legislative intent, and different

---

[162] See also section 2.3.3 on interpretive concepts.

ideologies and their prescribed purposes. For instance, lawyers can agree about the facts and that legal intentionalism is generally the correct interpretive method, while still disagreeing on normative grounds about what the counterfactual intention in the case at hand is.

The existence of theoretical disagreement in practice conclusively demonstrates that CTL cannot be correct—at least not when used as the basis of an account for actual indeterminacy in the law as done by many participants in the debate on vagueness in law. There are cases of legal disagreement without legal experts disagreeing empirically or verbally and without them being disingenuous or making mistakes. Legal experts genuinely and honestly disagree about the nature and methodology of law. These disagreements are based on different choices of legal interpretation and different (normative) assessments of context. The different weighings of the relevant conversational maxims or legal principles reflect their theoretical disagreements about legal interpretation and meta-interpretation.

In summary, linguistic content happens to be identical to legal content in many cases, even if the former does not constitute or determine the latter. Nobody denies that legal utterances are grounds of law. In other cases, however, linguistic and legal content come apart or there is at least consistent theoretical disagreement about the nature of linguistic content and its relation to legal content. This kind of disagreement has a direct bearing on the practice of legal interpretation. Linguistic content can thus not generally be said to be identical to or determine legal content.

As a consequence, certain claims about the role and value of indeterminacy in the law must be taken with a pinch of salt. Participants in the debate on vagueness in law should be aware that there is no way to entirely separate cases of theoretical disagreement from cases of linguistic indeterminacy. This should make us cautious when making or considering claims about the role and function of vagueness (and other forms of linguistic indeterminacy) in the law. The route from linguistic content to legal content is potentially indeterminate not only due to linguistic indeterminacy and the problem of context determination, but also because of different (maybe equally defensible and often implicit) theories of legal interpretation. Depending on different interpretive choices, language, intention, and purpose can be differently weighed and legal content thus be differently construed.

Linguistic indeterminacy can be rendered irrelevant by legal doctrine in some cases, but there are other cases in which linguistic indeterminacy translates into legal indeterminacy on the level of application or is mirrored by legal indeterminacy on the level of theory or meta-interpretation. In the remainder of this book, I will thus assume that linguistic content is at least decisive in the determination of legal content for many cases. But caution is called for to distinguish cases in which linguistic indeterminacy in fact translates into legal indeterminacy from those cases in which either linguistic indeterminacy does not or legal content is indeterminate due to non-linguistic forms of indeterminacy. Even in cases in which linguistic indeterminacy translates into legal indeterminacy, questions of legal theory and meta-interpretation tend to influence the debate and render linguistic questions less relevant.

2.5 Summary

This chapter had two functions. First, we prepared the theoretical ground for the discussion of linguistic indeterminacy in the law in chapters 3 and 5. I argued that legal utterances are typically normative, directed toward future events, addressed to heterogeneous audiences, and applied in a wide variety of circumstances.

These features of legal language are decisive for the use of linguistic indeterminacy in law, and they are exemplified in three paradigmatic kinds of legal utterances: the enactment of laws, rendering of verdicts, and formation of contracts. The strategic use of indeterminacy in these utterances will be discussed in detail in sections 5.1, 5.2, and 5.3, respectively.

Second, we examined the plausibility of the communication theory of law (CTL) as basis for an account of linguistic indeterminacy in the law. CTL entails that legal content is identical to or determined by linguistic content. CTL is either implicitly or explicitly assumed by many participants in the debate on vagueness in law. I argued that linguistic and legal content fall apart in some cases. It is thus possible that there are easy cases despite linguistic indeterminacy and hard cases despite linguistic determinacy.

More importantly, however, in the law there is, besides the linguistic forms of indeterminacy discussed in chapter 1, also indeterminacy on the level of legal content. This specially legal form of indeterminacy is not only due to gaps and contradictions but also theoretical and meta-interpretive disagreement. In particular, theoretical disagreement in legal practice renders linguistic indeterminacy (including semantic vagueness) less relevant than suggested by the debate on vagueness in law.

3

Indeterminacy in the Law

So far, we differentiated between the various forms of linguistic indeterminacy. We also discussed the characteristics of legal language, and I argued against the general validity of the communication theory of law (CTL), which entails that the content of the law is determined by or identical to the linguistic content of legal utterances. Bearing this in mind, we can now turn to a discussion of indeterminacy in the law. To put it precisely, we will tackle the question of what forms of linguistic indeterminacy do matter legally. The answer to this question will be important to our examination of the effects of indeterminacy on the interpretation and application of legal norms, which will be carried out in chapter 5 on strategic indeterminacy in the law.

In the following sections, I will demonstrate how a comprehensive differentiation of the various forms of linguistic indeterminacy, as shown in Figure 4, can shed light on the process of legal interpretation and construction. We will see that a range of claims that have been made about semantic vagueness, generality, and interpretation are mistaken and that it makes a significant difference to our assessment of indeterminacy in law which philosophical and linguistic toolkit we approach it with.

In section 3.1, I will first discuss cases of ambiguity in the law, arguing that polysemy—in contrast to both lexical and syntactic ambiguity—is its most relevant form. In section 3.2, I will argue that semantic vagueness is far *less* relevant than previously assumed, concluding that what is often taken to be the function of vagueness is in fact either standard-relativity or polysemy. Finally, I will analyze conversational vagueness in section 3.3 and pragmatic indeterminacy in section 3.4, showing that pragmatic forms of indeterminacy are *more* relevant in the law than one might have thought considering that they are essentially ignored by the legal and philosophical debate.

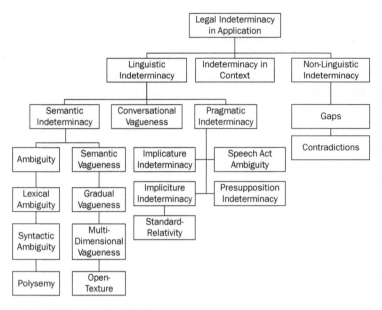

FIGURE 4 **Legal Indeterminacy in Application**

3.1 Ambiguity in the Law

The expression "ambiguity" is usually understood in the law as something like *uncertainty or doubtfulness of the meaning of language.* The US Supreme Court once defined "ambiguity" such that a "statute is ambiguous when reasonable minds differ or are uncertain as to its meaning."[1] This is not too dissimilar from our definition of "indeterminacy" in general:

(D1) An utterance *u* is (linguistically) INDETERMINATE in context *c* iff it is unclear to a competent and well-informed language user what is communicated by *u* in *c*.

In this section, we will not discuss the general notion of ambiguity as it is used in the law but concentrate on the notion of ambiguity developed in section 1.2, differentiating between lexical and referential ambiguity, syntactic ambiguity, and polysemy.

LEXICAL AND REFERENTIAL AMBIGUITY

The classic example of ambiguity in the legal literature is the famous case *Raffles v. Wichelhaus*, a textbook case in English contract law.[2] According to the contract

---

[1] See *Lockhart v. Cedar Rapids Community Sch. Dist.*, 577 N.W.2d 845 (1998), cited in Golanski (2002, 99).

[2] *Raffles v. Wichelhaus*, 2 H. & C. 906 (1864). Classically, legal scholars distinguish between two categories of ambiguity, namely, *ambiguitas latens* and *ambiguitas patens*. On one hand, *ambiguitas latens*

the parties signed, the goods that were to be sold should be transported on a ship called "Peerless." Unfortunately, there were two ships of that name, and disagreement arose because each party had a different ship in mind. Because of this, the content of the contract was disputed. Linguistically, the expression is *referentially* ambiguous. "Peerless," being a proper name, has, arguably, no lexical meaning at all. It just happened to be used to refer to two different objects.[3]

The court in *Raffles v. Wichelhaus* could not find a reasonable interpretation of the contract's terms that would determine the correct referent of the name "Peerless." As a consequence, there was no meeting of the minds, or *consensus ad idem*. The contracting parties did not agree to the same thing, and there was no binding contract. This is a simple case in which, by pure chance, a contract becomes indeterminate due to a referentially ambiguous expression.[4]

However, *Raffles v. Wichelhaus* is a rare case. Referential ambiguity and, even more so, lexical ambiguity hardly ever create indeterminacy in the law. The reason lies in the fact that the meanings or referents of lexically and referentially ambiguous expressions are unrelated and, consequently, not likely to be confused by competent and informed language users.

In particular, the meanings of lexically ambiguous expressions are so dissimilar that it is clear to any competent and informed language user which meaning must be the one expressed. Recall the taxi driver case from section 1.2.2. A taxi driver asks a client whether to turn left at the next junction. The client might say "Right!" in response, meaning either that the driver should turn *right* or that it is *right* to turn left. A failure of communication in this case would verge on situational comedy—and for good reason. When interpreting a statute containing the lexically ambiguous expression "bank," it would be absolutely ludicrous to find disagreement between some judges who take the statute to be about waterways and other judges who take it to be about finance. As Waldron (1994, 515) points out, "the problem of interpretation cannot get underway until we have at least a ball-park sense of the sort of message intended to be conveyed by the sounds and inscriptions that the legislator used."

---

is the phenomenon that more than one interpretation for an otherwise determinate legal expression presents itself because of extrinsic facts or evidence. On the other hand, *ambiguitas patens* is the phenomenon that more than one interpretation for a legal expression is equally plausible because the expression itself is ambiguous. The ambiguity in *Raffles v. Wichelhaus* is supposed to be *ambiguitas latens* because it is apparently an extrinsic fact that two ships with the same name existed. *Raffles v. Wichelhaus* illustrates why the classical distinction is problematic. There is generally both a linguistic and a contextual (or extrinsic) factor that accounts for any kind of actual ambiguity.

[3] If you are a descriptionist on proper names such as Russell (1905), the expression "Peerless" does in fact seem to be lexically ambiguous. Its ambiguity is then, presumably, latent for the simple fact that it is less transparently ambiguous than ambiguous general terms such as "bank."

[4] See Rosen (2011, 141–147) for a philosophical discussion of this case.

If it can be unclear whether a statute is about waterways or about finance, the legislature would have drafted it so poorly that it becomes questionable whether one can achieve an interpretation of *it* at all.

SYNTACTIC AMBIGUITY

Syntactic ambiguity is quite different in this regard. In section 1.2.1, we defined it thus:

(D6) An expression *e* is SYNTACTICALLY AMBIGUOUS iff *e* has two or more possible logical structures.

It seems that syntactic ambiguity is prone to generate indeterminacy in the law. For instance, in *California v. Brown*, the Supreme Court faced the question whether a jury instruction in a capital case violated the defendant's right to have the jury view his situation with compassion or sympathy.[5] The jury instruction stated: "You must not be swayed by mere sentiment, conjecture, sympathy, passion, prejudice, public opinion or public feeling." The matter of dispute was whether the adjective "mere" modified the term "sentiment" alone or all of the terms in the list. The outcome of the case depended on the precise scope of "mere" because of the legal relevance of the distinction between sympathy and mere sympathy.[6]

An empirical investigation by legal linguists would be desirable to establish the frequency with which syntactic ambiguity actually becomes an issue in legal interpretation. But it is also possible to give a general argument why syntactic ambiguity—in contrast to lexical and referential ambiguity—is likely to become a source of legal indeterminacy.

It is fairly easy to formulate a sentence without even noticing its ambiguous syntactic structure. In fact, it is practically impossible to eliminate all syntactic ambiguities from the law. The costs for doing so would simply be disproportional. As a result, many sentences in both ordinary and legal language are syntactically ambiguous, even though most of them are completely unproblematic due to the disambiguating role of context.

However, there are two factors that make syntactic ambiguity somewhat more interesting in the law than in everyday life communication. First, context in legal interpretation is, as we noted before, impoverished in contrast to context in verbal communication. Second, the law in its function to regulate the complex matters of human societies relies heavily on definitions and specifications of general terms.

---

[5] *California v. Brown*, 479 U.S. 538 (1987).

[6] For a detailed discussion of this case, see Solan (1993, 55–61).

As a consequence, the logical structure of sentences in legal texts tends to be complicated.[7]

Both factors systematically increase syntactic ambiguity in the law. The latter increases the occurrence of syntactically ambiguous expressions, while the former increases their generating actual indeterminacy. The mere frequency of syntactic ambiguities in legal texts is by itself no evidence that they actually matter in legal interpretation. However, there typically are different interpretations of a syntactically ambiguous expression that are sufficiently similar, though, to be within the scope of the assumed purpose of the law or intention of the lawmaker. Thus, they can reasonably be entertained by competent and informed lawyers and, at the same time, yield relevantly different legal consequences.[8]

This is also the case in *California v. Brown*. Both sympathy and mere sympathy are what can reasonably be assumed to be what is meant by the court in the context of its jury instruction. On the one hand, it was argued (by the court of appeals) that it is unconstitutional to deny the defendant the right to have "sympathy factors." It seems uncontroversial, on the other hand, that the jury's decision ought not to be based on sympathy alone. Thus, a hard case arises.[9]

POLYSEMY

Still more interesting for our purposes is polysemy. In section 1.2.3, we defined it in the following way:

(D8) An expression *e* is POLYSEMOUS iff *e* has two or more (related) senses of one lexical meaning.

An intriguing example of polysemy in the law is *United States v. Granderson*.[10] Ralph S. Granderson was a letter carrier who pleaded guilty to a charge of destroying mail. His potential prison term was up to six months. The court, however, sentenced him to five years of probation and a fine. During his probation, Granderson was found to possess cocaine, which on its own is punishable up to one year of imprisonment. The statute in question stated that

> if a defendant is found by the court to be in possession of a controlled substance ... the court shall revoke the sentence of probation and sentence

---

[7] See also section 2.1 on the features of legal language.

[8] For that reason, Dickerson (1975, 46) claims that syntactic ambiguity is "by far the most prevalent kind of ambiguity" in English legal texts.

[9] Structurally similar cases are, for example, *Sedima, SPRL v. Imrex Co., Inc.*, 473 U.S. 479 (1985) in which, according to Solan (1993), the syntactic ambiguity of "pattern of racketeering activity" was the source of legal indeterminacy; and *Staples v. United States*, 511 U.S. 600 (1994) in which, according to Cunningham et al. (1994), the scope of "knowingly" was unclear.

[10] *United States v. Granderson*, 511 U.S. 39 (1994).

the defendant to not less than one-third of the original sentence. (18 USC § 3565(a) (1988))

The district court construed the statute such that the defendant be sentenced to imprisonment of not less than one-third of the original time of probation, which amounted to twenty months of imprisonment for Granderson (one-third of the five years of probation). The court of appeals, however, vacated this prison sentence, construing the statute to require that Granderson be sentenced to a prison term of one-third of the original prison sentence that he could have received, which amounted to merely two months.

What does the expression "original sentence" mean? Justice Ginsburg, writing for the Supreme Court's majority, identified three possible senses of "original sentence." First, the verb phrase "sentence the defendant" and the noun phrase "original sentence" in 18 USC §3565(a) could refer to the same kind of sentence, namely, probation. Granderson would, then, be sentenced to additional twenty months of probation. Second, the verb phrase "sentence the defendant" could refer to imprisonment, and the noun phrase "original sentence" could refer to the original probationary sentence. Granderson would, then, be sentenced to a twenty months prison term, reinstating the district court's verdict. Third, the verb phrase "sentence the defendant" and the noun phrase "original sentence" could refer to the same kind of sentence, namely, imprisonment. Granderson would, then, be sentenced to two months in prison. The Supreme Court affirmed the construction of the court of appeals, adopting the third sense of "original sentence."

Cunningham et al. (1994) argue that the ambiguity of "original sentence" stems from a change in law in 1984.[11] Presumably, the legislators had different senses of "sentence" in mind when formulating the statute. According to Justice Ginsburg, Congress simply drafted the statute poorly.[12] In its pre-1984 sense, the expression "sentence" excludes probation, limiting sentences to incarcerations and monetary penalties. In its post-1984 sense, it includes probation as a kind of sentence. If this is correct, the expression "sentence" is indeterminate due to its vertical polysemy. It has two senses, which are related to each other such that the more general post-1984 sense strictly includes the pre-1984 sense.[13]

---

[11] It is noteworthy that the paper was published even before the Supreme Court issued its decision, and the Justices were certainly influenced by it.

[12] See Solan (1998, 114).

[13] Solan (1998, 113–115) seems to treat *United States v. Granderson* as a form of referential ambiguity such that the referent of "original sentence" is indeterminate. This is an implausible analysis of the case, however, since there are multiple clearly separable lexical senses of "sentence" that allow for different interpretations. On the other hand, there are no pragmatic, not to mention ostensive, elements in 18 USC § 3565(a), which would support Solan's analysis.

In general, we can say that vertical polysemy becomes a problem in legal interpretation when a legal utterance contains a polysemous expression that refers to some matter of fact X, and the disputed event can be considered an "X" in its broad sense; but it seems wrong to do so in the case at hand either (1) because the context of utterance makes the narrow reading of "X" more salient, (2) because the utterer seems to have meant "X" in its narrow sense, or (3) because the narrow reading of "X" is more plausible with respect to the overall purpose of the utterance.

Polysemy is a frequent, and generally underestimated, source of legal indeterminacy. Polysemous, and in particular vertically polysemous, expressions seem to account for many uncertainties in legal interpretation that have been indiscriminately dubbed "ambiguity" or "vagueness."[14] I will support this claim with a general argument structurally similar to the one for the relevance of syntactic ambiguity previously.

Polysemy becomes an issue in legal interpretation for two main reasons. First, the use of polysemous expressions is unavoidable because most general expressions have various different, but related, senses. General expressions are necessary for the law to capture the legally relevant aspects of human life. Additionally, it is often also desirable to use polysemous expressions because their context sensitivity allows them to be used in different contexts with an adaptable meaning. For instance, the polysemous expression "to have," which we discussed in examples (H1) to (H6) in section 1.2.3, can be used (among other things) in the sense of *possessing*, *carrying*, or *partaking*. The legal expression "sentence" can be used in different senses depending on the purposes of the statute. For instance, it is also ambiguous between the judgment pronounced by the judge and the punishment so imposed.[15] Almost all expressions can be used in at least some different senses. In contrast to lexical ambiguity, polysemy is an essential feature of language.

Second, if a polysemous expression is used in an utterance such that it can be reasonably understood in two different senses, in most cases both senses are sufficiently similar to be compatible with the assumed legislative intention or purpose of the law. If all but one of the senses would be obviously incompatible with any reasonable interpretation of the utterance, the fact that polysemy is essential to language would not entail that it be a significant source of legal indeterminacy. However, since what is said by an utterance using a polysemous expression in one sense is normally not strikingly different from what is said by an

---

[14] Another vivid example is *United States v. Santos*, 553 U.S. 507 (2008) in which the vertical polysemy of the expression "proceeds" caused indeterminacy since it can either mean specifically *net income* (the official gross revenues minus expenses) or generally *gross income* (which might also be received from illegal activity).

[15] Of course, "sentence" is also lexically ambiguous, but no Justice in *United States v. Granderson* would have dreamed that the legislature might have meant the linguistic entity when using the expression "sentence" in 18 USC § 3565(a).

utterance using the same expression in another sense, both interpretations can be reasonably defended by a competent and informed language user. If, additionally, the interpretations nonetheless yield relevantly different legal consequences, hard cases are certain to come up.

In a nutshell, polysemy is a prevalent form of indeterminacy in the law because (1) polysemous expressions are ubiquitous in legal texts; and (2) their senses are sufficiently similar to be reasonable, but sufficiently dissimilar to yield different legal consequences.

While lexical and referential ambiguity are marginal when it comes to legal indeterminacy, syntactic ambiguity and polysemy account for a significant number of hard cases in the law. Polysemy is even more interesting for our purposes than syntactic ambiguity since it is not as easily identifiable and resolvable. In chapter 1, we already noted the possibility of confusion between semantic vagueness and polysemy. Indeed, as we will see in section 3.2, many legal cases that have been given as examples of semantic vagueness are, in fact, instances of polysemy.

3.2 Semantic Vagueness in the Law

In jurisprudential discourse, the term "vagueness"—just as "ambiguity"—is used in a wide variety of ways. Some scholars mean polysemy, generality, or linguistic indeterminacy in general by the term. In many discussions of vagueness in law, all sorts of weasel words, indeterminate legal terms, as well as other context-sensitive and evaluative expressions are lumped together and generally treated as cases of vagueness. In these discussions, the vagueness of expressions such as "enterprise," "use," "sufficient cause," or "neglect" is considered to be the source of legal indeterminacy.[16]

It can be assumed that most authors discussing vagueness in the law have an understanding of "vagueness" that is rather similar to our definition of linguistic indeterminacy in (D1). However, there is also a number of philosophers, linguists, and legal scholars who explicitly claim to be talking about gradual vagueness, as defined in section 1.3.1:

(D13) An expression *e* is GRADUALLY VAGUE iff *e* allows for borderline cases due to *e*'s tolerance.

The accounts of two authors are particularly intriguing—both because of their prominence in the debate and the poignancy of their failure to correctly identify the source of legal indeterminacy. The linguist Lawrence M. Solan

---

[16] They are discussed by Solan (1993), Clare (1994), Engberg and Heller (2007), and Endicott (2011b), respectively.

and the philosopher Timothy A. O. Endicott cannot possibly—even under the most charitable interpretation—be taken to have a more general understanding of "vagueness." Both authors comprehensively discuss borderline cases and the Sorites paradox and survey at length the psychological, linguistic, and philosophical accounts of gradual vagueness—reviewing the debates and quoting the classical examples of gradually vague expressions such as "tall" or "heap."

But then they go on to talk about the vagueness of whole statutes, criticize the problems of enforcing vague laws, or praise the flexibility that vagueness is supposed to give to the law without arguing for or clarifying how it is that *gradual vagueness* could be responsible for this. If the legal cases cited by Solan and Endicott as examples of gradual vagueness are more closely scrutinized, it becomes evident that it is not—cannot be—the expressions' gradual vagueness that is the source of legal indeterminacy.

The problem about the debate on vagueness in law is, at bottom, that expressions such as "enterprise" or "neglect" are undeniably gradually vague but that actual borderline cases are rare and almost always disputed. The reason for this is that gradual vagueness is a property of an expression's meaning. Thus, before we can even ask whether something is a borderline case of some gradually vague expression, we need to determine the context more or less precisely, resolving ambiguities and pragmatic forms of indeterminacy. In any real life case, this is a very difficult task since in cases of unclarity, there will usually be disagreement about the implications of the whole utterance or the scope of some polysemous or syntactically ambiguous expression. Only once we have ruled out all the other forms of indeterminacy and determined the expression's extension relative to the context of utterance can we say whether some particular case is borderline or not.

In the philosophical debate on vagueness, this is not a problem since borderline cases are only imagined. The examples are highly idealized and abstract. The context is held fixed, and ambiguities and pragmatic forms of indeterminacy are stipulated away. Sometimes it can also legitimately be done in the legal debate. For instance, the fictitious vehicle in the park case discussed in section 2.3.4 is a legitimate idealization as long as we do not use it to prove a point about (actual) legal indeterminacy as defined in (D23). It becomes misleading, however, if we use it in arguments about the role or value of vagueness in the law.

In the next two sections, I will argue that Solan and Endicott overestimate the role of gradual vagueness by following too closely the philosophical debate and neglecting the context of real life cases. The laws they discuss and in which gradually vague expressions undoubtedly occur are indeterminate not because of their gradual vagueness, but, as I will show, mainly because of two other forms of indeterminacy: namely, polysemy and pragmatic indeterminacy. After discussing Solan's and Endicott's accounts, I will show in section 3.2.3 that gradual vagueness might nevertheless be a source of indeterminacy in the law.

3.2.1 SOLAN ON DEFINITIONS AND PROTOTYPES

In *United States v. Turkette*, the Supreme Court struggled with the meaning of the term "enterprise."[17] The defendant Novia Turkette distributed drugs as a member of a criminal network and was convicted for this activity under the *Racketeer Influenced and Corrupt Organizations Act* (RICO). The act was primarily intended to deal with organized crime. Its relevant section reads as follows:

> It shall be unlawful for any person employed by or associated with *any enterprise engaged in*, or in activities of which affect, *interstate or foreign commerce*, to conduct or participate, directly or indirectly, in the conduct of such enterprise's affairs through a pattern of racketeering activity or collection of unlawful debt. (18 USC § 1962(c), my emphasis)

Turkette claimed in his appeal that "enterprise" refers exclusively to legitimate businesses, not covering criminal networks as the one he was a member of. The court of appeals followed Turkette's understanding of "enterprise" and overturned his conviction. It held that RICO does not apply to associations that perform illegal acts only. The Supreme Court, however, reinstated Turkette's conviction, holding that the expression "enterprise" unambiguously referred to all associations or businesses—whether legitimate or not. Justice White, writing for the majority, argued that neither RICO's language, structure, nor legislative history limits its application to legitimate enterprises. Does the disagreement between the court of appeals and the Supreme Court perhaps indicate that criminal networks are borderline cases of "enterprise?" Is the gradual vagueness of "enterprise" the source of legal indeterminacy in *Turkette*?

Solan appears to think so. In criticizing the Supreme Court's ruling, he claims that it is "wrong to say that 'enterprise' could not be understood to include only legitimate businesses."[18] According to him, "there is nothing the least bit clear about what the word 'enterprise' means in RICO. ... [*Enterprise*] becomes a fuzzy concept at the margins."[19] The indeterminacy in *Turkette* is due to a "problem of conceptualization."[20] Solan (2005, 81) explains it in terms of prototype theory and (gradual) vagueness:

> Most words become vague when we are presented with situations that are close enough to the word's prototype that we are not ready to abandon the word as a fair description of the situation, but far enough away from the prototype that we are not certain. Often, these nonprototypical situations are the source of

---

[17] *United States v. Turkette*, 452 U.S. 576 (1981).

[18] See Solan (1993, 79).

[19] See Solan (1993, 107).

[20] See Solan (1998, 65–75).

disagreement among individuals judging the fit between the concept and the situation.

In *Turkette* the source of disagreement is, as Solan claims, such a non-prototypical situation—namely, a criminal network being a borderline case of "enterprise"—and, consequently, the expression's gradual vagueness. At first glance, Solan's explanation seems very convincing. At a closer look, however, we will see that it is (at its very best) confused.

The basic problem is that the context in *Turkette* is rich enough to allow for at least two salient interpretations of what "enterprise" means in RICO; and in both of them, a criminal network either clearly counts or clearly does not count as an enterprise. First, under the label of "definition," the statute elucidates what shall be included by "enterprise:"

> "[E]nterprise" includes any individual, partnership, corporation, association, or other legal entity, and any union or group of individuals associated in fact although not a legal entity. (18 USC § 1961(4))

Based on this elucidation, the Supreme Court in *Turkette* argued the following: "There is no restriction upon the associations embraced by the definition: an enterprise includes any union or group of individuals associated in fact."[21] Focusing on what it takes to be a definition of "enterprise," the Supreme Court's ruling that there is no indeterminacy in *Turkette* appears reasonable. The expression "enterprise" clearly includes criminal networks since it includes generally any group of individuals.

Second, however, a major purpose of RICO is presumably that the infiltration of organized crime into legitimate business be prevented. Taking this aspect of context into account, the interpretation of "enterprise" that was advocated by the court of appeals seems to fit much better what is meant by RICO.[22] If organized crime is to be prevented from infiltrating legitimate business, then it must be legitimate businesses to which RICO applies—not criminal networks.

This interpretation is further evidenced by other decisions on RICO. In *United States v. Anderson*, the court formulated a working definition of "enterprise" for the purposes of RICO, which was widely cited in subsequent cases and thus, apparently, entered RICO case law. It states

> [An enterprise is] an association having an ascertainable structure which exists for the purpose of maintaining operations directed toward an economic goal

---

[21] *United States v. Turkette*, 452 U.S. 576, 580–581 (1981).

[22] Whether one *ought* to take this aspect of context into account, depends, of course, on one's favored method of interpretation. See section 2.3.2 on the theories of legal interpretation.

that has an existence that can be defined apart from the commission of the predicate acts constituting the pattern of racketeering activity.[23]

According to this definition, the expression "enterprise" clearly excludes criminal networks.

One might argue that the meaning of "enterprise" in RICO is not determined by either definition. Instead, one ought to look at its actual usage in ordinary language. The definition in *Anderson* is not part of the statutory text but made up by a court, while the elucidation in *Turkette* is not really a definition to begin with. Most obviously, it reads "'enterprise' includes" and not "'enterprise' means," thus expressly not stating conditions for something being an enterprise.

Solan (1993, 107) complains that "the statute's definition is not really very helpful." Taken as a proper definition, any individual would be an enterprise, which surely is absurd. Accordingly, Cunningham et al. (1994, 1590) surmise that 18 USC § 1961(4) is merely "intended as a corrective against the possibility that the reader's preexisting understanding of *enterprise* might cause her to limit the word to legally constituted entities such as corporations and partnerships."

What then does "enterprise" mean? In ordinary language, too, it has at least two related senses, and depending on the context, it can be used to refer specifically to legitimate businesses or generally to any kind of business (or, even more generally, to some kind of undertaking). Cunningham et al. (1994) provide empirical evidence that the ordinary language expression "enterprise" is used in part in a narrower sense that corresponds to the definition in *Anderson* and in part in a broader sense that corresponds to the one in *Turkette*.[24]

Thus, the expression "enterprise," both in its legal and its ordinary language meaning, allows for two possible interpretations. It can be understood in a broad sense (sensu lato) or a narrow sense (sensu stricto). The interpretation of *Turkette* takes "enterprise" sensu lato to include any kind of business, both legitimate and illegitimate ones. The interpretation of *Anderson* takes "enterprise" sensu stricto to include only legitimate businesses. This is the phenomenon of vertical polysemy discussed in section 3.1. If this is correct, the source of unclarity in *Turkette* is the polysemy of "enterprise," and Solan's analysis of it as a case of gradual vagueness is misguided.

Two objections might be voiced against my analysis of *Turkette* and in favor of Solan's. First, one could argue that Solan's conception of vagueness is not limited to gradual vagueness but includes other forms of linguistic indeterminacy such as polysemy. Solan could then explain the unclarity in *Turkette* in more general terms

---

[23] *United States v. Anderson*, 626 F.2d 1358, 1372 (1980).

[24] See Kaplan et al. (1995) for a subsequent study on dictionary definitions and legal opinions on the meaning of "enterprise."

as a "problem of conceptualization," which does not distinguish between gradual vagueness and polysemy. As a result, my analysis of *Turkette* would not be strictly incorrect, but it would not be a critique of Solan's either.

But this is not an option. Solan is too clear about his understanding of the "problem of conceptualization," which he introduces with an example of a classical borderline case. Solan (1998, 65) asks us to consider the following dialogue:

A: "Is it raining?"
B: "No, it's just drizzling."

Solan claims that **B** might just as well have said: "Yes, but it's only drizzling." He claims that both answers are truthful to the question. The reason is gradual vagueness: "For the in-between experiences [such as] the drizzles ..., we become uncertain about whether the word *rain*, or another concept, is more appropriate."[25] Subsequently, Solan (1998, 117–118) gives a fairly long list of cases which he considers to be indeterminate due to the "vagueness" of some expression such as "vehicle" in *McBoyle v. United States* or "to use a firearm" in *Smith v. United States*.[26] Solan's analysis of these cases as a clash between a definitional and prototypical approach in legal interpretation already hints at the fact that the indeterminacy involved is due to there being different senses (of implicited content or polysemous expressions) and not borderline cases.

Solan (1998, 78) calls one of the problems of conceptualization in the law "overinclusion," contrasting it with "vagueness." While "vagueness" describes the problem of borderline cases, "overinclusion" describes the situation in which the expression clearly applies but is remote from its prototype. Often, there is a definition of an expression that is more general than what people ordinarily associate with it. For instance, robins are prototypical birds, but penguins are not.[27] Still, penguins are within the clear extension of "bird" due to how experts define it. Solan thinks that in many legal cases, we can decide between an interpretation that conforms with a general definition and one that is based on a prototype. Even in Solan's own analysis, the definition of "enterprise" includes criminal networks, while its prototypical meaning does not. This hits the mark of the problem, I think, but only demonstrates that it is not gradual vagueness that is effective in *Turkette*.

There are borderline cases of "enterprise." And, they are rather dissimilar to prototypical enterprises. But borderline cases are neither clearly within the

---

[25] See Solan (1998, 66).

[26] *McBoyle v. United States*, 283 U.S. 25 (1931) and *Smith v. United States*, 508 U.S. 223 (1993), respectively. We will see in section 3.4 that *Smith* is not a case of semantic vagueness but impliciture indeterminacy. Nor is *McBoyle* a case of semantic vagueness. It is polysemy—very much like *Turkette*.

[27] See section 1.5.4 on the relation between generics and linguistic indeterminacy.

extension nor clearly within the anti-extension of the term in its definitional or prototypical sense.

This is not the case in *Turkette*, however. In *Turkette*, "enterprise" does not become fuzzy at the margins. In the context of *Turkette*, a criminal network clearly falls within the extension in the definitional sense and clearly falls within the anti-extension in the prototypical sense of "enterprise." Solan's account is misguided because he treats *Turkette* as if it were a case of gradual vagueness.

The second objection is to insist that "enterprise" is a general and vague but unambiguous expression. One could argue that the expression "enterprise" has only a single core meaning, but with borderline cases such as criminal networks at its margin. If these borderline cases are not due to the expression's tolerance, they must be due to its multi-dimensionality. Evidently, "enterprise" is a multi-dimensional expression in which the dimensions of number of people, kind of their association, presence of some common goal, etc. can be more or less salient. Whether or not criminal networks are enterprises would then depend on which dimensions the context picks as salient. Then, the unclarity concerning the dimensions of "enterprise" would be the source of legal indeterminacy in *Turkette*.

My reply goes as follows. It is true that cases of semantic vagueness and polysemy are sometimes difficult to distinguish. In fact, this difficulty is to be expected since generality and polysemy cannot be sharply distinguished either.[28] There are quite a few cases in the law that exhibit this fuzziness between generality and polysemy. But *Turkette* is not a case like that. The expression "enterprise" can, in the context of the case, reasonably be understood in two different ways. In real life cases, the context cannot be completely fixed or fully determined. Moreover, an expression such as "enterprise" is not as semantically simple as the expressions "heap" or " tall," which are discussed as paradigm examples of gradual vagueness in the philosophical debate. The expression "enterprise" is general as well as gradually and multi-dimensionally vague. But it is also polysemous. The legal debate in *Turkette* reveals this.

Two senses of "enterprise" are discussed in *Turkette*, and even Solan acknowledges that there is a definitional and a prototypical understanding of it. His own words that "there is nothing the least bit clear about *what the word 'enterprise' means* in RICO" imply that "enterprise" has more than one possible sense in the context of RICO.[29]

If "enterprise" is polysemous in the context of RICO, then Solan must first single out the salient sense of "enterprise" and give reasons why a criminal network is a

---

[28] See section 1.2.3.

[29] See Solan (1993, 107, my emphasis).

borderline case of "enterprise" in *that* sense. Before the context is not sufficiently determined to resolve this ambiguity, gradual vagueness cannot even become an issue. The problem in *Turkette* is that the context does not determine a single sense of "enterprise" in which a criminal network could be a borderline case—whether the borderline case is due to gradual or multi-dimensional vagueness. The problem is, hence, not one about the unclear application of an unambiguous but vague expression, but about what meaning or sense an ambiguous expression has in a particular context. The indeterminacy in *Turkette* is, thus, due to polysemy and not gradual (or even multi-dimensional) vagueness.[30]

3.2.2 ENDICOTT ON EXTRAVAGANT VAGUENESS

According to Endicott, there are some expressions such as "neglect," "reasonable" or "substantial" that are extravagantly vague.[31] He is convinced that extravagant vagueness is "of central importance to the law-maker."[32] Not only is the use of extravagantly vague expressions a significant source of legal indeterminacy, but it actually fulfills a positive function.[33]

As we saw, they can be contrasted with transparently and ordinarily vague expressions. Transparently vague expressions are, for instance, "heap" or "tall." They are good candidates for philosophical discussions of gradual vagueness because they have a single salient dimension that is more or less instantiated. Examples for ordinarily vague expressions are "child" or "premises." They have multiple dimensions but do not seem to have the same inherent indeterminacy as extravagantly vague expressions.

Endicott's account of extravagant vagueness is heavily influenced by the philosophical debate on gradual vagueness. Not unlike Solan, Endicott introduces the phenomenon of vagueness by way of the classical examples and with reference to borderline cases and the Sorites paradox.[34] In Figure 5, for example, Endicott (2011a, 175) characterizes the vagueness of "child" by its having borderline cases. The figure clearly illustrates Endicott's classical notion of gradual vagueness. There are clear cases in which the vague expression "child" applies, there are clear ones in which it does not apply, and there are the borderline cases in between. After having introduced gradual vagueness in this way, he turns to the phenomenon of extravagant vagueness, characterizing it as follows:

---

[30] The most charitable reading of Solan's account is perhaps to say that he conflates (and confuses) semantic vagueness and polysemy. In another article, Solan (2004) seems to uniformly merge all cases of vagueness and polysemy under the term "ambiguity" in contrast to mere lexical and syntactic ambiguity.

[31] See section 1.3.2.

[32] See Endicott (2011b, 14).

[33] I will discuss the potential value and functions of indeterminacy in chapters 4 and 5 in full detail.

[34] See, for instance, Endicott (2001) or Endicott (2011a).

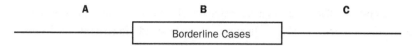

A: it is clearly true that a person is a child
B: it is neither clearly true nor clearly false that a person is a child
C: it is clearly false that a person is a child

FIGURE 5 **Endicott's Account of Vagueness**

> If an expression is extravagantly vague, it is possible for two competent users of the language, who understand the facts of the case, to take such different views that there is not even any overlap between the cases that each disputant would identify as borderline. ... Extravagant vagueness offers the possibility for deep controversy over the application of the law. (Endicott, 2011a, 176)

Extravagant vagueness seems to be an intense form of vagueness. Competent and informed language users not only disagree about the application of a vague term in a borderline case but also whether it is borderline in the first place. This indicates that Endicott understands extravagant vagueness as some form of higher-order vagueness. Endicott seems to think that extravagant vagueness is a special form of gradual vagueness that is prone to lead to deep disagreement.

Discussing the value of the extravagantly vague term "neglect," Endicott characterizes the indeterminacy of the *Children and Young Persons Act*, in which the term occurs, as gradual vagueness:

> "[Y]ou can see clearly that leaving a newborn baby alone all day would count as neglect .... Leaving a 15-year old at home alone for a few hours ... is not neglect. But there will be cases in between, for which the text of the statute gives no determinate guidance. (Endicott, 2011b, 16–17)

This is a problem for Endicott because gradual vagueness cannot have the effects that he attributes to extravagant vagueness. I think that Endicott is right when he claims that extravagantly vague expressions facilitate deep controversy. Competent and informed language users will disagree over the precise range of borderline cases. As a matter of fact, even transparently and ordinarily vague expressions usually have—as Endicott (2011a, 176) notes— no paradigm borderline cases. I disagree with Endicott, however, that this has anything to do with gradual vagueness. Both the actual indeterminacy generated by extravagantly vague expressions and their value for the law cannot be explained by their gradual vagueness, let alone their intensional gradual vagueness.[35]

---

[35] See definition (D11) in section 1.3.

Endicott oscillates between an extensional and intensional understanding of vagueness. Endicott (2000, 9) purports to understand "indeterminacy" such that "the law is indeterminate when a question of law, or of how the law applies to facts, has no single right answer." This characterization of "indeterminacy" is ambiguous between an extensional and intensional reading. It can mean that the law is (actually) indeterminate because there are particular hard cases in which judges struggle with and argue about their application. But it can also mean that the law is—and must be—(potentially) indeterminate because we can always come up with a new case in which the law does not determine a single outcome.[36] Gradual vagueness poses a problem with respect to potential indeterminacy. It threatens the *rule of law* theoretically. But it is extremely doubtful that gradual vagueness plays a significant role with respect to actual indeterminacy. Endicott confounds these two readings time and again when discussing the role of vagueness in the law.

His arguments against the epistemic theory of vagueness and legal interpretivism unequivocally show that Endicott is concerned with the problems of potential indeterminacy due to gradual vagueness. Endicott (2000, 57–75) discusses at length the consequences of the philosophical problem of vagueness—mainly the Sorites paradox—for legal theory and the concept of law. He argues that vagueness, despite appearances, need not be a threat to the *rule of law*. However, the philosophical problem of vagueness is a theoretical problem due to intensional vagueness. It is possible borderline cases that generate the Sorites paradox and threaten the principle of bivalence. Actual linguistic indeterminacy is mostly irrelevant to such considerations.

His concern for the Sorites and the *rule of law* explains why Endicott focuses on gradual vagueness, ignoring other forms of indeterminacy. His argumentative line of attack prompts him to do so. However, this leads to a misrepresentation of many of his examples from the law since his one-sided focus on gradual vagueness lets him turn a blind eye to other forms of indeterminacy and contextual factors in legal interpretation.

One could argue, as did Scott Soames (2011, 38–42) and Andrei Marmor (2014, 88–90), that the extravagantly vague expressions "neglect" and "substantial" are indeterminate not only due to gradual but also—and primarily—due to multi-dimensional vagueness as defined in section 1.3.2:

(D14)   An expression *e* is MULTI-DIMENSIONALLY VAGUE iff *e* allows for borderline cases due to incommensurability between *e*'s dimensions.

Both ordinarily and extravagantly vague expressions have multiple dimensions. If one of them is clearly instantiated while another is clearly not instantiated, the expression as a whole might neither clearly apply nor clearly not apply. There are

---

[36] See Fine (2015) for the related distinction between local and global vagueness.

borderline cases of intelligent people because they score extremely high on some dimension of intelligence and extremely low on some other.[37]

More importantly, the dimensions of a multi-dimensional term are typically not commensurable. A person can be borderline intelligent because the dimensions of intelligence on which she scores differently cannot uncontroversially be compared. For instance, we can imagine an autist who is borderline intelligent precisely because she is slow on the uptake in social interactions but highly capable of solving logical problems.

In contrast, the term "heap" has one salient dimension. Whether an arrangement of grains is a heap or not depends on its number of grains. Other dimensions of "heap"—such as the distance between grains—are significantly less salient. This accounts for the one-dimensionality of the transparently vague expression "heap."[38]

Just as with the term "intelligent," the extravagantly vague term "neglect" does not have a single salient dimension that could be the basis for a Sorites series. There are various dimensions on which an application of "neglect" depends. Often, the context provides some basis for a standard that can determine the salient dimensions. But even without any contextual background information, we can say that leaving a child unattended for six hours is more likely to be neglect than leaving it for two, and leaving a three-year-old child for the same amount of time is more likely to be neglect than leaving a five-year-old one.

How do we compare the child's age and the amount of time unattended to determine whether on the whole the parents' behavior constitutes neglect? Even if the dimensions were commensurable, there would be (possible) borderline cases in which one dimension is fully instantiated while another one is not instantiated at all. On the whole, the behavior is then neither clearly neglect nor clearly not neglect. Thus, the expression "neglect" is multi-dimensionally vague.[39]

But does this show that "neglect" in the context of the British *Children and Young Persons Act* is indeterminate due to multi-dimensional vagueness, as Soames and Marmor claim? Not necessarily since the expression is also both polysemous and general. The extension of "neglect" covers a broad range of very different kinds of behaviors. The statute explicates "neglect" as a behavior "likely to cause injury to [the child's] health if [one] has failed to provide adequate food, clothing, medical aid or lodging for him."[40]

---

[37] See also our discussion of this example in section 1.3.2.

[38] Recall, however, that no expression is completely one-dimensional. See section 1.3.2.

[39] See also Soames (2011, 38–42) and Marmor (2014, 88–90)

[40] See *Children and Young Persons Act* 1933 c. 12 (Regnal. 23 and 24 Geo 5), Part I s.1 (2).

There is an indefinite number of ways in which a parent can do this.[41] Consider, for example, the case of neglect when a child suffocates while in bed with an alcoholized parent.[42] But where does this indefiniteness come from?

H. L. A. Hart ascertains that

> Most difficulty in applying legal rules to concrete cases arises where (a) there is no difficulty in citing clear or standard cases to which the rule indisputably applies, but (b) in a given case a difficulty is precipitated because some feature present or absent in the standard case is absent or present in this case. (Hart, 1955, 258)

While this characterization of hard cases looks like one of multi-dimensional vagueness at first glance, it turns out not to be. There is no question of how similar this case is to the standard case—not even across dimensions. The question is rather whether a certain feature is intrinsic to the standard case or not. Recall that multi-dimensionality can lead to indeterminacy when it is either unclear (1) how the dimensions of the expression are to be weighed against each other in cases of conflict or doubt or (2) which dimension or which combination of them must be instantiated for its correct application. Only (1) concerns the existence of borderline cases. Only (1) is an instance of multi-dimensional vagueness. On the other hand, (2) is an instance of (multi-dimensional) polysemy. It concerns the question of which sense of "neglect" is adequate in the context of application or which conception of neglect is appropriate in this case.[43]

The indefiniteness of "neglect" cannot, however, be accounted for solely by its generality, multi-dimensionality, vagueness, or even polysemy. What makes most (legal) utterances with extravagantly vague expressions indeterminate is their, so to speak, extravagantly high context sensitivity. What is said by utterances containing expressions such as "neglect" or "substantial" can only be understood in relation to a contextually given standard.

As I argue in this section, expressions of this sort *generally* carry a special form of implicature. Implicatures can only reliably be made, however, if the context is sufficiently rich for certain pragmatic functions to operate. Otherwise, and this is typically the case for legal utterances, these expressions lead to indeterminacy.

The deep controversy and indefiniteness in the application of "neglect" is due to its standard-relativity as defined in (D20) in section 1.6. The expression "neglect" is standard-relative because some behavior is neglect only relative to a contextually

---

[41] This can also lead to conversational vagueness. See section 3.3.

[42] See *Children and Young Persons Act* 1933 c. 12 (Regnal. 23 and 24 Geo 5), s.1 (2)(b).

[43] See definition (D15) of multi-dimensional polysemy in section 1.3.2.

given standard. Most extravagantly vague expressions are standard-relative in a strong sense. As we saw in section 1.6, even an utterance such as

(E8) "Peter is tall."

is standard-relative. It implicites that Peter is tall *relative to a contextually valued standard*. In contrast, utterances containing the expression "neglect" require not only a comparison class with which to compare some behavior to determine whether it should count as neglect or not. A truly evaluative judgment is needed to determine the salience and weighing of the expression's dimensions. For this reason, the use of an expression such as "neglect" does not only tell us something about the state of affairs referred to but also about the social or moral environment of the speaker. The utterance

(E47) "Leaving a four-year-old child for two hours alone is neglect."

makes reference to a value system.[44]

As with "economy," "prudence," or "coward," the term "neglect" expresses a *thick concept* with both descriptive and prescriptive content.[45] In contrast, "tall" expresses a *thin concept* with only (or mostly) descriptive content. A contextually valued standard is necessary to understand what "tall" means in the context of utterance, but this standard usually does not require an evaluative judgment. It can be given by context. As such, it is an epistemic question about the context.

The expression "substantial" is different in this regard since something is substantial only relative to a contextually *valued* standard. It is not just an epistemic question. One could say that "substantial" expresses a thin concept with only (or mostly) prescriptive content.[46] Both, "neglect" and "substantial" are standard-relative in a strong way. They are *evaluative* terms. Most indeterminate legal terms in German law and most extravagantly vague terms are evaluative in this sense.[47]

---

[44] In most situations, the speaker expresses her own attitude by uttering it. However, this is not necessarily the case since one can merely state social or legal facts. See also section 2.1 on legal language, in particular the discussion of normativity in the law.

[45] See our discussion of thick concept terms in section 1.6.

[46] Supposedly, John E. Finn has called such expressions "mere verbal equations."

[47] See Herberger (1976) for the claim that the normativity of many legal terms (in particular, elements of a crime) stems from an emotive component in their meaning. Think of indeterminate legal terms such as "*Würde des Menschen*" ("human dignity") in art. 1 GG, "*Zumutbarkeit*" ("reasonableness") in § 10 SGB II, "*billige Entschädigung*" ("just compensation") in § 253 BGB, "*billiges Ermessen*" ("equitable discretion") in § 315 BGB, "*berechtigtes Interesse*" ("legitimate interest") in § 573 BGB, "*Härtefall*" ("case of hardship") in § 574 BGB, "*Treu und Glauben*" ("good faith") in § 157, and § 242 BGB, or "*gegen die guten Sitten*" ("contra bonos mores") in § 138 and § 826 BGB.

Interestingly, both Endicott (2005) and Marmor (2014) note that "neglect" is an evaluative expression, but neither of them seems to regard it as relevant.[48] However, evaluativity can hardly be overestimated when dealing with extravagantly vague expressions such as "neglect" or "substantial."

While "neglect" still has a fairly clear lexical meaning, "substantial" is so general that it can be considered as a mere placeholder for a contextually given or valued standard.[49] Endicott (2011a, 179–181) discusses a case in which this expression became hotly debated. In *Regina v. Monopolies and Mergers Commission*, a bus company merged with another, giving it an effective monopoly within a particular region of the United Kingdom.[50] The Monopolies and Mergers Commission found that this region was a sufficiently "substantial" part of the United Kingdom to cause concern that the newly created company may operate against the public interest.

But what does the expression "substantial" mean within the context of the case? It seems that "substantial" on its own does not mean anything really. This is partly due to its high generality, which—in many contexts—will require some form of completion impliciture as in this (previously mentioned) utterance:

(E29) "I am ready."

We do not know what is said by (E29) as long as we do not know what the speaker is ready *for*. The missing information is implicited by the context, which completes the content of the utterance.[51] A problem arises when the context is not sufficiently rich to figure out the implicited content. The speaker in (E29) might be ready for a party, for leaving the house, or for saying goodbye. Often, it does not matter what exactly it is that is implicited. Sometimes it does, however; and in *Regina v. Monopolies and Mergers Commission*, it did. The phenomenon of *evaluativity* explains why the court found that it needed to first identify a "criterion for a judgment" to determine what "substantial" even meant.

Evaluativity is an extremely important aspect when it comes to legal interpretation and must not be confused with semantic vagueness. It is a direct source of indeterminacy and controversy in the interpretation of extravagantly vague terms such as "substantial" and also in other more clearly evaluative, more general, and openly contested terms such as "social justice" or "democracy."

---

[48] Soames (2011) and Asgeirsson (2015) focus in their critique of Endicott solely on generality and (incommensurate) multi-dimensionality, and even Marmor (2011b, 147) takes semantic vagueness to be the source of "most cases of statutory interpretation that courts have to deal with."

[49] Its function would then be similar to indexicals. This seems to be the main reason why such terms are called "weasel words" by Gotti (2005) and many others.

[50] *Regina v. Monopolies and Mergers Commission*, 1 W.L.R. 23 (1993).

[51] See our discussion of Bach (1994) in section 1.5.4.

Walter B. Gallie's notion of *essentially contested concepts* is thus not only based on multi-dimensional polysemy but also on evaluativity.[52] This link between evaluativity and openness to controversy cogently explains why Endicott thinks of extravagantly vague expressions as potentially deeply contested.[53]

Concluding, it is very difficult to determine what the content of an utterance is in which an extravagantly vague term occurs. The polysemy, generality, and evaluativity contribute to the high context sensitivity of these terms. And, as we noted in the previous section, before we can even argue about whether some case is borderline or not, we need to determine the context. As a consequence of the high context sensitivity of extravagantly vague expressions, it is exceedingly difficult to determine whether some behavior is a borderline case of "neglect" or some region a borderline case of "substantial part of the United Kingdom." In *Regina v. Monopolies and Mergers Commission*, the question that the court needed to answer was what criterion or standard for "substantial" should be used. The question was one of context.

So far, I argued that extravagantly vague expressions matter in the law but not due to their vagueness. Do transparently and ordinarily vague terms matter? Transparently vague terms such as "heap" or "rich" are rarely found in the law. The reason is, as Marmor (2014, 87) stresses, that they can easily be replaced by numbers: "If Congress wanted to impose higher taxes on rich people, for example, it would define the regulation much more precisely, using income figures in dollar terms." Transparently vague terms have virtually *by definition* a salient dimension for which the legislature can set precise thresholds. This is not the case for ordinarily vague terms though. Marmor argues that they, too, tend to be irrelevant in the law. My arguments in the previous section against Solan's analysis of *Turkette* point in the same direction. However, the fundamental problem about cases of ordinary vagueness lies in the difficulty to detect them. At first glance, *Turkette* looks like a case of vagueness, but we then saw that it is not. In the next section, however, we will finally meet a genuine case of semantic vagueness.

3.2.3 SANDWICHES AND BURRITOS

I argued that Solan and Endicott confused gradual vagueness with other forms of indeterminacy and, as a consequence, picked unhappy examples for their discussions of vagueness in the law. However, that does not mean that semantic vagueness has no effect in legal practice at all.

---

[52] See Gallie (1956) and the discussion of essentially contested concepts in section 1.3.2. See also Waldron (1994, 526–540) for a discussion of contestability in the law.

[53] This is also true for "fair, just, and reasonable," "torture," "serious distress," and most other examples that Endicott gives; as well as for most thick concept terms such as "economy," "prudence," "coward," or "exploited."

It is notoriously hard to find borderline cases both in everyday life and in law. There is disagreement between competent language users about almost any borderline case. Vagueness is inherently higher-order. Typically, it is unclear whether some case is unclear. A (surmountable) problem is that many hard cases turn out to be merely relative borderline cases. Often, we do not know enough to say whether some unclarity is due to the vagueness of a term or due to ignorance about some aspect of context.

However, there is a more fundamental problem with regard to our linguistic practice in general. Most linguistic expressions are indeterminate in a variety of ways at the same time. They are polysemous, standard-relative, and multi-dimensionally and gradually vague. What is communicated by most utterances is not restricted to what is said, let alone to semantics.

The classical expressions such as "heap" are only good examples to introduce the phenomenon of gradual vagueness because we simplify and abstract away from other forms of indeterminacy. Also "heap" is polysemous, standard-relative, and multi-dimensional. We fix the context, set a standard, and focus on the salient dimension—which is legitimate in the philosophical debate on gradual vagueness. But not in a debate about *vagueness in law*.

Extravagantly vague expressions are especially unhappy examples in this regard since they are too complex to be good—that is, uncontroversial—candidates for gradual vagueness being the source of indeterminacy. We cannot sensibly abstract away the standard-relativity or multi-dimensionality of "substantial."

Unfortunately, transparently vague expressions are rarely used in the law at all. Because of this, we will have a hard time to find any case of gradual vagueness in the legal realm—apart from fictitious cases such as the vehicle in the park statute. But even the vehicle in the park statute is indeterminate due to the multi-dimensionality and polysemy of "vehicle," at least as much as it is due to its tolerance.[54] In fact, the example of the vehicle in the park statute is positively misleading because it presupposes that the context is fixed in a way in which it is rarely ever fixed in actual legal cases.

For that reason, I will focus on a case of multi-dimensional vagueness. In particular, I will now discuss a case in which the ordinary vague expression "sandwich" took center stage and, arguably, was indeterminate not due to any other form of indeterminacy.

In *White City Shopping Center v. PR Restaurants*, the Panera Bread restaurant leased space in the White City Shopping Center under a contract that forbade the shopping center to lease space to any restaurants whose annual sales of

---

[54] This is even more clearly the case in *McBoyle* in which the question had to be answered whether an airplane was a vehicle and that presumably inspired Hart's example of the vehicle in the park statute.

sandwiches might be expected to exceed 10% of the restaurant's income.[55] Later, the shopping center leased space to a Qdoba restaurant, which sold tacos, burritos, and quesadillas. This led Panera to file a declaratory-judgment action seeking to enjoin the new lease.

In the ensuing lawsuit, Panera argued that a burrito was a sandwich while White City argued that it was not. The court had to interpret the lease. The principle of contract interpretation that the court applied was that if "the words of the contract are plain and free from ambiguity, they must be construed in accordance with their ordinary and usual sense." It found that the term "sandwich" was unambiguous. Since the contract did not provide a definition for "sandwich," the court had to look for its ordinary meaning. Consequently, it turned to *The New Webster Third International Dictionary*, which says that a "sandwich" means "two thin pieces of bread, usually buttered, with a thin layer (as of meat, cheese, or a savory mixture) spread between them."

The court argued that burritos had no second slice, and it even doubted that the flour tortilla was bread. It came to the conclusion that burritos were not ordinarily thought of as "bread," and could thus not be regarded as sandwiches. Furthermore, the court could find no evidence that either Panera or White City intended tacos, burritos, or quesadillas to be considered as sandwiches. Thus, the court held that burritos are not sandwiches. Panera lost the case, and Qdobe could continue selling tacos, burritos, and quesadillas.

What form of indeterminacy caused the unclarity and controversy in *White City*? Again, the problem is that the expression "sandwich" is not only multi-dimensionally and gradually vague but also polysemous and general. One could argue that there is a broad sense of "sandwich" that includes burritos and a narrow sense that does not. Then, the court would have been mistaken in its claim that "sandwich" is unambiguous.

However, there is no evidence that the polysemy of "sandwich" played any role in *White City*. The issue was not which sense of "sandwich" was the salient one but which dimensions of "sandwich" were most relevant. The question was to what degree burritos instantiate the relevant dimensions of "sandwich." There are some dimensions which burritos fully share with sandwiches, such as containing a layer of meat or cheese, but others they share only to an imperfect degree, such as consisting of two pieces of bread. The result is that burritos are neither clearly

---

[55] *White City Shopping Center, LP. v. PR Restaurants, LLC*, 21 Mass. L.Rptr. 565 (2006). The original clause of the contract reads as follows: "Landlord agrees not to lease ... for [use as] a bakery or restaurant reasonably expected to have annual sales of sandwiches greater than ten percent of its total sales." See also a discussion of this case by Scalia and Garner (2012, 54–55), which ignited a lively online debate between Scalia and Posner about whether the decision in *White City* was justified.

nor clearly not sandwiches. This is evidenced by the United States Department of Agriculture, whose definition of "burrito" is the following:

> A Mexican style *sandwich-like* product consisting of a flour tortilla, various fillings, and at least 15 percent meat or 10 percent cooked poultry meat. The flour tortilla is rolled and may or may not have tucked ends. (USDA, 2005, 24, my emphasis)

Evidently, a product that is sandwich-like is not a clear case of a sandwich. Moreover, not even critics of the court's definition of "sandwich" claimed that burritos clearly are sandwiches (in a narrow or broad sense). Richard A. Posner (2012) criticizes the court's definition:

> A sandwich does not have to have two slices of bread; it can have more than two (a club sandwich) and it can have just one (an open-faced sandwich). ... The slices do not have to be slices of bread: a hamburger is regarded as a sandwich, and also a hot dog—and *some people* regard tacos and burritos as sandwiches, and a quesadilla is even more *sandwich-like*." (my emphasis)

Posner seems to have a broader understanding of "sandwich" than the court does. However, he does not say that burritos are sandwiches in some broad sense. He disagrees with the court that some dimensions of "sandwich" are as the court takes them to be.

At the bottom line, Posner emphasizes that tacos, burritos, and quesadillas are more sandwich-like than the court acknowledges. If some people regard them as sandwiches, and there is common agreement that they are sandwich-like, burritos cannot clearly be not-sandwiches either. Thus, one can reasonably claim that there is a unique salient sense of "sandwich" in the context of *White City* in which burritos neither clearly fall nor clearly do not fall in its extension.

In the end, however, whether a burrito is a borderline case of "sandwich" remains debatable to some degree. If the question of whether some case is borderline arises, there are usually (if not necessarily) other forms of indeterminacy present as well—in particular, it will typically be unclear what the relevant aspects of context are.[56] This will, however, make virtually any borderline case debatable. One can always come up with some technical sense of "sandwich" in which burritos clearly are or clearly are not sandwiches. When is the context ever sufficiently rich to enable one to say with certainty that a particular sense is the only possible one?

Nevertheless, if any real legal case is a case of semantic vagueness, then *White City* is. The lesson here is that vagueness will hardly ever play a significant role in

---

[56] See 1.6 for a discussion of context indeterminacy.

the law because of the problem of context determination and the context sensitivity of vague expressions.

3.3 Conversational Vagueness in the Law

We saw in section 3.2 that semantic vagueness is far less relevant to the law than the literature suggests. This result does not entail, however, that linguistic indeterminacy in general is irrelevant to the law. On the contrary, many examples cited as borderline cases turn out to be instances of other forms of indeterminacy.

In the beginning of chapter 1, I discussed the Jacksonville Ordinance Code. Its provisions were fantastically indeterminate at the time. It punished people for being "vagabonds" or "disorderly persons." I will now substantiate the claim that it is not semantic vagueness or ambiguity but primarily conversational vagueness that is the source of the ordinance's indeterminacy.

As we saw in section 1.4, generality is not itself a form of indeterminacy. It is a semantic property of expressions that can cause conversational vagueness. We defined conversational vagueness in the following way:

(D18) An utterance u is CONVERSATIONALLY VAGUE in context c iff u only borderline satisfies some Gricean maxim m in c.

Recall the telephone conversation in (E11) in which a general expression is used to make Kimberly's utterance conversationally vague:

Peter: Where are you?
Kimberly: East Coast.

Kimberly's answer is neither clearly relevant nor clearly not relevant to the conversation if Peter wants to know her location for the purpose of meeting her in person (and this is known to all participants in the conversation). Kimberly's answer is then not sufficiently informative to further that purpose. It is conversationally vague due to the generality of the expression "East Coast."

Does something similar happen when we want to know what kind of behavior exactly counts as "loitering" in the Jacksonville Ordinance Code? A relevant difference is that Kimberly's answer is a representative speech act while the Jacksonville Ordinance Code is an enacted statute that as a whole has directive illocutionary force. However, directive speech acts can exhibit conversational vagueness also. If Peter orders a steak by uttering "I will have the steak," Peter's order does not specify whether he wants it raw, medium, or well-done. Accordingly, the waiter might not know what exactly Peter wishes to be served. Depending on the context, Peter's order might not be sufficiently informative for the waiter to comply. The Maxim of Quantity will only be borderline satisfied, and his utterance will thus be conversationally vague.

General expressions are abundant in the law. In particular, constitutional and statutory provisions must, arguably, be phrased in general and all-inclusive terms. However, it depends on the purpose of conversation and circumstances of utterance whether generality results in conversational vagueness. Is it a significant source of legal indeterminacy? Does the Jacksonville Ordinance Code's generality lead to its being conversationally vague?

It seems to be a universal requirement of the law that laws refer to classes generally and not to individuals specifically. Hart formulated the reason for this:

> In any large group general rules, standards, and principles must be the main instrument of social control, and not particular directions given to each individual separately. If it were not possible to communicate general standards of conduct, which multitudes of individuals could understand, without further direction, ... nothing that we now recognize as law could exist. Hence the law must predominantly, but by no means exclusively, refer to *classes* of persons, and to *classes* of acts, things, and circumstances; and its successful operation over vast areas of social life depends on a widely diffused capacity to recognize particular acts, things, and circumstances as instances of general classifications which the law makes. (Hart, 1961/1994, 124)

General terms are thus a tool to efficiently control behavior in society. But it is also a matter of equality to use general terms. It is morally desirable that every member of society be treated equally (in relevant aspects) by the law. In many legal systems, it is, for this reason, unconstitutional to enact laws that are made for specific individuals. Both matters of fact and legal consequences must be described abstractly and generally.[57]

Paradigmatically general legal terms such as "vagabond" in the Jacksonville Ordinance Code or "neglect" in the *Children and Young Persons Act* are not only general, but (potentially) indeterminate in multiple ways. In the last section, we saw that it is neither the generality nor the semantic vagueness of "neglect" that provides on its own wide applicability to accommodate all circumstances in which a certain behavior possibly constitutes neglect. The term clearly is general, but it is also polysemous and standard-relative. Polysemy and standard-relativity allow—unlike the term's generality—different and often diverging interpretations of many general terms in statutory and constitutional provisions. As we saw in section 1.4, general terms are conceivable that entirely lack any form of indeterminacy. But although generality does not allow a margin of discretion in the interpretation, it typically enhances the effects of polysemy and standard-relativity by widening the term's extension and multiplying potential senses and standards.

---

[57] See Köhler (2010, 12–16) for this requirement in German law. See Bhatia (2005) for a broader discussion.

The primary function of generality seems to have nothing to do with indeterminacy, however. There are some authors who think that the function of vague terms lies in their generality only. Most prominently, Hart claims that semantic vagueness is merely a secondary effect of generality: "Uncertainty at the borderline is the price to be paid for the use of general classifying terms in any form of communication concerning matters of fact."[58]

Most general terms are vague, but their generality is the reason why we use them in legal texts. Most laws could still fulfill their function if they were phrased in general, but completely determinate, terms. We would loose the flexibility to apply them in one way or other since the legislature would determine all cases in advance by enacting such laws. This would require frequent reenactments to avoid overinclusiveness and underinclusiveness due to unforeseeability of a complex and changing social environment. However, this might be a price worth paying if fair notice and non-arbitrariness were thus achieved.[59]

Generality, then, has at least two basic functions. First, general terms can be applied to many different areas of law without the need to specify details. That way, they can provide purpose and guidance even if no detailed information is available. Second, they increase the margin of discretion that comes from linguistic indeterminacy such as polysemy or standard-relativity.

Hart relates these functions with two social needs. According to him

> all systems . . . compromise between two social needs: the need for certain rules which can, over great areas of conduct, safely be applied by private individuals to themselves without fresh guidance or weighing up of social issues, and the need to leave open, for later settlement by an informed, official choice, issues which can only be properly appreciated and settled when they arise in a concrete case. (Hart, 1961/1994, 130)

The first need corresponds to the principle of legal certainty as part of the *rule of law*. The second need results from considerations of equity.

Hart says that "vagueness" or "open texture" furthers the second need by either (1) power delegation to agencies that can transform general rules into more specific regulations or (2) power delegation to courts that can decide unforeseeable cases. When the legislature requires certain general standards in some industry, such as charging only a *fair rate* or providing *safe systems* of work, the first technique allows agencies to specify what is to count as a "fair rate" or "safe system" for a given area of law. The companies in that industry do not themselves need to apply the standards and run "the risk of being found to have violated them ex post

---

[58] See Hart, (1961/1994, 128).

[59] See chapter 5 on strategic indeterminacy in the law, in particular section 5.1.3 for a discussion of unforeseeability and arbitrariness in the law.

facto."[60] The use of due care in cases of negligence is an example of the second technique, which requires individuals to conform to it before it

> has been officially defined, and they may learn from a court only *ex post facto* when they have violated it [and] what, in terms of specific actions and forbearances, is the standard required from them. (Hart, 1961/1994, 132)

I take it that the most defensible reading of Hart (1961/1994, 131–132) is to interpret him as saying that generality in combination with *some form of indeterminacy* can be used for both techniques.

Concerning (1), *power delegation to agencies,* agencies are granted explicit discretion to specify general rules. Agencies have to decide what counts as a "fair rate" or "safe system," but this is a decision about the context-specific meaning of such expressions. They can decide which narrower sense of a general expression is to be used, which dimensions of a multi-dimensional expression are to be part of its meaning, or which standard of a standard-relative expression is to be applied—none of which can be facilitated by semantic vagueness.

Concerning (2), *power delegation to courts*, courts can decide discretionally in unclear cases because, again, they can decide the sense to be used, the standard to be applied, and the dimensions to be part of the expression's meaning. Unforeseen (including borderline) cases are the problem, not the solution. In such cases, other forms of indeterminacy can actually help because they allow justified discretion, whereas semantic vagueness leaves one without reason.[61] As Hart (1961/1994, 133) says:

> Our aim of securing people against harm is indeterminate till we put it in conjunction with, or test it against, possibilities which only experience will bring before us; when it does, then we have to face a decision which will, when made, render our aim *pro tanto* determinate.

Indeterminacy on the level of theory and in the determination of context allows judges to justifiably render many initially indeterminate laws legally determinate ex post. Potential indeterminacy in linguistic content dissolves when transformed into legal content—for example, by means of exploiting the discretion given by non-linguistic indeterminacy. General and multi-dimensionally polysemous terms ease such ex post determination.

While general terms are ubiquitously used in the law because of these positive functions, they can also create problems. Many hard cases in the law also result from conversational vagueness. If a judge is confronted with a case, the usual

---

[60] See Hart (1961/1994, 131).
[61] I will provide a more comprehensive argument for this claim in chapter 5, in particular, in section 5.1.5.

first step is to find relevant and applicable laws that determine its legal outcome. Sometimes there are no clearly relevant or applicable laws. Because of the *prohibition of denial of justice*, the judge has to make a decision notwithstanding. If she does not want to fall back to (moral or legal) principles, she can cite laws only borderline relevant to the case at hand. Even cases of non liquet or gaps can thus be decided by a ratio decidendi, which is at least superficially based on positive law. The judge can turn to a general clause that has some bearing on the case, even though it does not clearly determine an outcome. Such a conversationally vague law is not sufficiently relevant to determinately inform about the legal obligations in the case at hand, but it is something the judge can refer to in vindication of a decision. In the courtroom, this lack of information might be desirable for some parties; but in legal interpretation, it seems to rarely fulfill a function. It just happens that in some cases there are no clearly relevant or applicable laws to determine the outcome, and the conversationally vague law is better than none to justify *some* decision.

Because many gaps in the law result in the interpretation of conversationally vague laws by courts and agencies, the gaps are closed in an intransparent way. The decisions are cloaked under the guise of mere interpretation of already existing law, while in fact there is only a general phrase hardly relevant to the case at hand. When the US Supreme Court or the German Federal Constitutional Court interpret the Constitution or the Basic Law, respectively, they frequently make political decisions because its generality does not legally determine any particular outcome for the case at hand. As Roei Amit (2006, 278) puts it with respect to the prohibition of torture by the Israeli Basic Law and international law, "[t]hese general sources say nothing by themselves." Only in particular cases can it be determined whether a certain form of behavior constitutes torture.

Because laws are only conversationally vague with respect to particular cases, conversational vagueness is an issue for those who use, apply, or enforce the law. It is much less an issue for those who make it. Only in some cases will a law (even a constitutional article) be so general that it is borderline relevant for its purpose in all, or most, of its applications. One such case is, arguably, *Papachristou*. The Jacksonville Vagrancy Ordinance is, as we noted, fantastically indeterminate. It punished

> rogues and vagabonds, or dissolute persons who go about begging, common gamblers, persons who use juggling, or unlawful games or plays, common drunkards, common night walkers, ... persons wandering or strolling around from place to place without any lawful purpose or object, habitual loafers, disorderly persons.[62]

---

[62] Jacksonville Ordinance Code § 26–57, cited in Ribeiro (2004, 78).

The terms used to describe the elements of crime are undeniably vague. They are general and multi-dimensional. Most of them are polysemous, standard-relative, and thus sensitive to context. Some of them are evaluative in the strong sense. A judgment is needed to determine who ought to count as, for instance, a "disorderly person."

The main problem is, however, conversational vagueness. The ordinance fails to inform about what specifically it is that shall be punished. This is partly due to the terms being polysemous, standard-relative, and multi-dimensionally vague. But the ordinance is extremely general also as a whole—primarily due to the use of disjunction. Anybody could in principle be found to be within the extension of this disjunctive and general description of elements of crime.

But even on their own, terms such as "disorderly persons" are general enough to be clearly overinclusive. The legislature cannot possible mean to punish someone simply for being "disorderly." It is thus almost completely uninformative to say that "disorderly persons" shall be punished.

As a consequence, the ordinance effectively granted police and courts broad discretion to cleanse the city from vagrants and other unwanted persons. Presumably, the legislature deliberately used indeterminacy to achieve this end. But whether deliberate or not, conversational vagueness always has the effect to delegate power from the legislature to agencies or courts.[63] Such extremely conversationally vague laws as the Jacksonville Ordinance Code can thus be used to justify virtually *any* decision. And, for that reason, it was found unconstitutional in *Papachristou*.

3.4 Pragmatic Indeterminacy in the Law

In this section, I will investigate in more detail a cluster of forms of linguistic indeterminacy that has up to now received surprisingly little attention in the debate. Many indeterminate utterances exhibit a rather different form of indeterminacy from the ones discussed so far in this chapter. We called such utterances pragmatically indeterminate in section 1.5. They are not indeterminate due to underdetermination in semantic content or conversational vagueness but due to unclarity in pragmatically conveyed content.

When one utters

(E21) "Peter and Kimberly went to Paris."

one might implicate that they went together, but one might just as well be unclear about it. Such conversational implicatures are always cancelable. As such, there is always the possibility that the speaker did in fact not make an implicature. The speaker could either explicitly cancel it by adding, "But they went separately." Or,

---

[63] I will argue in depth for this claim in section 5.1.

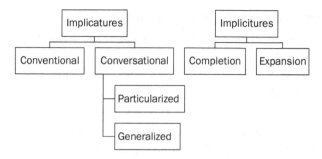

FIGURE 6 **Implicatures and Implicitures**

if the context is sufficiently determinate (if, e.g., everybody knows that Peter and Kimberly are not on speaking terms), it might even be clear that no implicature was made in the first place.

Sometimes, however, contextual information can point in opposing directions. Context sometimes allows both interpretations—that they went together and that they did not. Additionally, to this uncertainty about the existence of an implicature, there can be uncertainty about its content. In fact, it will usually not be entirely clear what exactly is conveyed by an implicature. When uttering (E21), the speaker might communicate that Peter and Kimberly traveled to and stayed in Paris together; but it is also possible that (E21) conveys (without making it explicit) that they traveled separately or that they traveled together, but split up once they arrived. Context can make conversational implicatures determinate, but it will usually be the case that some form of ambiguity or pragmatic vagueness lurks in the implicated content. What is implicated can thus be indeterminate either (1) if it is unclear whether an implicature was made or (2) if the content of the implicature itself is unclear. Analogously, what is implicited can be indeterminate either (1) if it is unclear whether an impliciture was made or (2) if the content of the impliciture is unclear.

Moreover, as depicted in Figure 6, there are three different types of implicatures as well as two different types of implicitures. An utterance can be implicature-indeterminate with respect to particularized conversational implicatures (PCIs), generalized conversational implicatures (GCIs), or conventional implicatures.[64] It can be impliciture-indeterminate with respect to expansion and completion implicitures. We will briefly discuss speech act ambiguity as a form of pragmatic indeterminacy as well. These forms of pragmatic indeterminacy are relevant to the law in varying degrees. We will discuss them one by one.

---

[64] See section 1.5.1 for a general discussion of implicature indeterminacy.

PARTICULARIZED CONVERSATIONAL IMPLICATURES

PCIs heavily depend on the context of the utterance. The definition of a PCI is

(D24) A speaker S CONVERSATIONALLY IMPLICATES that q by uttering u in context c iff

(1.) S observes the relevant conversational maxims in c,

(2.) the assumption that S meant that q is required to make sense of S's uttering u in c given the conversational maxims, and

(3.) S believes that S's audience can recognize condition (2) and can recognize that S knows that.

If S wants to conversationally implicate that q, S must know the conversational maxims and believe that her audience knows them, too. Moreover, S must believe that given the context of her utterance and the shared knowledge of the conversational maxims, uttering u conveys, ceteris paribus, that q is the case. Are these conditions satisfied in the law?

Condition (1) requires that the legislature (or other authors of legal utterances) be able to observe the conversational maxims. Conditions (2) and (3) require that agencies and courts (or other intended audiences) be able to recognize the context and conversational maxims to be such that something other than the utterance's literal content is conveyed, that is, they must be able to recognize the legislature's communicative intention.

There are two potentially problematic implications from these requirements for PCIs in the law. First, as we noted before, context must be sufficiently rich to enable the intended audience to recognize something other than the utterance's literal content to be what is meant by the legislature. Second, there must be conversational maxims that apply to the conversation in the first place.

At first glance, none of the three conditions are clearly satisfied in the law because both context and conversational maxims are of limited avail. The first problem is that judges are rarely in an epistemic position to know the legislature's communicative intention. This is a special case of the frame problem.[65] Recall that it is an open question whether the actual intention of the lawmaker matters or whether it is the illocutionary intention a competent, reasonable, and informed language user would be warranted in ascribing. This argument between the objective and subjective theory of legal interpretation is theoretically and practically undecided.[66]

---

[65] See section 1.6.

[66] See section 2.3.1 on the interpretive choices in legal interpretation.

Even if it were, in neither case is it entirely clear how to ascribe intentions to an institution, collective, or multitude of people—especially when the utterance was made in a very different context in the past. In many cases, it is certainly feasible and sometimes even straightforward to attribute an intention to a group of people.[67] Particularly in hard cases, however, it is anything but straightforward to determine the legislature's intention because to do so, knowledge about the context of utterance is required. But context will then rarely be rich enough to enable one to know what intention the relevant group of people had or what intention one would be warranted in ascribing.[68] Judges need to rely on secondary sources, which are all too often either inaccessible or unreliable. Moreover, it is not clear—not even theoretically—where a conversation begins and where it ends since the process of legislation is characterized by discontinuities and may reach deep into judicial interpretation. We do not know what legal provisions, other documents, debates in Congress, protocols, etc. form part of the context and how far back their history should be traced. It is not even clear what the parties of the conversation are. The actual drafters of many laws are not legislators themselves but collaborating administrative agencies, the respective ministries, special committees, lobbying groups, and so on.[69] The audience is a divided one, which consists of the general public (voters to be won over, potential criminals to be deterred, regular citizens to be guided), lawyers, judges, juries, and many more. As we saw in chapter 2, there is not one conversational context but at least two—a context of utterance and a context of application. How do we decide which one to give priority in cases of conflict?

The frame problem may be overstated for the law.[70] The context in the law might not be as rich as in ordinary conversation, but it is in fact (usually at least) rich enough to facilitate the use of implicatures. While there is usually no direct knowledge of the case at hand, there is documentation about it, witness accounts, legal materials on precedents, the possibility to comprehensively gather general and legal information, and so forth. Moreover, the required common ground is established by the language users' linguistic competence—in the law even more so than in ordinary conversation. Both speaker and audience know the same grammatical rules and lexical meanings of the expressions used. This is particularly true for lawyers trained in the use of the technical terms and interpretation principles of the law. Congress and courts are "conversant with [substantive]

---

[67] See Searle (2002) for a philosophical analysis of collective intentionality. See Sinclair (1997) for a defense of (the accessibility of) collective intentionality in the law.

[68] For supporters of the subjective theory, an additional problem is that sometimes, for instance, in the case of unwanted compromise, there does not exist any actual collective intention. See section 5.1.1.

[69] See Marmor (2008, 434–435).

[70] See also the *Argument from Pragmatics* in section 2.4.1 for a discussion of the possibility of pragmatically conveyed content in the law.

legal conventions."[71] These conventions form part of the "background ... against which Congress presumptively legislates."[72] The legislature can safely assume that judges know and apply the interpretation principles rooted in legal conventions and practice. These principles are the "conversational maxims" of the law, as Robyn Carston (2013, 16–23) argues.[73]

It can be objected to this claim, as Hrafn Asgeirsson (2012b, 195–198) does, that many legal provisions are addressed to ordinary citizens who lack legal competence. As a consequence, knowledge of legal principles cannot generally be assumed. What law communicates cannot be an implicature if the conversational maxims necessary to infer it are not common knowledge among a significant part of the audience.

Certainly, most citizens do not know the legal principles required to infer implicatures that might be communicated by a legal utterance. But even in criminal law cases—where the problem raised by Asgeirsson seems to be most pressing—the relevant legal content is usually mediated by courts, administrative agencies, lawyers, and the media to the general public. In fact, the situation seems to be the very reverse. People normally know the communicative or legal content of many criminal laws while being entirely ignorant about their literal content. They know it because lawyers and media inform them, and there is no reason to doubt that the legislature could not rely on the common ground shared by legal professionals.

Another objection is based on the fierce and consistent disagreement about the principles of legal interpretation.[74] If there are no uncontested principles of legal interpretation the legislature can assume its audience to know and apply, implicatures in the law are impossible. And even if there were theoretical agreement, they are not commonly adhered to in actual adjudication. For instance, the textualist Antonin Scalia frequently surprises with opinions that refer to the intentions of the lawmaker or the purpose of the law.[75] As Marmor (2011a, 96) and Francesca Poggi (2010, 34f.) claim, legislation, adjudication, and contracting are typically strategic forms of behavior. Legal conversations are not like ordinary conversations because the author of a legal utterance cannot rely on the good faith of its audience. But "if the parties effectively do not cooperate, if they do not assume that the statute is formulated according to the maxims, then

---

[71] See Manning (2003, 2467).

[72] See Manning (2003, 2468).

[73] Just as conversational maxims can explain both the existence of an implicature and the lack thereof by being either used as justification or flouted, the principles of legal interpretation can be analogously used to very opposite ends—a fact that legal realists such as Llewellyn (1962) demur.

[74] See also sections 2.3 and 2.4.3.

[75] See, for instance, Scalia's concurring opinion in *Green v. Bock Laundry Machine Co.*, 490 U.S. 504 (1989).

the legislator cannot reasonably rely on this cooperation to specify the meaning communicated."[76] In short, if legal communication is not a cooperative exchange of information, the Cooperative Principle does not apply to it. Hence, conversational maxims do not universally hold in the law and, consequently, implicatures are impossible (or impossibly difficult) to use and recognize.

This problem should not be overestimated, however. As we saw in section 2.4.1, ordinary conversation is at least as strategic as legislation. In fact, the legislature must be even more cooperative than participants in ordinary conversation to make law possible.[77] The limited extent of cooperation required for implicatures is clearly exhibited by the law.

In particular, some areas of the law require an increased level of cooperation. As Marmor (2008, 440) notes, in administrative law, implicatures are more likely used since the parties must act in closer coordination and, due to the proximity of the agents, the informational access to the context is more evenly shared. In general, the more information and background knowledge the audience shares with the author of the legal utterance, the more successful she can make an implicature.

Implicatures seem to frequently occur in contracts, too. Poggi (2010, 36–38) argues that they do so because contract interpretation includes the principle of *bona fides* ("good faith"). The principle justifies the assumption that the contracting parties demonstrate cooperative behavior and follow the conversational maxims. On the other hand, many business contracts, in particular, seem to defy the assumption of good faith. Many businesses operate highly strategically and with little concern for the interests of other stakeholders. Even though there exists the principle of bona fides in contract interpretation, it remains doubtful whether contracting really is more cooperative than other legal communication.

Interestingly, even if all arguments against the use of implicatures in the law are sound, they show at best that it is difficult to make and recognize them. This, however, is entirely compatible with a significant role of implicature *indeterminacy* in the law. There are numerous cases in which the issue is precisely about the existence or content of some implicature in the legal utterance.

The most straightforward cases of PCIs in the law are strategic ones in which different interpretations are anticipated. If the purpose of a law is unpopular with certain people but popular with others, it can be sensible to use implicature indeterminacy to address both groups with different messages.[78] For instance, the purpose of the *Alien Contract Labor Law* of 1885 was to stop the influx of cheap and unskilled labor from China, but Congress could not say this publicly. It would

---

[76] See Poggi (2010, 35).

[77] See my arguments in section 2.4.1.

[78] We will discuss this strategy at length in section 5.1.4 on double-talk.

have been politically inconvenient to be explicit about such a goal. Hence, the literal content of the law was such that it applied to "the importation and migration, of any alien or aliens, any foreigner or foreigners, ... under contract or agreement ... to perform labor or service of any kind;" whereas the political target was, undoubtedly, to restrict the importation of cheap and unskilled labor of Chinese immigrants. The arguments by the Justices in *Church of the Holy Trinity v. United States* indicate that there is indeterminacy with regard to the implicature that only cheap and unskilled labor be prohibited.[79] The law explicitly lists exemptions that demonstrate this occupational preference. However, this does not necessarily mean that the legal content includes this PCI.

Even more striking is the use of PCIs in areas of the law other than legislation. Consider the case of misleading in a court proceeding. If someone neither wants to lie nor say the truth but must say something, they can mislead by exploiting implicature indeterminacy.[80] Arguably, Bill Clinton used this strategy when he tried to avoid perjury in the Lewinsky trials by saying that "there's nothing going on between us," implicating that there is and never was a sexual relation between him and Monica Lewinsky.[81] Clinton's illocutionary intention was to communicate this implicated content. But, at the same time, he could later argue that what he *really* meant was merely that there was no sexual relation at the moment of utterance.[82]

Especially contracts appear to be frequently indeterminate with respect to PCIs. Peter M. Tiersma (1986, 209–211) discusses the case *Embry v. Hargadine*.[83] A written employment contract existed between Charles R. Embry and the dry goods company Hargadine. Shortly after it expired, Embry said at a meeting that he would seek work elsewhere unless his contract was renewed. Hargadine's president told Embry

(E48) "Go ahead, you're all right. Get your men out and don't let that worry you."

Embry thus remained with the company until he was fired a month later. Even though Hargadine's president denied having told Embry anything about a possible renewal of his contract, the court found that the words "don't let that worry you" constituted in effect an acceptance to Embry's offer to continue working for Hargadine. The indeterminacy about whether there was an implicature and its

---

[79] *Church of the Holy Trinity v. United States*, 143 U.S. 457 (1892).

[80] See Saul (2012, 118–126). See also Cotterill (2007).

[81] See also Tiersma (2004).

[82] According to Starr (2004, 128, note 1), he said at a later hearing about this implication, "It depends upon what the meaning of the word 'is' is. If ... 'is' means is and never has been, that is ... one thing. If it means there is none, that was a completely true statement."

[83] *Embry v. Hargadine, McKittrick Dry Goods Co.*, 127 Mo.App. 383 (1907).

possible content allowed Hargadine's president to mollify Embry by uttering (E48) without committing himself to anything. Or so he thought.

GENERALIZED CONVERSATIONAL IMPLICATURES

GCIs are even more likely to be relevant sources of indeterminacy in the law. Consider the following example:

(E49) "Peter is meeting a woman this evening."

(E49) normally implicates that the woman is not Peter's wife. Even though the implicature can be canceled just as a PCI, it is the default interpretation and does not need a lot of context to be made.

The best example of GCIs in the law is the use of statutory exceptions. Recall the *Alien Contract Labor Law* that restricted the immigration of cheap and unskilled labor. It included an explicit list of exemptions. The use of the term "unless" normally implicates that the list of exemptions is exclusive. However, the legislature can cancel the implicature by indicating that the listed exemptions are examples only and that there may be more. This is the interpretation reached by the Court in *Holy Trinity*.

Because courts can, as did the Court in *Holy Trinity*, easily ignore such implicatures, the argument has been made that there are no legal GCIs in the first place. Judges can interpret GCIs in divergent ways without predicament because there are interpretative principles that both justify literal and implicated content. But, as Marmor notes:

> The fact that judges tend to ignore these kinds of implicatures does not mean that the implicature is not there; judges tend to ignore them because they are skeptical, and perhaps rightly so, of a legislature's ability to determine in advance all possible justified exceptions to the general norm enacted. (Marmor, 2008, 442)

Other aspects of legal interpretation can supersede the linguistic content of the law. The principles of legal interpretation typically allow different outcomes based on the same linguistic data—giving judges some discretion.

In fact, however, many principles of legal interpretation capture precisely the conversational maxims that allow these implicatures to be made. The principle *expressio unius est exclusio alterius* ("the express mention of one thing excludes others") rules that items not on the list are assumed not to be covered by the law. This is the legal principle that captures the reasoning behind the implicature that was discussed, but rejected, in *Holy Trinity*. It is precisely the indeterminacy about the status and content of such GCIs that allows judges to use different legal principles to justify different interpretations.

Another interpretative principle eliciting an implicature is the principle *ejusdem generis* ("of the same kind"). A statutory provision granted the Illinois Department of Conservation the power to sell "gravel, sand, earth, or other material" from state-owned land.[84] The scope of the term "other material" became an interpretative issue in the case *Sierra Club v. Kenney*.[85] Literally, its extension includes virtually any substance. The Supreme Court of Illinois held, however, that the provision did not include timber because, it argued, the term "can only be interpreted to include materials of the same general type" as those listed.[86] Hence, the communicative content of the provision differs from its literal content due to the GCI elicited by the principle ejusdem generis.

GCIs might not only play a role when it comes to legal principles but could directly figure in the meaning of certain terms. Consider the expression of attitudes when using evaluative terms such as "neglect." Arguably, such thick concept terms are generally used to make GCIs, expressing evaluative judgments.[87] If that is correct, the evaluativity of "neglect," which we discussed in section 3.2.2, is at least partially based on the pragmatic indeterminacy of GCIs.

CONVENTIONAL IMPLICATURES

Conventional implicatures are part of a term's lexical meaning but not its truth-conditions. Because they are semantically encoded, they rely less (or maybe even not at all) on context. It may thus seem that the indeterminacy of conventional implicatures is more relevant in the law than of PCIs or GCIs. Surprisingly, the opposite is the case. Consider the following example:

(E50) "Peter is a politician, but he is quite honest."

(E50) conventionally implicates that the speaker believes that politicians are not generally honest or that it is surprising that a politician is honest. The term "but" conveys the semantically encoded implicature that there is some sort of contradiction or contrast.

Unlike PCIs and GCIs, the content of conventional implicatures is fairly specific and not cancelable. This makes them, however, less suited as a candidate for legal indeterminacy since their content is virtually context-independent. Conventional implicatures occur in the law as frequently as in natural language, but they do not generally become indeterminate.

---

[84] See Slocum (2016, 26).

[85] *Sierra Club v. Kenney*, 88 Ill. 2d 110 (1981).

[86] See *Sierra Club v. Kenney*, 88 Ill. 2d 110, 127 (1981).

[87] See Väyrynen (2013).

IMPLICITURES

Implicitures (including standard-relativity) are the most promising candidate for legal indeterminacy. In section 1.4, we came across what Endicott calls "pragmatic vagueness." Consider the 65 mph speed limit in California that allows a margin of discretion on part of the highway patrol. Evidently, a regulation that punishes everyone driving more than 65 mph is semantically precise. However, pragmatically it may be indeterminate whether someone driving, for example, 68 mph should be punished. This depends on the practices of the legal community such as the regulation's actual enforcement.

Pragmatic vagueness is, as we saw, a form of impliciture indeterminacy. In many conversational contexts an utterance of the form

(E51) "Do not drive faster than 65 mph!"

is used to pragmatically convey

(E52) "Do not drive faster than *approximately* 65 mph!"

(E52) explicates the content of an expansion impliciture made by (E51). The implicitures are—just as implicatures—based on conversational maxims. But even if actual enforcement is or would be such that driving as fast as, say, 68 mph is not actually prosecuted, the regulation (both its communicative and legal content) is pragmatically vague due to this impliciture.

Many alleged cases of ambiguity or vagueness are, as I argue, in fact cases of impliciture indeterminacy. We already came across the phenomenon of standard-relativity in section 3.2.2 on the evaluativity of many extravagantly vague terms. We found that standard-relativity—and not semantic vagueness—plays a significant role in many legal issues especially with respect to descriptively thin terms such as "reasonable" or "substantial." Apart from standard-relativity, which we identified as a form of completion impliciture in section 1.6, there are numerous instances of implicitures that give rise to legal indeterminacy.

Consider the very influential and intensively discussed case *Smith v. United States* in which the Supreme Court split on whether "using a firearm during and in relation to a crime of violence or drug trafficking crime" includes the use of trading a firearm for drugs.[88] The petitioner John Smith offered to trade his MAC-10, an automatic weapon, to an undercover officer for cocaine. As a consequence, he was charged with multiple firearm and drug trafficking offenses. In particular, the Court had to decide whether Smith "used" the weapon "during or in relation to" this crime and thus receive additional punishment. The relevant section of the statute in question says:

---

[88] *Smith v. United States*, 508 U.S. 223 (1993).

> Whoever, during and in relation to any crime of violence or drug trafficking … uses or carries a firearm, shall, in addition to the punishment provided for such crime of violence or drug trafficking crime, be sentenced to imprisonment for five years. (18 USC § 924(c))

Nowhere in 18 USC is "use" defined. This became a problem when courts had to deal with cases in which a firearm was not used in the traditional sense of brandishing or firing it. In essence, there are three less traditional senses that became relevant. There is the sense that (1) a firearm is "used" as an item of commerce, as in the guns-for-drugs exchange in *Smith*; the sense that (2) a firearm is "used" as passive protection for a narcotics stash; and the sense that (3) a firearm is "used" to embolden the defendant.[89] The courts have consistently interpreted the statute broadly enough to encompass all three of these non-traditional senses of "use."

In *Smith*, the majority of the Court acknowledged that there is a traditional sense of "use" that would render 18 USC § 924(c) inapplicable to the petitioner. Smith argued that he cannot be said to have "used" a firearm unless he used it as a weapon since that is how people would ordinarily understand the phrase "using a firearm." Justice Scalia argued:

> In the search for statutory meaning, we give nontechnical words and phrases their ordinary meaning. … To use an instrumentality ordinarily means to use it for its intended purpose. When someone asks "Do you use a cane?" he is not inquiring whether you have your grandfather's silver-handled walking-stick on display in the hall; he wants to know whether you walk with a cane. Similarly, to speak of "using a firearm" is to speak of using it for its distinctive purpose, i.e., as a weapon. To be sure, "one can use a firearm in a number of ways," … including as an article of exchange … but that is not the ordinary meaning of "using" the one or the other.[90]

Justice Sandra Day O'Connor, speaking for the majority of the Court, replied the following:

> That one example of "use" is the first to come to mind when the phrase "uses … a firearm" is uttered does not preclude us from recognizing that there are other "uses" that qualify as well. In this case, it is both reasonable and normal to say that petitioner "used" his MAC-10 in his drug trafficking offense by trading it for cocaine.[91]

---

[89] See Clare (1994, 817).
[90] See *Smith*, 242.
[91] See *Smith*, 230.

She argued that it is within the everyday meaning of the phrase to describe Smith's treatment of his gun as "using" it, by citing dictionary entries of "use." Moreover, it sounds perfectly natural to say that Smith used his gun in an attempt to obtain drugs by offering to trade it for cocaine. The Court was convinced by these arguments and held that the exchange of a gun for drugs constituted the "use" of a firearm "during and in relation to" a drug trafficking crime for the purposes of the statute.

Scalia adopted the traditional or, as Solan would call it, prototypical sense, whereas the majority, in contrast, ascribed a broad, or definitional, meaning to "use." Legal scholars have analyzed the indeterminacy in 18 USC § 924(c) as either semantic vagueness or polysemy if they specified it at all.[92] Based on our findings in section 3.2.1, it is implausible to attribute vagueness any role in the issue.

Polysemy, on the other hand, certainly has at least theoretical attraction. The phrasing of the problem by the courts themselves suggests that there are several senses of the ambiguous expression "to use a firearm." In particular, it appears to be vertically polysemous because it can be used in a broad sense (to include the commercial exchange of the weapon) and a narrow sense (to be limited to brandishing and firing it), the former including the latter.

Note that in neither sense is Smith's action a borderline case of using a firearm. In the narrow sense, Smith clearly did not use the gun; while in the broad sense, he clearly did. The unclarity about the application stems from different evaluations of the context—triggering either the narrow or the broad interpretation.

There are some scholars who claim that there is no indeterminacy involved in *Smith* at all. Moshe Azar (2007, 135), for instance, argues that only one interpretation—the narrow one—is feasible since the other does not take into account the context. But this is precisely the issue in *Smith*—what is the relevant conversational context? Both the majority opinion and the dissent consider several aspects of context. They argue about the rationale of the law, its purpose, and the intention of the lawmaker. Both refer to the meaning of "use" in dictionaries and ordinary conversation. Both take into account other parts of the USC and bring them in relation to § 924(c).

It is true that dictionaries do not tell us what an expression means in a particular context. Even if one is "taking seriously the entire available context," unclarity about the communicative content of the statute remains. If the content were clear, reference to the law's rationale would not be necessary, which, according to Azar (2007, 136), entails that "one cannot but conclude that the meaning of 'uses ... a firearm' ... falls along the lines of Scalia's narrow meaning."

---

[92] See Solan (1998, 82) for the claim that it is vagueness and Clare (1994) for the claim that it is polysemy.

By the same token, one could argue just the other way round. Only the broad interpretation is feasible because it captures the lexical meaning of the expression while the other relies on speculation about context, intention, and purpose. This is evidenced by the very different subsequent rulings concerning § 924. In *Bailey v. United States*, the Court ruled that a defendant must "actively employ" a firearm in a manner that makes the firearm an operative factor in the crime to violate § 924, re-interpreting "to use a firearm" in its narrow sense and nullifying the implications of *Smith*.[93] Accordingly, in *Watson v. United States*, the Court decided that a transaction in the opposite direction does not violate § 924, holding that one does not "use" a gun by receiving it in exchange for drugs.[94]

I will not try to argue here for any particular resolution of *Smith*. I mention these interpretative problems to show that there is actual indeterminacy in *Smith*. It is rooted in the language of 18 USC § 924 and, as I argue now, is a form of impliciture indeterminacy.

According to Soames (2008a), the court confused the lexical meaning of the text and the statute's content—what is said by it. The "ordinary meaning," which both O'Connor and Scalia try to determine, is ambiguous between lexical meaning, which can be found in dictionaries, and literal content, which can only be determined relative to the context of utterance. Scalia's response to the majority's critique of his argument shows this:

> The Court asserts that the "significant flaw" ... is that "to say that the ordinary meaning of 'uses a firearm' includes using a firearm as a weapon" is quite different from saying the ordinary meaning "also excludes any other use." The two are indeed different—but it is precisely the latter that I assert to be true. The ordinary meaning of "uses a firearm" does not include using it as an article of commerce. I think it perfectly obvious, for example, that the objective falsity requirement for a perjury conviction would not be satisfied if a witness answered "no" to a prosecutor's inquiry whether he had ever "used a firearm," even though he had once sold his grandfather's Enfield rifle to a collector.[95]

Soames seems to be correct in his assessment that neither majority nor dissent recognized the difference between "ordinary meaning" as literal meaning found in the dictionary and "ordinary meaning" as literal content understood by ordinary people. Even though Soames's analysis highlights this important aspect, this is not the heart of the problem.

---

[93] *Bailey v. United States*, 516 U.S. 137 (1995).

[94] *Watson v. United States*, 128 S.Ct. 697 (2007).

[95] See *Smith*, 242, note 1.

The source of indeterminacy in *Smith* lies in the communicative content of § 924. The term "use" is general, and its lexical meaning is thin. As a consequence, an utterance such as

(E53) "Peter used the hammer."

is almost trivially true—if we do not add information about the context.[96] Peter could have used the hammer to do *anything*—as a door prop, to fight off a burglar, or to bang a nail into a wall. The context of utterance usually provides the appropriate impliciture.

We normally draw such inferences unconsciously. Scalia is right to emphasize that in most cases, there is an impliciture that Peter used the hammer *as a hammer*.[97] Hence, the lexical meaning of "to use a firearm" and even what is said by § 924 is reasonably clear. What is not clear is what is communicated by it since only the context can tell us how to pragmatically expand the expression "use a firearm."

But the determination of context is precisely the issue here. Depending on how the context is framed, the impliciture can be expected to be recognized or not. And only if it can, an impliciture is made.[98]

In *Smith*, the immediate co-text of the expression can determine one or the other reading. By framing the interpretative problem as one about determining the meaning of "to use a firearm during and in relation to a drug trafficking crime," the majority took into account the broader circumstances of drug trafficking, which allows the term "to use a firearm" to include also non-traditional uses of firearms such as commercial exchanges. The majority's choice of co-text resulted in the interpretation of "to use a firearm" as *to use a firearm for some purpose*.

In contrast, the dissent framed the interpretative problem as one about the expression "to use a firearm," omitting the phrase "during and in relation to a drug trafficking crime" from the interpretative analysis. Because no contextual information is added, the sense of "to use a firearm" that comes first to mind makes the expansion impliciture salient, resulting in Scalia's interpretation of "to use a firearm" as *to use a firearm as a firearm*.[99] However, since there is no single way to choose the co-text, § 924 is pragmatically indeterminate with respect to *Smith*.

One might think that this analysis of *Smith* corroborates Solan's distinction between prototypes and definitions.[100] According to Solan (2001, 258), Supreme Court cases such as *Smith* "can be seen as battles among justices over definitions

---

[96] See our discussion of impliciture indeterminacy in section 1.5.4.

[97] See section 1.5.4, where I called this an expansion impliciture, following Bach (1994).

[98] See condition (3) in definition (D24) in section 3.4.

[99] See Sinko (2015, 11).

[100] See section 3.2.1.

versus prototypes." The prototypical meaning of an expression captures the ways in which it is most frequently used and understood, whereas a dictionary definition gives a broad description of the various ways in which it can be used and understood.[101] The definitional meaning might be identified with the lexical meaning of the term and the prototypical meaning with the impliciture.[102] Thus, the indeterminacy effective in *Smith* could be the polysemy of "to use," contrary to my analysis.

The persuasiveness of my argumentation ultimately depends on where one draws the line between semantics and pragmatics. The main advantage of analyzing *Smith* as a case of impliciture indeterminacy is that one does not multiply senses above what is necessary.[103] The term "to use" would have myriads of lexically encoded senses. Apart from the theoretical worry of *Ockham's Razor*, a multitude of senses seems to require that we represent them cognitively in some way. But this is implausible—at least for the term "to use." It is much more likely that we represent one or maybe a few senses of "to use" and all other content is pragmatically derived based on contextually available information.

Matters are different with respect to instances of vertical polysemy such as in the case *Turkette*, which we discussed previously and in which two clear and lexically traceable senses of "enterprise" can be identified. However, there are also borderline cases between impliciture indeterminacy and vertical polysemy, such as in *Frigaliment v. B.N.S.* in which the issue was whether the term "chicken" as used in a sales contract refers only to young chickens that are suitable for broiling and frying or whether it refers generally to any chicken that meet the contract specifications on weight and quality.[104] One can reasonably argue both for the claim that the term "chicken" is general and carries an indeterminate impliciture in the context of the sales contract and for the claim that its meaning contains both senses but context does not disambiguate.[105]

As most cases, *Smith* is sufficiently complex to also allow an analysis in terms of indeterminacy on the level of legal theory. The question would be of how to generally determine the legal content of a statute. Should it be based on the literal meaning of the words used, as the majority argued; on what the ordinary person would take it to communicate, as Scalia argued; or on what the legislature actually

---

[101] See also Solan (1995, 1074–1076).

[102] The basic problem in Solan's analysis is that he does neither properly distinguish between lexical meaning, what is said, and what is communicated, nor, consequently, between semantic vagueness, polysemy, and pragmatic indeterminacy.

[103] See Asgeirsson (2012b, 180–184) for basically the same argument.

[104] *Frigaliment Imp. Co. v. BNS Intern. Sales Corp.*, 190 F. Supp. 116 (1960).

[105] The case *Shrum v. Zeltwanger*, 559 P.2d. 1384 (1977), also involving the sale of animals, is intriguingly similar to this one. The buyer understood the term "cows" to mean female bovines that had produced calves (the narrow sense), whereas the seller meant any female bovine including heifers (the broad sense).

intended, as is manifest in the unanimous opinion authored by O'Connor in *Bailey v. United States*? As I argued in section 2.4, this sort of theoretical disagreement makes it impossible to adhere unconditionally to the communication theory of law. While uncertainty about the line between semantics and pragmatics (both in theory and with respect to *Smith*) remains a minor issue, the additional problem of indeterminacy on the level of legal theory might be seen as overshadowing many linguistic considerations.[106]

SPEECH ACT AMBIGUITY

A special case of implicature indeterminacy is speech act ambiguity. We differentiated between various kinds of legal performatives in chapter 2. For instance, an utterance might be a promise or just a loose statement about one's plans, thus not quite amounting to a contract offer. As a consequence, sometimes it remains unclear at what point a contract is made. Whether it is intentional or not, this leads to contract lawyers spending a lot of time on the determination of what a contract is and when it begins.[107]

Recall, for instance, the indeterminate PCI made by Hargadine's president in *Embry v. Hargadine* (1907):

(E48) "Go ahead, you're all right. Get your men out and don't let that worry you."

Due to indeterminacy in implicated content, (E48) can be understood as an acceptance of Embry's offer to continue working for him or simply as a general reassurance without social or legal commitments. (E48) is thus speech-act-ambiguous between a (legally enforceable) contract acceptance and mere appeasement.

In section 2.2.2, we saw that verdicts have to fulfill different functions with conflicting aims. There is reason to believe that to mitigate this, their illocutionary force is "ambiguous" between representatives and declarations. Verdicts are subject to truth and falsity, and at the same time, they make something to be the case. Because of indeterminacy in other legal utterances, judges cannot satisfy both the *principle of legal certainty* and the *prohibition of denial of justice* when deciding hard cases. The conflict between these principles may require a certain amount of indeterminacy in the speech act itself for judges to be able to sincerely fulfill their duties.[108] This structural speech act ambiguity allows judges to justifiably and sincerely make difficult decisions even when they cannot (clearly) be based on the law.

---

[106] See Polich (1994) and Gilbert (1997).

[107] See section 2.2.3.

[108] See Lanius (2013).

3.5 Summary

In this chapter, I examined the role of linguistic indeterminacy in law. I established that some forms of linguistic indeterminacy are central to at least some legal problems despite the communication theory of law (CTL) not being unconditionally true. I investigated the role of lexical and syntactic ambiguity, polysemy, as well as gradual and multi-dimensional vagueness in the law. I related the legal functions of generality and conversational vagueness; and finally, I surveyed the different types of pragmatic indeterminacy.

The examination showed that semantic vagueness is less relevant to the law than the debate on vagueness suggests. Most cases considered to be clear examples of vagueness by the participants in the debate turn out to be indeterminate due to polysemy or standard-relativity at closer inspection.

There is a structural reason for this finding. Before an actual case can be said to be borderline or not, one has to determine what is said. This requires, however, to fix the context and rule out most other forms of indeterminacy. In most cases, there are other forms of indeterminacy present that can be resolved in different ways to avoid borderline applications. In many complex environments (such as legal cases), the frame problem creates indeterminacy in the context itself. This is aggravated by the fact that legal content can, as we saw in chapter 2, differ from linguistic content. If it does, semantic vagueness is (in most cases) rendered moot.

There are thus two basic reasons why the role of vagueness is overestimated by many participants in the debate. First, most examples given by them are not in fact instances of vagueness because they structurally neglect the role of context and other forms of indeterminacy. Second, they uncritically presuppose the correctness of CTL. Its incorrectness, however, casts doubt on the role of linguistic indeterminacy in law in general.

4

Functions of Indeterminacy

Law enactments, renderings of verdicts, and contracts formations are strategic forms of behavior. Individuals and institutions use such legal speech acts to accomplish particular goals. They have different beliefs and interests and varying degrees of power. Laws, verdicts, and contracts are there to mitigate these interests and expand or limit this power.

Legislators, judges, contract negotiators, but also business spokespeople, diplomats, and philosophers—they all use language strategically if their interests require it. They are concerned not only with the illocutionary functions of their speech acts but also with their (sometimes long-term) perlocutionary effects. If they deliberately control a speech act's perlocutionary effects by first weighing pros and cons and then deciding for the wording that achieves the best overall outcome, they use language strategically.

Arguably, most speech acts in casual conversation are not strategic. It is of relatively little importance how others react to one's views on the weather, for instance. But there are situations in which each term matters—politicians' speeches, arguments in philosophical papers, or verdicts of judges. In particular, legal speech acts have consequences that tend to matter for a large number of people. Exactly which consequences they have depends on, among many other factors, how they are framed. And although legal content is, as we saw in chapter 2, neither identical to nor determined by the linguistic content of legal speech acts generally, the language used directly impacts on how most legal cases are decided and people are guided by the law.

It has been argued that it is advantageous to both avoid using and strategically use linguistic indeterminacy. As we established in chapter 1, linguistic indeterminacy has the immediate (illocutionary) effect of unclarity. Unclarity, in turn, can have very different effects depending on the circumstances of the utterance. In this chapter, I will investigate such perlocutionary effects of indeterminate utterances—whether they are to be dreaded or praised. Does vagueness give law its "much needed flexibility?" Or does it erode the very core of the law by threatening fair notice, legal certainty, equality, and other principles of the *rule of law*?

Both questions will be fully answered in chapter 5. In this chapter, I will address the issue of the value of indeterminacy in more general terms. First, I will give a short introduction to signaling games in section 4.1. Second, I will show in section 4.2 how some forms of indeterminacy can be represented within this game theoretic framework by means of semantic spaces. Third, in section 4.3, I will analyze the conditions for the use of indeterminacy by discussing Barton L. Lipman's influential proof for the disutility of indeterminacy. After that, I will turn to positive accounts of the use of semantic vagueness, conversational vagueness, ambiguity, and pragmatic indeterminacy in section 4.4. Finally, in section 4.5, I will compare the different forms of indeterminacy with respect to their utility in strategic speech.

4.1 Signaling Games

Legislation has an illuminating analogy to marksmanship, as Michael S. Moore (2012) points out. When there is wind, an archer who aims directly at the target will almost certainly miss it. Just as the archer has to take into account the wind in her calculations of the course of the arrow to hit the target, the legislature has to take into account the reactions of authorities, citizens, and judges. Public opinion, political constellations, theories of legal interpretation, ideologies, etc. influence how a statutory bill will be received, what its legal consequences will be, and what it will politically and socially achieve. Just as the archer would miss the target if she ignored the wind, a contract may fail to be closed or result in breach or annulment if diverging interests, contract law, political stances and ideologies of potential judges, etc. are ignored.

The objectives of legislators, judges, and contract drafters can frequently not be achieved directly. Game theory (or, more precisely, the theory of signaling games) provides answers to questions of which strategies should be chosen (how laws, verdicts, or contracts should be phrased) such that the agents' (legislators, judges, or contract drafters') objectives are optimally realized given the environment. Originally, signaling games were introduced by David Lewis (1969) to explain meaning based on a non-normative conception of convention. Lewis's analysis has its roots in the later works of Ludwig Wittgenstein and were furthered in philosophy and linguistics by Lauri Carlson (1985), Robert C. Stalnaker (2006), and Brian Skyrms (2010) among others. In general, communicative actions can be investigated with the tools of signaling games with respect to their utility. Since we are interested in the utterances' overall outcome (i.e., their value), not only their legal content but also wider political and social (perlocutionary) effects are to be considered. While these effects generally do in turn depend on the utterances' legal effects, they can also be due to linguistic content independently from legal content. The tools of signaling games thus provide arguments for and against the use of (indeterminate) utterances in the law, despite the communication theory of law (CTL) not being unconditionally correct.[1]

Formally fleshed out and applied foremost in economic science by A. Michael Spence (1973), signaling games are usually defined in the following way:

(D25)   A SIGNALING GAME is a 2-agent-2-turn-game with incomplete information such that the better-informed agent S (the sender) observes state $\omega \in \Omega$ and sends message $m \in M$, while the less-informed agent R (the receiver) observes message m and chooses action $a \in A$.

In other words, based on information about the world, the speaker makes an utterance to which the hearer reacts. The outcome depends on the state of the world to which only the speaker has access to; it depends on the utterance itself, which might be costly to send; and it depends on the action that the hearer performs in response to the utterance. To put it precisely, the utility of both agents depends on state ω, message m, and action a.

It is usually assumed that there are less messages than states (i.e., $M < \Omega$).[2] State space Ω contains all possible states of the world, message space M contains all messages that S can possibly send, and action space A contains all actions that R can possibly perform. For reasons of conciseness, we will assume that Ω, M, and A are discrete and finite.[3] That is, there is a limited number of individual states of the world as well as finitely many messages and actions available to the agents.

Speech acts are individual moves within a signaling game such as sending message m by S. If an agent sends a message or chooses an action, she does so based on her expected outcome. Each agent has a utility function that represents her gain in relation to any $\omega \in \Omega$, $m \in M$, and $a \in A$. In the classical signaling game, S chooses message m given the state ω that S observes, while R chooses action a given message m that R receives from S. Both choose the strategy that maximizes their respective utility function. That is, any agent chooses the best strategy with respect to her preferences given the available information.

---

[1] See chapter 2 for a critical discussion of CTL.

[2] This assumption is warranted since individual objects can be described in potentially infinitely many ways, as Keil (2006) points out. A recent overview about game theory and the pragmatics of language can be found in de Jaegher and van Rooij (2013).

[3] This assumption is not entirely realistic, but all conclusions can be generalized to models with continuous and infinite Ω, M, and A.

An agent is *incompletely* informed if she does not know the outcomes and strategies available to other agents.[4] In a signaling game, R does not know which state the world is in but can be informed by a message from S, who does know.[5] The *informational content* of a message is traditionally conceived as a proposition, that is, a set of possible worlds or situations. However, in signaling games, it makes sense to conceive of informational content as the way in which the message affects probabilities. The *quantity of information* is the degree to which the message moves probabilities.[6]

To see the difference, consider a game in which probabilities are initially equal for two states. Message m_1 moves probabilities for state ω_1 to $9/10$ and for ω_2 to $1/10$, while message m_2 moves them to $1/10$ and $9/10$, respectively. By considerations of symmetry, both messages have the same quantity of information—they move probabilities to the same degree. However, they differ in informational content because probabilities are moved in opposite directions.

At first glance, informational content plays a role only in representative speech acts because only they are used to inform. However, directive and commissive speech acts are also often conditional on matters of fact and make more or less determinate presuppositions. R needs to know under what conditions certain obligations kick in.

But even unconditional commands or promises inform in some way about something. If S commands R to perform some action, S wants R to know what her illocutionary intention is, that is, in game theoretical parlance, what her *type* is. Hence, Ω does not comprise only states of the world, but it can also include mental states of S (S's types)—for instance, that S wants R to perform action a. A statute can inform about the legislature's intention to make citizens pay their taxes and punish them for tax evasion.

Directives and commissives can also signal information that goes beyond illocutionary intention. For instance, by signaling harsh punishment, a criminal statute's wording can incentivize to perform (or refrain from) certain actions, for example, to comply or even overcomply. Such compliance would be the directive's perlocutionary effect.

Commands and promises can be phrased in indeterminate terms just as representations. They give more or less information about the speaker's intention or about the obligations created. The legislature can send the message (enact the

---

[4] In contrast, an agent is *imperfectly* informed if she does not know other players' moves. There is perfect, but incomplete, information in classical signaling games.

[5] Signaling games are so called because S "signals" R this information. They are sometimes contrasted with screening games, in which the lesser informed agent acts first and tries to "screen" the information available to the better informed agent. See Stiglitz and Weiss (1990).

[6] See Skyrms (2010, 34).

statute) that certain goods are to be taxed 10%. Whether some business will react by paying the new tax or by evading it depends on its expected gain from and informational access to its actions' consequences. Indeterminacy can affect both informational content and quantity of information.

My primary goal in this chapter is to make use of game theoretic models *not* to find the best strategies of indeterminacy in communication but to make explicit which conditions are in principle required for its use. Before we analyze the conditions under which indeterminate messages can be strategically used in a signaling game, we need to find a way to properly represent indeterminacy and distinguish between its various forms.[7]

4.2 Indeterminacy in Signaling Games

In chapter 1, I differentiated various forms of linguistic indeterminacy. With regard to their potential strategic value, I will focus now on three basic effects. First, semantically vague terms allow for borderline cases in which there is unclarity and disagreement about their application. Second, general terms are non-informative (with respect to some aspect relevant to the conversation) when used in a conversationally vague manner. Third, some terms allow for multiple interpretations due to ambiguity (including polysemy, lexical ambiguity, and syntactic ambiguity).

Each form of indeterminacy can be visualized and represented in what I call *semantic spaces*.[8] They are a modified notion of conceptual spaces based on the geometrical account by Peter Gärdenfors (2004). Conceptual spaces are multi-dimensional spaces in which points refer to objects and areas to concepts. They have multiple dimensions that correspond to the fundamental properties by means of which objects and concepts can be compared. The concept of *heap*, for instance, can be represented (in a highly simplified way) by an appropriate area on the dimension of number of grains. A particular object can then be said to be a heap depending on its position on this dimension.[9]

Since we are not concerned with concepts but with terms and utterances in which they are used, we will translate Gärdenfors' cognitive model of

---

[7] There are justified doubts about the usefulness of game theoretic models especially when applied to everyday situations like natural language communication. I hope, however, that most of them will be resolved by the specific approach taken here, as it does not aim to describe communication. Rather, it aims to make explicit under what circumstances a particular set of strategies (such as indeterminate messages) can in principle be useful.

[8] Linguists sometimes use another, slightly related, notion of semantic spaces within the framework of natural language processing. See Lowe (2001).

[9] The concept of *heap* is reduced here to one dimension; but more dimensions, such as the arrangement of grains, can easily be added. All concepts include similarity relations to other concepts—a basic feature of Gärdenfors' account that I willfully ignore here. Gärdenfors defines concepts essentially in terms of conceptual similarity to their prototypes.

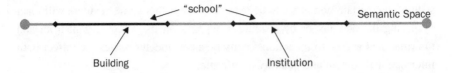

FIGURE 7 **Ambiguity in Semantic Space**

conceptual spaces into a linguistic model of semantic spaces. Conversational vagueness (in its form of generality), semantic vagueness, and ambiguity, on one hand, can be modeled in a straightforward way. Pragmatic indeterminacy, being a property of whole utterances, on the other hand, cannot directly be incorporated in the model. I will discuss this form of indeterminacy in section 4.4.4 separately.

It should be noted, however, that pragmatic indeterminacy has basically the same effects as ambiguity. Both allow for multiple, distinct, interpretations of what is communicated. A pragmatically indeterminate utterance can do so on the level of what is presupposed, what is implicited, what is implicated, or its illocutionary force—analogously to ambiguity that allows for two or more different interpretations of what is said. For instance, a term can have two or more senses—either because it is polysemous or because it carries an indeterminate impliciture.[10] In contrast, a general utterance communicates a particular content which, however, is not informative or relevant enough for the purposes at hand; while a semantically vague utterance communicates a particular content that is unclear due to a borderline application of the vague terms used.

We will now model ambiguity, generality, and vagueness in one-dimensional semantic spaces and explore how each can be employed within the framework of signaling games.

AMBIGUITY

Ambiguity causes unclarity about the message's interpretation by R. More precisely, an ambiguous message can be interpreted by R in different ways—leading potentially to different reactions. An ambiguous term can be understood in different ways either because of its syntactic or semantic properties.

Recall the polysemous term "school," which can be used either to refer to the building or the institution. Depending on the context of utterance, it can be used in one or the other sense. The term "school" is therefore split in two areas within the semantic space, as illustrated in Figure 7.

---

[10] We saw this in section 3.4 for the example of "chicken" in the context of the case *Frigaliment v. BNS*, in which it is unclear whether the different senses of the term result from polysemy or impliciture indeterminacy.

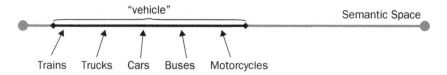

FIGURE 8 **Generality in Semantic Space**

Used in message *m*, the ambiguous term "school" may have the effect that *m* does not pick out a single set of states from state space Ω. *R* might be uncertain whether the state of the world is either a member of the set $\{\omega_i, \ldots, \omega_j\}$ or $\{\omega_k, \ldots, \omega_l\}$. In the case of vertical polysemy, for instance, one set is the subset of the other; but *R* may not know about a number of states (those that are only members of one set) whether they are referred to by *S* or not.

GENERALITY

A general message is indeterminate in the sense that *R* is insufficiently informed by it for the purposes of the conversation. *R* does not know enough about the state of the world (including the intentions of *S*) to react properly to the message.

Also, a general term can be understood in different ways because *R* can specify it in different ways. For instance, the term "vehicle" can be used to refer to either trucks, buses, trains, or motorcycles, but also to all of them at once. This is a case of vertical polysemy due to the generality of the term.

But even if it is clearly used for all of them at once, the message can be conversationally vague because *R* needs, for some purpose, more specific information about the kind of vehicle referred to. Both these features of generality can be captured by the model. As illustrated in Figure 8, the term "vehicle" covers a broad area (covering potentially relevantly different points) in the semantic space.

Used in message *m*, the general term "vehicle" may have the effect that *m* picks out an overly big set of states from state space Ω. If *S* is assumed to be truthful, *R* knows that the state of the world is a member of the set $\{\omega_i, \ldots, \omega_j\}$ but may not know specifically which state the world is in. If *R*'s knowing this makes a difference for the purpose of the conversation (namely, for *S* and *R*'s expected outcomes), *m* is conversationally vague.

SEMANTIC VAGUENESS

A semantically vague message is usually understood in the same way by both *S* and *R*. However, if the object referred to by the vague term is a borderline case, different interpretations or unclarity can result.

Consider the term "vehicle" again. It can be used to refer to trucks, trains, and buses, but sometimes also to motorized floor strippers, segways, or surfboards.

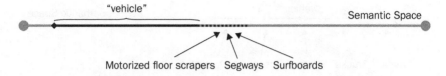

FIGURE 9 **Vagueness in Semantic Space**

Whether such objects are included in the extension of "vehicle" is unclear, however. Vague terms are characterized by the area's fuzzy margins within the semantic space, as illustrated in Figure 9. There are points or areas in the semantic space in which it is undefined whether the term applies or not.

Used in message m, the vague term "vehicle" may have the effect that m picks out a set of states from state space Ω that is not well-defined. There might be some states $\omega \in \Omega$ which neither clearly are nor clearly are not members of the set picked out by m. In other words, m picks out a fuzzy set. Either S and R agree that there is no fact of the matter or they understand m differently in these cases.

Based on these simple representations of ambiguity, generality, and semantic vagueness, I will analyze the strategic use of indeterminate messages in the following sections. As noted in chapter 1, terms or expressions are not indeterminate in themselves but rather become indeterminate through their use in speech acts, utterances, or messages. Any term can be used either determinately or indeterminately. What is then the effect of ambiguous, general, and vague terms when indeterminately used in utterances?

4.3 The Disutility of Indeterminacy

In ordinary conversation and especially in legal discourse, indeterminacy seems to be a bad thing. H. L. A. Hart (1961/1994, 207) maintains that laws are such that their subjects are "expected to understand and conform to the rules without further direction." This expectation seems to be warranted only if laws are sufficiently clear and determinate.

As mentioned in chapter 2, we value legal certainty and fair notice. They might even be part of the concept of law. For this reason, law has established principles such as the prohibition of arbitrariness and the *void for vagueness* doctrine. A prevalent and almost universally accepted demand on the phrasing of legal texts is perspicuity, precision, and clarity.

Laws, verdicts, and contracts have the function to tell people what their rights and duties are, that is, what they are allowed and required to do and not to do. If the language used is indeterminate, it seems that laws and contracts cannot properly fulfill this function since people do not know what they should and should not do. A defining feature of legal language is its being designed for the very particular purpose of guiding behavior, and it has to achieve this goal in a complex environment while addressing a widely heterogeneous audience in a context-impoverished environment. It is, for that reason, commonly held that lawmakers, judges, and contract drafters should try to avoid unclarity whenever possible.

The desideratum of clarity is—not only according to Lon L. Fuller but also to Joseph Raz and many others—a legal principle imbedded in the *rule of law*. Without clarity, law cannot fulfill its function of guiding the conduct of its subjects: "An ambiguous, vague, obscure, or imprecise law is likely to mislead or confuse at least some of those who desire to be guided by it."[11] It seems thus that indeterminacy is—contrary to having value—detrimental to the law's own purpose.

Moreover, it is doubtful what function indeterminacy could possibly have even in everyday communication. After all, clarity is an important goal to both speakers and listeners in most conversations. The reason appears to be, as H. Paul Grice (1989b) emphasizes, that clarity is part of the mutual cooperation required for successful language behavior. Evidently, clarity is crucial if there is an interest in communication. What is the purpose of uttering something to somebody if the utterance does not result in knowledge of what is communicated? Since indeterminacy entails unclarity, and unclarity is generally to be avoided, it is natural to assume that indeterminacy is to be avoided too. By modus tollens, if clarity is a virtue, then determinacy is a virtue too. Consequently, determinacy is a goal that should be pursued by the speaker—a demand on communication that is encapsulated by the Maxim of Manner.

4.3.1 LIPMAN'S PROOF

There is a famous proof by Lipman (2009) that precision is always preferable to vagueness in contexts of cooperation. He gave a very simple and straightforward proof that vague messages can never generate a higher outcome than precise ones when interests are aligned.

It can be illustrated by the following scenario:

> S asks R to pick up an acquaintance, Mr. X, at the airport. S knows Mr. X's height precisely, while R is able to perfectly and effortlessly measure heights. The heights of the other people at the airport are uniformly distributed. The outcome for both S and R is 1 if R picks up Mr. X and 0 if R picks up anybody else.[12]

---

[11] See Raz (2009a, 214).

[12] See Lipman (2009, 6–7). See also van Deemter (2010, 261).

Under these assumptions the vague message

(E54) "Mr. X is tall."

cannot be preferable to the precise message

(E55) "Mr. X is 176.2 cm."

(E55) allows R to pick up Mr. X with almost complete certainty, given that the probability that two persons at the airport have exactly the same height is negligible. At best, (E54) can achieve as good a result as (E55). Vagueness thus cannot have an advantage over precision and, in some cases, will be strictly worse.[13] Lipman concludes that we use vague terms not because vagueness has any value but because we are boundedly rational.[14]

Does Lipman's proof really show that vagueness has no value? There are two aspects about Lipman's proof that are potentially problematic. The first one is his representation of vagueness. Even though he defines vagueness with reference to the Sorites paradox in the beginning of his paper, he does not consistently distinguish it from other forms of indeterminacy—neither in his proof nor in his discussion.[15] We will return to this potential problem in section 4.4.1 on strategies of semantic vagueness.

The second aspect concerns several assumptions explicitly and implicitly made by Lipman. Each of them will point us toward a possible (strategic) use of indeterminacy.

Assumption 1

Lipman explicitly assumes that messages are costless. Messages are unverifiable and do not incur costs to either S or R.[16] This is not always plausible. By increasing the costs of determinate messages, indeterminacy becomes the preferable strategy

---

[13] Concretely, Lipman shows that for any joint mixed strategy (σ_1, σ_2) where the supremum is attained, every joint pure strategy (s_1, s_2) in the support of (σ_1, σ_2) is a pure Nash-equilibrium such that the expected utility $EU(s_1, s_2) = sup_{(\sigma_1, \sigma_2)} EU(\sigma_1, \sigma_2)$. The proof goes as follows. Let (σ_1^*, σ_2^*) be a joint mixed strategy where the supremum is achieved. Trivially, (σ_1^*, σ_2^*) is an equilibrium. Since it is optimal, strategy σ_1^* gives the same payoff as any pure strategy in its support. So, there is a pure strategy s_1 such that (s_1, σ_2^*) is an equilibrium. The same is true for the optimal strategy σ_2^*. Hence, there is a joint pure strategy (s_1, s_2) where the supremum is achieved. That is, (s_1, s_2) is an equilibrium.

[14] Individuals are boundedly rational when their rationality is limited by, for instance, the available information or their cognitive capacities. For more details, see the discussion of different forms of bounded rationality as causes of contractual incompleteness in section 5.3.2.

[15] Lipman (2009, 1) explicates his understanding of vagueness with reference to Sainsbury (1997): "I will say that a word is precise if it describes a well-defined set of objects. By contrast, a word is vague if it is not precise."

[16] Lipman's example is thus a form of *cheap talk*—a notion coined by Farrell (1987), who defines cheap talk as games in which messages are costless, non-binding, and unverifiable.

even if interests are perfectly aligned and all other assumptions are held fixed. In ordinary language, there is time and energy involved in phrasing carefully and consciously avoiding indeterminacy. It requires putting oneself in the shoes of one's audience and anticipating how one's utterance will be received. This may be cognitive costs only, but actual money could be needed when hiring someone to write a clear and unambiguous speech, for instance.

Especially in the law, there is ample reason to believe that precise and specific drafting actually increases costs. We might thus want to be unclear simply for reasons of efficiency. It requires effort to communicate. It requires even more effort to communicate clearly. It seems, ceteris paribus, to be both physically and cognitively harder to articulate clearly than to do so unclearly; and it similarly seems harder to use precise and specific expressions than to rely on general and vague ones.[17]

Assumption 2

Lipman implicitly assumes that agents have full knowledge about the starting point and rules of the game. This is clearly not plausible under most circumstances. We do not always know who the other participants in the conversation are or what they are capable of. People do not always share the same background knowledge about the world. Such asymmetric information about the background and context of the message can affect directly how it is understood or interpreted.

We saw that especially in the law, there are different theories of legal interpretation that yield different understandings of legal utterances. But even in ordinary conversation, there are different ways to understand utterances due to different background beliefs. Agents frequently have (at least slightly) different views about the kind of conversation in which they engage. This does, however, not only change the interpretation of (unavoidably indeterminate) utterances but may also require intentional indeterminacy to bridge gaps between divergent beliefs.

Assumption 3

Lipman implicitly assumes that agents have full knowledge about their own and other agents' preferences. This is not always plausible either. Usually we do not know the interests of all members of our audience in great detail. We can only anticipate how they might react to what we say.

There is uncertainty not only with respect to the preferences of others but even one's own preferences are not always known to oneself. Sometimes one is

---

[17] I will discuss this hypothesis in detail in section 4.3.2.

in error about what is in one's best interests and will later regret one's choices.[18] Well-placed indeterminacy might mitigate the repercussions of such blindness to one's own and other people's preferences.

Assumption 4

Lipman implicitly assumes that agents have perfect, even if incomplete, information. They are aware of every move in the game and know the likelihood with which everything will happen. Some events are unforeseen, however, because of cognitive or computational limitations. Some events may even be unforeseeable. If the speaker herself does not have the relevant information, an indeterminate utterance is legitimate even under complete cooperation. This is also true if the speaker does not possess the relevant conceptual resources such as children, non-native speakers, or people who lack the terminology required for the situation.[19] In the case of unforeseen contingencies, probabilities cannot be calculated and uncertainty results.

Assumption 5

Lipman explicitly assumes that there are no conflicting interests between the agents. His assumption is that participants in most ordinary conversations cooperate and do not act against each other. However, the conclusion that he draws from this assumption is clearly too strong. Even in ordinary conversation, it is rarely ever the case that *all* relevant interests are *perfectly* aligned. There are common interests, otherwise there would be no sense in having the conversation in the first place; but there are usually *some* interests that diverge or conflict with each other even in the most cooperative information exchange.[20]

Assumption 6

Lipman explicitly assumes the standard model of a signaling game in which there are only two agents involved. However, there are often, especially for written utterances as in the law, multiple audiences who might have conflicting interests among themselves or between them and the speaker. They might also have different assumptions about interpretative methods or background and context information. In particular in the law, audiences are often heterogeneous both with respect to their interests and beliefs.[21]

---

[18] This is especially the case when the regret is due to cognitive dissonance—which rarely is transparent to us. See Cooper (2007).

[19] See Cotterill (2007) or Bazzanella (2011).

[20] See section 4.3.3 in which I argue that people do not need to fully cooperate either in ordinary conversation or in the law to successfully communicate.

[21] See section 2.1 on the feature of language in the law.

Assumption 7

Lipman implicitly assumes that language is a form of information exchange. However, messages are not always descriptions of the world. In ordinary conversation, as well as in the law, there are all sorts of speech acts. We utter directives, declarations, and commissives that are made to have an impact on the world. Indeterminacy might have pragmatic functions impossible to represent in a model such as Lipman's, which is designed to model information exchange.[22]

These remarks are not intended to make a case against Lipman's proof, which does not aim to demonstrate the disutility of indeterminacy in general. Lipman clearly understands (at least some of) the limits of his model. On the contrary, the discussion of his explicit and implicit assumptions is intended to show in what areas and under what circumstances indeterminacy can possibly have a value—if Lipman's proof is in principle considered to be convincing.

4.3.2 THE VALUE OF SEMANTIC VAGUENESS

A number of authors, including Lipman himself, argue that vagueness has a value. As a matter of fact, we often do use language in ways less determinate than possible. In particular, we often use vague terms when we could have used more precise ones instead. These authors try to explain why we do so. They are convinced that not only some form of indeterminacy has a positive function but that semantic vagueness in particular is valuable. I will now discuss a series of arguments given in favor of this view.

The Argument from Perception and Memory

It has been argued that vagueness is useful because it more adequately represents our perceptual experience.[23] The unclarity caused by vagueness is in fact a perfectly accurate reflection of the vague language's object. There is no need for more precision. Friedrich Waismann (1965, 210) illustrates this claim with the example of rain:

> The picture of the rain I see is blurred. ... I could not say of any exact description—e.g. for a description mentioning an exact number of raindrops—that it describes my experience exactly.

Indeed, it would violate both the conversational Maxims of Quantity and Relation to mention the number of raindrops when describing the experience of rain. Even though a message informing about the exact number of raindrops would

---

[22] For example, empirical studies suggest that indeterminate utterances are more frequent in speech acts of apologies and requests. See Urbanová (1999) who argues that indeterminate speech acts are closely connected with informal politeness.

[23] See Russell (1923), Wittgenstein (1953), and Waismann (1965) for this claim.

be more precise, it would also be *more informative* than required and, as a result, *less relevant* for the purposes of the conversation. There are some contexts in which the highest possible precision is pursued, as in science or logic. But the standard of precision is adjustable. It depends on the object and purpose of the conversation. As such, in virtually all contexts of ordinary conversation it is significantly lower.

Furthermore, absolute precision is arguably—due to the imperfection of measurement—impossible anyway. At least for continuous scales like time there is always another decimal place to add—exacting ever more precise measurement.[24] There is no sense in which someone is *completely* punctual. But also, for most other scales, there is usually a certain point from which onward precise measurement becomes increasingly difficult or outright impossible, such as the measurement of position and momentum of particles due Heisenberg's Uncertainty Principle. As a consequence, it would be futile to even strive for absolute precision. As Charles S. Peirce is supposed to have said, "[v]agueness is no more to be done away with in the world of logic than friction in mechanics."[25]

Not only our limited perception seems to require vagueness in language but also our cognitive limitations with respect to memory.[26] Consider the following scenario by Kees van Deemter (2010, 263):

> Suppose I told you that 324,542 people perished in some cataclysmic earthquake. For a while, you might remember the exact death toll. In the longer term, however, details are likely to be corrupted (if you remember the wrong number) or lost: the next day, you may only recall that the victims numbered in their hundreds of thousands; a year later, you may only remember that there were many.

Van Deemter concludes that human memory retains only the gist of information due to evolutionary economization of memory space. By itself the earthquake scenario does not quite show, however, that it is semantic vagueness that does the trick. If details are corrupted or lost, one can always choose a general expression instead of a more specific one. The term "many" happens to be both vague and general. Even if you cannot remember whether there are hundreds or merely tens of thousands, you are usually still able to say whether there are more than 1,000 (or some other number).

However, something seems to draw (most of) us to vague terms such as "many" when our memory is fading. What is it about "many" that we tend to prefer it to other equally easily truth-assessable but perfectly precise expressions? It seems that two cognitive mechanisms described by Alan Baddeley (2007) support van

---

[24] See Swinburne (1969, 288).

[25] Cited in McNeill and Freiberger (1993, 136).

[26] See Waismann (1978), van Deemter (2010), and Kluck (2014) for this claim.

Deemter's conclusion. First, there is *semantic coding*, by which only the meaning of an expression is retained while the expression itself is forgotten. Second, there is *chunking*, by which a handful of items are clustered together as a unit. Chunking is clearly connected to generality. We lump together specific information into general "chunks." Semantic coding, however, could be the source of semantic vagueness. Maybe we really think "vaguely." Maybe, it is easier for our memory to retain a fuzzy image than a clear-cut one. Let us assume for the sake of the argument that this is the case.

Unfortunately, however, even if both arguments are sound, they do not show what they purport to do. Maybe our perception and memory are such that we cannot but think and speak vaguely. Maybe semantic vagueness is a necessary feature of human thought and language. If one does not have sufficient information and wants to be truthful, one cannot help oneself but to be less precise than desirable. But this does not entail that imprecision fulfills a positive function. If the arguments were successful, semantic vagueness would still be a defect, albeit an unavoidable one.

The Argument from Cognitive Costs

Lipman assumes in his proof that messages are costless. However, as noted previously, there is some reason to believe that vague messages can be processed more easily than precise ones and, for that reason, cause less *cognitive costs*.[27] It is arguably easier to pronounce the term "many" than "324,542 people." It is arguably also easier to hold the thought in mind or to learn the term.

It appears that we generally use language according to some form of the mini–max principle; that is, we are as unclear and inarticulate as possible in order not to waste energy, while at the same time as clear and articulate as necessary to still get the message across. Hence, the goal of avoiding unclarity has to be balanced with the goal of not wasting energy. This principle is a reformulation of the so called "false" Zipf's law.[28] If that is true, any formal proof for the value of vagueness based on cognitive costs becomes trivial. The agents' expected utility increases simply because costs decrease.[29] But what is the actual value of semantic vagueness?

While it might be both informationally and economically best to use a vague expression, its vagueness does not become actual in most situations. Semantically vague terms do usually not generate actual borderline cases.[30] It might thus be the case that the costs of using precise terms outweigh the expected costs of vague ones

---

[27] See sections 5.1.1 and 5.3.2 for a discussion of the costs of indeterminacy in the law.

[28] It is not to be confused with Zipf's law in mathematical statistics. See Zipf (1949).

[29] In the classical model by Spence (1973), sending a message is costly by itself, and one could increase the costs for precise messages by stipulation.

[30] See section 1.3 for a detailed discussion of this claim.

because the likelihood of actually encountering borderline cases is negligible. The risk of running into borderline cases is merely tacitly assumed.

Moreover, it is not even entirely clear whether semantic vagueness reduces cognitive costs even in clear cases. Experiments by Matthew J. Green and van Deemter (2011, 6) do, according to the authors' own conclusion, "more to cast doubt on the cost reduction hypothesis than to confirm it." What is effective here seem to be other linguistic properties of the vague terms. Consider again replacing the term "many" with the expression "more than 1,000" when reacting to van Deemter's earthquake scenario. What is done by going from "324,542 people" to "more than 1,000" is a pruning away of details—which may not be available anymore or which may simply be irrelevant.[31] The same effect is present when going from "324,542 people" to "many." The vague term "many" is more general than the precise "324,542 people." In contrast to "more than 1,000," it is also shorter, grammatically less complex, and devoid of mathematical concepts. These properties alone adequately explain why "many" is cognitively less costly than "324,542 people."

While it arguably is cost-efficient to use vague terms, it is doubtful that their vagueness is the reason for it. But even if it were, cognitive costs could not show that semantic vagueness itself is valuable, that is, that borderline cases are effective. In the same way as the previous argument, the *Argument from Cognitive Costs* fails to show how semantic vagueness could have a positive function.

The Argument from Language Change and Learning

A common argument for the value of vagueness is that it makes language more adaptable. In particular, it has been argued that the gradual widening of a term's extension along a Sorites series over time and by a significant group of speakers can facilitate a change in meaning that satisfies the communicative needs of a language community. We can reformulate it in the following way:

(P1) Gradual vagueness entails tolerance.
(P2) Tolerance allows for gradual change in meaning.
(P3) Gradual change in meaning is useful.
(C)   Gradual vagueness is useful.

Renate Bartsch seems at first glance to support the *Argument from Language Change*:

Semantic norms carry the possibility of change with them. Because of this, we can adjust our language to change in our physical and social world. If vagueness and context-dependence of meanings were not part of the meanings

---

[31] See also the discussion of the *Argument from Communicative Success*.

of words, language would be a less efficient means of communication. (Bartsch, 1984, 372)

Bartsch claims that vagueness and context-dependence of meaning make language more efficient by facilitating semantic change. Gradual change in meaning allows us to adjust our language efficiently to a changing world. (P3) seems to be uncontroversial.

Nora Kluck (2014) argues, based on Bartsch's claim, that semantic vagueness facilitates adaptability of language. She considers the Sorites susceptibility in such changes as evidence for (P2). Indeed, meaning does change gradually, and this is the reason why we can create Sorites series from an old meaning to a new one. But does this entail that it is the Sorites susceptibility that facilitates the change?

The same mechanism is, according to Kluck, used in language learning. Consider a child who does not yet know the correct expression for some object. She could remain silent, giving away even the chance to be understood. Alternatively, she could overgeneralize, making herself at least potentially understood. Kluck claims that semantic vagueness facilitates overgeneralization and undergeneralization because it allows the child to freely move in the borderline area, so to speak. The child can use a term that only borderline applies to the case at hand if she does not know a better term that would clearly apply. The strategy of overgeneralization is better than no communication at all.[32] Thus, overgeneralization and undergeneralization are communicative strategies in language learning relying on the use of semantic vagueness.

Unfortunately, even if this is correct,[33] the argument fails to show how semantic vagueness could have a positive function. It shows at best that vagueness is not necessarily disadvantageous. Strikingly, it is not disadvantageous when its main effect is mitigated. It is not disadvantageous when we can figure out that the term must apply *even though* it is (semantically) a borderline case. Hence, the *Argument from Language Learning* fails to show that semantic vagueness has a value.

On closer examination, the *Argument from Language Change* also fails. Bartsch actually attributes the possibility of change to polysemy and other forms of context-dependence, explicitly denying any role of semantic vagueness in it:

> Vagueness due to gradualness does, to my knowledge, not play a role in semantic change, while vagueness due to contextual indeterminateness of a relative term can give rise to metonymic relationships in the structure of meaning. (Bartsch, 1984, 374)

---

[32] See also the following discussion of the *Argument from Communicative Success*.

[33] It is doubtful that it is since a child also overgeneralizes in clear cases of non-application. Semantic vagueness is neither logically dependent on the phenomenon of overgeneralization and undergeneralization nor empirically correlated.

While there might be some small contribution of vagueness to language change, other properties of language are clearly more efficient to facilitate long-term adaptability—as, for instance, the figurative use of words. Context-dependence is by far more useful for this end than semantic vagueness, which at best can smooth the transition actuated by other processes. There is thus no positive argument for the claim that Sorites susceptibility or tolerance allow for gradual change in meaning. (P2) is unwarranted. Hence, neither Sorites susceptibility nor strategies of overgeneralization and undergeneralization entail that semantic vagueness plays any interesting role in supporting language change or learning.

The Argument from Communicative Success

Semantic vagueness may be necessary and sometimes a flaw of language, but it does not preclude successful communication and is thus not a defect per se, as some philosophers are keen to point out.[34] Consider an argument made by Wittgenstein. He asks us to take into account the conversation's purpose and shake off any ill-advised longings for *the* ideal of exactness:

> Now, if I tell someone: "You should come to dinner more punctually; you know it begins at one o'clock exactly"—is there really no question of exactness here? After all, one can say: "Think of the determination of time in the laboratory or the observatory; there you see what 'exactness' means." "Inexact" is really a reproach, and "exact" is praise. And that is to say that what is inexact attains its goal less perfectly than does what is more exact. So it all depends on what we call "the goal". Is it inexact when I don't give our distance from the sun to the nearest metre, or tell a joiner the width of a table to the nearest thousandth of a millimetre? No single ideal of exactness has been envisaged. (Wittgenstein, 1953, § 88)

Wittgenstein's point is that the goal of perfect precision is, even if it were attainable, not a generally reasonable one. The purpose of most conversations can be furthered by using vague terms. Conversations demand different "ideals of exactness" depending on their purpose. What counts as perfectly precise in one conversation is unacceptably vague in another one. It depends on the conversationally given degree of granularity.[35]

There is nothing to say against this claim. It is as convincing as it is modest. Communication would obviously be hindered by always telling the time exactly to the nanosecond. Doing it would achieve nothing. However, not doing it does not

---

[34] See Black (1937), Hempel (1939), Wittgenstein (1953), Peirce (1960), and Quine (1960).
[35] See section 1.6 and also the discussion of the *Argument from Perception and Memory*.

entail that one must use semantically vague language. Recall our example from section 1.4:

(E16) "At 5pm."

If used as an answer to the question of when to meet, (E16) normally communicates that the meeting takes place at 5pm plus or minus a few seconds or minutes. If the degree of granularity is sufficiently coarse-grained, (E16) could even communicate that it is 5pm plus or minus an hour. Strikingly, all expressions used in (E16) are precise. What is "vague" is the implicited content. This is what we called pragmatic vagueness in section 1.4.

As Manfred Pinkal (1995) argues, a coarse-grained degree of granularity can actually facilitate stability in judgment. For instance, if we were to describe someone by her precise height measured to the tenth decimal place, the description would need to be adjusted on a regular basis. Otherwise, it would not fit the subject who is slightly changing in height every day. Hence, it is better to be less precise. It is better to utter the vague (E54) instead of the precise (E55) after all. "Mr. X is 176.221cm" might easily be wrong if Mr. X—as all humans—slightly changes in height over the course of a day. The judgment on the more coarse-grained degree of granularity is thus more stable because it is not susceptible to such small changes. Some writers conclude that it is semantic vagueness that facilitates this stability in judgment.[36]

However, a coarse-grained degree of granularity is not identical to semantic vagueness. Stability is primarily guaranteed by a broader scope in judgment. It is true in more (possible) states of affairs. The statement

(E56) "The meeting starts at 5pm."

will be accepted as true or appropriate if it does so at 4:55 or 5:10. In contrast, if the speaker had said that the meeting starts at 5:03, she could be reasonably criticized if it started at any time other than 5:03 plus or minus a minute or so. Borderline cases are not what makes such less than fully precise utterances useful. It is their unspecificity.

As Manfred Krifka (2009) points out, it is often beneficial for both speaker and hearer to describe the world at a more coarse-grained degree of granularity. It is both linguistically and cognitively easier to process (E16) than

(E57) "At 5:03."

Cognitive costs seem to rise with the degree of granularity. While this might be due to lack of precision, as we noted in our discussion of the *Argument from Cognitive Costs*, the main reason seems to be the possibility of chunking.[37] A

---

[36] For instance, van Rooij (2011) and Kluck (2014) explicitly claim this.

[37] See our discussion of the *Arguments of Perception and Memory* before.

coarse-grained degree of granularity allows for both the use of less precise terms and loose interpretation.

In general, the more fine-grained the degree of granularity, the less (pragmatically) vague the utterance can be interpreted. If the speaker uses several decimal places, there is no room for the hearer to interpret her utterance loosely. The reason is the Maxim of Quantity. The speaker would not have added the information if it were not required.

Conversely, the lack of decimal places indicates (in combination with other factors) that a few minutes more or less do not matter. Pragmatic vagueness does thus not hinder communication if the degree of granularity is sufficiently coarse-grained. However, the use of less precise terms and loose interpretation do not imply that semantic vagueness is functional. An imprecise term such as "many" is not only semantically vague, but also general, that is, "many" covers much more cases than "324,542." A more coarse-grained degree of granularity thus also allows for more generality—a property of language that clearly does make information processing easier.

The most famous version of the *Argument from Communicative Success* is advanced by Rohit Parikh. Parikh (1994) shows that even if borderline cases actually arise and unclarity results, as long as the conversational purpose is not (seriously) obstructed, vague messages can be useful. He shows that vague messages still succeed in promoting the conversation's goal—also under perfect alignment of interests. Parikh interprets vagueness such that vague terms have an extension that is slightly different for different language users such that there is disagreement between them in some cases (sc. borderline cases).

Parikh asks us to consider two language users S and R. S wants R to bring her the topology book. She tells him only that it is blue. Due to its vagueness the semantic space of the term "book" is not divided in the same way into $blue_S$ books (within S's semantic) and $blue_R$ books (within R's semantic). The extensions of the homonymous terms "$blue_S$ books" and "$blue_R$ books" merely overlap. As long as they do so sufficiently, that is, if there are not too many borderline cases, R obtains sufficiently useful information to more quickly find the correct book and bring it to S. If R searches all $blue_R$ books first and then the others (maybe less and less blue ones), he will more quickly find the correct book with higher probability than if he has to search all books more or less randomly. R will thus save time by searching all $blue_R$ books, even though this is not what S intended.

Parikh convincingly shows that communication in vague terms can be valuable in the sense that it is better than no communication at all. However, it is also clearly the case that S and R would communicate even better if the extensions of "$blue_S$

books" and "blue$_R$ books" would overlap entirely, that is, if the terms used were precise.[38]

Parikh's representation captures an important aspect of vagueness. What could be problematic, however, is that language users in fact do not usually have unconsciously idiosyncratic idioms that they assume to be precise. It is possible for language users to explicitly disagree in borderline cases what the term's extension is or explicitly agree that they face a borderline case in which there is no fact of the matter. Semantic vagueness does not merely consist in incompletely overlapping extensions between idiolects. But if we accept for the sake of argument that this captures at least an aspect of semantic vagueness, we can conclude with Parikh that this property of vague terms is useful inasmuch as it does not preclude successful communication.

In sum, neither Pinkal, Krifka, or Parikh's arguments show that the *existence of borderline cases* fulfills any positive function. What Parikh shows is only that a semantically vague message is better than no message at all. Parikh presupposes that vagueness is a necessary feature of natural language, which presumably it is, and he argues, based on this presupposition, that natural language can *despite* its vagueness be used to successfully exchange information. Parikh cannot—and does not even try to—explain why we should use vague terms when we could turn to more precise ones. His argument does not aim to show why we are sometimes more vague than necessary.

Nor do Pinkal and Krifka seem to rely on actual vagueness when they argue that sometimes a more coarse-grained degree of granularity is useful. Either (in the case of Pinkal) the term's unspecificity improves communicative success by making judgments more stable or (in the case of Krifka) the gains provided by ease of expression outweigh the risks due to possible borderline cases. In neither case, however, is it borderline cases themselves that serve a positive function.

The Argument from Inefficiency

It is also often argued that semantic vagueness is valuable because precision is inefficient. In particular, it is said that the use of precise terms requires unnecessary and inefficient measurement.[39] Vagueness, on the other hand, makes ordinary language expressions fit for everyday use. Without vagueness, we would have to measure all day long the number of grains, the height of people, and the wavelength of light when all we want is to talk about heaps, tall people, and blue books.

The argument can be reconstructed as follows:

---

[38] This was also shown by Lipman (2009). See his proof in the beginning of section 4.3.1.

[39] See, for instance, Kluck (2014).

(P1) Precision requires measurement.

(P2) Measurement is inefficient.

(C1) Precision is inefficient.

If understood in the intended sense, (P2) is certainly true. It certainly would be inefficient to measure the number of grains each time we want to determine whether some arrangement of grains is a heap.

While (P1) also has some initial appeal, at closer inspection it must be rejected. Precision does not *generally* require measurement. It is even conceivable to have a completely precise language without the need of any additional measurement. The basic tenet of the epistemic theory of vagueness is that ordinary language expressions have precise boundaries that cannot be known. A lot may be said against this theory, but it is not inconsistent in and by itself. The replacement of the vague term "blue" with "blue*" whose extension is determined by a precise range in the wave length spectrum, would not require any new measurements. Most of the time, we use language such that it clearly applies. For that reason, no measurement would be necessary because most of the time we would not even be in the vicinity of the sharp boundary. We could most of time use "blue*" just as we use our ordinary language expression "blue."

Moreover, it is correct that measurement is necessary if the case at hand is close to the sharp boundary of a precise term, and we want to be certain about its application to it. In contrast, if the case is close to the fuzzy boundary of a vague term, we are necessarily ignorant about its application. Both precision and vagueness thus result in ignorance if we are close to the boundary of the term's extension. But precision has the additional advantage that ignorance can be resolved by measurement. Precision does not require measurement but makes it possible. (P1) is incorrect.

Gottlob Frege's analogy of the hand is sometimes cited as support for a variant of the *Argument from Inefficiency*:

> The ... shortcomings result from a certain softness and changeability of language which ... is a precondition of its viability and versatility. In this respect, language can be compared to the hand which, despite its ability to adapt itself to most diverse tasks, does not suffice. We created artificial hands, tools for special purposes which work in such precision in which the hand could not. And by what is this precision facilitated? Exactly by the rigidity, the parts' unchangeability, the lack of which makes the hand so versatilely skilled.[40]

---

[40] Translated from Frege (1882, 52): "Die ... Mängel haben ihren Grund in einer gewissen Weichheit und Veränderlichkeit der Sprache, die ... Bedingung ihrer Entwicklungsfähigkeit und vielseitigen Tauglichkeit ist. Die Sprache kann in dieser Hinsicht mit der Hand verglichen werden, die uns trotz ihrer Fähigkeit, sich den verschiedensten Aufgaben anzupassen, nicht genügt. Wir schaffen uns künstliche Hände, Werkzeuge für besondere Zwecke, die so genau arbeiten, wie die Hand es nicht vermöchte. Und wodurch

Natural language is "soft" and "changeable." It is multi-functional just like the human hand. In contrast, tools such as screwdrivers are rigid. They can only be used for particular purposes—and the same is true for the tools of formal logic. The precision of screwdrivers and formal logic is facilitated by their rigidity. Supposedly, the multi-functionality of natural language is based on its semantic vagueness since it is the precision of logic that makes it so useful for its purpose. However, this is a non sequitur. Let me show why.

Frege's analogy—understood in this way—will lead to the following argument:

(P3) Formal languages are useful because of their precision.

(P4) If formal languages are useful because of their precision, natural language must be useful because of its lack of precision.

(C2) Natural language is useful because of its vagueness.

Frege's analogy does not aim at the vagueness of natural language, and it is hard to see how Frege himself could have understood it in this way. His analogy applies to other properties of natural language—which happens to also contain vague terms. Natural language is multi-functional because of generality, polysemy, and various pragmatic features. We can use the same terms for different purposes because they are polysemous—not because they are vague. We can use the same terms to express different contents because we make implicatures and implicitures. We use metaphors and irony. Vagueness cannot do this. And it is extremely doubtful that Frege thought it did.

(P3) is arguably correct. The exactness of formal languages stems from their precision. Also, (P4) seems to be warranted. Frege's analogy suggests that formal and natural languages have complementary functions. They certainly do have them. Formal language is useful because it is precise. Natural language is useful because it is multi-functional. However, there is no explanatory link between the effects of precision in formal languages and the effects of vagueness in natural language. Lack of precision does entail much more than semantic vagueness. It certainly does not imply that the adaptability and efficiency of natural language stems from vagueness.[41] To draw the conclusion (C2), an additional premise is needed. We would need the premise that the usefulness of imprecision entails the usefulness of vagueness.

---

wird diese Genauigkeit möglich? Durch eben die Starrheit, die Unveränderlichkeit der Teile, deren Mangel die Hand so vielseitig geschickt macht."

[41] While it is true that semantic vagueness correlates with context sensitivity and precision correlates with context insensitivity, there is no necessary connection. It is conceivable, as Åkerman and Greenough (2010) show, that vague terms are completely context-insensitive, and equally conceivable that precise terms are context-sensitive. Think of interpretations of adjectives such as "tall" within formal semantics. The adjective "tall" is perfectly precise in this framework, but it is still context-sensitive because it is relative to some (precise) standard.

The misguided use of Frege's analogy highlights one of the fundamental problems that inhere in many arguments for the value of vagueness. If we replace a precise term with an imprecise one, we rarely get a term that is vague but in all other respects just as the original one. First, experiments by Green and van Deemter (2013, 5) indicate that it is not the semantic vagueness of an imprecise term that makes it easier to process utterances than a co-referring precise one, but "that the observed benefits may be due to factors other than vagueness itself that the vague forms bring along with them: factors like avoiding numbers and permitting comparison tasks."[42]

Second, other forms of indeterminacy are systematically confused with semantic vagueness. Consider the term "many" again. As pointed out previously, it is not only vague but also more general than the original "324,542." Moreover, it is relative to a contextually valued standard and can thus vary in its extension in a way "324,542" or "more than 1,000" cannot. Nor do these precise expressions lean themselves toward figurative or other pragmatic uses as do terms such as "many."

Furthermore, if a speaker calls the number of perished people "many," she might not only say something about the earthquake but give also a value judgment. She could provide information about her values and assessment of the state of affairs.[43] As Frank Veltman put it, the speaker adds an opinion.[44] She can implicite that the number of deaths in the earthquake is high relative to other earthquakes that she considers comparable or high relative to how much she can stomach. The audience can learn more from her uttering "many" in addition to or instead of "324,542." The terms "more than 1,000" and "324,542" cannot be used to make such a judgment.

For some reason, it seems to be particularly difficult to keep semantic vagueness and standard-relativity apart. Even van Deemter, who writes on the value of semantic vagueness with matchless accuracy, seems to oscillate between both phenomena. He is quite explicit about his intention to talk about vague terms in the philosophical sense that they "allow borderline cases."[45] Nevertheless, he asks the following questions:

> "'Why do people make such frequent use of words whose meaning is difficult to pin down?' and 'What do these words mean?' 'Why is it that their meaning varies so much from one context to the next?'" (van Deemter, 2010, 2)

---

[42] See also Kennedy (2011) for the relation between semantic vagueness and comparisons.

[43] Jucker et al. (2003) show, for instance, that imprecise speech acts better convey the speaker's attitude and inform also about her assumptions about the audience's beliefs in addition to what is said.

[44] This is discussed by van Deemter (2010, 266–267) and van Rooij (2011, 129–130). Both refer to an inaugural lecture by Veltman (2002).

[45] See van Deemter (2010, 8).

The first two questions seem to point to polysemy or multi-dimensionality, while the third aims toward standard-relativity or context sensitivity more generally. He describes semantic vagueness and context sensitivity as two sides of the same coin. Van Deemter argues that terms such as "indecent" or "vehicle" are vague "because context affects the interpretation of these words in ways that are impossible to foresee: their precisification depends on who is it that does the precisifying."[46]

However, the unforeseeability of how context affects a term's interpretation has hardly anything to do with semantic vagueness. Surely, both terms are vague and can be precisified differently by different persons in different contexts. But before they can precisify them, they need to determine a context of application or precisification. This requires them to settle on a particular sense of "indecent" or "vehicle." The impossibility to foresee in which ways context affects the interpretation of these terms stems from their property of being context-sensitive—not from their property of allowing for borderline cases.

4.3.3 INDETERMINACY AND COOPERATION

In section 4.3.2, I surveyed arguments made for the value of vagueness. My hope to show that semantic vagueness has a positive function in communication has been curtailed. Many prima facie promising lines of argument could not be sustained. Some of these arguments indicated, however, that even though semantic vagueness might not have a positive function, other forms of linguistic indeterminacy do have one.

In section 4.3.1, I discussed seven assumptions explicitly and implicitly made by Lipman in his proof for the disutility of indeterminacy. In this section, I will scrutinize Assumption 5 that the interests of participants in a conversation must be aligned. Does linguistic indeterminacy in general threaten the Cooperative Principle and is thus without positive function in conversation?

As noted previously, indeterminacy itself seems to be a threat to cooperation because it directly violates the Maxim of Manner. It causes unclarity and thus hinders communication. Lipman's proof shows that indeterminacy is disadvantageous if interests are aligned. But does the Cooperative Principle really entail alignment of interests?

In fact, there is rarely full cooperation in either law or ordinary communication. As we saw in section 2.4.1, cooperative language behavior does not entail that our interests are perfectly aligned. It makes perfect sense to cooperate for some sort of linguistic behavior even if our common interests are only marginal. As Robyn Carston (2013, 17) points out, "the producer of language wants to get a certain message across to an audience and the audience wants to grasp that meaning." Nothing else is needed for the kind of cooperative behavior necessary for communication.

---

[46] See van Deemter (2010, 269).

Moreover, the conversational maxims are not guidelines for good communication. They can be flouted precisely to ensure it. Kent Bach (2005, 19) argues "Although Grice presented them in the form of guidelines for how to communicate successfully, I think they are better construed as presumptions about speaker's intentions." Thus, the Maxim of Manner can be seen as a presumption about what the audiences can rely on—which in turn can be exploited by the speaker. Unclarity appears to be inherently bad in argumentation and, in particular, in legal and philosophical argumentation.[47] But in most contexts, the Maxim of Manner is either a presumption of polite conduct or a means to make implicatures or other non-explicit and defeasible inferences. According to Frans H. van Eemeren and Rob Grootendorst (1992, 50), the Maxim of Manner "does not mean the speaker must be completely explicit but it does mean he must not make it impossible, or all but impossible, for the listener to arrive at the correct interpretation."

A minimal overlap of interests often suffices to ensure communication. We need a common goal, only enough to keep talking to each other—as, for example, diplomats trying to avoid war. And even in less antagonistic contexts, clarity is often not even expected. Consider, for instance, the following utterance by the former Chairman of the Federal Reserve, Alan Greenspan:

(E58) "If I seem unduly clear to you, you must have misunderstood what I said."[48]

Who would expect people in positions such as Alan Greenspan's to be perfectly clear? Whoever does can be criticized with good reasons for being naive. But even conversations between acquaintances, friends, and lovers are often based on small common ground, leaving room for disagreement over many questions. If two lovers try to make a date to go to the movies, their preferences about time, place, movie, or even the kind of relationship that they want to have may collide in the process of coordination. We successfully communicate all the time despite not so perfectly aligned interests.

Although legal communication is typically a form of strategic behavior, a surprisingly high degree of cooperation is maintained there, too.[49] Timothy A. O. Endicott (2014) even claims that the law is more cooperative than ordinary language because in the law there are established principles and roles that determine certain forms of behavior. The basic purpose of a verdict, for instance, is much clearer than the basic purpose of a casual conversation in the train. In fact, most ordinary conversations are characterized by diverging beliefs, interests, and purposes. There is an "unlimited plethora of purposes" in ordinary conversations,

---

[47] See Walton (1996, 34).

[48] Cited in Geraats (2007, 37).

[49] See section 2.4.1.

some of which are highly strategic.[50] We cooperate even when we are engaged in conversation for strategic purposes and with conflicting interests and beliefs.

Such conflicts preclude neither in law nor ordinary conversation the cooperation required to successfully cooperate in Grice's sense. It is such conflicting beliefs and interests on other questions that—as we will see in the next section—makes indeterminacy a useful tool for communication.

In general, if any of Lipman's seven assumptions is lifted, there is plenty of room for indeterminacy to be justifiably used in a framework of Gricean cooperative language behavior. In the remainder of this chapter, and in chapter 5, we will see a number of constructive arguments of how (and which forms of) indeterminacy can be strategically used.

4.4 Strategies of Indeterminacy

Section 4.3.3 made clear that strategic use of indeterminacy is not limited to clearly strategic communication. As we saw, the sense in which cooperation is required for successful communication is rather weak. In most conversations, even those in which there is no reason to act strategically or to doubt the participants' cooperativeness, interests are not perfectly aligned. In many other conversations, even when interests are perfectly aligned, there are differences in beliefs, expectations, or ideologies.

In this section, I will thus examine the role of indeterminacy in signaling games with diverging interests. We will show how each form of indeterminacy can become a useful communicative strategy if Assumption 5 of Lipman's proof is dropped. In chapter 5, I will investigate in detail how indeterminacy is strategically used in an environment (i.e., the law) in which the other assumptions are also lifted.

Let us start with a simple signaling game as defined in (D25) in section 4.1 with sender S and receiver R. S observes either state ω_1 or ω_2, based on which she sends the precise, unambiguous, and specific message m_1 or m_2 to R. Both states occur equally frequently, that is, with probability $\pi(\omega_1) = \pi(\omega_2) = 1/2$. R chooses action a_1, a_2, or a_3 based on the message received from S.

Imagine now that both S and R work in a company. S knows that an important deal will be either closed by a certain time or not. Let ω_1 be the state of the world in which the deal is not closed and ω_2 the one in which it is.

State	Interpretation	Probability
ω_1	Deal not closed	1/2
ω_2	Deal closed	1/2

[50] See Endicott (2014, 54).

R is supposed to schedule and organize a meeting to discuss the specifics of the deal. However, the meeting only makes sense if the deal is not closed yet. *R* can hold the meeting at the scheduled time, cancel it, or postpone it. Let a_1 be *R*'s action to hold the meeting, a_2 be his action to cancel it, and a_3 be his action to postpone it.

Action	Interpretation
a_1	Holding the meeting
a_2	Canceling the meeting
a_3	Postponing the meeting

What are the preferences of *S* and *R* for each action given the state of the world? When do they prefer the meeting to be held, canceled, or postponed? Consider the utility functions for *S* and *R* as depicted in Table 1.

The first number in each row represents the utility of *S*, and the second one represents the utility of *R*. The numbers themselves do not have any significance apart from ranking the agents' preferences. In state ω_1, for instance, *S* prefers *R* to choose action a_1 over a_2 or a_3.

In this game, interests are perfectly aligned. *S* prefers any action under the same circumstances and to the same degree as *R*. It is easy to see that there is only one Nash-equilibrium.[51] Only when *S* sends m_1 in ω_1 and m_2 in ω_2, while *R* chooses a_1 when receiving m_1 and a_2 when receiving m_2, does neither of them have any incentive to deviate from their strategy.[52] This means that *S* tells *R* that the deal is closed iff the deal in fact is closed, while *R* holds the meeting if it is not closed yet and cancels it if it is. The game in Table 1 is thus a classical coordination game.

It is also easy to see that this game is very similar to the one described by Lipman in section 4.3.1 and that it does, as Lipman's game, not allow for the strategic use of indeterminacy. Sending less determinate messages cannot result in better payoffs for either *S* or *R*. In the following sections, I will modify this example by introducing a conflict of interests. As a consequence, indeterminacy can be useful

---

[51] Nash-equilibria are combinations of strategies that are best responses to each other. Each agent chooses a strategy such that no other agent has an incentive to deviate from her chosen strategy. In other words, Nash-equilibria are combinations of stable strategies. Note that in this chapter, I will discuss only pure Nash-equilibria. In the examples used, mixed Nash-equilibria always realize weakly worse outcomes.

[52] Strictly speaking, there are two (pure) Nash-equilibria. The other equilibrium is when *S* sends m_2 in ω_1 and m_1 in ω_2, while *R* chooses a_1 when receiving m_2 and a_2 when receiving m_1. They are obviously equivalent, though.

TABLE 1

Signaling Game 1

$u(\omega,a)$	a_1	a_2	a_3
ω_1	3,3	0,0	2,2
ω_2	0,0	3,3	2,2

in the sense that it helps to realize a strictly better outcome (for both S and R) than any determinate strategy does.

4.4.1 STRATEGIES OF SEMANTIC VAGUENESS

So far, we saw many ways in which semantic vagueness is not useful. In particular, in section 4.3.2, I argued that most of the arguments for the utility of semantic vagueness are unsound. In this section, I will analyze a game theoretic model aiming to show the value of vagueness. Maybe I can show that semantic vagueness has a positive function at least under some limited circumstances.

In addition to dropping Lipman's Assumption 5, we need to alter his representation of vagueness. Lipman modeled vagueness as a mixed strategy. This introduces an element of randomness and thus might be said to capture the arbitrariness of application in borderline cases. There is, however, neither unclarity in the message itself nor cases (or states) in which the message unclearly applies. The element of randomness is solely on the level of strategy. The sender S sends message m with some element of randomness, but the message received by R is perfectly precise. We thus need to model vagueness in a different, more truthful, way.

The best game theoretic model so far proposed to represent vagueness is by the concept of *noise*. Competent language users can faultlessly disagree about the application of a vague term in a borderline case. Semantic vagueness may thus be seen as *noise* in m such that S and R understand m in some cases (sc. borderline cases) differently.[53]

As in the precise game before, imagine that S knows about the closing of the deal and R holds, cancels, or postpones the meeting. This time let us assume that the interests between S and R diverge in the way depicted in Table 2.

The outcomes for R are unchanged with respect to *Signaling Game 1*. As before, R likes the meeting to be held (a_1) when the deal is not closed yet (ω_1) and he likes it to be canceled (a_2) when it already is (ω_2). Moreover, R prefers postponing the meeting (a_3) in cases of doubt. In contrast, S now has a private agenda—she always

---

[53] We will use the concept of *noise* as developed, for example, by Matthews and Mirman (1983) and Carlsson and Dasgupta (1997). See Board et al. (2007) and Board and Blume (2013) for its application to vagueness.

TABLE 2

Signaling Game 2

$u(\omega, a)$	a_1	a_2	a_3
ω_1	3,3	1,0	0,2
ω_2	6,0	5,3	0,2

prefers the meeting to be held to its being canceled or postponed. While R (as before) benefits somewhat from postponing the meeting, S strictly opposes it now.

In this game, there are two Nash-equilibria. They are the combined strategies in which S either always sends m_1 or m_2, and R always chooses a_3. R cannot trust S since S does not communicate to R when ω_2 occurs but tries to provoke R into choosing the less useful a_1. As a consequence, communication breaks down, and R acts independently from the messages that S sends. If S can send only messages that precisely refer to either of the two states, S has no incentive to be truthful and R has no incentive to trust S. S's expected utility is $u_S^* = 0$, and R's expected utility is $u_R^* = 2$, which is the maximal expected utility that S and R can achieve by using determinate messages.

The situation changes, however, if we allow S to send a semantically vague message m such that in a borderline case, R either understands m differently than S or is unclear about what S means by m. We will thus assume that there is some probability that R reacts to m as if m means something else or as if m does not mean anything.

In game theoretical parlance, for any vague message m_i there is the probability $\mu(m_i|m_i)$ such that m_i is correctly understood as m_i and probability $\mu(m_j|m_i)$ such that m_i is understood as the different message m_j. Although S wants to signal the occurrence of state ω_i to R, there is the possibility that R understands S to signal the different state ω_j or is uncertain whether m_i refers to ω_i or ω_j. In other words, a semantically vague message m is *noisy*.

In effect, this means that how S understands a *noisy* message can come apart from how R understands it. Let us assume that R interprets m_1 half of the time correctly as m_1, sometimes mistakenly as m_2, and is the rest of the time uncertain about its content (interpreting it as m_Δ). Let us further assume that R interprets m_2 half of the time as m_2 but is the other half of the time uncertain about its content.

Now, when R receives m_1, he understands that the deal is not closed (ω_1), and when R receives m_2, he understands that the deal is closed (ω_2). When R receives m_Δ, however, he is uncertain whether ω_1 or ω_2 obtains. As a result, when S sends m_1, she knows that R will half of the time understand it correctly but sometimes misunderstand it or be left uncertain about its meaning. When S sends m_2, she knows that R will half of the time understand it correctly and half of the time be left uncertain about its meaning.

In this example, m_1 and m_2 are representative speech acts. The representative

(E59) "The deal is closed."

allows for borderline cases when the deal is closed. For instance, (E59) might considered to be not clearly untrue if the deal is orally agreed on, but not yet in writing. As such, the hearer remains ignorant about the exact nature of the state of the world when hearing (E59) applied to a borderline case.

The example can be modified to account for the other kinds of speech acts discussed in chapter 2. Directives such as

(E60) "Cancel the meeting!"

allow borderline cases for R to comply with S's command. For instance, R might think that (E60) requires him to cancel the meeting only half of the time because (E60) is semantically vague—allowing R to hold or postpone the meeting in borderline cases. In effect, R does not know what action is required or he is free to perform any action in certain (sc. borderline) cases.

Similarly, a commissive such as

(E61) "I support you if you cancel the meeting."

allows borderline cases for the meeting to be canceled. With respect to borderline cases, (E61) gives insufficient information on S's commitments. In effect, R does not know what S is committed to do.

In all three kinds of speech acts, semantic vagueness has the effect of leaving out information in certain cases. This effect is perfectly captured by the concept of *noise*. S might wish to withhold information because it would negatively affect her payoffs if R would know precisely about the real state of the world. The utility functions in Table 2 show that it would not suit the interests of S to fully inform R about ω. This is the reason why communication broke down before.

Now, however, due to semantic vagueness, S has no incentive anymore to be insincere. S sends the semantically vague message m_1 when observing state ω_1 and the semantically vague message m_2 when observing state ω_2. As a result, R can trust S and react to message m_1 with a_1 and m_2 with a_2 while choosing a_3 if uncertain (i.e., when observing m_Δ). The reason is that S and R's expected utilities roughly re-align due to the unclarity created by the semantic vagueness of message m.

In this model, we can show that both S and R's expected utility is strictly greater when using semantically vague messages than the respective utility in the best equilibrium with precise messages.[54] Thus, vague messages can be useful in cases

---

[54] A proof is given in Appendix A.1.

of conflicting interests. *S* states truthfully when the deal is closed, even though she does so vaguely. The vagueness allows *R* to trust *S* and hold the meeting when the deal is not closed, cancel it when the deal is closed, and postpone it when he is uncertain.

What does this example tell us about the possible use of semantic vagueness in real communication? Unfortunately, this is not at all clear. Similarly to Lipman's proof, we do not know whether we represent semantic vagueness with any degree of accuracy.

First, borderline cases behave differently than cases in which a message is misunderstood or not understood at all. As we noted in section 4.2, language users can knowingly disagree about the application of a vague term in borderline cases. Borderline cases are not just any unclear cases. They occur at the margin of a term's extension. While *noise* may represent some aspect of vagueness, it does not account for borderline cases as *particular* cases in which the term neither clearly applies nor clearly does not apply.

Second, and more importantly, differences in understanding can have different sources. There are other reasons why one might misunderstand a message than its semantic vagueness, as Kris de Jaegher and Robert van Rooij (2010) point out. They argue that the game theoretic concept of *noise* does not adequately capture the natural language phenomenon of vagueness because it is designed to model the very different phenomenon of garbling messages. In the original example by Joseph Farrell (1993), sending *noisy* messages is interpreted as sending unreliable carrier pigeons that sometimes fail to arrive. De Jaegher and van Rooij draw, as a consequence, a tentative comparison between *noise* and potentially misunderstood irony.

I agree with de Jaegher and van Rooij in their critique and that it is presumably easier to deliberately achieve *noise* by way of other forms of indeterminacy such as pragmatic indeterminacy. However, there is so far no better game theoretic model to represent semantic vagueness. *Noise* is, as I will argue in section 4.4.3, a more faithful model of semantic vagueness than de Jaegher and van Rooij's alternative concept of *imperfectly correlated equilibria*.

My discussion of the arguments for the value of semantic vagueness in section 4.3.2 indicated that language may be necessarily vague, but its vagueness is not necessarily a problem. There are no conclusive arguments, however, that vagueness has any additional positive value. Vagueness does neither effectively reduce cognitive costs, facilitate language change or learning, nor make communication more successful or efficient. At best, there might be some limited value in the uncertainty created by vagueness (as *noise*) when dealing with conflicting interests. In general, the possibility of borderline cases is a necessary evil to condone.

4.4.2 STRATEGIES OF CONVERSATIONAL VAGUENESS

Many supposedly strategic uses of semantic vagueness are in fact functions of the generality of vague terms. The utility of general messages has been shown for many contexts and purposes.[55]

Recall (E11) in which Kimberly does not specify her exact location in a conversation on the phone. Her utterance is indeterminate because it does not fully satisfy the Maxim of Relation:

(E11) PETER: "Where are you?"   KIMBERLY: "East Coast."

In semantic space, we represented generality as broadness in area. A general message is a message that can truthfully be sent in many different states in Ω. If all states referred to by the general message lead to the same outcome, no indeterminacy occurs because no conversational maxim is violated. A general message is only indeterminate if the receiver R is dependent on information about specific states that are not distinguished by it. In the following example, R is reliant on such information, allowing the sender S to strategically use generality as a source of conversational vagueness.

The representative speech act in (E11) does not distinguish between NYC, Miami, or Boston. Its conversational vagueness results in ignorance of facts. In contrast to semantic vagueness, which has a similar effect, S can exploit R's ignorance by means of generality in a more directed way because S can anticipate which events falling under the general term are not known to R.

Generality can be used to exploit such informational asymmetry not only in representatives but also directives and commissives. For example, the directive

(E62) "I will have the steak." (to the waiter)

does not distinguish between raw, medium, and well-done steaks. The waiter remains partially ignorant about the wish of the speaker or what she ought to do. And, similarly, the commissive

(E63) "Damages due to vehicles are excluded." (as part of an insurance contract)

does not distinguish between cars, trucks, and motorcycles. The insuree remains partially ignorant about the intentions of the insurer. He lacks relevant information on what exactly the insurer takes herself to be committed to.

Conversational vagueness in all three speech acts results in lack of relevant information. Let us return to the original example of representatives in which S and R plan a meeting. As before, R can choose between holding, canceling, and

---

[55] See, for instance, most influentially, Milgrom and Roberts (1982), Crawford and Sobel (1982), or Cho and Kreps (1987). See also my discussion of generality in the law in section 3.3.

postponing it. But S now observes one of three states—the deal is not closed, the deal is closed, or the Executive Board opposes the meeting. Each state occurs with the same probability, that is, $\pi(\omega_1) = \pi(\omega_2) = \pi(\omega_3) = 1/3$ (see following chart).

State	Interpretation	Probability
ω_1	Deal not closed	1/3
ω_2	Deal closed	1/3
ω_3	Executive Board opposes meeting	1/3

We use the utility function in Table 3 with the three states ω_1, ω_2, and ω_3 as well as the three actions a_1, a_2, and a_3.

TABLE 3
Signaling Game 3

$u(\omega, a)$	a_1	a_2	a_3
ω_1	3,3	6,2	2,2
ω_2	2,0	2,6	2,2
ω_3	0,0	0,0	2,2

In words, S prefers R to cancel the meeting iff the deal is not closed and is indifferent iff the deal is closed. R wants to hold the meeting iff the meeting is not closed and to cancel it iff it is closed. Both S and R want to postpone it iff the Executive Board opposes it. The conflict is about R's canceling the meeting or not.

In states ω_1 and ω_2, interests conflict because S prefers action a_2 in ω_1 while R will choose action a_3; and S prefers action a_3 in ω_2, while R will go for action a_2. As a consequence, R cannot trust S. As long as S can send specific messages only, there will be no effective communication. R will not believe messages sent by S in ω_1 and ω_2 because S does not report them truthfully.

This results in R always choosing a_3 since this maximizes his utility. The combined strategies where S sends any message m and R chooses a_3 independently from m are the only Nash-equilibria in this game with specific messages, yielding a maximal expected utility of $EU_S^* = EU_R^* = 2$. Thus, no matter what S tells R, R always postpones the meeting, which is clearly sub-optimal for both S and R.

Now consider the possibility in which S can send the general message that the Executive Board does not oppose the meeting, namely S can send the general message $m_{1\vee2}$, which unspecifically reports ω_1 and ω_2. The message effectively partitions the state space Ω by differentiating between the combined state $\omega_1 \cup \omega_2$, on one hand, and the single state ω_3, on the other, but not between the individual states ω_1 and ω_2. The expected utility of S and R is then maximized for a_2 if the "general" state $\omega_{1\cup2}$ persists.

In this way, generality facilitates credible communication. S sends $m_{1\vee2}$ in both ω_1 and ω_2 such that R performs a_2; and she sends m_3 in ω_3, such that R performs a_3. This is the only Nash-equilibrium in this game with general messages, and it is strictly greater than any Nash-equilibrium achievable for specific messages.[56] This shows that it can be advantageous for both S and R to not share some information.

It is important to remember that generality can but does not need to result in conversational vagueness. Generality is often deliberately employed without being conversationally vague. If S herself does not have knowledge specific enough to adequately inform R, she can resort to generality. If S does not know what sort of vehicle the car rental agency will provide, she will best resort to the general expression "vehicle" instead of risking saying something false. However, by doing so, S will typically not be conversationally vague or indeterminate in any other form but using the general expression determinately and in accordance with the purposes of the conversation.

In other cases such as the one discussed previously, conversational vagueness is in fact used for strategic purposes. When Peter asks Kimberly where she is, and she answers "East Coast," Kimberly's motivation is to avoid answering his question by being intentionally unspecific.[57] Similarly, as we saw in section 3.3, conversational vagueness is not only a problematic sideeffect of general norms, but can itself have an important function in law. Just as in natural language, it can—as we will see in chapter 5—be used (among other things) to facilitate compromise in legislation and to exploit informational asymmetry in contracting.

4.4.3 STRATEGIES OF AMBIGUITY

In chapter 1, I distinguished between lexical ambiguity, syntactic ambiguity, and polysemy. They are forms of ambiguity because they allow a message to be interpreted in one or another way. This effect can be intentionally exploited.

---

[56] Appendix A.2 contains a formal proof of this claim. A more general proof for the utility of generality is given by Crawford and Sobel (1982). They assume continuously many states of the world that S observes and continuously many actions from which R can select. The basic idea is that this continuous state space is partitioned by m, and the more coarse-grained the partition is, the more general m is. Crawford and Sobel show that the higher the degree of conflict between S and R, the more general m must be to still facilitate truthful communication.

[57] Another—very different—reason for being conversationally vague is social status and its signaling by means of language. For instance, according to Stenström et al. (2002, 88), "[i]n the teenage world it is cool to be [conversationally] vague, and it is cool to demonstrate that one cannot be bothered to be precise." Many utterances by teenagers are intentionally not clearly relevant to the purpose of the conversation or overly obscure or uninformative. They use conversational vagueness strategically to signal, for instance, "coolness."

One reason to strategically use ambiguity is when the speaker herself lacks the relevant information but does not want to admit it. A famous example for this use of ambiguity is the prophecy of the Oracle of Delphi that was consulted by Croesus before he attacked Persia. The Oracle's ambiguous message was the following:

(E64) "If you cross the river, a great empire will be destroyed."

Believing the prophecy favorable, Croesus attacked Persia. Unfortunately for him, it was his own empire, namely, Lydia, that was destroyed by the Persians. The expression "a great empire" can in the context of the utterance refer to either Persia or Lydia. Strategic ambiguity is used here to deal with the uncertainty and unforeseeability of the future.[58]

Similar to the representative in (E64), which allows for different interpretations of the ambiguous "a great empire," the directive

(E65) "You must not be swayed by mere sentiment, conjecture, sympathy, passion, prejudice, public opinion or public feeling."

allows for an interpretation that restricts the scope of "mere" to "sentiment" and a different one that extends it to include all elements of the list. The syntactic ambiguity of this jury instruction had the effect that the jury remained ignorant about what it ought to do.

Just as the commissive

(E66) "I will deliver 1,000 chickens."

allows the interpretation of "chicken" as referring only to young chickens suitable for broiling and frying or referring generally to any chicken.[59] Again, the polysemy of "chicken" has the effect that the hearer does not get the relevant information on what the speaker is committed to. Both speaker and hearer remain ignorant about their promissory obligations.

In general, an ambiguous message (whether a representation, directive, or commissive) is used in two or more different (sets of) states that are discontiguous. In contrast, unambiguous—even if conversationally or semantically vague—messages are used in a single (contiguous) set of states.[60]

---

[58] It is noteworthy that the Oracle's utterance is also conversationally vague. What is (literally) said is only borderline relevant to Croesus's request. Moreover, the utterance is ambiguous only on the level of what is implicated. Thus, strictly speaking, the utterance is pragmatically indeterminate with respect to its implicated content.

[59] We discussed both (E65) and (E66) in section 3.1.

[60] More precisely, the area of an unambiguous message in state space is convex, that is, each point between two points that are elements of the message's area is also an element of the message's area. In general, it is thus possible for an ambiguous message to be used in a single set of states, which is non-convex though, that is, there are points not in the set that lie between points within the set. Polysemous messages could adequately be represented in this way, for example.

I will incorporate this property of ambiguous messages in the example by differentiating between contexts in which messages are sent and in which S and R can disagree over the interpretation of a message, that is, where they can disagree to which state m refers or which action of R m requires. In particular, this will be modeled by *correlated equilibria*, which were introduced by Robert J. Aumann (1974) and applied to indeterminacy by de Jaegher (2003).[61]

Let us first consider a signaling game with unambiguous messages in which the actions that R can perform are the same as before, namely, R can either hold, cancel, or postpone the meeting. There are two states that can occur with the same frequency such that $\pi(\omega_1) = \pi(\omega_2) = 1/2$. Either the Supervisory Board approves of the meeting or the Executive Board approves of it (see the following chart).

State	Interpretation	Probability
ω_1	Supervisory Board approves of meeting	1/2
ω_2	Executive Board approves of meeting	1/2

The payoffs of both S and R depend on that state of the world and R's action according to the utility function given in Table 4.[62]

TABLE 4
Signaling Game 4

$u(\omega, a)$	a_1	a_2	a_3
ω_1	3,3	1,0	0,2
ω_2	1,0	0,3	$-1,2$

In words, both S and R want to hold the meeting (a_1) iff the Supervisory Board wants it, too (ω_1). However, if the Executive Board wants it to take place (ω_2), only S still wants to hold the meeting (a_1) while R would rather cancel it (a_2). Again, R prefers to postpone the meeting (a_3) if uncertain about whether the Supervisory or Executive Board want it to take place.

Evidently, there is no effective communication because S prefers R to choose action a_1 in every state, that is, S prefers R to hold the meeting under any circumstances. Because of that, R cannot trust S and will thus always choose action a_3. The best Nash-equilibrium for precise messages is the combined strategy in

---

[61] Even though de Jaegher (2003) aims to model semantic vagueness, it will become clear in the course of this section why it is a suitable model for context sensitivity—that is, for ambiguity or standard-relativity, but not for vagueness.

[62] The example is based on de Jaegher and van Rooij (2010).

which S either sends always m_1 or m_2 and R always performs a_3. For this case, S's utility is $u_S^* = -1/2$ and R's is $u_R^* = 2$.

Assume now that S can send an ambiguous message m_1 ("The Board supports the meeting."). It is ambiguous because it can be used to refer to the state that the Supervisory Board wants the meeting to take place (ω_1) or the state that the Executive Board wants it (ω_2). Let us assume that S can send either this ambiguous message or the unambiguous m_2 ("The Executive Board supports the meeting.").

We use the concept of *correlated equilibria* to incorporate the ambiguity of m_1 in the game. Assume that S sends and R receives m in a particular context c, which they perceive slightly differently. The context c_S that S perceives and the context c_R that R perceives are correlated, but not perfectly so.

Let us assume for reasons of simplicity that there are only two possible contexts for S and R, respectively, that is, S is either in context c_{S1} or c_{S2}, and R is in either c_{R1} or c_{R2}. Even though contexts c_{S1} and c_{R1} as well as contexts c_{S2} and c_{R2} do not always match, they give some clue about the other agent's perception. Accordingly, S sends message m depending on state ω and context c_S while R chooses action a depending on message m and context c_R. Ambiguous messages can thus be interpreted differently in different contexts.

The probabilities with which S and R can perceive both contexts as the same and with which they perceive them differently will vary depending on the situation. S and R might have different opinions about what the relevant aspects of context are or different knowledge about some relevant aspect and, as a result, interpret m differently. We might say that in some contexts, the Supervisory Board is more salient while in other contexts, it is the Executive Board.

Now, if contexts can be perceived differently, a better outcome for both S and R is possible. S may send the ambiguous m_1 ("The Board supports the meeting.") in some contexts of state ω_1 and some contexts of state ω_2. However, in some contexts of state ω_2 (in which she does not take the Executive Board to be salient enough), for example, she may send the unambiguous m_2. It is possible to show that there is a Nash-equilibrium such that S and R successfully communicate with ambiguous messages because neither of them has any incentive to deviate from their strategies. Indeed, we can show that the expected utility for both S and R in this Nash-equilibrium with ambiguous messages is greater than in the best equilibrium with unambiguous messages.[63] Thus, we can show in this model that ambiguity has a positive function.

De Jaegher and van Rooij (2010) try to use this model with *imperfectly correlated equilibria* to show that semantic vagueness has a positive function. They

---

[63] Appendix A.3 contains a formal proof of this claim. It is based on a proof by de Jaegher and van Rooij (2010).

presuppose that language users will interpret a semantically vague utterance differently in borderline cases. The existence of borderline cases—as supervaluationists such as Kit Fine (1975) or David Lewis (1986) argue—can be seen as some kind of hyper-ambiguity. After all, someone can say in a borderline situation of rain that it rains, while somebody else can say that it does not rain, and apparently nobody is mistaken. It thus appears that vague terms have indefinitely many meanings. They are hyper-ambiguous.

It is certainly correct that language users understand both ambiguous and semantically vague utterances differently based on the context. The difference between semantic vagueness and ambiguity lies in the nature of unclear cases, however. Whereas borderline cases occur at the margins of a term's extension and are hard to anticipate due to changes in context, unclear cases due to ambiguity can more easily be foreseen.

Moreover, indeterminacy due to ambiguity is usually in some way correctable.[64] Ambiguity (in particular, multi-dimensional polysemy) can reflect non-linguistic disagreement, for instance, about political ideology or legal theory. In contrast, borderline cases cannot be resolved. There are no (knowable) facts. Different applications in borderline cases do not represent anything. They merely result from a (moderate) mismatch between word and object.

De Jaegher and van Rooij assume that messages are vague in the sense that in different contexts, S and R can interpret a borderline case differently, that is, a borderline case for vague message m is a state ω if m is interpreted differently in c_S than in c_R. Even if we leave doubts about the nature of borderline cases aside, there are two problems with this characterization of semantic vagueness. First, semantic vagueness does not merely consist in the property of there being cases in which unclarity or disagreement reigns. Semantically vague terms are characterized by fuzziness in their application. As we saw in section 1.3.1, semantically vague terms do not only allow for borderline cases but also for borderline cases of borderline cases.

Second, and more importantly, borderline cases have not only the effect that people come to reach different conclusions about a term's applicability, but often even a single speaker is hesitant or undecided whether to apply the term. In other words, semantic vagueness does not only concern disagreement between language users but also uncertainty within a single language user. The general problem with de Jaegher and van Rooij's aim to capture semantic vagueness with this model is that borderline cases are not just cases in which different people understand a term differently. This feature alone does not differentiate semantic vagueness from other forms of indeterminacy. Strikingly, the defining feature of this model is that agents disagree about the context that they are in. But this is indeterminacy due to

---

[64] See Solan (1998, 116). See also Solum (2010b, 97–108).

context sensitivity (as ambiguity or standard-relativity), not semantic vagueness. De Jaegher and van Rooij's model can thus more fruitfully be used to show the strategic use of ambiguity and other forms of indeterminacy due to context sensitivity.

Before I turn to pragmatic indeterminacy in section 4.4.4, let us now look at differences between the forms of ambiguity. On one hand, lexically ambiguous expressions are basically never used strategically. Because of the unrelatedness of meaning, they rarely pose a problem since context can easily disambiguate them. As we saw in chapter 3, lexical ambiguity does not normally cause actual indeterminacy in the law—and for the same reasons, it does not in ordinary discourse either.

Syntactic ambiguity is, on the other hand, pervasive. Consider a politician who says

(E67) "I oppose taxes that hinder economic growth."

It is possible to interpret (E67) such that she generally opposes taxes because they hinder economic growth, but it is also possible to interpret (E67) such that she opposes only those taxes which she believes will hinder economic growth. The politician might hope that everyone will interpret (E67) in the most desirable way. As a result, the politician could rally support from opposite groups by pleasing them all.

However, the opposite is also possible. Everyone might interpret (E67) in the most undesirable way, leaving the politician without any support. It depends on the context and beliefs of the particular interpreter how (E67) is interpreted. But this can be anticipated. Thus, used carefully, syntactic ambiguity might well have the desired effects.

Polysemy is equally pervasive. It can be used strategically in many ways because utterances containing polysemous expressions leave (interesting) questions open to context. Laws containing polysemous expressions can be differently applied to many different cases—cases that might be anticipated by the lawmaker incorrectly or not at all. Context sensitivity allows the flexible and adapted application of laws—both in the form of polysemy and standard-relativity.

The term "rich" is both polysemous and standard-relative. Depending on the context, someone having 10.000 Euro on her bank account might be rich or not rich, or someone having an income of 100.000 Euro annually might be rich or not rich. One can leave open the standard by which someone will be measured to be rich, but it can also be left open which sense of wealth one is talking about. In both cases, its context sensitivity can be used to remain indeterminate between two (or more) possibilities.

In the next chapter, we will see how this form of indeterminacy fares in the legal domain, focusing on examples such as "reasonable," "deliberate," and "vehicle." The effects of syntactic ambiguity, polysemy, and standard-relativity are adequately represented in the model with *imperfectly correlated equilibria* mentioned earlier. In section 4.4.4, I will examine the strategic use of pragmatic indeterminacy and compare it with ambiguity.

4.4.4 STRATEGIES OF PRAGMATIC INDETERMINACY

Consider the case of criminal C who is stopped by police officer P for speeding. C can either try to bribe P or let P check C's papers and risk arrest. There are high stakes in both possibilities depending on whether P is honest or dishonest. If C does not bribe P, C will be arrested for and charged with his crimes. If C bribes P, and P is honest, C is arrested for and charged with both his crimes and the bribery. C goes free if and only if C bribes P and P is dishonest.[65] If the outcomes are weighed as in Table 5 and both possibilities are expected to be equally likely, neither (b) bribing P nor ($\neg b$) not bribing P is preferable.

TABLE 5

Bribery Game

$u(\omega, m)$	b	$\neg$b
Honest	−2	−1
Dishonest	0	−1

But now suppose that C can use indeterminate language. Let us assume that, on one side, the speech act performed by C can be interpreted by a dishonest P as a bribe, in which case C goes free. On the other side, an honest P will either not recognize it as a bribe or not be able to hold C to it, in which case C is only arrested for and charged with thievery. Table 6 shows that phrased in indeterminate language, the bribe is now strictly preferable since it gives an expected utility of $-1/2$.[66]

TABLE 6

Indeterminate Bribery Game

$u(\omega, m)$	ib	$\neg$b
Honest	−1	−1
Dishonest	0	−1

The form of indeterminacy effective here is clearly neither semantic nor conversational vagueness. Of course, there are many ways to offer a bribe. Stephen Pinker et al. (2008, 834) consider three variants. The most direct and determinate way to bribe is by means of a straightforward, if-then proposition like

---

[65] See Pinker et al. (2008) for a similar scenario. See also Parikh (1991) who first used game theory to model the use of implicatures.

[66] Even if there are only honest police officers, indeterminate bribing would still be weakly better than not bribing. However, this does not take into account that even an indeterminate bribe probably involves some risk of being held accountable for attempted bribery.

(E68) "If you let me go, I will give you $50."

Alternatively, one can be less direct and determinate by means of a leading question such as

(E69) "Is there some way to take care of it here?"

Finally, even less direct and determinate is a general remark as in

(E70) "I've learned my lesson; you don't have to worry about me doing this again."

Both (E69) and (E70) are potentially indeterminate because of the implicatures they carry. They are—in contrast to (E68)—indirect speech acts. Criminal C can always deny having tried to bribe the officer. The less direct the speech act is, the less certain the officer can be that bribery was attempted. C can exploit this speech act ambiguity to discriminate between honest and dishonest police officers.

Polysemy can be used for this end, too. In fact, the effects of polysemy and pragmatic indeterminacy are strikingly similar—the main difference being that polysemy is on the level of semantics while pragmatic indeterminacy is on the level of pragmatics. Both allow for two (or more) different interpretations of what is communicated, and these interpretations heavily depend on the determination of context. For this reason, the model in section 4.4.3 captures pragmatic indeterminacy just as well as ambiguity. Speaker S and receiver R rely on the context to reach an interpretation that potentially differs from the interpretation reached by the other. Both ambiguity and pragmatic indeterminacy can be used in the same way to facilitate successful communication in conflicts of interests.

Conversely, and analogously to the bribery example, many polysemous terms can be used to gain plausible deniability. Consider the following examples by van Deemter. He says that one is used to hearing

> consumer products being recommended for being "powerful" (when it's a vacuum cleaner or a car engine), "healthy'" (when it's food), "fast" (when it's a car or a phone), or "excellent value" (when it's pretty much anything), even though it would be very difficult to test such claims, because the words are essentially undefined. It is easy to see why such claims are left vague: if you claim that your product is better than some particular alternative, in some well-specified respect, you might be proved wrong, with potentially unpleasant consequences.[67]

What does van Deemter mean when he says that such terms are "essentially undefined?" It is hardly semantic vagueness that precludes comparison "in some well-specified respect." Van Deemter's own phrasing of the argument suggests that the value of such terms lies in their high degree of generality. They can be applied

---

[67] See van Deemter (2010, 6).

in a broad range of circumstances. Their true function, however, stems from context sensitivity, that is, either polysemy or pragmatic indeterminacy. The advertiser can always argue that she meant "powerful" relative to a standard or in a sense different from what some consumer might have thought. The term's generality merely increases the wiggling room created by its polysemy and standard-relativity.

Similarly, William P. Alston argues that a diplomat might say that her country does "strongly oppose" a certain action by the foreign government because of the vagueness of the term "strongly." Alston claims that it leaves the other country guessing and allows "choosing an alternative in the light of day-to-day changes of the situation."[68] It is evident that the possibility to choose different interpretations depending on the circumstances is not due to semantic vagueness. One can interpret "strongly" in different ways because it is polysemous and standard-relative. Depending on the standard for or sense of "strong," very different actions can be "strongly opposed."[69]

Both the diplomat and the advertiser are confronted with the same challenge as the criminal. The advertiser wants to maximize the sales of vacuum cleaners, cars, and phones while maintaining plausible deniability in case that an unsatisfied consumer sues for damages. The diplomat wants to signal opposition to a foreign government without closing any doors permanently. These cases exemplify what John L. Austin famously calls "taking refuge in vagueness."[70] He explicates that "the more precise you are, in general the more likely you are to be wrong, whereas you stand a good chance of not being wrong if you make it vague enough."[71] One can thus take "refuge in vagueness" also to avoid commitment. The less specifically an event is described, the less likely the description will turn out to be false.

Alston's example of the diplomat highlights yet another function of standard-relativity. It is not only valuable to gain plausible deniability in cases of uncertainty about other agents' interests and beliefs, but it can also be used to facilitate flexibility in cases of uncertainty about the future. I will discuss this use of standard-relativity at length in chapter 5 with respect to the law.[72]

---

[68] See Alston (1964, 86).

[69] Recall also the corrupt politician in (E15) from section 1.4.

[70] Note that Austin understands "vagueness" in its general sense, meaning *indeterminacy*. Of course, this can also be achieved by hedging or using general terms. See Brown and Levinson (1987, 117).

[71] See Austin and Warnock (1962, 126).

[72] Other uses of pragmatic indeterminacy, which I will not discuss, are cases in which indeterminate questions are used to provoke indeterminate answers, as Janney (2002) shows with respect to the famous case *People of the State of California vs. Orenthal James Simpson* (1994).

4.5 Comparison of the Strategies

In the previous sections, I argued that all forms of indeterminacy can facilitate successful communication when interests diverge by introducing unclarity. Unclarity comes in different flavors, however, as we saw in chapter 1. Different forms of indeterminacy, one would expect, have different functions and can be used for different ends.

Indeterminacy is due to its constitutive effect of unclarity also an epistemic phenomenon. It sometimes reduces the quantity of information but often changes the entire informational content. A merely general message decreases only the quantity of information, but most other forms of indeterminacy affect information in a more fundamental way. They result in uncertainty.

There are, in the immortal words of Donald Rumsfeld, two forms of unknowns, namely, the "known unknowns" and the "unknown unknowns."[73] As Frank H. Knight (1921) puts it, there is risk and uncertainty. When we know what we do not know, we can assess the risk and assign probabilities to different outcomes. When we do not know what we do not know, we can neither assess risk nor assign probabilities; we are uncertain.[74]

Linguistic indeterminacy is sometimes closer to risk (in the case of clear-cut polysemy) and sometimes closer to uncertainty (in the case of semantic vagueness). In cases of ambiguity, we usually know that there are different possibilities and even whether one interpretation is more likely than another. In contrast, as Michael E. McCloskey and Sam Glucksberg (1978) show, there is persistent disagreement between and inconsistent applications within language users when categorizing borderline cases. There is second-order uncertainty (we do not know that we do not know) in borderline cases, whereas we usually know that we do not know the meaning of an expression or some fact of the world. James A. Hampton et al. (2012) call this the *Rumsfeld Effect*. Thus, the unclarity caused by semantic vagueness is more like uncertainty, unforeseeability, or unawareness—and less like risk.

In cases of generality, it can go either way. As I will show in section 5.3.4 with respect to insurance contracts, generality can be used to exploit someone's unawareness of specific cases. Generality then results in uncertainty. However, if generality is merely used to cover different states, as in the example discussed in section 4.4.2, it only increases the risk experienced by the hearer since he knows which states are covered—remaining only ignorant about the states' individual probabilities.

---

[73] See Rumsfeld (2011, xiii).

[74] See also Lindley (2006).

This difference is important since people react differently to risk and uncertainty—which can be most clearly seen in Ellsberg's paradox. Daniel Ellsberg (1961) shows that people prefer to bet on the outcome of an urn with 50 black and 50 white balls to an urn with 100 total balls for which the number of black and white balls is unknown. This is striking because the probability is the same in both scenarios, namely, 50 %. Thus, other things being equal, people prefer known unknowns (risk) to unknown unknowns (uncertainty).[75]

This is one reason why not all forms of indeterminacy can be used strategically equally well. Other reasons are (1) the ease with which they can be recognized, (2) the level on which they manifest themselves, (3) the kind of cases that they affect, and (4) the difficulty with which they can be resolved. Semantic vagueness concerns borderline cases at the fringe. They result in uncertainty and are hard to predict due to other forms of indeterminacy that affect context. Polysemy and pragmatic indeterminacy often concern pivotal cases. They sometimes result in risk, but due to the frame problem can also cause uncertainty. The resulting unclarity can be on the semantic or the pragmatic level. Usually it is easier to recognize the existence of different semantically provable senses than different standards or other merely contextual features. If generality results in unclarity, it does so on the pragmatic level in form of conversational vagueness. The unclarity can be either risk or uncertainty depending on the awareness of what specific cases are covered by the general term.

A potential problem of the formal models that we used in this chapter and will continue to use in chapter 5 is that they do not properly capture the differences between the forms of indeterminacy. They abstract away from many (potentially relevant) details. However, they can nevertheless tell us something about the effects of some properties of some forms of indeterminacy. They can point us toward possible functions of indeterminacy—as Lipman's proof does.

The signaling games considered in section 4.4 share the assumptions made by Lipman that there are only two agents who have full knowledge about the game, context and background of utterance, their preferences, and the likelihood of all future events. The signaling games are instances of cheap talk because they are based on the assumption that messages are mere unverifiable information carriers that are costless to send and receive.

So far we dropped only one assumption. Once interests are not perfectly aligned anymore, determinacy and credibility become increasingly incompatible. The games show that communication can be perfectly efficient if messages are indeterminate. Under conflicts of interests, indeterminacy can be more efficient than determinacy. If we further weaken Lipman's assumptions, more ways to use

---

[75] This phenomenon is also misleadingly called "ambiguity aversion."

indeterminacy become apparent. The assumptions suggest that indeterminacy is potentially useful when

    (1) determinate messages are more costly than indeterminate ones.

    (2) agents are not fully informed about their possibilities and differ in their access to context and background of the utterance.

    (3) agents are not fully informed about their preferences.

    (4) some events are uncertain (due to unforeseeability or unawareness).

    (5) interests are not perfectly aligned.

    (6) there are more than two agents.

    (7) messages themselves (as speech acts) affect the outcome.

Lipman tentatively discusses options (1), (3), and (4). First, concerning option (1), indeterminacy might result from some form of bounded rationality. People learn, represent, remember, and process indeterminate information easier than more determinate information. We discussed this in section 4.3.2 on the value of semantic vagueness and will return to it in section 5.3.2 on incompleteness in contracts.

Second, concerning option (3), indeterminacy might simply reflect the agents' preferences. As Lipman (2009, 12) puts it, "it is not that people have a precise view of the world but communicate it vaguely; instead, they have a vague view of the world." Agents often do not precisely know what their preferences are and thus, cannot but send indeterminate messages. We hinted at this in section 4.3.2 in our discussion of the *Argument from Perception and Memory*.

Third, concerning option (4), indeterminacy might be useful under unforeseen contingencies.[76] It allows agents to wiggle out of some unwanted situation by gaining plausible deniability: "If agents fear that circumstances may arise that they currently cannot imagine, they may wish to avoid being too precise in order to avoid being trapped later."[77] We will discuss Austin's strategy of "taking refuge in vagueness" in section 5.1.3 on informational asymmetry in the law.

All forms of indeterminacy can be strategically used to facilitate communication when interests conflict, as we saw in the previous sections. It can be found, for instance, in the courtroom when intentionally withholding information as a witness or defendant without giving the impression of not being cooperative.[78] While the illocutionary effect of indeterminate utterances is risk and uncertainty, this is one of their perlocutionary functions. It concerns option 5.

---

[76] This is the case even if interests are perfectly aligned as long as there are different expectations about an uncertain future. See Lanius (2011).

[77] See Lipman (2009, 11–12).

[78] See section 3.4 on the role of PCIs in the law.

Based on Lipman's other assumptions, we will identify more such perlocutionary functions of indeterminacy in chapter 5. Besides facilitation of compromise, the most evident are cost reduction (re 1); power delegation and deferral (re 2 and 3); exploitation of asymmetrical information and incitement of compliance (re 4 and 5); and double-talk and plausible deniability (re 6 and 7).

In chapter 5, I will discuss these seven options with respect to the three legal performatives analyzed in section 2.2. In particular, I will discuss different kinds of costs that might be reduced by indeterminacy—such as drafting costs, litigation costs, social costs (saving face, plausible deniability), or renegotiation costs (sections 5.1.1, 5.1.4, 5.2.3, and 5.3.2). I will also discuss conflicting interests within S as an institution, such as a parliament or court, and between S and R (sections 5.1.1 and 5.2.1); informational asymmetry between S and R (sections 5.1.3 and 5.3.4), double-talk directed to different audiences (section 5.1.4), compliance by R (sections 5.1.4 and 5.3.3), and unforeseeability or unawareness (section 5.3.4). Throughout I will argue that indeterminate language can and is strategically and successfully used by lawmakers, judges, and contract drafters.

4.6 Summary

In this chapter, I used the tools of signaling games to examine the potential use of linguistic indeterminacy. There is a game theoretic proof by Barton L. Lipman that vagueness cannot in principle have a positive function if interests are aligned. We used this proof to identify conditions under which indeterminacy in general (if not semantic vagueness) can be strategically used.

Unfortunately, we could not show that semantic vagueness in particular has a value. On one hand, we found that most arguments for the value of semantic vagueness are unsound. On the other hand, even our best game theoretic model of vagueness only shows that some form of *noise* is beneficial under some conditions. Thus, while we could establish that most forms of linguistic indeterminacy have a positive function if there is a conflict of interests, there is still considerable doubt about any potential value of semantic vagueness.

On the positive side, we could clearly show the possibility to strategically use conversational vagueness, ambiguity, and pragmatic indeterminacy. We focused on how indeterminacy can be used to allow cooperation despite conflicts of interests. But by lifting more of Lipman's assumptions, we indicated also other ways in which indeterminacy is advantageous such as cost reduction, power delegation, deferral, exploitation of asymmetrical information, incitement of compliance and other desired behavior, double-talk, as well as plausible deniability. In chapter 5, I will analyze these ways to strategically use linguistic indeterminacy in the law.

5

Strategic Indeterminacy in the Law

Intentional indeterminacy is a common part of everyday communication. People use indeterminacy to avoid direct confrontation, mislead, or not commit themselves. We saw in chapter 4 that people can use conversational vagueness and ambiguity to facilitate communication when conflicting interests would otherwise preclude it. We also saw how people can use pragmatic indeterminacy to gain deniability in bribery attempts or advertisements. Products are ascribed "high quality" because what high quality is depends on contextually valued standards and weighings of the multiple dimensions of quality. Such advertisements are catchpenny because the standard-relativity of "high quality" effectively limits liability.

In this chapter, I will examine different strategies of indeterminacy in the law. Legal language has various features that make it particularly suited for the study of strategic indeterminacy. As we saw in chapter 2, legal utterances are typically (1) normative, (2) directed toward future events, (3) addressed to heterogeneous audiences, and (4) applied in a wide variety of circumstances.[1] As Andrei Marmor emphasizes, the language of the law is also typically strategic.[2]

Obviously, not all indeterminacy in legal texts is strategic in nature. A major reason for indeterminacy in law is poor drafting. Legal texts are, however, not poorly drafted only when their authors are incompetent or fail to spend sufficient resources. As we noted in section 1.3.3 on open texture, some indeterminacy cannot be avoided. It is, strictly speaking, impossible to make a completely determinate utterance. As Eugene Wambach (1894, 83) puts it with respect to the law:

---

[1] See section 2.1, in particular.

[2] See section 2.4.1 on the *Argument from Pragmatics*.

It is so difficult to word statutes clearly, that, even regarding a question that certainly was in the mind of the legislative body, the words of a statute are often so ambiguous as to require judicial interpretation or construction.

Particularly the law, which is directed toward social behavior in present and future, cannot be free from indeterminacy. The unavoidable polysemy, open texture, and pragmatic indeterminacy of natural languages will inevitably produce some hard cases.

I will investigate under what circumstances indeterminacy can be strategically used when a more determinate utterance is in principle available, however. Because this investigation cannot be comprehensive, I will focus on three cases that are especially noteworthy because of their legal features. First, I will analyze the strategic use of indeterminacy in laws (section 5.1). How do legislators use indeterminacy when drafting statutory bills? Do they primarily use it to facilitate compromise and resolve conflicts of interests? Do they use it to delegate power to other legal institutions? Or do they use it to positively guide people's behavior, as some have argued?

Second, I will analyze the strategic use of indeterminacy in verdicts (section 5.2). Do judges use indeterminacy to secure compliance when the issues involved are controversial? Do they use it to save face when they are likely to be overruled by higher courts or other political stakeholders?

Third, I will analyze the strategic use of indeterminacy in contracts (section 5.3). Do contracting parties use indeterminacy to save transaction costs? Do they use it to incentivize their co-contractors to outperform their contractual obligations? Or do they use it to mislead less-informed co-contractors about the content of the agreement?[3]

While investigating these functions of indeterminacy in the law, I will continuously ask the question: What is really doing the job here? What form of indeterminacy can actually be used as a means to, say, facilitate compromise?[4]

5.1 Delegating Power in Laws

According to Isaac Ehrlich and Richard A. Posner (1974), the potential value of indeterminacy in laws draws on a number of factors. The most important ones are (1) the costs of lawmaking, (2) the costs of law application, (3) the

---

[3] Besides laws, verdicts, and contracts, other interesting kinds of (strategic) legal utterances are constitutional provisions or agency regulations. For a discussion of (strategic) indeterminacy in constitutional provisions, see Moreso (1998). For a discussion of strategic indeterminacy in agency regulations, see Haubrich (1995) or Slocum (2010).

[4] See my discussion of this question in communication in general in section 4.4.

overinclusiveness and underinclusiveness of laws, and (4) compliance to the law.[5] The costs of lawmaking comprise the time and money required to agree on and draft laws. The costs of law application comprise the time and money required to use, enforce, and determine laws after their enactment. Overinclusiveness and underinclusiveness of laws concerns cases in which their linguistic content and intended legal content or assumed purpose come apart. Compliance concerns the rate at and degree to which those addressed by the law actually behave according to it. In this section, I will discuss the utility of indeterminacy with respect to these four basic factors in the light of the heterogeneity of the addressees of the law.

The legislature in a democracy typically consist of representatives pursuing different and potentially conflicting interests. Before a law can be enacted, an internal conversation is required to collectively agree on its content. This conversation takes place within the legislature between the individual representatives.[6] Its outcome, if successful, is a single speech act or message sent by the legislature as an institution.

The receiver of this speech act or message is an even less homogeneous group than the legislators. While the legislature more or less uniformly makes the law, there are two relevantly different communities at the receiving end.[7] First, citizens are those who use the law. The legislature aims to guide their behavior, and, in a properly functioning legal system, citizens also want their behavior to be guided by the law.[8] Second, courts and agencies are those who enforce, apply, and determine the law. Administration departments, police agencies, judges, and juries find facts and make decisions based on the law. Sometimes, this involves settling open questions.[9]

This heterogeneity of sender and receiver plays a crucial role for the utility of strategic indeterminacy. The variance within the legislature requires indeterminacy if, as I will argue, internal conflicts of interests cannot be solved or can only be solved at too high a price. Indeterminacy in laws is in general a delegation of power from the legislature to agencies and courts. The use of indeterminacy to resolve conflicts of interests and lower the costs of lawmaking is, as I will argue in section 5.1.1, the main reason for power delegation by indeterminacy. In particular, what has been called "incompletely theorized agreements" are best facilitated by multi-dimensionally polysemous and standard-relative terms.

---

[5] See also Diver (1983, 73–74).

[6] This internal conversation is, of course, heavily influenced by expert committees and other third parties such as lobbying groups. I will come back to this.

[7] See Bentham (1776, 430). See also our discussion of laws as legal performatives in section 2.2.1.

[8] This is, arguably, one of law's functions. Some have argued that the only function of law is to inform about legal consequences. See section 2.2.1 for a short discussion.

[9] Anderson (2006, 231) differentiates, in total, five different communities: those who make the law, those who use it, those who enforce it, those who apply it, and those who determine it. For our purposes, the tripartition is entirely sufficient.

The *Sherman* and *Clayton* acts, which I will analyze in section 5.1.2, are striking examples of how these forms of indeterminacy can be used to delegate power.

It is less clear whether indeterminacy is useful in dealing with the fact that laws are directed toward future events in a wide variety of possibly unforeseeable circumstances. Surely, legislators cannot always reliably anticipate the nature of such events. If they are to some degree ignorant about the probable consequences of legislation, they might be able to use indeterminacy to improve its aim. If, for instance, courts can access data unavailable to the legislature, it seems sensible to delegate questions that cannot be answered within the legislature to the better-informed judiciary—reducing the overinclusiveness and underinclusiveness of the law. It is true that if the costs of law application are lower than the costs of lawmaking, power delegation by indeterminacy is, ceteris paribus, advantageous. However, as I argue in section 5.1.3, even when courts are better informed, indeterminacy does not automatically reduce overinclusiveness and underinclusiveness and, hence, the costs of law application.

In section 5.1.4, I will examine whether indeterminacy can also be used as double-talk to strategically address different audiences to improve compliance, gain plausible deniability in cases of unpopular choice, and enhance the autonomy of individual citizens. And, finally, I will argue in section 5.1.5 that none of these functions of indeterminacy can reasonably be attributed to semantic vagueness, contrary to what most participants in the debate on vagueness in law suggest.

5.1.1 CONFLICT AND COMPROMISE

As noted previously, legislation consists of two different conversations. Let us first consider the internal conversation within the legislature. The legislature is typically composed of people with different, usually opposing, ethical and social beliefs and political interests.[10] There are numerous agents, often hundreds of members of parliament, who represent the diverging interests of a large population. They sometimes persistently disagree on ethical and social values and how to implement them. However, even the most antagonistic opponents share some beliefs and interests. We can call this common ground "overlapping consensus," following John Rawls (2005). The legislators might agree on particular changes to, say, abortion law, while still in deep disagreement about the nature of personhood.

---

[10] See, for instance, Jhering (1872) or Heck (1933), whose approaches to law are based on the conflict of interests. Note that internal conflicts can equally result from sincere and deep disagreements in beliefs as well as collisions of cold-blooded interests.

Even if a full consensus on the underlying philosophical questions is impossible, an overlapping consensus can often be reached.[11]

When beliefs and interests are irreconcilable, a law can still be enacted if based on an overlapping consensus by leaving some questions undecided. The result is what Cass Sunstein (1995) calls an "incompletely theorized agreement." Consider two parties in the legislature debating a controversial bill. Party A wants to enact a law l with legal content $p \wedge q$. Party B wants to enact a law with legal content $p \wedge \neg q$. There is no way to agree on the matter of q. However, another course of action is feasible:

- A wants to enact l intending it to communicate $p \wedge q$.
- B wants to enact l intending it to communicate $p \wedge \neg q$.
- A and B act collectively, intending their collective speech in enacting l^* to communicate p but remain undecided about q or $\neg q$.[12]

Assume that both A and B want to enact a law regulating abortion in the 1970s.[13] Both parties agree that some forms of abortion are to be penalized while others should be exempt from punishment. They disagree about voluntary abortion in the first three months. A wants to criminalize such early abortion by making q law. B wants to decriminalize it by making $\neg q$ law. Instead of failing to enact the law entirely, they let a modified law l^* pass, which is indeterminate as to whether early abortion is unlawful.[14]

Irrespective of the actual, perlocutionary, intentions of the legislators, the speaker (in this case, a collective entity) illocutionarily intends what her speech act is meant to communicate. A and B have illocutionary intentions about what the legal content of the enacted law should be.[15] If these intentions overlap, a partially indeterminate collective illocutionary intention can be formed. The agreement reached is incompletely theorized.

---

[11] An overlapping consensus is (at least with respect to justice) for Rawls (2005, 387–388) not just a tactical agreement for pragmatic ends but has moral value and justification in itself.

[12] See Marmor (2011b, 154), who developed a similar notion to Sunstein's incompletely theorized agreements, calling them "tacitly acknowledged incomplete decisions."

[13] Think of the political debate in the United States shortly after *Roe v. Wade*, 410 U.S. 113 (1973) or in Germany shortly after the Federal Constitutional Court's decision in 1975 (BVerfGE 39, 1) declaring the legal reform of §§ 218 to 220 StGB in 1974 to be unconstitutional.

[14] In Germany, this was the case for the modified indicator solution in 1976, which was a compromise between the liberal parties, favoring a general decriminalization of early abortion, and the conservative parties, favoring a general criminalization but allowing exceptions based on (medical and criminological) indicators. Today, after reforms in the 1990s, German abortion law with its extended indicator solution is largely uncontroversial.

[15] Rosen (2011, 133) calls them legal intentions. According to him, they are intentions "to bring about certain changes in the law by means of their pronouncements." See section 2.4.1.

Sometimes, the agreement reached is based on an overlapping consensus on many particular instances, but it is incomplete because it remains silent on the underlying principle to do so. For instance, *A* and *B* agree that it is wrong to kill a fetus in the later stages of pregnancy, but they disagree about the moral reasoning behind it. Sometimes, and presumably more frequently in the law, there is consensus on the underlying principle or general purpose of the law, while specific applications are contested:

> Such agreements are incompletely theorized in the sense that people who accept the principle need not agree on what it entails in particular cases. People know that murder is wrong, but they disagree about abortion. They favor racial equality, but they are divided on affirmative action. Hence there is a familiar phenomenon of a comfortable and even emphatic agreement on a general principle, accompanied by sharp disagreement about particular cases. (Sunstein, 1995, 1739)

This sort of incompletely theorized agreement is facilitated by general, polysemous, and standard-relative terms such as "serious risk" or "discrimination." The standard of seriousness that the risk must have to the physical health of the mother to allow abortion or the exact form of discrimination that the *Civil Rights Act* seeks to prevent depends on the interpreter's framing of context. The indeterminate terms allow the parties to reach incompletely theorized agreements because they may be disambiguated and specified after the enactment.[16]

By using indeterminacy, the legislature can enact statutes that would otherwise fall victim to the incongruity of interests. A collective decision can be made that would not be possible if all questions needed to be answered. In this way, indeterminacy secures majority support for otherwise unenactable statutes. Strategic indeterminacy may thus be considered an indispensable tool of conflict management.[17]

The use of incompletely theorized agreements has not always been viewed so favorably, however. Carl Schmitt (1993), for instance, saw in the Constitution of the Weimar Republic the result of a dangerous incompletely theorized agreement due to its large number of "dilatory formula compromises." Such compromises enable both parties to accommodate their interests in an indeterminate formula, putting off any real agreement. As a result, they generate confusion, Schmitt argues, since

---

[16] Sunstein also considers incompletely theorized agreements based on mid-level principles. The parties disagree both on the general principle and particular cases, but find common ground on a mid-level principle. This can in the same way be analyzed with respect to the potential value of indeterminacy, however.

[17] The strategic indeterminacy in diplomatic agreements is sometimes called "constructive ambiguity"—a term credited to Henry Kissinger.

the relevant illocutionary intentions are to leave crucial matters open.[18] According to Schmitt, dilatory formula compromises represent tactical victories to preserve private interests but hinder social welfare.[19] If so, they are rather different from Rawl's overlapping consensus.

While the Weimar Republic is certainly a negative example and possibly a case in which incompletely theorized agreement led to political failure, there is no necessary connection between incompletely theorized agreements and the confusion and deterioration of society or law. On the contrary, if there are irresolvable conflicts of interests between parties, incompletely theorized agreements can facilitate collective action when otherwise it would break down entirely.[20] The alternative would be paralysis or open conflict—both of which are less preferable than compromise. The crucial question is whether and how the matters left open by an incompletely theorized agreement can be resolved later on. But this is entirely contingent.

Other enterprises of incompletely theorized agreements did not turn out so bad—for example, the US Constitution.[21] Even though it was created in a time of tense conflict between states and federal government and the result of fierce negotiation and compromise, its indeterminate rules effectively guide conduct, albeit in a flexible way. Scott Soames explicates:

> The overly general content of the constitutional provision keeps the normative goal clearly in mind, while signaling to relevant actors that although care must be taken to adhere to the goal, the actions counted as doing so may not always be those that strictly conform to the literal content of the provision ..., but rather are, to a certain extent, up for negotiation. (Soames, 2011, 51)

The reason for the US Constitution's success lies for the most part in the subsequent political negotiations of its contents and implications. Moreover, a formal resolution of the underlying conflicts would not resolve the tension at the more fundamental level of social practices. A more determinate constitution would not only lose its legitimacy, as Thomas W. Merrill (2000, 979–980) argues. It would

---

[18] They are, according to Schmitt (2008, 84), "an external, semantic jumble of substantively irreconcilable matters" based on a formula "that satisfies all contradictory demands and leaves, in an ambiguous turn of phrase, the actual points of controversy undecided."

[19] Schmitt (2008, 87) explicitly claims: "If the Weimar Constitution contains nothing besides such dilatory compromises, ... its statutory provisions would only mean a tactical victory, which was achieved by some party coalition in a favorable moment in order to protect its partisan special interests against shifting parliamentary majorities." See also Günther (2006, 26–28).

[20] This can most plainly be seen in article 165 of the Weimar Constitution in which, according to Günther (2006, 82), incompletely theorized agreements (or dilatory formulas) were used to cover deep disagreements about the institutional organization of the Republic.

[21] The framers had, according to their own testimony, different understandings of the text. See Kesavan and Paulsen (2003, 1162).

also lay the conflicts open, while blocking further discussion. As Jeremy Waldron (1994, 539) puts it, "sometimes the point of a legal provision may be to start a discussion rather than to settle it."

But even if the conflict would be resolvable and the effects of indeterminacy entirely negative, the use of indeterminate terms might still have some value to the legislators. As Robert Batey (1998) argues, there is a balancing act between the need to pass a statute despite conflicting interests and the chilling effect of indeterminacy on protected or desirable conduct. Incompletely theorized agreements reduce decision costs because they shortcut protracted and potentially unending discussions on controversial issues. If the benefits of incompletely theorized agreements outweigh the drawbacks of law enforcement becoming arbitrary and fair notice being lost, indeterminacy is still strategically valuable.

Incompletely theorized agreements save time and energy also for a related reason. It requires cost-intensive drafting to phrase a law (or any legal text) such that it clearly applies to all relevant cases. Optimally, a law is specific enough without irrelevant details and precise enough without convoluted definitions; it is able to effectively guide behavior by adequately stating both matters of fact and legal consequences. It is expensive to achieve expedience. It requires well-trained lawyers, experts, and time. Thus, if another, more determinate, utterance is too costly, other things being equal, indeterminacy is the better strategy. This can be due to conflicts of interests within the legislature or high transaction costs.[22] As Ralf Poscher (2012, 132) says, indeterminacy allows us to postpone decisions. If luck has it, the postponed decisions may never have to be made because the controversial cases do not in fact arise.

But law cannot even in principle be fully determinate. The world is too complex to anticipate everything.[23] As Wambach (1894, 83–84) puts it,

> while it is conceivable that all questions which have heretofore arisen may be grasped by the legislative mind and may now be set at least by a carefully chosen language, it certainly is inconceivable that every question which has not yet arisen can be foreseen, and it is still more inconceivable that all unforeseen future questions can be provided for by the words of legislators who do not think of them.

---

[22] See section 5.3.2 for a detailed discussion of transaction costs. The notion of *costs* used here is the game theoretical, broad one, comprising all forms of information, decision, adjustment, and enforcement costs. It is questionable whether the legislature in fact cares much about monetary costs when drafting laws. What seems more important are the costs incurred by disagreement and time—in particular when there is political pressure to "get some bill passed," as we will see was the case in *Sherman*.

[23] The futility to foresee every case is nicely illustrated by Stumpff (2013), who compares the law to a fractal. See also section 5.3 on the incompleteness of contracts.

Some cases cannot be foreseen. Other cases could be foreseen in principle but are too difficult to foresee or controversial to determine ex ante the content of the law. Thomas Aquinas puts it in a nutshell:

> No man is so wise as to be able to take account of every single case, wherefore he is not able sufficiently to express in words all those things that are suitable for the end he has in view. And even if a lawgiver were able to take all the cases into consideration, he ought not to mention them all in order to avoid confusion: but should frame the law according to that which is of most common occurrence. (Aquinas, 1912, II-I, Q. 96, Art. 6, 1869)

The most probable and least controversial cases are those that legislators should aim for. For all other cases, there is still hope that they will eventually be decided ex post to their own benefit (or that of society).

Recall the two parties disagreeing on the law on abortion. Despite the impossibility to assert all its interests in the enactment of law l^*, party A might hope to realize its interests ex post in the expectation that courts will determine l^*'s legal content to A's advantage.[24] This is an additional incentive not to be completely clear about the illocutionary intention of the collective speech act. A wishes that her true intentions prevail and what is received by the audience is in fact message q. If the risk that the legal content determined by the courts be $\neg q$ is small, other things being equal, it is preferable for A to use indeterminate language.

This strategy is even more compelling if A is not a party or representative within the legislature. The internal conversation of the legislature is invariably influenced by third parties such as lobbying groups. If lobbyists pre-formulate statutory texts, under most circumstances they don't do so in the open. By using indeterminacy, they can further their goals without making their exertion of influence transparent. A highly professional lobbying group might even better anticipate future judicial decisions than the legislature. If it can, it is able to use indeterminacy to deceive the general public and the legislature by letting the courts decide ex post in its favor.

In section 5.1.2, I will consider two related cases in which strategic indeterminacy facilitated collective legal action. Both the desire to overcome the conflict of interests and the hope to change the legal content ex post were material to the deliberate use of indeterminacy in the US antitrust *Sherman* and *Clayton* acts.

5.1.2 AN EXAMPLE: SHERMAN AND CLAYTON

The *Sherman Act* of 1890 is a striking example of an incompletely theorized agreement due to conflicting interests. It was a landmark federal statute in US

---

[24] See Lovell (2010, 40), who claims that "[t]wo legislators with opposite policy preferences may cast the same 'yes' vote for legislation because each predicts that judges will make rulings favorable to his or her position."

antitrust law and formally aimed at breaking up large corporations for the benefit of consumers. In the words of Senator Orville Platt, however, Congress actually intended with *Sherman* only "to get some bill headed 'a bill to punish trusts' with which to go to the country."[25] As a result, its formulation was not as determinate as it might have been. Consider section 1 of *Sherman*, which states "Every contract, combination in the form of trust or otherwise, or conspiracy, in restraint of trade or commerce among the several States, or with foreign nations, is declared to be illegal."

Literally, this section outlaws any contract or firm. As Justice Louis D. Brandeis puts it in *Chicago Board of Trade v. United States*, "[e]very agreement concerning trade, every regulation of trade, restrains. To bind, to restrain, is of their very essence."[26] Since virtually nobody honestly believes that *Sherman* bans all firms and contracts, courts have found that a Rule of Reason be applied such that facts and circumstances of each particular case determine whether trade is restrained for the purposes of the Act. The effective indeterminacy in *Sherman* is thus pragmatic and concerns the scope of "restraint of trade."

While Antonin Scalia argues in *Business Electronics Corp. v. Sharp Electronics Corp.* that "restraint of trade" is a reference to the antitrust case-law prior to *Sherman*, for all ends and purposes, he draws the same conclusion as his predecessors:

> The term "restraint of trade" in the Sherman Act, like the term at common law before the statute was adopted, refers not to a particular list of agreements, but to a particular economic consequence, which may be produced by quite different sorts of agreements in varying times and circumstances.[27]

The indeterminacy in *Sherman* thus effectively delegated to the courts the task "to learn how businesses and markets work and formulate a set of rules that will make them work in socially efficient ways."[28] And, members of Congress and Senate anticipated this. Representative David B. Culbertson complained shortly before its enactment that "[j]ust what contracts, what combinations in the form of trusts, or what conspiracies will be in restraint of trade ... will not be known until the courts have construed and interpreted this provision."[29] Senator George Edmunds established that the *Sherman* bill "would leave it to the courts in the first instance to say how far they could carry it."[30] Reed Dickerson (1983,

---

[25] Cited in Thorelli (1954, 229).

[26] *Chicago Board of Trade v. United States*, 246 U.S. 231, 238 (1918).

[27] See *Business Electronics Corp. v. Sharp Electronics Corp.*, 485 U.S. 717 (1988).

[28] See Hovenkamp (1985, 52).

[29] Cited in Graber (1993, 53).

[30] Cited in Graber (1993, 52).

1144) concludes thus that "the legislature, through the devices of vagueness and generality, has consciously delegated to the courts authority to supplement substantively the statute."[31] What Dickerson calls "the devices of vagueness and generality" is, however, neither semantic vagueness nor generality.

Of course, the term "restraint of trade" is vague and general, but it also carries an impliciture.[32] As in Kent Bach's example (E27), which we discussed in section 1.5.4, some semantic information must be added to render the utterance plausible:

(E27) "You're not going to die." (by a mother to her son who cut himself with a knife)

While the mother communicates in (E27) that her son is not going to die *from a knife cut*, Congress communicated in *Sherman* that every contract in *unreasonable* restraint of trade be illegal. One could say that the impliciture pragmatically adds "unreasonable" to "restraint of trade."

Despite changing rationales, the Supreme Court has interpreted the Act in this way ever since. As Margaret H. Lemos (2015, 92) puts it, "the Supreme Court long has held that the operative question is whether the conduct at issue restrained trade *unreasonably*." What "unreasonable" means, however, depends strongly on the standard of reasonableness the court determines.[33] The indeterminacy effective in *Sherman* is thus the implicited standard-relativity of "unreasonable."

This will become even clearer when we look at the *Clayton Act* of 1914, which sought to preclude the application of antitrust legislation against organized labor.[34] Even though *Sherman* was aimed at large corporations, it ended up being frequently applied to labor organizations.[35] Over more than two decades and in several unsuccessful bills, the American Federation of Labor (AFL) tried to remedy this defect of *Sherman*. The result of this political campaign was the enactment of *Clayton*.

After promising to the AFL to provide relief for the unfavorable consequences of *Sherman*'s indeterminacy, T. Woodrow Wilson became President in 1912. The ensuing negotiations about the *Clayton Bill* between the AFL and Democrats were fierce. Wilson opposed a clear exemption for the activities of labor organizations because he did not want to rebuff business during the recession that began in 1913.[36]

---

[31] See also Rhodes et al. (1978).

[32] See section 1.5.1 for a discussion of impliciture indeterminacy in ordinary language and section 3.4 for a discussion of its role in the law.

[33] See our discussion of the standard-relative term "substantial" in section 3.2.2.

[34] See 15 USC §§ 12–38. and 29 USC §§ 52–53.

[35] See Frankfurter and Green (1930, 139–141).

[36] See Jones (1957) for a discussion of Wilson's stance in the negotiations.

Despite these conflicting interests, the House Judiciary Committee had to phrase the bill such that both Wilson and the AFL would be willing to endorse it. The first draft simply remained silent on the issue. Its section 6 said that

> nothing contained in the antitrust laws shall be construed to forbid the existence and operation of ... labor ... organizations ..., or to forbid or restrain individual members of such organizations ... from carrying out the legitimate objects thereof.

The AFL feared, however, that the courts would construe the section to exempt only the existence of labor organizations from antitrust legislation but not their activities. In effect, this would not have changed anything since their existence was never legally threatened. Eventually, Committee Chair Edwin Webb came up with a compromise. He added the following sentence: "Nor shall such organizations, or the members thereof, be held or construed to be illegal combinations or conspiracies in restraint of trade under the antitrust laws."

The such amended bill went to the Senate and was, with some minor changes, successfully enacted. The underlying disagreement, however, was immediately revealed by the very different interpretations given by the two parties. The AFL maintained that it fully exempted both labor unions and their activities from antitrust laws, while the members of Congress following Wilson claimed labor organizations' activities were not exempted if they restrained trade by departing from their legitimate objects.

Even before the bill went to the House floor, members of Congress were aware that it would leave the courts to decide this question. Representative Andrew Volstead, for instance, noted:

> Some of the friends of labor say that the amendment does exempt organized labor from the provisions of the Sherman antitrust law, but its enemies say that it does not exempt organized labor. Who knows? No man on the floor of this House. Who will determine? The Courts.[37]

Despite this, neither the AFL nor Congress wanted to phrase the bill in any more determinate language. This is particularly striking, since a more determinate alternative had been proposed by representative Robert Thomas. It said: "The provisions of the antitrust laws shall not apply to agricultural, labor, consumers, fraternal, or horticultural organizations, orders, or associations."[38]

The leaders of the AFL rejected this proposal out of fear that in this form, *Clayton* would not be enacted at all. Consequently, the bill passed as the *Clayton Act* with the following section 6:

---

[37] Cited from Lovell (2010, 118).
[38] Cited from Lovell (2010, 119).

> That the labor of a human being is not a commodity or article of commerce. Nothing contained in the antitrust laws shall be construed to forbid the existence and operation of labor ... organizations ..., or to forbid or restrain individual members of such organizations from lawfully carrying out the legitimate objects thereof; nor shall such organizations, or the members thereof, be held or construed to be illegal combinations or conspiracies in restraint of trade under the antitrust laws.

By the time of its enactment, *Clayton* was celebrated by AFL leaders as "the most important legislative victory ever achieved by the American labor movement."[39] And, at first, the rulings in lower courts seemed to confirm their assessment.[40] But in *Duplex v. Deering* (1921), the Supreme Court transformed the AFL's victory into total defeat.[41] It ruled that the antitrust provisions in *Sherman* fully applied to the activities of labor organizations. Justice Mahlon Pitney argued:

> There is nothing in the section to exempt such an organization or its members from accountability where it or they depart from its normal and legitimate objects, and engage in an actual combination or conspiracy in restraint of trade. And by no fair or permissible construction can it be taken as authorizing any activity otherwise unlawful.[42]

Because *Clayton* did neither define nor clarify in any other way the expressions "illegal," "legitimate," and "unlawful," the Court had to determine what would count as *illegal* or *unlawful restraint of trade* for the purposes of the act. It came to the conclusion that its section 6 mandates judges "to continue to apply the widely known (and widely resented) judge-made standards that judges had developed prior to passage of the Clayton Act."[43]

Both *Sherman* and *Clayton* draw on the question of what (unreasonable, unlawful, illegitimate, or illegal) restraint of trade is. *Clayton* made the impliciture in *Sherman* explicit, but preserved the standard-relativity of its content. Consequently, even after *Clayton*, the courts had broad discretion in determining what "restraint of trade" meant for the purposes of the acts.[44]

This power delegation and even the specific ruling in *Duplex* (1921) were neither unforeseen nor unexpected. Members of Congress anticipated this and other

---

[39] See Lovell (2010, 99).

[40] See *Duplex Printing. Press Co. v. Deering*, 247 F. 192 (1917); and *Duplex Printing. Press Co. v. Deering*, 253 Fed 722 (1918).

[41] *Duplex Printing Press Co. v. Deering*, 254 U.S. 443 (1921).

[42] See *Duplex Printing Press Co. v. Deering*, 254 U.S. 443, 496 (1921).

[43] See Lovell (2010, 105).

[44] See *Apex Hosiery Co. v. Leader*, 310 U.S. 469, 492–493 (1940).

interpretive questions that later arose. They understood that the language of the act would grant judges discretion to decide substantive questions of policy.[45] The AFL, too, was aware that the Supreme Court could and possibly would decide against their interests.

There was simply no majority in Congress to produce more determinate legislation. The conflict of interests within the legislature and between the different political groups was hence resolved by delegating contested issues to the courts. The legislative process and the debates in Congress suggest that the courts made choices that the legislature could not or did not want to make at the time of enactment.[46]

In summary, the effective form of indeterminacy in *Sherman* and *Clayton* is standard-relativity. Its strategic use in both acts is evident because (a) legislators were aware of the indeterminacy, (b) they associated it with the future role of the courts, and (c) they rejected alternative legislative proposals that offered to clarify the language and limit the discretion of the courts.[47] The legislators used indeterminacy (1) to cover the conflict of interests between them and (2) in the hope that the courts would interpret the acts ex post in their favor, respectively.

In section 5.1.3, I will consider a third reason to delegate power by indeterminacy. The legislators can use indeterminacy (3) if courts or agencies are in a better position to determine the content of the law. Thus, we shift our focus from the legislature to the addressee of law enactments.

5.1.3 INFORMATIONAL ASYMMETRY

As Timothy A. O. Endicott (2011b) claims, both precise and semantically vague norms bring with them forms of arbitrariness. A precise norm facilitates predictability of result, uniformity of treatment, and limitation of discretion.[48] But its precision establishes a measure that cannot perfectly commensurate with the (assumed) purpose of the rule. Some legal decisions based on precise norms are arbitrary because they lead to injustice or absurdity. Manfred Pinkal (1995, 154) calls this the "problem of intuitively untenable overprecisification." Some cases are within the scope of the norm when they should not be and some are not when they should. A precise speed limit, for instance, will prohibit some instances of perfectly safe driving while allowing some instances of unreasonably dangerous speeding. Such false negatives and false positives exist due to the complexity

---

[45] See Lovell (2010, 160).

[46] See Lovell (2010, 154–155).

[47] See Lovell (2010, 41) for this claim with respect to *Clayton*.

[48] According to Schauer (2009, 36–60), this is primarily achieved by the classical rule-based legal decision-making approach and stare decisis.

and unforeseeability of the world. They induce what Posner (1973) calls "error costs."

If we wanted to avoid (or at least reduce) them, we would need judges having discretion to overturn the legal norm by interpreting it *contra legem*, that is, by revising it on the basis of something other than the norm itself (as moral or economic considerations). Such discretion would bring with it the same form of arbitrariness that is generated by semantic vagueness, however. A semantically vague norm leaves its application in borderline cases to the judgment of individual persons. This can enhance conformity with the purpose of the norm, but it carries again the danger of arbitrariness. Here, the legal decision is arbitrary in the sense that it may be unjust or absurd due to the capriciousness of a single person. There might be no rule at all, but mere chance, or, even worse, prejudice and discrimination. John F. Decker (2002, 243) complains:

> Vagueness is a concept that appears heavily dependent on the "I know it when I see it" test, where one begins with a conclusion and thereafter works backward for rational support. Vagueness challenges require a highly subjective mode of analysis that involves an unpredictable assortment of paths a court might take in arriving at a ruling.

Semantic vagueness, and indeterminacy in general, lead to discretion on part of the audience. In borderline cases, the audience is free to figure out for themselves what to do. There is no (knowable) fact of the matter. The legislature, by enacting a semantically vague law, effectively grants discretion to decide borderline cases and thus delegates power to some other institution.[49] Hans Kelsen (1934, 105) argues that indeterminacy is the lawmaker's delegation of certain questions to those who use and apply the law, whether this is the purpose for which an indeterminate law is enacted or not. An indeterminate law thus provides limits in which law application is possible.[50]

The power delegation in *Sherman* and *Clayton* resulted from the incapability of the legislature to agree upon a more complete set of decisions. The use of incompletely theorized agreements in such cases is either a practical necessity or at best a short-term advantage since the decision is, as Schmitt (2008) emphasizes, merely delayed. Such delegation may not always be fully intended since it stems from the legislators' inability to agree on a more complete decision. *Sherman* and *Clayton* show how this use of indeterminacy can backfire—at least for the AFL. Arguably, the strategy worked rather smoothly for Wilson and the Democrats.

---

[49] See Lemos (2008) or Leib and Serota (2010).

[50] See Kelsen (1934, 94).

In other cases, however, power delegation results from the fact that the case at hand was not and maybe could not have been foreseen.[51] As Supreme Court Justice Benjamin N. Cardozo famously put it "the ideal [legal] system ... would be a code at once so flexible and so minute, as to supply in advance for every conceivable situation the just and fitting rule. But life is too complex."[52] Due to the unforeseeability of events and excessive costs to specify all contingencies, it is neither possible nor advisable to try to anticipate and resolve all questions of implementation in advance.[53] From an economic point of view, the indeterminate law's utility both in cases of conflict resolution and unforeseeability depends on the ratio between the legislative costs ex ante and expected costs after legislation. Indeterminacy is useful if the expected costs are lower or have to be paid by someone else.[54] If we assume that the interests within the legislature were perfectly aligned, under what circumstances does it still make sense to use indeterminate language and delegate power to other decision-makers?

The traditional suggestion is that there is sometimes a need to leave technical questions to experts in agencies or courts.[55] More generally, one can say that agencies and courts have an informational advantage over legislators on some issues. On one hand, the necessary information is directly available to them while the legislature has to make laws in the light of a not completely foreseeable future.[56] On the other hand, agencies and courts arguably have expert knowledge about the implementation of certain laws or in certain areas of the law. Consider the professional environment of the police. Discretion and individual judgment is needed to focus on crimes that can be fought.[57] Even though discrimination based on gender or race is a serious problem, discretion in law enforcement is essential for

---

[51] See Kelsen (1934, 105). It seems to be the primary reason to delegate power that is assumed by the political economy literature on legislative delegation. See Epstein and O'Halloran (1999) or Huber and Shipan (2002).

[52] See Cardozo (1921, 143).

[53] See Posner (1983, 812). See also Maurer (2011, §7, note 14), who says that discretion and indeterminate legal terms exist due to unforeseeability. Consider common law terms such as "reasonable person," "good faith and fair dealing," or "serious carelessness"; and indeterminate legal terms such as "*wichtiger Grund*" in § 314 BGB, "*angemessener Betrag*" in § 343 BGB, "*berechtigtes Interesse*" in § 573 BGB, or "*angemessene Frist*" in § 281 BGB. Due to their polysemy and impliciture indeterminacy, they can be used in contexts in which it is difficult or even futile to specify the facts of the case or the legal consequences in any detail.

[54] This depends, of course, on what we assume costs to include. There are variables such as time, money, and reputation, but also clearly incommensurable factors such as the level of overinclusiveness and underinclusiveness of and compliance to the law. See section 5.3.2. Recall also note 22 previously.

[55] This has been classically proposed by Landis (1938). For a modern game theoretic analysis, see Spence and Cross (2000) for agencies and Rogers (2001) for courts.

[56] See Rogers (2001), who analyzes power delegation based on uncertainty of matters of fact and judicial attitudes.

[57] See LaFrance (2011).

a functioning legal system. Minor crimes are often not worth pursuing. It is usually ineffective, for instance, to prosecute small time drug dealers, even though they commit crimes on a daily basis, because the true problem are the organizers and backers of their crimes; and, usually in a matter of days, imprisoned drug dealers are replaced by new ones. Due to their practical experience and expert knowledge, the police know arguably best if, when, and how to strike against such crimes. Police agencies are thus in a better position than the legislature to find out what crimes are worth pursuing.[58]

While it makes sense to delegate the task of answering specific and technical questions to an agency such as the police, part of whose function it is to answer such questions, it is not quite so clear why courts should be able to decide them better than the legislature.[59] Endicott (2011b, 26) argues that power delegation to judges is justifiable because (1) they have special expertise to develop the law, (2) they can develop the law incrementally and revise general rules that turn out to be damaging in particular unforeseen cases, and (3) the law's effectiveness depends on the judicial process of hearing both sides of an argument.

Endicott does not say anything about the kind of special expertise that courts might have. James R. Rogers (2001) argues, however, that generally courts have special expertise in finding facts. Due to the informational access to the specifics of the cases at hand, they can decide them individually on the basis of equity. This informational advantage depends also on conditions (2) and (3) just mentioned. If courts can approach each case on its own and develop the law case by case, informational access is increased—just as it is if all participants in a case can be heard. Moreover, courts might have special expertise when the new law draws upon already established common law. Arguably, this was also the case for *Sherman* and *Clayton*.

Unfortunately, it is not entirely clear whether power delegation in these acts is justified all things considered. As Lemos (2015, 99) claims, "courts may seem like better delegates when the job consists of building on a body of law that courts themselves constructed." But it really comes down to the question of whether they indeed can achieve socially and politically better results than Congress could and whether these better results can justify the use of indeterminacy. Power delegation to agencies and courts appears to be sensible when they can decide some questions better than the legislature because of either special expertise or direct acquaintance with the actual facts of the case.

---

[58] Another reason is, arguably, the enforcement of crimes that threaten important legal rights. Ideological crimes (such as terrorist attacks) are usually persecuted with more effort and public attention than crimes of passion.

[59] See Epstein and O'Halloran (1998) for a discussion of the expertise agencies have and Congress lacks.

However, these gains are easily outbalanced if they do worse in other matters. Poor judgment, mistakes, and bias are basic problems. But the inherent lack of control makes abuse and discrimination incessant menaces. While legislators must fear not to be re-elected, police officers and judges rarely face the consequences of their professional decisions. They sometimes have incentives to arrest or convict someone who is not clearly or even clearly not a criminal to advance their careers.

Concentrated power in the hands of agencies and courts constitutes itself a problem because, in contrast to legislators, they are neither democratically legitimated nor democratically controlled. Legislators thus have reason to shy away from indeterminacy because of its threat to the separation of powers and the *rule of law*. If the legislators value these principles, they might refrain from delegating power by indeterminacy even when agencies and courts could make the socially and politically better decision. Thus, it is by no means clear that indeterminacy in laws is useful for reasons of better decision-making abilities in agencies and courts—all things considered.

But suppose that it is: why does the legislature not grant discretion to agencies and courts explicitly? It could do so, for instance, by using "can" clauses, and this could lessen the problems of abuse and discrimination because the discretion granted is made transparent and revisable.

There are several reasons to prefer indeterminacy, however. On one hand, explicit discretion is in many legal systems almost exclusively limited to the determination of legal consequences. If the legislature wants to grant discretion to courts with respect to the determination of matters of fact because, for instance, it has insufficient knowledge about their precise nature, this can only be done by linguistic indeterminacy.[60]

On the other hand, an indeterminate utterance is often indeterminate on multiple orders.[61] This is an advantage, in particular, when the delegation of power itself must not be obvious. George I. Lovell (2010, 40) points out: "The circumstances that make it likely that legislators will create deliberate ambiguity also make it likely that legislators will deceptively advertise such statutes as ones that make clear choices." If an utterance is indeterminate, there is often not only disagreement about its content but also whether it in fact is indeterminate. Since discretion and

---

[60] For instance, German agencies can be granted explicit discretion with respect to the determination of legal consequences ("*Ermessensspielraum*"). See Held-Daab (1996). In contrast, discretion granted to agencies with respect to the determination of matters of fact ("Beurteilungsspielraum") can only result from indeterminacy. According to German legal theory, only the existence of *indeterminate legal terms* allows the use of *Beurteilungsspielraum*. See Koch (1979). See also Herdegen (1991) for a comparison between *Ermessensspielraum* and *Beurteilungsspielraum*.

[61] Due to the uncertainty on different levels, Vermeule (2006) calls legislative power delegation the "delegation lottery."

power delegation are potentially problematic due to *rule of law* and separation of powers concerns, legislators will typically balk at open delegation of power. If the desired delegation of power would not be viewed favorably by stakeholders or the general public, as in *Sherman* or *Clayton*, indeterminacy is preferable to explicitly granting discretion. A related reason concerns the expectation to realize one's interests ex post. This is—or at least can seem—much more likely if the indeterminacy of the text is responsible for the discretion and, at the same time, suggestive of one or the other outcome.

In summary, by using indeterminacy to delegate power to other parties, legislators can at least gain short-term relief. Sometimes, they cannot agree among themselves and hope to realize their interests ex post through the courts. This can be called "symbolic legislation" because it does not resolve the underlying conflict and delays its real resolution. Sometimes, difficult decisions are not made because it would be inefficient to do so. This is the case when decision costs are disproportionally high in cases in which the likelihood that problematic cases arise is negligible or the conflict is truly irreconcilable, or when other parties can make them with less difficulty due to special expertise or better decision-making abilities.

5.1.4 DOUBLE-TALK AND COMPLIANCE

The legislature can also delegate unpopular choices by indeterminacy. The use of indeterminate language deflects potential blame from legislators, as they can afterward claim that the controversial decision was made by someone else. Agencies and courts can thus help to shield legislators from the electoral consequences of their decisions.[62] Besides (1) formal conflict resolution, (2) the expectation to change legal content *ex post* in one's favor, and (3) informational asymmetry, this is a fourth possible advantage of power delegation by indeterminacy. By delegating to agencies and courts, (4) legislators can gain plausible deniability. I will investigate this function of indeterminacy in section 5.2 at full length with respect to adjudication.

In this section, I will first examine the strategy to use indeterminacy (5) to improve compliance by addressing different audiences with different messages. Such double-talk also deflects blame but in a different way. All too often, compliance by those who execute or enforce the law is more important than compliance by those directly addressed by it. We will critically discuss, then, (6) the role of indeterminacy in citizens' overcomplying with the law; and, finally, (7) its utility to enhance their autonomy.

---

[62] See Hirschl (2000) discussing this form of power delegation to courts and Aranson et al. (1982) to agencies.

Legislators are also politicians trying to win the next election. They can try to promote their re-election by pleasing opposing audiences by means of double-talk. Recall the case in which a law is enacted to regulate abortion in the United States in the 1970s. Assume that this time there is no conflict of interests within the legislature and that law l^* literally says that abortion is permitted if there is a serious risk to the mother's life. Assume further that this implicates that abortion is prohibited if there is no such risk. If there is no extra-textual clarification, the legal content of l^* is indeterminate since what is said and what is implicated are relevantly different. At least for certain regions in the United States, one can assume that radical opponents to abortion will care more about the political message, while abortionists will be more concerned with its legal content.

If the law is interpreted by the courts such that what is said becomes the law, and news and political discussions revolve around what is implicated, both opponents and abortionists will hear what they want to hear and re-elect the governing party.[63] As a result, the legislature implicates that politics is taking abortion seriously, but it makes only a very limited number of abortions actually illegal. The implicature indeterminacy causes the legal and political message to come apart and allows the courts to specify and determine the legal content ex post.

In *Clayton*, something very similar happened as a matter of fact. Recall the first sentence of section 6, which says

"That the labor of a human being is not a commodity or article of commerce."

When the Senate introduced this sentence, AFL President Samuel Gompers was thrilled by its political message. He saw its words as "sledge-hammer blows to the wrongs and injustice so long inflicted upon the workers."[64] AFL leaders and other skeptics took this sentence to implicate that the act would exempt also the activities of labor organizations. This implicature indeterminacy finally made (at least in part) the enactment of *Clayton* possible. Gompers and some Senators hoped that the sentence's introduction would exert moral pressure on the courts to adopt a pro-labor interpretation. However, it never did enter any judicial opinion and had no legal effect at all.

Double talk might potentially be used in another, maybe more noble, way. According to Meir Dan-Cohen (1983), double-talk can enable legislators to guide action more efficiently. Recall that the illocutionary function of most law enactments is directive, and there are two basic kinds of legal directives. Dan-Cohen calls them conduct and decision rules. The former aim at guiding the

---

[63] This inference is supported by what Korobkin (2000, 46) calls the "self-serving bias," which has the effect that indeterminacy tends to be interpreted in favor of the interpreter. The stronger the bias, the more trustworthy the speaker is.

[64] Cited in Lovell (2010, 122).

conduct of the general public while the latter direct authorities in their application of the former.[65]

Consider the defense of duress. If a crime is committed under threat, the law wants to exculpate the defendant because she was unlawfully coerced by a third party. At the same time, the law does not want to prompt citizens to lightly commit crimes simply because they feel pressured. For instance, being tailgated in traffic can constitute duress for the purposes of the German § 240 StGB, but it should not be taken as an excuse for speeding. A similar, but slightly more serious, example is blackmail, which should not be considered carte blanche to commit crimes oneself. The problem is that when duress is known to be granted, citizens will easily succumb to threats that they should and could have resisted; or, worse, they will try to deceive the law by pretending to be pressured.

Is it possible to exculpate victims of duress without giving such undesirable incentives? According to Dan-Cohen (1983, 639–645), the solution might be indeterminacy. By way of double-talk, the law can maintain deterrence such that people do not commit crimes out of weakness or fear while exempting those from punishment who do so under actual duress. Indeterminacy thus effectively separates decision and conduct rules.[66] The polysemous and standard-relative terms "danger" and " threat of an appreciable harm" in § 240(1) StGB might cause the judiciary to enforce the more lenient decision rule by interpreting it broadly—exonerating those under duress.[67] At the same time, interpreted narrowly by the citizens, the conduct rule incentivizes them to withstand all threats but the most serious. The result is that fewer people commit crimes since there seems to be no way to avoid punishment.

Even though this strategy seems to work in principle, it is much more limited than Dan-Cohen suggests. For once, there is no guarantee that judges would in fact understand the indeterminacy of "duress" as a deliberate strategy of the legislature. Judges might have a hard time to differentiate conduct and decision rules if they are separated by indeterminacy. As a matter of fact, judges frequently complained about the "open-ended nature" of duress.[68] Thus, it can always turn out that judges do not or cannot play along.

But even if they do, will people really continue to believe that they will be punished when courts consistently exonerate actual defendants? Maybe the strategy

---

[65] See section 2.2.1 on a discussion of laws as addressing two audiences with two sets of rules.

[66] Dan-Cohen (1983) calls this phenomenon "selective transmission."

[67] § 240(1) StGB reads: Whoever unlawfully with force or threat of an appreciable harm compels a human being to commit, acquiesce in or omit an act, shall be punished with imprisonment for not more than three years or a fine.

[68] See, for instance, *State v. Toscano*, 74 N.J. 421 (1977).

works for a while, but after a number of cases in which defendants were exculpated, it must be publicly known that duress will be granted in certain cases, must it not?

Interestingly, this is not quite so clear. Indeterminacy makes it less likely that citizens can rely on the law with confidence, and this is even the case if indeterminacy causes a great deal of case law, making it incrementally less indeterminate. The reason is that the case law's sheer volume and complexity precludes the ordinary citizen's access to the content of the law. The law creates another kind of double-talk due to the distinction between ordinary and legal language—quite unrelated to indeterminacy.[69]

However, as Richard Singer (1986, 85) points out, in a democratic system such as the United States, publication of opinions is prevalent; and there is no strict separation between officials, knowing the decision rules, and the general public, knowing the conduct rules. Hence, in one way or another, it will be known to the general public that duress is generally granted. Less democratic systems such as Nazi Germany or the Soviet Union, on the other hand, do not face this problem. The Nazi Criminal Code, for instance, criminalized "asocials."[70] The indeterminacy of this offense deters risk-averse citizens from many acts that may or may not be "asocial." Because totalitarian regimes do not publish all legal decisions, and its ruling classes are more strictly separated from those addressed by the law, the knowledge of the decision rules can be limited to officials. Whether this sort of strategic indeterminacy is morally desirable is another question, however.[71]

The rationale in the Nazi Criminal Code reveals another problem with this strategy. Some people, to comply with the law, will endure hardships that they could—and should—have averted because they think that duress will not be granted. Dan-Cohen (1983, 638) rather optimistically suggests that benefits foregone due to overcompliance are more than offset by the danger of reduced obedience to the law caused by openly permitting the defense of duress. But even if Dan-Cohen is correct, overcompliance in the case of duress is undesirable because people suffer more than necessary. If thugs repeatedly beat up and bully a witness to suborn him to perjury, for instance, overcompliance would make him endure the

---

[69] See Dan-Cohen (1983, 661–664).

[70] See Ayaß (2012). In *Erlass zur vorbeugenden Verbrechensbekämpfung* of 1937 "asocial" is defined as "anyone who shows by being inimical to society, though not by criminal behavior, that he does not want to fit into society" (translated from the German: "wer durch sein gemeinschaftswidriges, wenn auch nicht verbrecherisches Verhalten zeigt, dass er sich nicht in die Gemeinschaft einfügen ... will"). Not dissimilar is the Soviet Criminal Code, which criminalized "parasites."

[71] Maybe a limited case can be made for laws in democracies aimed at particular social classes with less access to legal institutions such as the vagrancy law of Jacksonville discussed in chapter 1. However, such laws are morally not much more desirable than the respective laws in Nazi Germany or the Soviet Union.

attacks and withstand the coercion. He would sustain serious psychological and physical harm only to avoid conviction for a minor crime.

In other cases, overcompliance might actually be desirable. Endicott (2011b), Soames (2011), and Waldron (2011) argue that indeterminacy can give incentives to positively overcomply with the law. Soames (2011, 41) offers the following argument. A college administrator faces financial crisis and requires cuts by all departments. She considers two alternatives. She could order all departments to (a) cut at least 10% or (b) make the maximum reductions possible and indicate that those who are not sufficiently forthcoming will lose their graduate programs. Alternative (a) is precise and specific. Alternative (b) is semantically and conversationally vague.[72] According to Soames, the indeterminacy in alternative (b) incentivizes departments to leave a margin of error by making cuts larger than 10%.

The problem for this argument is that the effect on compliance goes both ways. The margin of discretion due to indeterminacy can lead to undercompliance as well as overcompliance. Moreover, the margin of discretion is only necessary if deterrence matters. As Richard Craswell and John E. Calfee (1986) show, overcompliance is generally not achieved if deterrence is low. Laws are normally enacted in reaction to some behavior that needs to be regulated. Hence, there are some subjects whose interests are ex ante in conflict with the law. If all subjects behaved desirably, there was no need to enact the law in the first place. For some laws, such as traffic regulations or tax laws where deterrence matters and moral considerations are at best marginal, one can say that a rational individual will violate the law if her gain by doing so is greater than the expected punishment, which is the product of (1) the subjective probability of the individual's being convicted and of (2) the cost to her of the penalty in the case of conviction. The probability of conviction, in turn, is the product of (1a) the probability that her behavior will be deemed illegal and of (1b) the probability that, if so, she will be convicted for it. Thus, she will violate the law if she either considers the penalty tolerable or if the probability of conviction is low. Perfect enforcement of the law is practically impossible, and punishments are not always sufficiently harsh to effectively deter. In a nutshell, if sentences are either insufficiently harsh or enforcement insufficiently effective, individuals with something to gain by violating the law will do so.

How could indeterminacy possibly help in such a case? At first glance, indeterminacy reduces the probability that some behavior will be deemed illegal, thereby reducing the probability of conviction and, consequently, incentivizing to undercomply. The reason is, again, a potential conflict of interests. Hence, even if

---

[72] Alternatives (a) and (b) reflect the difference between what is often called "rule" and "standard." There is no need to dwell on the *rules v. standards* debate here. See Schlag (1985) and Kaplow (1992) for discussions.

indeterminacy does improve compliance in some cases, it is clearly a double-edged sword. If a legal norm is indeterminate and punishment for non-compliance is low, the incentive is, ceteris paribus, to undercomply, since the expected costs are negligible.

Only if the legal norm is indeterminate and the punishment for non-compliance is high, the incentive is, ceteris paribus, to overcomply since the expected costs are substantial. The driving force of Soames's example is the harsh penalty for non-compliance. The departments are effectively deterred by the potential loss of their graduate program. The harsh penalty even outweighs the lower probability of conviction due to the indeterminacy of alternative (b). If the penalty is not regarded sufficiently harsh, there is no incentive to overcomply. On the contrary, pharmaceutical companies, for instance, frequently appear to underfulfill indeterminate contract terms precisely because liability is reduced by their indeterminacy.

Whether indeterminacy gives rise to undercompliance or overcompliance depends thus on the expected punishment costs, that is, the severity and probability of punishment as well as the individual's degree of risk aversion. However, as Dan-Cohen's example shows, overcompliance itself is problematic when the exact allocation of resources matters. Overcompliance results in losses if resources are unnecessarily spent only to be on the safe side. Playing it safe can be costly.[73] Consider the college administrator in Soames's example who might dislike exceedingly large cuts by the departments because the college as a whole would suffer if departments cannot provide the required standard of education and research anymore. In this case, overcompliance is less preferable and it is best to opt for the determinate alternative (a), ordering all departments to cut at least 10%.

According to Endicott (2011b, 27), indeterminacy might be valuable for three related reasons. It might create incentives to (1) avoid the creation of risks, (2) contract out of liability such that costs be allocated to the least risk-averse agent, and (3) seek creative alternatives to exclude liability. For instance, the heads of department might try to reduce liability not only by overcomplying the administrator's order but by ensuring in some other, possibly innovative, way that their particular graduate programs will not be lost.

Endicott himself provides no articulate reason why indeterminacy leads to creativity. But deterrence seems to be the deciding factor again. If expected punishment costs are low, there is no incentive to seek (creative) alternatives. If they are high, there certainly is an incentive to find ways to avoid liability, but this is the case whether the law is indeterminate or not. How could an indeterminate law incentivize more creativity than a determinate one?

---

[73] As we saw in chapter 4, it is in some cases even more costly to provoke complete non-compliance than to risk overcompliance or undercompliance due to indeterminacy. We will discuss this effect also in section 5.3.3 on incentives of indeterminacy in contracts.

Perhaps, creativity is enticed simply because of the increased uncertainty of a potential lawsuit. Dan L. Burk (1999, 139) argues that "uncertainty itself makes litigation potentially expensive, and so there are incentives to find some other method of clarification." Subjects will then want to contract out of liability in some, more or less creative, way.[74] However, this is only the case if they are sufficiently risk-averse. Even if punishment is likely and severe, a risk-seeking subject might want try her luck and undercomply.

In any case, the fact that they have to determine on their own what the law says requires them to reason about it. As Joseph Raz (2009b, 302) says, interpretation necessarily has a creative element. In contrast, a determinate norm could be applied without much reasoning. So maybe indeterminacy causes people to think about their legal obligations more than determinacy.

The fact that subjects need to determine on their own what the law says has, as Waldron (2011, 59–70) argues, another, maybe related, effect. It lets them decide self-determinedly how to comply with the law. It entices subjects to "behave *as if they were* citizens in a larger, ongoing community talking about fairness."[75] Indeterminacy in laws directly improves the guidance of action because it requires reasoning by the subjects of what is required of them under the circumstances. Even though they can later be corrected by a police officer or judge, at first they need to figure out for themselves what is reasonable to do. This is, presumably, due to the standard-relativity of terms such as "reasonable." Because subjects have to determine the standard of reasonableness in each case on their own, their actions are more self-determined. The interpretation of the law requires a subject's own assessment or judgment with regard to the situation she is in. She has to assess or judge the circumstances that would make it unreasonable to, for instance, resist duress or make further cuts in the college department.

Waldron's argument may be strengthened by the following example. Consider the rule that parents have to pay $5.00 for every 15 minutes after the kindergarten's closing time in which they have not picked up their kids and compare it with the rule that kids should be picked up by closing time without specifying a penalty. Psychological research suggests that the incentive given by the first rule is that parents will leave their kids at the kindergarten longer because they do not feel responsible anymore. They calculate the costs and consider it a price, not a penalty.[76] Only if the rule specifies a sufficiently high price will parents pick up their kids in time. This suggests that responsibility induced by standard-relative terms can sometimes counteract the loss of deterrence in cases of indeterminacy.

---

[74] They are also, as we will see in section 5.3.3, more likely to settle a dispute.

[75] See Poirier (2002, 152).

[76] This has been shown in an experiment by Gneezy and Rustichini (2000).

Waldron concludes that indeterminacy in the law respects the individual subject's autonomy. The self-determination facilitated by the need to reason for oneself in cases of standard-relativity gives autonomy to the individual. Waldron's argument touches a crucial point. There are some limited circumstances in which indeterminacy can enhance self-determination and improve law's guidance of action. If the individual—just as an agency or court—knows better how to deal with the case at hand and is pushed into reasoning about her situation, she might reach the better decision.

However, there are many important ways in which indeterminacy does not respect autonomy. It potentially leads to arbitrariness in the assessment of the officer or judge who must later assess the individual's prior judgment. It fails to give fair notice of what is permitted and prohibited. It frustrates to some degree our wish to be guided by the law. In many cases, it causes estrangement because citizens feel abused or disempowered due to lack of notice and understanding.

It is no accident that many laws contain determinate provisions that precisely and specifically state matters of fact and legal consequences accompanied by a provision in general, multi-dimensional, and standard-relative terms stating the normative goal of the law. However, this does not mean that it is its indeterminacy that is functional. Compliance and guidance of action is improved by adding interpretational backing in cases of underinclusion or overinclusion. In section 5.1.5, I will revisit the question of which forms of indeterminacy can and which cannot be strategically used in legislation.

5.1.5 FORMS OF INDETERMINACY REVISITED

Clearly not all forms of indeterminacy are equally suited for the same strategic ends. Some can be used to facilitate collective action by incompletely theorized agreements in the face of conflict. Some can be used to improve compliance by double-talk. Some might even be used to allow for autonomy and self-determination.

Standard-relativity played, as we saw, a deciding role in *Sherman* and *Clayton*. But also conversational vagueness, polysemy, and implicature indeterminacy can be effective for the formal resolution of conflicting interests. All these forms of indeterminacy allow the delegation of contested issues to other parties. This facilitates incompletely theorized agreements because the parties can determine different standards, senses, or implicatures. Constitutions are full of standard-relative, polysemous, and highly general terms for the simple reason that they are "made for people of fundamentally differing views."[77] For the same reason, these forms of indeterminacy can be used to achieve compliance in reluctant agents, as we will see in more detail in section 5.2 on the strategic indeterminacy in verdicts.

---

[77] See Holmes's dissent in *Lochner v. New York*, 198 U.S. 45, 76 (1905).

We also saw that standard-relativity and implicature indeterminacy can effectively be used for double-talk. One part of the audience understands the utterance one way, the other part understands it the other way. Moreover, standard-relativity might enhance the autonomy of citizens by allowing them to determine on their own what is reasonable under the circumstances. Even though we did not analyze it here, it is certainly conceivable that syntactic ambiguity and speech act ambiguity have some such functions in the law as well.

However, a potential value of semantic vagueness seems rather questionable. The examples given by Endicott, Soames, and Waldron for the value of indeterminacy with regard to compliance and autonomy are mainly uses of standard-relativity. The problems arising from conflicting interests and overinclusiveness and underinclusiveness are not remedied by semantic vagueness either but by effectively delegating power to other parties due to standard-relativity, polysemy, and generality.[78] Examples are § 157 BGB and § 242 BGB on good faith or § 826 BGB on unconscionability. The indeterminate legal terms involved in these clauses (i.e., *"Treu und Glauben," "Verkehrssitte,"* and *"Sittenwidrigkeit"*) are all standard-relative, polysemous, and general. Nevertheless, Endicott (2011a, 178) and with him many others claim that semantic vagueness is used to deal with the "vast variety of ways" in which legal norms must be applied.[79] Recall Endicott's example of "neglect" in the *Children and Young Persons Act*, which we discussed in section 3.2.2. According to Endicott (2011b, 26), its semantic vagueness grants discretion to courts on how to decide borderline cases and to social service officials on whether to take action protecting the child in borderline cases.

Undeniably, semantic vagueness causes discretion—as all forms of indeterminacy do. But borderline cases are hardly the ones that matter. The "complex and open-ended undertaking" of the law cannot be furthered by using vague terms, contrary to what Endicott (2011a, 179) suggests. As we saw in section 3.2, there is no way to know whether one faces a borderline case before having determined the context. But this means that one has to specify and disambiguate all relevant terms as well as rule out any pragmatic indeterminacy. The "I know it when I see it" test mentioned by Decker in section 5.1.3 thus cannot be due to semantic vagueness since the required "subjective mode of analysis" draws on the variability of context. But this is precisely *not* the issue in borderline cases. The unclarity generated by borderline cases cannot be controlled except through other forms of indeterminacy. As a result, cases in which semantic vagueness can directly be used are (and must be) rare.

---

[78] In German legal theory this device is usually called *"Generalklauseln"* ("sweeping clauses"). See also Garstka (1976).

[79] Other proponents of this view are Alexy (1995) and Soames (2012). For instance, Alexy (1995, 24) says that semantic vagueness is "the practically most important case of semantic discretion."

Gradually vague, one-dimensional terms might be good candidates to create borderline cases in a controlled way, but they are easily replaced by precise definitions with a threshold effectively eliminating semantic vagueness. The more clearly borderline cases can be made out, the easier it is to replace the vague term with a precise one.[80] Other terms with more than one dimension typically are highly context-sensitive due to multi-dimensional polysemy and standard-relativity. The extension of such terms is too heterogeneous to anticipate in any reliable way the occurrence of borderline cases. As a result, borderline cases are necessarily inconsequential for strategic considerations if compared to these other forms of indeterminacy.[81]

Moreover, in borderline cases, judges and officials lack justification for their decision. After all, one cannot know what the law says in such a case. This lack in justification can be redressed by determining the context in different ways to shift the borderline area. This is possible, however, not because "neglect" is vague but because different standards or senses of the vague, but also polysemous and standard-relative, term "neglect" can be chosen.

Roy A. Sorensen argues that instead of semantic vagueness, it is relative borderline cases that have a positive effect. Relative borderline cases can be used, according to Sorensen (2001, 397), to promote "cognitive division of labor." He claims that the resolution of relative borderline cases "get[s] delegated to officials with the best knowledge of local circumstances, practices, and standards."

Unfortunately, this is as implausible as semantic vagueness. Relative borderline cases have *by definition* a determinate answer. It is only epistemic resources that the decision-maker lacks. Once she has invested enough time and effort, all relative borderline cases are gone. Although they might play some role in cases of double-talk due to the epistemic uncertainty involved, they can neither grant discretion nor give autonomy.

Terms such as "neglect" have absolute as well as relative borderline cases, but this is not the reason why they are used. As Soames (2011, 39) puts it thus:

> Although it is no accident that such terms are vague, the legal utility of such terms, as opposed to more specific substitutes, is only partly due to their vagueness, while being partly due to other semantic features, the possession of which contributes to their vagueness.

---

[80] See Asgeirsson (2016) for a similar point. See also Marmor (2014, 87).

[81] Recall the *Argument from Inefficiency* in section 4.3.2. The fact that sometimes precision is disadvantageous does not entail that in such cases semantic vagueness is advantageous. As we saw, there are many properties of imprecision that—unlike semantic vagueness—clearly have positive effects. By using imprecise terms, one can add an opinion, avoid the difficulty of dealing with numbers, or exploit the terms' standard-relativity or generality. These features of imprecise terms more than satisfactorily explain why precision is to be avoided. Because of this, Endicott's argument is a non sequitur.

Soames attributes the utility of vague terms to their multi-dimensionality and generality. Strikingly, neither is itself a form of indeterminacy. Both can be used to include unforeseeable and complex events because they allow broad applicability. However, purely general and multi-dimensional terms alone cannot in principle grant discretion either. Only in combination with (multi-dimensional) polysemy or pragmatic indeterminacy can such terms track change and function as tools of delegation. A judge or official can determine the sense or standard of "neglect" to fit the context. Polysemy and standard-relativity not only redress the justificatory problems of semantic vagueness, but they would effectively give discretion even in cases of perfect precision.

Moreover, there is an incentive to determine the sense or standard in such a way that "neglect" either clearly applies or clearly does not apply. Anything else would cast doubt on the proposed interpretation. Thus, the required discretion is at best supported by semantic vagueness in some way.[82]

While semantic vagueness may have a minor role to play when it comes to discretion or double-talk, it can impossibly improve self-determination. Borderline cases are at the fringes of a term's meaning, but the disagreement turns on its core meaning.[83] If anything, we gain self-determination by being able to determine our own standards.

Nor is it vagueness that makes terms such as "neglect" or "racial equity" the fix points for moral and political disagreement.[84] We disagree about neglect and racial equity in part because we ascribe different conceptions or senses to the terms. Differences in moral views on neglect are often reflected by different standards on the different dimensions of "neglect." Generality and multi-dimensionality might boost the effects of standard-relativity and polysemy. But, as Waldron (1994, 537) says, "many unanticipated cases where flexibility is desirable have nothing to do with [semantic] vagueness." Semantic vagueness cannot possibly respect autonomy, guide disputes, or track changes in value judgments.

5.2 Saving Face in Verdicts

In this section, I will continue the line of argument that it is not semantic vagueness but rather pragmatic indeterminacy, and especially standard-relativity, that is the

---

[82] Although Soames (2012) explicitly notes this, he considers the "important positive value" of semantic vagueness to be evidence for his own philosophical theory of vagueness.

[83] See also Schiffer (2001).

[84] According to Rodgers (1998, 6), these terms function also as key words for political concepts that help to legitimize public life and explain government to citizens. *Interpretive concepts*, as seen by Dworkin, can track such disagreement because they allow for different conceptions due to the different senses and standards of the polysemous and standard-relative terms that express them. See section 2.3.4. Endicott (2011a, 184) seems to acknowledge that they do not have this function due to semantic vagueness.

form of indeterminacy most relevant for strategic purposes in the law. In particular, I will show that this form of indeterminacy can be used to (1) find compromise within the court, (2) secure compliance with its verdict, (3) delegate power to better informed agents, and (4) gain deniability and deflect blame.

Recall that verdicts have the dual illocutionary force of representative declarations. They structurally exhibit a particular kind of speech act ambiguity. On one hand, verdicts are decisions that declare something to be the case, and, as a result, share some properties with laws; for example, that they create or change legal content. As such, indeterminacy can be used in similar ways as in legislation. I will examine such a case in section 5.2.1 on the decision in *Brown v. Board of Education of Topeka*, which demonstrates the strategic use of indeterminacy in a directive legal speech act for functions (1), (2), and (3) just listed.[85]

On the other hand, verdicts are applications of the law. They can be correct or incorrect because they ought to represent already existing law. A possible use of semantic vagueness might be found in the gradual change in the meaning of legal terms—a phenomenon that we will examine in section 5.2.2 on the indeterminacy of the term "violence" in German Federal Constitutional Court opinions.

Finally, in section 5.2.3 we will consider the use of indeterminacy by courts when they are in danger of being criticized or losing reputation. In this case, indeterminacy is used rather differently, that is, for function (4): By wording their verdicts in indeterminate terms, courts can gain plausible deniability, deflect blame, save face, and avoid clear revision by higher courts or parliament.

5.2.1 AN EXAMPLE: WITH ALL DELIBERATE SPEED

Oliver Brown, a black welder and pastor from Topeka, sued in *Brown v. Board of Education of Topeka* (1954) that racial segregation in public schools violated the constitutional right for equal education.[86] The Supreme Court held that racial segregation indeed violates the 14th Amendment of the Constitution. Whether black and white schools in fact have the same standards of education or not, the forced segregation of black school children impedes their development and equal chances. Racial desegregation is "inherently unequal," concluded the Court.

---

[85] *Brown v. Board of Education of Topeka*, 349 U.S. 294 (1955).

[86] *Brown v. Board of Education of Topeka*, 347 U.S. 483 (1954). The class action *Brown* was introduced into the philosophical debate on vagueness by Tappenden (1994). It consists of five individual cases. *Gebhart v. Belton* from Delaware, *Brown v. Board of Education* from Kansas, *Briggs v. Elliott* from South Carolina, *Davis v. County School Board of Prince Edward County* from Virginia, and *Bolling v. Sharpe* from the District of Columbia. The Supreme Court heard them together because each raised the issue of the constitutionality of segregation in public schools.

The verdict in *Brown* (1954) did not offer any instructions of how to remedy the inherent inequality of segregation. This was done one year later in *Brown* (1955). In that case, the Supreme Court famously ruled that states must desegregate public schools "with all deliberate speed."[87] The indeterminacy of this instruction is striking. Why did the Court choose this formulation?

In both cases Chief Justice Earl Warren secured the verdict's unanimity.[88] Warren's wish for consensus provides the first reason for the indeterminacy, which is—as in many instances of indeterminacy in statutory laws—the need (1) to find compromise.[89] Warren wanted neither concurring nor dissenting opinions.[90] For this reason, he had to convince all of his colleagues to agree on the same opinion. Some of the Justices had very divergent views, as not all of them considered even *Plessy v. Ferguson* as legally incorrect.[91] Thus, as Dennis J. Hutchinson (1980, 56) notes, "Warren faced the difficult task of accommodating in one statement eight other views that had been far from harmonious at conference."

Justice Hugo L. Black believed it to be best if the Court remained silent on the issue of how to desegregate to give discretion to the states. He was convinced that the Court could not achieve anything on the short term.[92] Black wanted a direct order granting the plaintiffs admission to the schools, but nothing more. Also Justice William O. Douglas believed that a symbolic gesture would be sufficient. Justice Felix Frankfurter disagreed and argued for an incremental transition to racial integration guided by the Court. Both Frankfurter and Douglas believed that "it was essential that whatever the Court ordered should be obeyed."[93]

Outside of the Court the disunity was even greater. The South was expected to ferociously resist any attempt to desegregate. This was an additional reason for the verdict's unanimity, which Warren intended to be a signal to society. The second reason for indeterminacy is thus the need (2) to secure compliance.[94] Frankfurter, in particular, wanted to appease the South by using the phrase "with all deliberate speed."[95] As Warren expressed it:

---

[87] Apparently, the expression was coined by Justice Holmes in *Virginia v. West Virginia*, 222 U.S. 1 (1911).

[88] See Balkin and Ackerman (2001, 37).

[89] See Schwartz (1983) and Cray (1997), discussing the desire to craft a unanimous decision as a reason for strategic indeterminacy.

[90] See Ulmer (1971, 702).

[91] The US Supreme Court upheld in *Plessy v. Ferguson*, 163 U.S. 537 (1896) the constitutionality of racial segregation in public facilities under the *separate but equal* doctrine.

[92] See Balkin and Ackerman (2001, 40).

[93] See Powe (2000, 53). This already hints at our fourth reason for indeterminacy in verdicts, namely, to save face. We will discuss this reason in section 5.2.3.

[94] The effect is the same as in our game theoretic models in chapter 4 in which we showed that indeterminacy facilitates communication when conflicting interests would make it impossible otherwise.

[95] See Balkin and Ackerman (2001, 42).

There were so many blocks preventing an immediate solution ... that the best we could look for would be a progression of action; and to keep it going, in a proper manner, we adopted that phrase, all deliberate speed.[96]

For the same reason, the Justices wanted the opinion to be short and comprehensible to the general public. Judicial decisions are not only a matter of political acceptance through the relevant agents but also of public relations. It was important that the majority of society supported the verdict.

The result was the compromise that states should desegregate with "all deliberate speed." Desegregation should be monitored by the district courts; and only individual lawsuits, but not class actions, against insufficient integration were to be admitted. The Justices feared that anything more radical and determinate would lead to such strong opposition that the verdict would not be implemented at all.[97]

Determinacy can lead to full non-compliance if interests are not fully aligned, as we saw in section 4.4. Indeterminacy, on the other hand, can help to achieve a certain objective, which may otherwise be difficult to achieve, for instance, because it is not accepted by the majority of the legal or political community. Recall the notion of incompletely theorized agreements, which

> may permit acceptance of a general aspiration when people are unclear about what the aspiration means, and in this sense, they can maintain a measure of both stability and flexibility over time. At the same time, they can conceal the fact of large-scale social disagreement about particular cases. (Sunstein, 1995, 1739)

As laws, indeterminate verdicts can reduce political and legal opposition. Gregory S. Kavka (1990, 312) argues that "policies which will probably provide substantially more overall benefit than harm can be accepted by most citizens as policies that promote the general welfare." Indeterminacy creates uncertainty as to what the legal content of the policy is and, consequently, who will gain or loose from it. In particular, the Supreme Court and the legislature can mollify each other if they are not in full opposition to their respective political agendas by leaving certain difficult issues untouched.[98] But,

---

[96] Cited in Scheiber (2007, 17).

[97] See Balkin and Ackerman (2001, 41).

[98] This allows a party also to save face in cases in which another party can later overrule its policy by declaring the law unconstitutional or by amending the Constitution. See section 5.2.3 for a detailed discussion. This may sound paradoxical since sometimes it is precisely its indeterminacy that causes the Supreme Court to rule a statute unconstitutional. However, to be considered void for vagueness, the indeterminate statute must frustrate an average citizen's understanding of its legal content, which is not necessarily its effect. Also, the risk of a statute being declared void for vagueness might be negligible in comparison to other more substantial unconstitutionality charges. Finally, the mentioned uses of strategic indeterminacy give the

as Sunstein and Kavka point out, it also helps to reduces disagreement in society generally.

Moreover, the Justices were convinced that the implementation of *Brown* could only be enforced by the district courts. They needed to delegate the supervision of desegregation to them partly because the differences between schools required individual decisions by better-informed institutions that were closer to the facts of the case. Warren thus ordered his clerks to draft "a short opinion embodying the view that most of the details should be left to the district courts."[99]

Analogously to legislation, indeterminacy in verdicts can be used to delegate power. In *Brown*, power was delegated to the district courts who were granted discretion of how and when to enforce desegregation. The district courts did, as the Court believed, know better how to approach the problem. As Jeffrey K. Staton and Georg Vanberg (2008, 506) emphasize: "Determining which specific policies will achieve integration and with which side effects presents a technical challenge requiring specialized knowledge."[100]

Thus, similarly to the legislature, courts can delegate power to technical experts. For courts, the lack of technical information might even pose a greater problem than for the legislature or agencies. The latter can often rely on specialized committees and extensive staff and are thus better positioned to design the specific policies necessary to actually bring about what is legally required. Courts, in contrast, do not have such resources. The third reason for indeterminacy is, accordingly, the need (3) to delegate power to better informed parties.

Brown (1955) shows that an indeterminate expression such as "all deliberate speed" can be strategically used by a court to facilitate compliance by unwilling agents and gain acceptance for the decision in general terms. It also contributed to resolve disagreement and conflicts of interests within the Court and delegated technical questions to lower courts.

But what form of indeterminacy was effective in fulfilling these functions? Consider the following possible formulations (F) that the Court could have used:

(F1) "with all deliberate speed"
(F2) "promptly"
(F3) "within 10 years"
(F4) "as soon as conditions x, y, and z are satisfied" (where x, y, and z specify all relevant factors)

Justices themselves reason to not strictly apply the *void for vagueness* doctrine. See Dan-Cohen (1983, 639) for a similar point.

[99] See Balkin and Ackerman (2001).

[100] See also Vermeule (2000, 76).

The Court chose (F1) for a reason. Why did Warren not use another formulation? We have now a preliminary answer to this question. (F1) is more congruent with the verdict's purpose than (F3) because (F3) runs the risk of overinclusion or underinclusion. It is simply too precise. (F1) is more applicable than (F4) given the lack of information and variance of factors. (F4) is too specific for the options of the Court. (F2) might have been the best choice if resistance were not anticipated to be wide and fierce, coming not only from large parts of the white Southern population and their schools but also from the enforcing authorities themselves. Hence, given the likelihood of complete non-compliance, (F1) is also preferable to (F2).

Generality and imprecision are important to avoid overinclusion or underinclusion and to achieve compliance and gain acceptance. One could argue that (F1) is an instance of the strategic use of semantic vagueness, as Jamie Tappenden (1994) does. The Supreme Court intentionally chose the vague term "deliberate" to allow lower courts to decide borderline cases at their discretion. When the Court ruled that schools be integrated with all deliberate speed, it could not anticipate how long it would take even progressive schools under the best possible circumstances. Hence, one might think that it used a general and vague expression, deciding on an indeterminate time period.

Vagueness may be functional if borderline cases play a role in either (1) facilitating compromise, (2) securing compliance, (3) delegating to better informed parties, or (4) gaining deniability. The relevance of borderline cases is, however, extremely doubtful for the entire subsequent legal history of *Brown*.

In general, even if a vague term is strategically used, its semantic vagueness may not serve a function, as Sorensen (2001, 398) shows:

> Merely showing that a vague predicate serves a function is not sufficient for showing that its vagueness serves a function. I can show that a gray fan belt serves a function in an automobile without showing that its grayness serves any function. Granted, the grayness may serve a function. Perhaps the grayness distinguishes the fan belt from other belts because its grayness is part of a color-coding scheme. But simply to assume that the grayness has a function would be an instance of the fallacy of division. The whole artifact can be functional without each of its properties being functional.

As we saw in section 5.1, Sorensen (2001, 397) draws the conclusion that the "relative borderline cases are doing the work and the absolute borderline cases are epiphenomenal." It would indeed not be surprising if we wrongly attribute the function of relative borderline cases to absolute ones. We often cannot tell apart absolute from relative borderline cases—at least not at first glance. As I showed, however, not even relative borderline cases can do the job because they do not allow for discretion.

The expression "with all deliberate speed" does not have only relative and absolute borderline cases. On the semantic level, the expression is polysemous as well as vague. On the pragmatic level, it is conversationally vague due to the generality of "deliberate." But there are also several forms of pragmatic indeterminacy involved.

One form of linguistic indeterminacy stems from the adjective construction of "deliberate speed." As in the expression "vegetarian cook," it is not clear what the relation between the adjective "deliberate" and the substantive "speed" is. A cook can *eat* or *prepare* vegetarian food to count as a "vegetarian cook." Speed can be deliberate because it is *used carefully* or prudently, or because it is *slow*.[101] As we noted in section 1.2, this form of indeterminacy can be seen as either syntactic ambiguity, polysemy, or impliciture indeterminacy. But in any case, there is an (additional) impliciture. Both "used carefully" and "slow" are relative to a contextually valued standard.

The standard-relativity of "deliberate" and the resulting indeterminate impliciture mark context as the decisive factor. The context might include current values in society as well as economic and social facts at the schools. The courts have to decide what is deliberate in individual cases. They have to determinate the contextually valued standard of "deliberate." There are certainly some borderline cases, once the context is determined. However, the unclarity resulting from these borderline cases does not allow *directed* delegation of power.

Most importantly, due to the interaction of pragmatic mechanisms such as this impliciture and indeterminacy in context the extension of the term "deliberate" can be stretched. The opponents of desegregation can argue that ever longer time periods constitute "deliberate speed." This possibility to stretch the extension of a term might appear to be connected to the Sorites reasoning with vague terms. Indeed, it can be used in slippery slope arguments similar to Sorites reasoning. However, as I will show in section 5.2.2, slippery slope arguments are not always based on semantic vagueness. In *Brown*, it is its context sensitivity that allows for the stretchability of the term.

"Deliberate" is a *weasel word* similar to "social." Nobody really knows, according to Friedrich A. von Hayek and Alfred Bosch (2001, 132), what "social" means in expressions such as "social instability" or "social uncertainty."[102] "Social" is a general term that can gain various narrower senses depending on how and where it is used. It is polysemous and standard-relative, expressing different conceptions when attached to different substantives. In a nutshell, the

---

[101] See Ogletree (2005, 10).

[102] See Pei (1978), who traces the expression "weasel word" back to US President Theodore Roosevelt. See also Nussbaumer (2005).

generality and context sensitivity of "deliberate" allows for its wide applicability, stretchability, and flexibility.

The context indeterminacy in *Brown* proves it futile to seek evidence for or against philosophical theories of semantic vagueness in legal practice. Tappenden (1994), for instance, tries to use *Brown* to prove the epistemic theory wrong but fails because he cannot identify the context of *Brown*. Other authors, too, argue for the adequacy of philosophical theories of vagueness by "applying" them to the law.[103] We can now see why they are unable to prove other philosophical theories of vagueness wrong by citing indeterminate legal utterances. Their context is changing from application to application. As a result, what is communicated by "with all deliberate speed" is changing, too. As Sorensen correctly concludes, its vagueness is merely epiphenomenal.[104]

However, by the same reasoning, one cannot exclude that semantic vagueness ultimately has *some* function. One cannot with certainty say which cases are hard due to semantic vagueness or ultimately another form of indeterminacy.[105] Sorensen's argument mentioned previously shows this—but nothing more.

Sorensen presents another argument, however, which can be paraphrased in the following way:

(P1) Delegation of power is valuable only if delegates are in a better position to resolve the case than the delegator.

(P2) In borderline cases, no one is in any position to resolve them.

(C) Delegation of power by way of absolute borderline cases cannot be valuable.

Hrafn Asgeirsson (2012a) rejects Sorensen's claim by arguing that delegation of power is valuable even if delegates are not in a better position to resolve a borderline case than the delegator. He rejects (P1). Borderline cases prompt judicial discretion, but this discretion is due to an implicit or explicit change in question. In a borderline case, one asks not whether some x is F but whether x should count as F.

Sorensen assumes that "being in a better position" must be understood epistemically. However, one can be in a better position to resolve a case even if one does not have better knowledge. If one understands "being in a better position" as having better tools to find an answer or having lower decision costs,

---

[103] See, for instance, Anderson (2006), Soames (2012), or Gruschke (2014).

[104] Schiffer (2001, 423) argues against the usefulness of applying philosophical theories of vagueness to the law by stressing that nothing would follow from any such theory because all that is of relevance to the lawyer is the "platitude that if p is indeterminate, then one cannot know either p or not-p."

[105] For instance, Greenawalt (2001), Raz (2001), Glenn (2007), Asgeirsson (2012a), and Lanius (2013) argue that semantic vagueness might still have some function.

it becomes evident that district courts deciding actual (borderline) cases can have better resources and more information to answer the normative question of when and how integration should proceed than the Supreme Court.

Asgeirsson's reasoning is valid. But his argument fails to show that it is semantic vagueness that serves a function. The delegation of power resulting from vagueness cannot be anticipated by the delegator due to the accompanying context sensitivity of most legal terms. As we saw in section 4.4.1, (at least) some effects of semantic vagueness may arguably facilitate conflict resolution, compliance, and the reduction of decision costs. This does not entail, however, that it can be used strategically in a directed manner. And it is hard to find instances of semantic vagueness even for non-strategic uses. As we saw in chapter 3, the indeterminacy in such cases can rarely be linked with vagueness and instead frequently is clearly traceable to generality, standard-relativity, or polysemy.

In *Brown*, compliance is achieved (among other things) by exploiting the generality, standard-relativity, and polysemy of "deliberate." While a specific instruction would evoke open resistance in a reluctant agent, the probability for compliance is greater if the instruction is generally phrased such that the agent has some liberties as to how exactly to comply. Particularly in *Brown*, the Justices needed to ensure compliance not only with potentially unwilling schools but mainly with those agents who were to enforce the ruling. If a new precedent set by the Supreme Court is highly unpopular with other political agents such as agencies or lower courts, it will not or only to some lessened degree be enforced by them.

This is a special case of the *principal agent problem*. If there is a conflict of interests between principal and agent, the latter might not comply with the former's order. In such a case, agencies and lower courts resist to implement or enforce a new policy that they oppose. Phrasing the verdict in general, standard-relative, and polysemous terms can turn out to be advantageous for the court since it allows agencies and lower courts to implement or enforce it with (broad) discretion, thereby effectively reducing the conflict of interests.

But did the indeterminacy in *Brown* have even a positive effect? The lower courts implementing *Brown* essentially opted for two interpretations. First, to comply with the Supreme Court's ruling, they assigned pupils to schools on the basis of residence rather than on the basis of race. Second, they allowed for freedom of choice, that is, they gave pupils the right to choose between white and black schools irrespective of their race. However, neither had the effect of integration: "[F]reedom of choice plans became the dominant judicially sanctioned mechanism of implementing a view of *Brown* that remedied the constitutional violation, but did not stop the segregation."[106] The utility of indeterminacy in *Brown* thus appears to be doubtful—especially when we look at how desegregation unfolded in the last decades. It continues to be criticized from both proponents and

---

[106] See Ogletree (2005, 125).

opponents of desegregation. The verdict's indeterminacy seems to have been, just as in *Clayton*, only a short-term advantage. Is Schmitt right after all? In the end, "the most recalcitrant judge and the most defiant school board were allowed to set the pace," as Jack W. Peltason (1961, 55) complains. Was the predominant effect of indeterminacy in *Brown* undercompliance?

Consider the verdict's effects in light of the odds. The Supreme Court Justices knew that they did not have the backing of either the Eisenhower administration or Congress to render a more determinate verdict. President Dwight D. Eisenhower privately expressed his fear that the desegregation mandated by *Brown* would lead to social disintegration.[107] This is evidenced by non-compliance and occasionally open resistance of state governments and district courts to desegregation, as the so called "Little Rock" incident shows vividly.[108] The resistance might have been even greater if the verdict had been phrased in more determinate and thus threatening terms.

While the *Civil Rights Act* of 1964 strengthened the liberal policy of *Brown*, only a few years later, President Richard M. Nixon claimed that the Court had tried to force integration "too far too fast" and that he wanted to undo its decision.[109] And so he did. By appointing William H. Rehnquist as Justice, he put a staunch opponent of desegregation on the Supreme Court. As a consequence, desegregation is still an issue—more than 60 years after *Brown*.

The sustained opposition and severe criticism from both sides at least show that *Brown* could have been a worse decision for both proponents and opponents of desegregation. It was a compromise intended to preserve social peace. The Justices in *Brown* wanted to promote civil rights without endangering society. They did so by strategically using indeterminacy.

In sum, the indeterminacy of *Brown* created uncertainty about the time that schools had to integrate. This allowed the Justices to grant discretion and delegate power to lower and future courts. This may also have increased acceptability to opponents and compliance by reluctant authorities. Since courts in cases such as *Brown* are effectively lawmakers, their use of indeterminacy is not entirely dissimilar to its use in legislation.[110] In section 5.2.2, I will examine

---

[107] See Patterson (2001, 82).

[108] In 1957, the governor of Arkansas called out the National Guard to prevent the integration of the Central High School in Little Rock. After the intervention of the federal government and the Supreme Court, he continued to openly resist integration and won four more campaigns for governor.

[109] See Haldeman (1995, 126).

[110] A structurally similar, but less famous, example is *Goodyear Dunlop Tires Operations, S.A. v. Brown*, 564 U.S. 915 (2011), which sought to precisify the Alien Tort Statute (ATS) with respect to the indeterminate term "essentially at home." Its opinion said, "A connection so limited between the forum and the foreign corporation, we hold, is an inadequate basis for the exercise of general jurisdiction. Such a connection does not establish the 'continuous and systematic' affiliation necessary to empower North

the role of semantic vagueness in verdicts over a longer period of time, using the example of German supreme court decisions on the notion of *violence* in § 240 StGB.

5.2.2 SORITES REASONING

At the beginning of the 1980s the peace movement in Germany protested against the deployment of US weapons, occupying the entrances to US military bases. The protests and occupations were exceptionally peaceful. Police and military were informed about them beforehand, and protesters were trained to remain peaceful and never resort to violence even in self-defense. Despite the peacefulness of the protests, the Higher Regional Court in Stuttgart and Federal High Court of Justice legally classified them as "violence."[111]

Eike von Savigny (1991, 63) argues that this classification was made possible by a series of verdicts, each of which legally classified as "violence" (V) a borderline case of violence, thereby shifting its extension more and more into the range of clear non-violence:

(V1) If the defendant, without himself behaving violently, can exercise violence by using a dog in order to intimidate a night watchman, as was decided in an earlier case, then he can exercise violence by using only a little of his own physical strength in locking up a police man (RG 27, 405; RG 69, 327).

(V2) If blocking the path of a cart by advancing toward it in the middle of the road is exercise of violence, as was decided in an earlier case, then all the more so is firing in the air with a loaded gun (RG 60, 157).

(V3) If firing in the air with a loaded gun is exercise of violence, as was decided in an earlier case, then so is firing in the air with a blank gun (RG 66, 353).

(V4) If exercise of violence is constituted by behavior involving natural muscular force, as was decided in an earlier case, then so it is by behavior involving other natural forces, like the chemical force of a narcotic (BGH 1, 145) or the kinetic energy of a motor car (BGH, NJW 1953, 672).

(V5) If it is sufficient for the exercise of violence that a force has effects on the victim, as was decided in earlier cases, then violence can be exercised by the effect of psychological forces (BGH 19, 263).

Carolina courts to entertain claims unrelated to the foreign corporation's contacts with the State." The reason for the opinion's indeterminacy appears to be its striving for acceptance by public opinion, academics, politics, and peers, and its uncertainty about whether time was ready for a clear rejection of ATS.

[111] See OLG Stuttgart, NJW 1984, 1909, and BHG, NJW 1986, 1883, respectively.

Von Savigny takes this process to be (evidently) parallel to the fallacious Sorites reasoning based on semantic vagueness. The term "violence," which is central to § 240 StGB on *Nötigung* (constraint or duress), is certainly vague and, thus, susceptible to the Sorites paradox. Each step appears to be justifiable, and yet the conclusion is absurd. Von Savigny (1991, 64) complains: "The result has been that the courts can now punish any kind of constraint, under the label of violence, provided they do not like it."

The path from (V1) to (V5) is certainly some form of slippery slope mechanism in the sense that some event *A*, which on its own is considered to be desirable, ends up materially increasing the probability that another event *B* is brought about, which is considered to be undesirable or absurd. As von Savigny (1991, 63) frames it:

> Each single decision argues for the claim that the present case, as compared to a case decided earlier, is not significantly different, and from this reasoning incorrectly concludes, first, that it is a case of violence, too; and, second, that there is now a new precedent for the courts to appeal to in the same fallacious way next time.

It appears that the German courts in their decisions from (V1) to (V5) used the *small change deference heuristic*. They deferred to precedents that were only marginally different from each case at hand. Because the difference was sufficiently small, most observers did not complain when the judges drew a new line. This is what led from the reasonable rulings in (V1) to the strikingly less reasonable ruling in the "*Laepple*" verdict (BGHSt 23, 46). Based on the ruling in (V5), which extended the term "violence" to include all forms of physical and psychological violence, the judges in *Laepple* assumed that a protester resorts to violence if she "starts a psychologically determined process" by means of her mere physical presence. They concluded that a train operator who is forced to do or omit something (such as stopping the train) in order not to run someone over is the victim of "violence."[112]

The interpretation of § 240 StGB established by *Laepple* was then applied to the peaceful protests in the early 1980s.[113] Each application of the term "violence," von Savigny argues, is a borderline application that shifts the whole borderline area further toward cases that in the beginning would have been considered to be clearly non-violence. Thus, the reasoning from (V1) to (V5) is an instance of Sorites reasoning, or so it would seem.

---

[112] See Busse (1991, 268).

[113] It was found unconstitutional, however, in a later Federal Constitutional Court decision (BVerfGE 73, 206).

But is the absurd conclusion that von Savigny complains about really facilitated by the term's vagueness? There are two reasons to doubt that the slippery slope mechanism in (V1) to (V5) is actually due to the Soriticality of "violence."

First, the verdicts in (V1) to (V5) have been rendered over a period of more than 70 years. During this time, the meaning of the expression "violence" changed not only in the legal domain but also in public discourse. As we know from section 4.3.2, language change may be eased by semantic vagueness but is essentially independent from it. Other factors such as figurative language use, context-dependence, and true overgeneralizations cause language change all by their own.

Second, and more importantly, there is not a single slippery slope mechanism, but there are many ways in which a desirable event can make successively less desirable events more likely. The difficulty in drawing a line or making a distinction can stem from a term's vagueness, but there are many other causes as well. Eugene Volokh (2003) subsumes vagueness based slippery slopes under a more general phenomenon that he calls "small change tolerance slippery slopes," which he in turn differentiates from a number of other types of slippery slopes. While the likelihood of an ultimately undesirable event may be increased by the semantics of the terms involved, many causal factors contribute to its occurrence.

Virtually all legal terms are vague. If Sorites reasoning were the sole cause to effectuate event B, judges would be able to draw the absurd conclusion that everything counts as X for any legal term "X." But this is clearly not possible for most legal terms even over longer periods of time. Other mechanisms are required. The following causal effects arguably also played a relevant role in the process from (V1) to (V5).

First, each decision altered the attitude that many lawyers had toward standards of violence. Each decision caused judges and other observers of legal practice to change their opinion of what counts and should count as violence—independently of the existence of borderline cases.

Second, each decision extended the set of precedents. Because more and more precedents can justify a beforehand absurd decision, it becomes more likely. The set of precedents can be extended by the just mentioned altering of attitudes or simply by the general human apathy to small changes. Even if each tiny change matters, if it matters only a little, people will rarely stand up against the decision. This *small change apathy* makes possible what the economist Alfred E. Kahn (1966) famously calls "the tyranny of small decisions."

Third, the decisions from (V1) to (V5) first may well have created and then sustained a political momentum driving the courts to the "absurd" conclusion when deciding the peaceful protests in 1984. Such momentum has nothing to do with semantic vagueness. Each decision causes other decision-makers to make further decisions. Just as with the Domino Effect mentioned in section 1.3.1, one small step can cause the next one, leading to a process that cannot easily be stopped.

Furthermore, it is by no means clear that the meaning of "violence" actually was changed by the decisions from (V1) to (V5). One could argue that "violence" is merely standard-relative and its standard has changed. A change of standard causes a change of the (contextually determined) extension. Thus, "violence" might change its extension just as many other standard-relative and evaluative terms change in their extension through applications and over time.[114]

If that were correct, then one could explain the slippery slope mechanism from (V1) to (V5) without reference to semantic vagueness at all. Strikingly, von Savigny does not even argue that semantic vagueness is the relevant factor in the slippery slope from (V1) to (V5). Instead, he argues (convincingly) that the different conceptions of violence are standard-relative.[115] This, however, only shows that the extension of "violence" depends on a contextually valued standard; it does not show that either standard-relativity or semantic vagueness are in any way functional in the verdicts from (V1) to (V5).

5.2.3 DENIABILITY AND SAVING FACE

The linguistic indeterminacy in *Brown*, on one hand, did not only reflect indeterminacy already in the US Constitution but also facilitated a unanimous opinion due to conflicting interests within the Court—analogously to the incompletely theorized agreements in the legislative process we saw in section 5.1.1. The Justices also intended it to increase the compliance of those who needed to enforce it. Unfortunately, there is no comprehensive way to show that it actually did so. I argued that the (intended) wide applicability, stretchability, and flexibility of the terms used result from pragmatic indeterminacy in combination with generality and polysemy.

Nor is the slippery slope mechanism underlying the decisions of the German courts on *Nötigung* based on semantic vagueness. For the most part, it even appears to be entirely unrelated to linguistic indeterminacy in general. Instead, causal factors, such as successive changes in the decision-makers' attitudes, arguably effectuated the gradual changes in the application of the term "violence."

Another function of indeterminacy can, however, be shown clearly in verdicts. Sometimes judges—just as legislators—want to elude responsibility.[116] Certain decisions involve uncertainty and potential threat to them as individuals or

---

[114] Balkin (2011) argues that terms such as "equality" are evaluative in the sense specified in section 3.2.2 and that this indeterminacy is a strength of such terms. Balkin's theory of *living originalism* incorporates into the original meaning of the Constitution the expectation that it will evolve with later developments. Balkin takes seriously the fact that an answer to the question of what does "equal protection" mean is influenced by the respondent's values.

[115] See von Savigny (1991, 62–63). He calls it more generally "context-relativity."

[116] See Gruber (1993), who discusses the use of indeterminacy by politicians for the same effect.

the institution of the court. Between judges and legislators, for instance, there are seesaw changes and conflicting interests. A judicial decision might be ignored or otherwise not complied with. Parliaments, agencies, and other political stakeholders sometimes evade or challenge even supreme court decisions.

Constant non-compliance can undermine a court's ability to make policy in general. Judges will lose influence once they have rendered too many verdicts that were openly defied or ignored. To prevent this, they can choose indeterminacy "when they expect defiance in order to protect the court against open institutional challenges."[117] Courts are strategic institutions seeking to maximize their effectiveness as institutions. Both the US Supreme Court and Federal Constitutional Court of Germany used indeterminacy to avoid defiance by other policymakers in the past.[118]

In general, indeterminacy can help judges to deal with their limited abilities in policymaking under uncertainty and fear of potential revision. While the highest courts can save face in front of the public and maintain institutional prestige in the face of political opposition, lower courts can save face by avoiding revision by higher courts.[119] But how exactly can courts save face with indeterminacy? How can it be used to gain deniability in verdicts without rendering them ineffective?

As we saw in section 5.1.4, indeterminacy generally incites non-compliance. There are two primary reasons. The receivers of indeterminate directives are less likely to comply because (1) they do not know exactly what they are supposed to do, and (2) they are less likely to be punished for non-compliance. Why do courts then render verdicts that potentially increase non-compliance?

Staton and Vanberg (2008) argue that courts risk non-compliance because indeterminacy does not only generally increase it, it makes it also harder to prove. It is harder to tell whether someone fails to comply because it is harder to tell which actions are consistent with the indeterminate directives given. This difficulty to prove non-compliance is a (perlocutionary) effect of indeterminacy which enables courts to save face and gain plausible deniability.

---

[117] See Staton and Vanberg (2008, 507).

[118] According to Vanberg (2005), outright parliamentary defiance of the German Federal Constitutional Court is more common than defiance of Supreme Court rulings by state and federal legislatures in the United States. For instance, a Federal Constitutional Court decision in 1995 (BVerfGE 93, 1) banning the display of crucifixes in schools was ignored by the Bavarian legislature. In contrast, the federal states in the United States have complied with a similarly unpopular Supreme Court decision banning prayer from public schools. In general, the US Supreme Court can more easily afford to make unpopular decisions without fearing legislative resistance than the Federal Constitutional Court of Germany.

[119] For instance, Staton (2006) shows that courts have an endogenous incentive to promote their decisions to the public.

The following scenario, adapted from Staton and Vanberg, shows this. Assume that a court reviews a policy and renders a verdict. Besides declaring the policy legally valid or invalid, the verdict also demands that the law be applied according to its ruling and suggests implications for future policy choices. The verdict can, however, vary in how clearly it articulates such demands and suggestions. In response to the court's verdict, the legislature implements a certain policy.

Formally, there is a sender S (the court) and a receiver R (the legislature). S can be interpreted as giving instructions m (the verdict) to R. Doing this, S uses a language that is more or less determinate about its implications for R. In the model, this degree of determinacy is represented by a parameter ζ. Finally, based on S's message m, R performs action $a \in A$.

The outcome for S depends on the severity of R's deviation from S's verdict m, its determinacy ζ, and S's concern about R's compliance with it. While R cares about the potential costs of deviating from m, the court is concerned about the costs of being defied. Both depend on the determinacy ζ of the court's verdict m. Ceteris paribus, the court S is more concerned when (1) its decision m lacks public support, and (2) the public is likely to become aware of any possible defiance by the legislature R. Whether the legislature openly opposes a judicial decision thus depends on how popular the court's verdict is and how transparent defiance would be to the public. If the court is not concerned at all about compliance, the degree of determinacy in its instructions will be irrelevant to its decision.

Staton and Vanberg's model entails that S can use an indeterminate m to mask potential resistance by R, even though it also encourages R to further diverge from S's instructions. S has to balance three (sometimes opposing) goals. S has to (1) deal with policy uncertainty, (2) uphold pressure for compliance, and (3) mask potential non-compliance to its decisions. How S will tackle this balancing act depends fundamentally on its leverage. If leverage is high, indeterminacy may primarily be used to deal with policy uncertainty. If leverage is low, however, indeterminacy may also serve the purpose of hiding non-compliance.

More precisely, depending on S's leverage over R, S's concern for compliance, and the divergence between S and R's preferences, S will try to find a different balance between determinacy and indeterminacy. On one hand, if the potential costs to R for defiance are relatively small, a greater concern for compliance will generally make indeterminacy more desirable because S prefers R to diverge to some degree from its instructions m instead of fully and openly opposing them. Thus, a concerned court should employ indeterminate language when it expects the legislature to defy its instructions if they were phrased in more determinate terms.[120]

---

[120] This finding corroborates my results from section 4.4.

If *R*'s potential costs for defiance are relatively great, on the other hand, and preferences only moderately diverge, *m* should be more determinate the greater *S*'s concern for compliance is. As long as the agents' preferences do not diverge too greatly, *S* should force *R* to fully comply with its determinate instructions *m*. When preferences diverge more, however, and *S*'s concern for compliance surpasses a certain point, *S* should mask possible non-compliance by issuing a completely indeterminate *m*. The risk and potential costs that the public becomes aware of the legislature's defiance of the court's verdict are simply too great then.

In short, the court should try to make the legislature comply with its instructions by phrasing them in determinate terms when preferences diverge moderately. If preferences diverge severely, and the court's concern for compliance is sufficiently great, however, it should try to save face by masking its inability to ensure compliance through indeterminate language in its verdict. Indeterminacy is thus a tool for courts to exercise control over the degree to which non-compliance will be detected.[121]

This result by Staton and Vanberg can be applied to our discussion of *Brown* in section 5.2.1.[122] The instructions in *Brown* were completely indeterminate because they did not impose any enforceable demands on the legislature. The Court's concern for compliance was high. It thus made sure that non-compliance would not be detected since its reasoning was, as we saw, that "it was essential that whatever the Court ordered should be obeyed."

The model shows that the value of indeterminacy depends on certain conditions. If the court has at least some leverage over the enforcing agencies, and divergence of preferences is neither too great nor too small, a concern for compliance requires—from the court's point of view—strategic indeterminacy in the verdict.

What the model does not show, however, is that semantic vagueness has some function in judicial opinions. Although Staton and Vanberg call their model "a model of judicial opinion vagueness," the parameter ζ does not represent anything similar to semantic vagueness. Semantic vagueness is not a variable degree of unspecificity. As we saw in section 1.3, vague terms are characterized by the property of having borderline cases and fuzzy boundaries, neither of which is represented by parameter ζ. The courts want to allow for different interpretations of their instructions—making it harder to verify non-compliance. Is this due to the messages' semantic or conversational vagueness, or some other form of indeterminacy? Staton and Vanberg's model seems to point to conversational vagueness due to generality because ζ does not *specify* what possible actions by the legislature count as compliance.

---

[121] A formal proof is given in Appendix A.4.

[122] See also Staton and Vanberg (2008, 508, note 11).

However, ζ can also be interpreted as the wide applicability and stretchability of polysemous and pragmatically indeterminate expressions. Judges—like other people—frame their political and moral disagreements in verbal disagreements about interpretive issues. There is prima facie reason to assume that many cases in which language is discussed in legal disputes are in fact cases of conflicting political and moral views.[123] Interpretive concept terms are, as we saw, multi-dimensionally polysemous. When a verdict is about a politically, socially, or morally contested issue, the court can use multi-dimensionally polysemous terms to address the greater part of society without inflaming too much debate and causing defiance or open resistance.

A different strategy is the practice of many legal professionals to use indeterminate language to signal dominance.[124] Indeterminate speech acts can have the perlocutionary effect to bring about an emotional or intellectual bonding to the speaker. A striking example is the so called guru effect:

> It is not just that insufficiently competent speakers refrain, as they should, from passing judgment on what they don't understand. All too often, what readers do is judge profound what they have failed to grasp. Obscurity inspires awe. (Sperber, 2010, 583)

This effect is attributable to judges, who by using indeterminacy in verdicts make the impression of wisdom and grandeur. Judicial rhetoric can exploit indeterminacy to hide the lack of good argument, save face, and gain plausible deniability.

Conversational vagueness seems to work best for these purposes if combined with other techniques. The "guru effect" develops its full impact in combination with legal jargon, which the layman cannot easily understand. Conversational vagueness is also more effective to save face in combination with the practice of judges to say as little as necessary to justify a verdict. The court can simply remain silent on controversial issues. Sunstein (1996, 7) calls this practice "decisional minimalism."

For the same reason, judges usually prefer to treat hard cases as if they were easy ones. They frequently "attempt to mask the fact that a case is hard in the first place."[125] All too often, all nine Supreme Court Justices agree that the meaning of a statute is "plain" but disagree what its plain meaning is, resulting in a five-to-four

---

[123] See Plunkett and Sundell (2013a). See also sections 1.3.2, 2.3.4, and 5.1.5.

[124] Along the lines of Nietzsche (1883, 71): "They muddy the water, to make it seem deep." ("Sie trüben ... ihr Gewässer, dass es tief scheine.")

[125] See Solan (1993, 208).

ruling over the case.[126] This helps not only to strengthen the court's own case, but it further reduces the cost of non-compliance because it appears that the verdict is determinate, even when in fact it is not.

Judges have a strong incentive to hide unclarity and pretend that a case is easy. Judges worry about their professional future, how they are perceived by their peers, possible revision of their rulings, and potential dilemmata between the principles of legal certainty and prohibition of denial of justice. This is why decisional minimalism is favorable, or as Poscher (2012, 36) puts it: "It is considered a virtue of a judge not to decide more than needed in a given case. *Obiter dicta* are a privilege—usually of the highest courts—and to be consumed with outmost moderation." Decisional minimalism helps judges to avoid commitment and exposure, in particular, in combination with indeterminacy in what formally is decided.

In sum, the use of indeterminacy in verdicts has many parallels to its use in laws. Our discussion of *Brown* demonstrated that indeterminacy can facilitate compromise within the court and ensure compliance outside of it. The gradual shift over time in German decisions on § 240 StGB toward a widening of the extension of "violence" resulted not from semantic vagueness and presumably not even linguistic indeterminacy in general but from non-linguistic factors such as changes in attitude. However, some forms of linguistic indeterminacy effectively assist judges to save face and gain plausible deniability by reducing the detectability of non-compliance.

In the next, and final, section, we will discuss the use of indeterminacy in contracts. There are some parallels to legislation and adjudication, but we will also explore a function of indeterminacy not encountered so far.

5.3 Exploiting Unawareness in Contracts

Analogously to laws and verdicts, we can ask why indeterminacy occurs and how it is best used in contracts. Contracts are a subspecies of legal texts that have intensively been studied with respect to strategic behavior. Economists have long asked questions about the utility of particular types of contracts and their phrasing. They use the tools of game theory to study contracts within the framework of contract theory.

From the perspective of this theory, contracts are agreements between two or more parties that voluntarily agree under uncertainty. This includes arrangements that define, influence, or coordinate the possibilities of strategic interaction.[127] The

---

[126] See Cunningham et al. (1994, 1564). According to Sunstein (2014), there is a relatively stable frequency (about 20%) of five-to-four splits in the Supreme Court's opinions over the last decades.

[127] See Schweizer (1999, 58).

contract theoretic notion of contracts is thus wider than both the legal and speech act theoretic one.

From a speech act theoretic perspective, contract formation is substantially different from the enactment of laws and rendering of verdicts. There are two (or more) contracting parties, namely, an offeror and an offeree. The former proposes to do something in exchange for something being done or promised by the latter. The formation of a contract is then the combination of offer and acceptance, that is, of two commissive speech acts.

When exactly offer and acceptance constitute a legally enforceable contract and what exactly its legal content is depends on the laws of the respective legal system. Contract law determines which commissive speech acts (and thus which contract theoretic arrangements) are legally enforceable contracts and how they are to be interpreted.[128] Within these limits, the contracting parties can decide for themselves what their obligations are to each other, that is, what the contract's legal content shall be.

Consider contract formation as a signaling game as discussed in section 4.1. Analogously to sender S's sending message m to which receiver R responds, offeror S chooses a particular phrasing of contract C that offeree R accepts or rejects.[129] Contract C is formed iff R accepts S's offer.

Contract C can be incomplete. In standard contract theory, the incompleteness of C is defined in the following way:

(D26) A contract C is INCOMPLETE if C does not unequivocally determine for every contingency the (legal) rights and duties of the contracting parties.[130]

This definition entails that C can be incomplete without being linguistically indeterminate. Linguistic indeterminacy renders C incomplete because it will be unclear to the parties what their legal obligations are in some contingencies. But one can also conceive of a contract that sets out precise and unambiguous rules for some contingencies, but other contingencies are not regulated at all—similar to gaps in the law. Contract theory does not differentiate between different kinds of incompleteness such as those resulting from linguistic indeterminacy, gaps, or contradictions.

The resolution of all three kinds of legal indeterminacy is in some way interpretive. They require "efforts to determine how the parties would have

---

[128] See section 2.2.3 for a discussion of the speech act theoretic and legal perspective on contracts.

[129] That is, S makes R a take-it-or-leave-it offer. Alternatively, the game can include the option of R making a counter-offer. In general, the game can be extended to include multiple stages with actions such as renegotiation, investment, or litigation. See our discussion of the stages of contracting in section 5.3.2 later.

[130] According to the classical definition by Hart (1995, 23), an incomplete contract "will be silent about the parties' obligations in some states of the world and will specify these obligations only coarsely or ambiguously in other states of the world."

resolved the issue that has arisen had they foreseen it when they negotiated their contract."[131] However, there is an important difference between gaps, on one hand, and linguistic indeterminacy and contradictions on the other. Gaps can be filled by reference to default rules such as industry practice or recognized customs of trade.[132] This form of incompleteness can effectively be lessened by contract law.

Contract law determines the legal content of contracts in addition to and sometimes instead of the contract's communicative content. Contracts would generally be complete if contract law could fully determine everyone's legal obligations for every contingency. However, there is the same (unavoidable) indeterminacy in laws regulating the formation of contracts as there is in contracts themselves.[133] As a matter of fact, many interpretation principles in both German and US contract law are phrased in *sweeping clauses* such as the statues on good faith or unconscionability, deliberately introducing indeterminacy.[134]

More importantly, however, default rules cannot resolve linguistic indeterminacy and contradictions, which require legal interpretation. They must be resolved by reference to the parties' intentions, the contract's purpose, or by some other (established) means to break the tie (such as the contra proferentem rule). Incompleteness due to linguistic indeterminacy and contradictions may thus have a different function from incompleteness due to gaps.

In the classical models, contracts are assumed to be complete. They determine the contracting parties' rights and duties for every contingency. As a matter of principle, there cannot be real-world contracts that are complete as defined in (D26). Contracts are finite entities, but the set of contingencies is infinite. Real-world contracts are rarely contingent even on publicly available information. The relevant question is thus not why there are incomplete contracts but why most contracts are *more incomplete than necessary*.[135] Why do they leave questions open that could have been answered?

---

[131] See Posner (2005, 1586).

[132] An example is § 157 BGB on the interpretation of contracts, which relies on the notion of *Verkehrssitte* (common usage).

[133] Additionally, most default rules established by contract law are, according to Schwartz and Scott (2003, 594), "useless or inefficient" from the point of view of contract theory.

[134] They are stated in UCC § 1-304 and § 2A-108, as well as § 242 BGB and § 826 BGB, respectively. Of course, nor is § 157 BGB on the interpretation of contracts different in this regard. See Dubroff (2012) on the concept of good faith in US contract law or Kilian (1976) on § 157 BGB in German contract law. See also our discussion in 5.1.

[135] Some contract theorists argue that courts should interpret gaps and indeterminacy in ways to penalize the parties for writing incomplete contracts. See Ayres and Gertner (1989), for instance. Do they presuppose that complete contracts are feasible? They do not. They presuppose that C must determine the legal obligations for every *foreseeable and relevant* contingency. Thus, C would still count as incomplete according to (D26).

The strategic use of indeterminacy can be shown even more clearly in contracts than in laws and verdicts. Many contracts are negotiated between parties that pursue their interests professionally and are based on economic theory. They measure the contract's expected utility in terms of financial payoff. As a consequence, the effect of indeterminacy can directly be analyzed in terms of (quantifiable) costs. In section 5.3.2, I will examine strategic indeterminacy in contracts as a means to reduce costs.

Indeterminacy is also assumed to change the incentives of contracts. We saw that indeterminacy in laws can increase or decrease compliance. Indeterminacy in contracts can incentivize different forms of behavior in ways analogous to laws but also particular to contracts. In section 5.3.3, I will survey the use of indeterminacy to strategically deal with incentives.

The nature of contracts as combinations of speech acts by two (or more) agents makes room for asymmetries that call for exploitation. One contracting party may be in a better position at the moment of contract formation or expect to be so in the future than the other one. Informational asymmetry between parties may be an opportunity for one party to use indeterminacy to gain advantage over the other. In section 5.3.4, I will finally discuss indeterminacy as a means to exploit unawareness. But let us first start with an example of linguistic indeterminacy in an insurance contract.

5.3.1 AN EXAMPLE: VEHICLES

Indeterminacy in a contract became an issue for the court in *Cincinnati Insurance v. German St. Vincent Orphan Association*.[136] For renovation purposes, St. Vincent removed, in 1998, the old flooring in its orphanage. It used a motorized floor stripper, which pulverized and scraped up the old vinyl flooring. This generated thick clouds of dust containing asbestos, which spread throughout the orphanage's first floor.

St. Vincent had insurance for building and personal property loss with Cincinnati Insurance and wanted to recover damages for the harm caused by the spread of asbestos. Cincinnati Insurance, however, rejected the claim. In the following lawsuit, a controversy ensued about the meaning of particular terms used in the insurance contract. It contained, for instance, the following clause, specifying the covered causes of loss:

> SPECIFIED CAUSES OF LOSS CLAUSE: Fire; lightning; explosion; windstorm or hail; smoke; aircraft or *vehicles*; riot or civil commotion; vandalism; leakage from fire extinguishing equipment, sinkhole collapse; volcanic action; falling objects; weight of snow, ice or sleet; water damage.

---

[136] *Cincinnati Insurance Co. v. German St. Vincent Orphan Association, Inc.*, 54 S.W.3d 661 (2001).

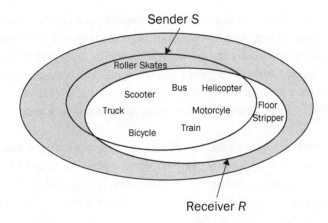

FIGURE 10 **Strategic Vagueness**

All expressions used in this clause were undefined. They are polysemous, general, and vague. The crucial question in *St. Vincent* was whether a motorized floor stripper constitutes a "vehicle" for the purposes of the contract. The floor stripper used to scrape the flooring in the St. Vincent orphanage resembled a riding lawn mower or golf cart. At first glance, such a floor stripper seems to be a borderline case of "vehicle," as depicted in Figure 10. In fact, *St. Vincent* is the example of indeterminacy in contracts most similar to a borderline case that I could find. St. Vincent (receiver *R*) considers the floor stripper a vehicle, while Cincinnati Insurance (sender *S*) does not. They disagree about the extension of "vehicle" in this case. But is it really a borderline case?

St. Vincent and Cincinnati Insurance offered arguments for their differing applications of "vehicle." Cincinnati Insurance argued that the term as used in the contract must be read as "a conveyance for transportation of goods and/or passengers on public highways," which the trial court confirmed. But the court of appeals reversed. It found that the floor stripper served as "a means of . . . transporting" its operator, and highway travel is not a necessary element of "vehicle." It is unclear what the constitutive elements of "vehicle" are. The term seems thus to be (vertically and multi-dimensionally) polysemous.

The term "vehicle" as used in the contract includes trucks, cars, buses, motorcycles, trains, and so on. It is clearly general. The *Specified Causes of Loss Clause* is not conversationally vague due to generality, however. Instead, the generality intensified the vertical polysemy of "vehicle," as depicted in Figure 11. According to St. Vincent and the court of appeals, "vehicle" in the context of the contract must be understood in its broad sense to include the floor stripper. According to Cincinnati Insurance and the trial court, it must be understood in its narrow sense to exclude it.

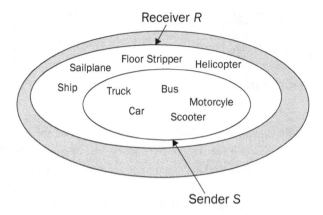

FIGURE 11 **Strategic Polysemy**

If the interpretation of "vehicle" in its narrow sense were accepted, a floor stripper would clearly not be a vehicle. However, this interpretation is at best dubious. There is no evidence in the contract for it, and it can hardly be a general definition of "vehicle" due to the fact that many clear instances of "vehicle" are not used on public highways (such as trains, ships, or airplanes).

Additionally, there remains some doubt about a floor stripper being a "vehicle" even in its broad sense. There are prototypical cases of "vehicle" in this sense such as cars and trains, but floor stripper is a rather unusual one. Its unusualness results from an impliciture indeterminacy. The definition of "vehicle" as "a means of carrying or transporting something" does indeterminately carry an impliciture that it must be designed for the (primary) purpose of carrying or transporting something. But this does not clearly apply to floor strippers, as they are designed for the (primary) purpose of stripping floors.

One could alternatively argue that having the (primary) purpose "of carrying or transporting something" is a dimension of "vehicle," which is neither clearly instantiated nor clearly not instantiated in floor strippers. Then floor strippers' being unusual cases of "vehicle" would be explained by the term's multi-dimensional vagueness. However, it is precisely the issue whether having the (primary) purpose "of carrying or transporting something" is in fact a dimension of "vehicle." Thus, the source of unclarity in *St. Vincent* is not semantic vagueness but either multi-dimensional polysemy or impliciture indeterminacy. At best, it may be said that gradual vagueness on the contested dimension of having the (primary) purpose "of carrying or transporting something" complicates it further.[137]

---

[137] The case is in fact even more complicated yet. It was also debated whether asbestos was either dust or a form of pollutant (as defined by the contract), since "dust" and "pollutants" were specifically excluded from coverage.

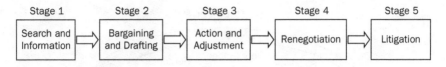

FIGURE 12 **Contractual Stages**

Thus, the multi-dimensional polysemy of "vehicle" caused the incompleteness of the contract in *St. Vincent*. Its indeterminacy was increased by the term's generality and vagueness as well as by pragmatic indeterminacy in the contract. It seems now that Cincinnati Insurance should have used precise thresholds and more specific definitions of its contract vocabulary to avoid litigation. Why did it not do so? The term "vehicle" as used in the contract can be seen to exclude or include floor strippers. The insurance contract by Cincinnati Insurance did not determine this issue in advance.

It is obvious that Cincinnati Insurance could have chosen more determinate terms. It could have defined the terms more specifically and more precisely. But it left the contract in certain respects incomplete. Contractual incompleteness affects costs (section 5.3.2), incentives (section 5.3.3), and is a means to exploit informational asymmetry (section 5.3.4). These three factors will help to explain why Cincinnati Insurance may have done wisely in not using more determinate terms after all.

5.3.2 COSTS

Insurance companies want to keep down drafting costs, enforcement costs, and the likelihood of litigation. They want to allow for the possibility of bailing out from expensive coverage cases. They want to keep premiums up and coverage down. They want to attract low-risk insurees and repel high-risk ones. In short, insurance companies want to draft cost-efficient insurance contracts.

In general, the efficient drafting of contracts depends on factors at different stages. At a first stage, the contracting parties S and R may gather information. After that, at the second stage, they will bargain and draft contract C. At a third stage, they may or may not comply with its terms. Finally, they can renegotiate and legally enforce C at the fourth and fifth stage. Costs are incurred at each of these stages, as depicted in Figure 12.

Traditionally, contract theory analyzes the possibility of renegotiation and the verifiability of contract terms. Indeterminacy matters with respect to both the likelihood of and position in renegotiation as well as the costs of verification. Ceteris paribus, indeterminacy raises the likelihood of renegotiation because some aspects of the contract are not fully determined and must potentially be renegotiated. It is, however, entirely contingent on whether indeterminacy

FIGURE 13 **Transaction Costs**

strengthens or weakens the parties' renegotiation position. Finally, it reduces the contract's verifiability because third parties cannot ascertain what exactly the parties' contractual obligations are. These factors concern the last two stages of contracting in which a particular form of transaction cost is incurred, namely, enforcement costs.

In general, transaction costs are costs incurred when making an economic exchange. As depicted in Figure 13, they consist of information costs, decision costs, adjustment costs, and enforcement costs.[138] Information costs are costs incurred (at stage 1) when investigating whether C is likely to be profitable. Decision costs are costs incurred (at stage 2) when finding an agreement with the other party. As such, they include drafting costs and the costs of facilitating compromise. Adjustment costs are costs incurred (at stage 3) when unforeseen contingencies set in after C is formed but before terminating, renegotiating, or legally enforcing it. Enforcement costs are costs incurred (at stage 4 or 5) when securing compliance with the terms of C.

Transaction costs are an elegant way to explain why contracts are more incomplete than necessary. Oliver D. Hart (1995, 23) identifies three forms of transaction costs as sources for contractual incompleteness. First, it is hard for the parties to *think* far ahead. Second, even if individual plans are made, it is hard for the parties to *negotiate* about them. Third, even if the parties can make and negotiate the plans, it is hard to *write* them down in a way such that also a third party (e.g., a court) can understand and enforce them.

Classically, incompleteness is seen as a necessary evil.[139] In classical models, the contracting parties know the expected utility for all foreseeable contingencies and all possible actions ex ante. Based on this information, they choose a contract design that determines for these contingencies and actions what is legally required from all parties. Once the contract design is determined, nature "chooses" ex post which contingencies in fact set in, and this can be observed by the contracting parties.

Clearly, these are not realistic assumptions. Modern contract theory identifies bounded rationality as the main reason for contractual incompleteness. People do not always take into account all relevant information and process it according

---

[138] Dahlman (1979) differentiates between search and information costs, bargaining and decision costs, as well as policing and enforcement costs.

[139] See, for instance, Williamson (1979).

to logic and probability theory. Contingencies can be misinterpreted or missed altogether. Some contracts are incomplete simply because the contracting parties do not know better. If it is impossible to obtain the information required to make the language of the contract more determinate, the use of indeterminacy can be explained, but it is not strategic. We cannot foresee every contingency. The contract's incompleteness thus cannot be avoided.[140]

Here the difference between gaps and linguistic indeterminacy matters. While the unforeseeability of the future necessarily results in gaps in the contract, the contracting parties can be strategic in their way of dealing with this. They can use indeterminacy to account for the possibility of gaps. Examples are material adverse change (MAC) clauses; *force majeure* clauses; or exclusion clauses such as, for instance, the one in *St. Vincent*. They are designed to enable the contracting parties to terminate the contract or otherwise free them from liability or obligation if some extraordinary (unforeseen) contingency occurs. These clauses are indeterminate for a number of reasons, one of which is to allow wide applicability and flexibility by means of the terms' polysemy and impliciture indeterminacy.[141]

Bounded rationality does not imply irrationality. A behavior is also boundedly rational, for instance, when a search for alternatives is completed as soon as one has found an acceptable solution, even though there might be a better one.[142] The information is often not impossible but merely too hard or costly to obtain.[143] The behavior is then boundedly rational due to the cognitive costs incurred when trying to make contingencies explicit or known.[144] If it is too hard to *think* far ahead, the agent does not consider some contingencies for good reasons because not considering them saves time and energy.[145]

What contingencies are specified in the contract depends on the information costs incurred for specifying them. The contracting parties might spend more on

---

[140] See Maskin and Tirole (1999). This is similar to the use of indeterminacy due to limitations in perception and memory as well to cognitive costs. See section 4.3.2 on the *Argument from Perception and Memory* as well as the *Argument from Cognitive Costs*.

[141] See sections 5.1.3 and 5.2.1 for a similar point with regard to laws and verdicts, respectively.

[142] Simon (1959, 262–263) argues that human beings usually try to "satisfice" instead of maximize their preferences.

[143] Consider the Louisiana Treaty from 1803. It is the single greatest real estate deal in history. It effectively doubled the size of the United States. Napoleon Bonaparte offered Louisiana to the US emissaries James Monroe and Robert Livingston and sold New Orleans and all of the Louisiana Province for 15 million dollars in cash. The Treaty, however, did not determine the exact boundaries and contents of Louisiana. The subject matter of the Treaty remained indeterminate because, arguably, the contracting parties were ignorant about the exact nature of territories. They were uncertain where the boundaries ran because they had not properly explored the territories yet. For instance, it was unclear whether the deal included Spanish held West Florida, the vast areas west of Rio Grande, and the Oregon Territory.

[144] See Tirole (2009).

[145] According to Posner (2005, 1582), there are no complete contracts also because "perfect foresight is infinitely costly."

investigating contingencies (e.g., thinking of and enumerating unlikely cases or quantifying risks) than they would save by taking them into account. Consequently, contracts can also be too complete.[146] In other words, it can be inefficient to write a contract as complete as possible.

Incompleteness of contracts is in many instances analogous to indeterminacy in legislation and adjudication.[147] Contracts can be efficiently incomplete for various reasons. Indeterminacy can reduce information costs not only in laws but also in contracts.[148] Similarly, indeterminacy provides a solution for conflicts of interests and beliefs in laws, verdicts, and contracts.[149] The contracting parties can form incompletely theorized agreements in contracts in the same way as in laws or verdicts.

Difficulties in finding an agreement between contracting parties with conflicting interests or beliefs are analyzed within contract theory classically as the incursion of decision costs. The more interests or beliefs diverge, the greater the decision costs.[150] The greater the decision costs, the more incomplete contracts must be to facilitate (incompletely theorized) agreement. In other words, the harder it is to *negotiate*, the more efficient incompleteness becomes.[151]

However, even if all relevant contingencies were foreseeable and could be agreed on, it would still be too costly to list and describe them. It costs time and money to draft a concise and specific contract. It is costly to draft it in a way such that a court will understand and be able to verify its terms. It is thus more efficient to not account for all contingencies, even if they were in principal foreseeable and agreeable by all parties, because they are too costly to include in the contract or to verify in case of litigation. Ceteris paribus, the more contingencies to account for, the greater the drafting costs. In other words, the harder it is to *write* the contract, the more incomplete it should be.

Information and decision costs can be reduced by ignoring contingencies. Similarly to legislating or adjudicating, it is too costly to detail in advance specific obligations for possible applications in terms of anticipating, agreeing on, and writing them down. These costs are incurred at the first and second stage. After these stages, however, other costs must be taken into account to determine the (long-term) efficiency of incompleteness.

---

[146] There are numerous case studies about the efficiency of incomplete contracts. See, for instance, Crocker and Reynolds (1993) about the strategic incompleteness of Air Force engine procurement contracts.

[147] See Hadfield (1994b), who compares incompleteness in contracts and laws.

[148] See section 5.1.3. It does so arguably also in verdicts.

[149] See sections 5.1.1 and 5.2.1.

[150] See Scott and Triantis (2005) or Craswell (2005).

[151] It can also be shown that the more asymmetric the information between S and R is, the more incomplete the contract becomes. See Spier (1992).

Circumstances can change after the contract is formed. An exogenous shock might occur or the parties make investments—both of which can change the contract's expected utility. For example, a material change of circumstances (such as a financial crisis) may decrease profits of Cincinnati Insurance. It may try to raise the premium as a consequence. The insuree may in return try to terminate the deal, which can result in renegotiation or litigation.

But even if the contracting parties neither renegotiate the contract nor litigate, adjustment costs are incurred. Either insurer or insuree has to compensate for the loss due to the material change of circumstances. Incompleteness can help to alleviate this loss. It has been argued that indeterminacy reduces the risk of error though overinclusiveness and underinclusiveness.[152] Unforeseen contingencies will not simply be excluded when they should have been included or vice versa. There will be less false positives and false negatives because contractual obligations in unforeseen contingencies can be decided ex post. Indeterminacy might thus reduce adjustment costs.

As we noted in section 5.1.4, however, the effect of indeterminacy can also be just the opposite. Someone has to decide eventually. If no agreement is reached, courts have to understand and verify the contract terms. Indeterminacy in the contract's language increases the uncertainty of the legal decision (in addition to factors such as possible bias, incompetence, or corruption of judges). It renders interpretation more protracted and less certain, thereby increasing the costs of litigation.[153]

Some contract theorists argue that courts should interpret contractual incompleteness such as to maximize the joint profits for the parties.[154] If courts would do that, the ex post costs of indeterminacy would be, so the argument goes, suspended. There are two worries about this argument.

First, the parties would still face the costs of litigation and uncertainty. Even if judges would render only verdicts with the best possible outcome for both parties, someone would still have to pay the legal costs. The judges would need to determine what is the best possible outcome—a process that itself involves costs.

Second, and more importantly, it is doubtful that courts have the requisite technical expertise. The legislature may be able to effectively delegate power to agencies because agencies typically have some informational advantage. But, as we saw in section 5.1.3, courts do not. While there is some room for debating whether courts have technical expertise when settling indeterminacy in laws under certain conditions, they typically have no informational advantage when it comes to the completion of contracts. As Gillian K. Hadfield (1994a, 162) points out,

---

[152] See section 5.1.3.

[153] See Choi and Triantis (2010, 852).

[154] See Goetz and Scott (1981), for instance.

generalist courts "possess only limited competence in any one area." Due to the diverse subjects and private nature of contracts, they are usually in a strictly worse position to determine the best solution for contractual incompleteness than the contracting parties themselves.[155] It is thus doubtful that judges can in general complete contracts efficiently.

If litigation is generally more expensive when indeterminacy must be resolved by limitedly competent or unpredictable judges, the parties might still use indeterminacy to stall the decision in hope of a more favorable position when renegotiating. They might thus defer negotiation to some later stage. Some indeterminacy in contracts may be due to *strategic renegotiation design*, as Avery W. Katz (2005, 173) calls it. Contracting parties strategically defer decisions to the renegotiation stage in which they expect to make them more efficiently. This captures what Austin called "taking refuge in vagueness."[156]

Moreover, parties might want to leave a strategic handle to keep a good litigation position when negotiations yield worse results than expected. When some questions are open to dispute, it is easier to find a reason to litigate (and to effectively threaten it). If the contract is complete, the party that wants to terminate the deal will have a hard time convincing the other party or even his lawyers that there is ground to litigate. Thus, indeterminacy can be used to strengthen one's renegotiation position.

According to Jean Tirole (1999), incompleteness is efficient because of unforeseeability at the information and drafting stage and the possibility to renegotiate incompletely theorized agreements ex post. Agents are unwilling to completely and determinately commit themselves before knowing ex ante unforeseeable contingencies. If an unforeseen event occurs, the parties can either adjust to the situation within the contract terms' limits, renegotiate, or litigate.

The crucial question is how contract C should be drafted to maximize, for example, Cincinnati Insurance's overall expected utility. Should C be more or less complete? The phrasing of C affects the costs incurred at all five stages. At the first and second stage, information and decision costs comprise the money and time for Cincinnati Insurance to have lawyers and economists assess risks and find legal definitions and threshold values. At the third stage, potential exogenous shocks or material changes of circumstances determine Cincinnati Insurance's adjustment costs and how good its negotiation position will be. This depends on Cincinnati Insurance's informational access and how well C has anticipated the events. At the fourth and fifth stage, the enforcement costs include the uncertainty of as well as the time and money spent on renegotiation and litigation. Whether the insuree will

---

[155] See Katz (2005, 171) for a similar point.
[156] See section 4.5.

terminate C, accept renegotiation offers, or litigate depends (among other things) on C's degree of determinacy.

The expected adjustment and enforcement costs directly affect the completeness of the optimal contract. If expected adjustment, renegotiation, and litigation is less costly than information and drafting, a less complete contract is more efficient. This means that indeterminacy generally induces a shift of costs from the drafting and negotiation to the litigation or renegotiation phase, that is, from stages 1 and 2 to stages 4 or 5. The choice between more or less indeterminate phrasings of the contract can thus be represented as a trade-off in transaction costs. While determinate phrasings increase information and decision costs ex ante, indeterminate phrasings increase enforcement costs ex post.

In detail, indeterminacy is more preferable when contingencies are remote such that expected enforcement costs are low but less preferable when adversarial litigation is likely or likely to be protracted. Indeterminacy is also less preferable when courts are less informed than the parties themselves because it raises the prospect of costly judicial error (increasing enforcement costs). In general, renegotiation is more efficient than litigation, that is, it is better to defer than to delegate. Analogously to the legislature, which can delegate to better informed agencies, contracting parties can "delegate" to their better informed future selves. This deferral has two basic advantages. First, information and decision costs are generally lower ex post when more information about both the state of the world and the other party are available. Second, unregulated issues can turn out never to be a problem because the relevant contingencies never actually occur.[157] Deferral to renegotiation by indeterminacy is generally less costly than both delegation to courts and ex ante determinacy.

In this section, following the conventional analysis, I argued that indeterminacy shifts transaction costs from the information and decision stages to the renegotiation and litigation stages. In the next section, I will survey different (more controversial) arguments that have been made for the use of indeterminacy in contracts to incentivize desirable behavior.

5.3.3 INCENTIVES

So far, I discussed direct costs and benefits of incompleteness in contracts. There are also indirect costs and benefits, however. I now discuss six ways of using indeterminacy to provide positive incentives. Indeterminacy may be used (1) to provide incentives to overcomply or undercomply, (2) as double-talk, (3) as cheap

---

[157] It is thus possible that neither renegotiation nor litigation costs are actually incurred. See Choi and Triantis (2010, 853). See also section 5.1.1 for basically the same point with respect to legislative delegation.

talk, (4) to signal willingness to renegotiate, (5) to enhance reputation, and (6) as adverse signaling.

First, indeterminacy can reduce and increase compliance. As we saw in section 4.4, it increases compliance when the alternative is total or near non-compliance. However, as we saw in section 5.1.4, indeterminacy generally decreases compliance because other agents with conflicting interests or beliefs can exploit the discretion granted by it. These two effects notwithstanding, indeterminacy may provide additional incentives to overcomply or undercomply.

In particular, semantic vagueness is said to have such effects. When precise thresholds are agreed on, there is no incentive to overcomply or undercomply because the contracting parties will maximize their utility according to the threshold. In contrast, when vague terms are agreed on, the parties have to cope with the risk to just closely miss the point of safety and face litigation when they calculate too narrowly. For a risk-averse agent, it is thus profitable to leave a margin of error to avoid the borderline area altogether.

Hadfield (1994b) argues that precision causes some individuals to ignore a contract clause entirely if they are forced to steer to the same, cost-inefficient, safe harbor. In contrast, a semantically vague contract clause does not set sharp thresholds. As a result, there can be a gradual reduction of probability of liability evoking different responses from different individuals approaching an outcome that is closer to the optimum. Thus, semantic vagueness "softens the impact of judicial error on individual incentives without abandoning entirely the effort to control private behavior."[158]

Hadfield is correct in blaming precision for providing undesired incentives. She is also correct in attributing semantic vagueness some function in correcting false incentives. Individuals can choose their optimal behavior within the borderline area at their own discretion. However, as we saw in section 4.3.2, it is first and foremost the lack of precision that is functional. The gradual reduction of probability of liability results from different forms of context sensitivity such as standard-relativity. A borderline area is often perceived as such only because there are different views about the sense or standard in question, the relevant aspects of context, and the communicative content in general. This is what in actual situations will effectively generate uncertainty and discretion. Semantic vagueness may thus theoretically provide a remedy to moral hazard, but other forms of indeterminacy are actually effective.[159]

Semantic vagueness is often associated also with the function of avoiding other negative incentives of precision. A precise threshold leads generally to fewer

---

[158] See Hadfield (1994b, 545).

[159] Moral hazard is, for instance, the problem when insurees drop precautions because they know that they are covered by the insurance anyway; leading to more occurrences of events insured than usual.

lawsuits because it gives certainty. However, it may also psychologically anchor an undesired value. For instance, if damages in an insurance contract are capped at one million dollars, more claims for damages close to that value will be made. According to Daniel Kahneman (2012, 127), the cap tends to have the effect of anchoring it at that level. This increases lawsuits in general and makes them more costly, even though it prevents claims for damages of more than one million dollars. The cap gives false incentives by eliciting unreasonable claims just below the threshold value because the anchor tends to pull them up to the cap.[160] However, this has nothing directly to do with either semantic vagueness or indeterminacy in general.[161] Even though a semantically vague standard avoids the problem, what is effective is simply the lack of precision.

Second, one might think that, in contrast to laws, double-talk is rather pointless in contracts. Laws have to apply to many different individuals. As we saw, this may require indeterminacy to allow for different incentives to different people. This is normally not the case in contracts that address the contracting parties only. However, taking into account potential third parties who need to decide controversial issues, such as judges or arbitrators, one can easily imagine that the offeror might want to send different messages to the offeree and the judges. Thus, if enforceability is at issue, indeterminacy might prove useful to facilitate double-talk and deniability, as contracts create and change legal norms for the contracting parties (very much as laws do for the whole population).[162]

Double-talk can also be used to address one and the same agent differently depending on his type. Recall the bribery example that we discussed in section 4.4.4. It is a commissive speech act similar to a contract offer. A criminal wants to bribe a dishonest police officer but not an honest one. Thus, the criminal uses indeterminacy to simultaneously address the dishonest police officer with a bribe and the honest one with mere small talk. Analogously, if the offeree settles for products of a certain quality only, but the offeror does not know its degree, the offeror can offer "high quality" and (gradually) increase the quality until the offeree is satisfied. This is a classic strategy in bargaining, by way of which the offeror does not offer more than necessary.

Third, an offeror can also use indeterminacy to signal the high quality of products or services in different ways.[163] Depending on interpretation standards and the parties' access to information, the offeror can get a better deal by pretending attractive conditions through indeterminate language. Describing products as "high quality" is cheap talk. One advertises quality without committing to it, that is, without direct costs. It is evident, however, that this strategy can easily backfire

---

[160] See also Pogarsky and Babcock (2001).

[161] See also our discussion of the *Argument from Inefficiency* in section 4.3.2.

[162] See section 2.2.3 on contracts as legal performatives.

[163] Recall the example in the introduction of this chapter.

since cheap talk is by no means a reliable form of signaling quality. On the contrary, many potential offerees will shy away from offerors using cheap talk because they suspect they are being cheated.

Fourth, it has been argued that because of the potential for high litigation costs caused by indeterminacy, only companies who are unlikely to enter into a lawsuit will use indeterminate language. As Albert H. Choi and George G. Triantis (2010, 888) put it, the "cost of litigation can weed out bad cases from good cases." By framing the insurance contract in indeterminate terms, Cincinnati Insurance may signal that it is willing to award damages or at least to renegotiate instead of litigating. If this is understood by potential insurees, they will consider Cincinnati Insurance more attractive than other insurance companies because they are less likely to litigate. The increased attractiveness allows Cincinnati Insurance to charge higher premiums as a result. Unfortunately, this strategy works only if indeterminacy does effectively signal lower litigiousness. It is doubtful, however, that the litigation likelihood of many companies using indeterminate language is actually lower; and, even if this were the case, that the clients' perception of them is actually improved by this.[164]

Fifth, a similar strategy seems to work for contract terms that are unenforceable due to their indeterminacy. Arnoud W. A. Boot et al. (1993) show that it can be preferable to use legally unenforceable, discretionary, terms in contracts to enhance reputation. Indeterminacy can be used as a signal of trustworthiness when legally unenforceable promises are kept. In the long run, holding up to one's end of the bargain even if one cannot be forced to demonstrates one's reliability. Such increased market reputation would allow Cincinnati Insurance to charge higher premiums.[165]

Again, there are some worries about the strategy's usefulness. First, it is doubtful whether indeterminacy makes any real difference for the question of reliability. Whether the contract is phrased in indeterminate terms or not, an offeror's reputation will, ceteris paribus, be better if she generally sticks to bargains; and it will, ceteris paribus, be worse if she does not. Second, market reputation is a good thing, but it comes at a price. It will often be more profitable to enforce a contract (especially if enforcement is certain) than to keep an unenforceable promise. This will be the case even if unenforceability has the positive side effect to increase reputation in the long run. Moreover, it seems that

---

[164] Certainly, Choi and Triantis (2010) do not provide any evidence for the claim that indeterminacy signals lower litigation likelihood.

[165] See also Triantis (2001, 1070), who examines three effects of "vagueness" related to this strategy. The description of "high quality" in research papers does not distinguish between bestsellers and attention in academic journals, it admits non-verifiable factors, and it creates uncertainty as of which one of three factors has the most weight (sales, reviews, or contribution to knowledge).

reputation can be more effectively increased by other means than indeterminacy. All things considered, it is thus doubtful that by using indeterminate terms the offeror can benefit from such uncertain and long-term advantages as increased reputation.

Sixth, for many areas of business—but especially for insurance—there is the risk of adverse selection. There is the tendency that insurees who are likely to actually make a claim will contract insurance with companies that offer clear and determinate policies. The more determinate the policies, the more attractive they are for such insurees. If the insurer does not want to adversely signal attractiveness, she can use indeterminate language. This repels costly clients, at least if we assume that they are also risk-averse. Hence, Cincinnati Insurance may count on being selected by insurees who are not above-average to make a claim because they do not know ex ante what its insurance covers.

In sum, indeterminacy can strategically be used to provide different kinds of incentives, but none of the six strategies here considered is unconditionally beneficial. There are strings attached to each one of them. Under the right conditions, however, indeterminacy might well provide the incentives desired. In the following and final section, I will turn to a less problematic strategy to use indeterminacy, which is specific to contracts as commissive speech acts.

5.3.4 UNAWARENESS

In game theory, indeterminacy has been formalized in a number of ways. We modeled the different forms of linguistic indeterminacy in section 4.4 as *noise, coarseness,* and *imperfectly correlated equilibria.* Indeterminacy in contracts has been analyzed in even more simplified ways as, for instance, by focusing on its effect to decrease information and decision costs or increase enforcement costs.[166] If contract theorists are more specific in their accounts of indeterminacy, they focus on the use of conversational vagueness, such as Luca Anderlini and Leonardo Felli (2004), Juliet P. Kostritsky (2005), or Xiaojian Zhao (2011).

The most obvious effect of conversational vagueness is non-informativeness. The contracting parties can use a general term and be confident that many (also unforeseen) cases will be included. In contracts, as in laws and verdicts, generality can be used to achieve all-inclusiveness. For the same reason, generality also reduces information and decision costs. It is cheaper to draft a contract in which less contingencies are specifically enumerated and instead covered by a general term. Conversational vagueness is indirectly advantageous here. By specifying the terms of the contract, one would have to gather more information about possible contingencies and their probabilities, spend more care on the drafting process, and

---

[166] This is done by Choi and Triantis (2010), for example.

potentially negotiate harder with a more openly adverse offeree. However, it is not always clear whether the resulting conversational vagueness is itself valuable or simply the unwanted by-product of the valuable effects of generality.

I will discuss in this final section a strategic use of conversational vagueness particular to contracting. The so far mentioned uses of indeterminacy in contracts do not differ much from uses of indeterminacy in legislation and adjudication. However, there are some uses specific to contracts due to their nature as combinations of commissive speech acts. For example, one party can strategically withhold information by using what is sometimes called *intentional vagueness*.[167]

Recall the case *St. Vincent*. Cincinnati Insurance offered an insurance to St. Vincent against damages due to fire and vehicles but not pollutants. The insurance contract specifies covered causes of loss in which Cincinnati Insurance awards damages to St. Vincent and exclusions in which it does not.

I will now analyze the utility of conversational vagueness in such an insurance contract under unforeseen contingencies, based on a model by Zhao (2011). Let us call Cincinnati Insurance insurer S and St. Vincent insuree R. S knows all three possible states of the world. They are the events in which R's orphanage suffers no damage (ω_1), damage due to fire (ω_2), or damage due to vehicles (ω_3):

State	Interpretation
ω_1	No damage
ω_2	Damage due to fire
ω_3	Damage due to vehicles

Assume that R only foresees two states, namely, the contingencies of there being no damage (ω_1) and there being damage due to fire (ω_2), but is unaware of the possibility that there may be damage due to vehicles (ω_3). All events foreseen by R can be directly referred to in R's language. In contrast, R cannot directly refer to events that R does not foresee. In general, foreseeability determines richness of language. However, even though an event might not be expressible in R's language, R may still be able to refer to it by some general term "X."

If R foresees only the two states ω_1 and ω_2, but has the general term $X = \{\omega_2, \omega_3\}$, R's language is limited to expressions such as "there will be damage due to fire," "there will be no damage," "there will be damage," and "there will be no damage or damage due to fire." What R cannot specify in the contract is that "there will be damage due to vehicles." In other words, event ω_3 is not directly expressible in R's language.

---

[167] See, for instance, Allon and Bassamboo (2009) or Board and Blume (2013).

For states that R does not foresee, he will be more or less aware of the unawareness. This awareness of unawareness is the degree to which one does not know that one does not know.[168] But despite this unawareness of unawareness, R can use a heuristic to determine the probability of each event expressible in his language. For all foreseen events ω, R's subjective probability of ω is the ratio of its weight to the sum of the weights of all foreseen events and the general event that comprises the residual unforeseen contingencies. In contrast, R can determine the probability of the general event by the ratio of its weight to the sum of all weights.

Formally, there are three cases now. There is the (unlikely) case that R correctly anticipates the probability of any unforeseen contingency. R gives the correct weight to the general event that precisely corresponds to the probability of the sum of all unforeseen contingencies. He is perfectly aware of this unawareness by correctly estimating their probability. In other words, he perfectly knows that he does not know about some events.

Let us now consider the (slightly more likely) case that R believes that ω_1 and ω_2 are the only possible contingencies and that he would be fully aware of any others if there were any. In other words, he does not know that he does not know about some events.

However, there is also the (much more likely) case that R is only somewhat aware of his unawareness and has some inkling that he does not know about some events. R might be aware that there are other contingencies in X apart from the events he foresees, but he *underestimates* their existence. Or, it may also be the case that R is aware that there are more contingencies in X, but he *overestimates* their existence. In both cases, R knows that he does not know about some events but misjudges their probability.

When S offers the insurance contract C to R, R can become aware of more contingencies, which may affect R's degree of awareness of the unawareness. The contract C can then be said to be conversationally vague with respect to the general term X if the agent is still unaware of some contingencies in X after C has been proposed. This definition fits well with our definitions of generality and conversational vagueness in section 1.4.

When will S prefer a conversationally vague contract? In our example, R knows about the risks of fires and wants to be insured against them, but he is also generally concerned about other causes of damage, too. The utility for R will depend on the monetary gain for running the orphanage in the light of possible damage and the insurance fee that he pays to S, while the utility for S will depend on the insurance premium she offers to R. If the contract is determinate, then all contingencies are

---

[168] See our discussion of the *Rumsfeld Effect* in section 4.5.

listed:

$$
C^{\{\omega_1,\omega_2,\omega_3\}} = \begin{pmatrix} \omega_1, & t_{\omega_1} & \text{no damage} \\ \omega_2, & t_{\omega_2} & \text{damage due to fire} \\ \omega_3, & t_{\omega_3} & \text{damage due to vehicles} \end{pmatrix}
$$

R will either accept or reject the contract depending on the objective probabilities of all three events. If the contract is conversationally vague, on the other hand, then some contingencies are not listed:

$$
C^{\{\omega_1,\omega_2\}} = \begin{pmatrix} \omega_1, & t_{\omega_1} & \text{no damage} \\ \omega_2, & t_{\omega_2} & \text{damage due to fire} \\ \omega_3, & t_{\omega_3} & \text{other damage} \end{pmatrix}
$$

The conversationally vague contract has the same mapping as the determinate one, but it is framed differently. Event ω_3 is framed generally as "other damage." In this case, R will either accept or reject the contract depending also on his subjective weights for the general event of other damage.

It can be formally shown in this model that S will prefer to propose the conversationally vague contract to the precise one for a particular degree of R's awareness of unawareness.[169] If R is sufficiently aware of his unawareness, S cannot profit from the vague contract. If R is not, however, conversational vagueness pays off because the insurance benefit in case of damage due to vehicles will be sufficiently low. R may underestimate the probability of damage due to vehicles, which allows S to offer relatively lower insurance benefits for this contingency. The same is true for the case when R overestimates the likelihood of unforeseen contingencies. S profits then from charging a relatively more expensive insurance premium for the contingency of damage due to vehicles. In either case, insurer S exploits the insuree R's unawareness by using general terms to cover unforeseen contingencies.

In sum, S has an incentive to propose a conversationally vague contract if the existence of unforeseen contingencies are either sufficiently underestimated or overestimated. Furthermore, psychological evidence suggests that virtually nobody highly overestimates the existence of unforeseen contingencies.[170] This allows us to conclude that as the degree of the awareness of unawareness increases, the efficiency of conversationally vague messages decreases. Hence, it makes sense for S to employ general terms in the contract when R is sufficiently unaware of his unawareness of unforeseen contingencies.

---

[169] A formal proof is given in Appendix A.5.

[170] See Johnson and Hershey (1993) and Tversky and Koehler (1994). See also Kahneman (2012, 325).

In particular, S can increase her profits by either charging high premiums or providing low coverage for generally framed contingencies that R is unaware to be unaware of. For instance, Cincinnati Insurance can try to exclude as many cases as possible from coverage by using general exclusion clauses. If it is unknown to the insuree that there is a non-negligible risk of damage by certain types of vehicles, Cincinnati Insurance can use the general term "vehicle" instead of enumerating specifically what counts as vehicles for the purposes of the contract. If insurees generally estimate the likelihood of damage due to vehicles to be smaller than it actually is, they will (wrongly) believe that damage due to vehicles can reasonably be excluded from coverage. In effect, this raises Cincinnati Insurance's profit because insurees are willing to pay more for less coverage.

We said that a contract is conversationally vague in relation to a general term that will not be understood fully by an agent after the contract has been proposed. The insuree will not know whether some relevant contingencies will be covered or not. But does semantic vagueness not have the same effect?

Semantic vagueness seems to be useful here, too, since borderline cases are equally unforeseen by the insuree. This is true. However, borderline cases are generally not foreseen by the insurer either. Moreover, they come with the risk that they can be decided either way. An insurer can use unforeseen cases by phrasing the contract in general terms that include cases that are far from the prototype but still clearly fall within their extension. Consider the term "bird," which clearly includes penguins, even though one rarely thinks of penguins when talking about birds. They are not salient. A borderline case is equally not salient. But in contrast to clear, albeit non-prototypical, cases, borderline cases are difficult to anticipate and can easily backfire.

The same is the case for the multi-dimensional polysemy of "vehicle" in *St. Vincent*. At the end of the day, Cincinnati Insurance had to award damages to St. Vincent for the harm caused by the floor stripper to the orphanage. The court found that a floor stripper constitutes a vehicle for the purposes of the contract.[171] Thus, generality can be strategically used to exploit unawareness in insurance contracts—but not semantic vagueness or polysemy even if they have the same ex ante effect of unforeseeability.

5.4 Summary

In this final chapter, I examined the use of indeterminacy in laws, verdicts, and contracts. I identified five basic functions of indeterminacy.

---

[171] It ultimately decided in favor of St. Vincent, however, based on the contra proferentem rule due to another indeterminacy in the contract.

First, indeterminacy can facilitate the finding of compromise in the light of conflicting interests and beliefs. Legislators, judges, and contracting parties can form incompletely theorized agreements to make communication possible where it would break down otherwise. This reflects the results from the game theoretic models in chapter 4.

Second, indeterminacy can be used to counter the overinclusiveness and underinclusiveness due to an unforeseeable and complex world by using the informational advantage of other parties such as agencies and courts. Indeterminacy can mitigate both conflicts and unforeseeability because it delegates power to potentially better informed parties, as we saw for the *Sherman* and *Clayton* acts, or defers the decision to a later stage, as in contracts with *strategic renegotiation design*. Laws as directives are particularly suited for the use of indeterminacy as power delegation.

Third, indeterminacy can in general be used to reduce drafting costs. However, since it also increases adjustment or enforcement costs, indeterminacy results at best in a strategic and efficient shift in transaction costs from the information and decision phase to the renegotiation and litigation phase. This shift in transaction costs is efficient if, for instance, the occurrence of hard cases is unlikely or adjustment or enforcement costs are comparably low due to informational gains in time.

Fourth, indeterminacy can be used as double-talk in laws, verdicts, and contracts. Under certain circumstances, the legislature can address law enforcement agencies and ordinary citizens differently, improving compliance without imposing unjust or inefficient punishment. Courts can save face and gain deniability by framing their verdicts in indeterminate terms. Contract offerors can allow for different interpretations by offerees and possible third parties such as courts, providing positive incentives. Verdicts as representative declarations are specifically suited for this use of indeterminacy because of their dual function to both find legal facts and change legal status.

Fifth, indeterminacy can be used to improve compliance. The most effective way to do so seems to be by exploiting asymmetrical information. If an agent is unaware of being unaware of some contingencies and either overestimates or underestimates their likelihood, another agent can maintain this informational disadvantage by employing indeterminate terms and turn it into a direct advantage by increasing the other agent's compliance. Contracts as commissives in which the other party commits itself are especially suited for this use of indeterminacy.

This examination of the strategic use of indeterminacy in law also confirmed the main line of argument in this book. While there are numerous functions of indeterminacy, there is no evidence that semantic vagueness has any value in the law. The forms of indeterminacy that I positively identified to be valuable in the law are polysemy, conversational vagueness, and pragmatic indeterminacy.

SUMMARY AND CONCLUSION

Let us return to the case *Papachristou* that we discussed in the very first chapter. What were the sources of indeterminacy in the Jacksonville vagrancy ordinance? What were its effects? And why did the legislators of Jacksonville frame it in this way?

We now have well-founded answers to these questions. The generality, standard-relativity, and polysemy of expressions such as "night walker" facilitated unjustifiably broad discretion by the agencies of law enforcement. As a result, the ordinance was declared unconstitutional. The Supreme Court held:

> This ordinance is void for vagueness, both in the sense that it "fails to give a person of ordinary intelligence fair notice that his contemplated conduct is forbidden by the statute," ... and because it encourages arbitrary and erratic arrests and convictions[1]

The Court found the ordinance unconstitutional due to its "effect of the unfettered discretion it places in the hands of the Jacksonville police."[2] This effect of indeterminacy poses a challenge to important legal principles. It threatens the *rule of law*, the principle of legal certainty, and the separation of powers.

The findings in this book strongly suggest, however, that indeterminacy also fulfills important functions in a legal system. I identified five basic ways in which indeterminacy can be used strategically. First, indeterminacy in general facilitates compromise and the (formal) resolution of conflicting interests and beliefs. Second, indeterminacy can be used to delegate power to other agents or defer a decision to a later stage. This may allow a more informed and less costly approach to difficult cases. It confers to the law "flexibility," which is so frequently demanded, but may also threaten the separation of powers and the *rule of law*. Third, indeterminacy directly reduces costs when drafting a legal text. Fourth, indeterminacy can be used

---

[1] *Papachristou v. City of Jacksonville*, 405 U.S. 156, 162 (1972).
[2] *Papachristou v. City of Jacksonville*, 405 U.S. 156, 168 (1972).

as double-talk to address different audiences with different messages as well as to save face and gain plausible deniability. Fifth, indeterminacy can be used to improve compliance by, for instance, signaling quality or exploiting unawareness.

In *Papachristou*, several of these functions were effective. The legislators of Jacksonville might have strategically used indeterminacy in the ordinance (1) to formally resolve conflicting interests and beliefs about the way to deal with vagrancy, (2) to tacitly grant the Jacksonville police discretion to determine individually who was a "vagrant," (3) to reduce costs by indeterminately describing the elements of the offense instead of determinately defining them, (4) to allow proponents and opponents to understand the purpose of the ordinance in different ways, or (5) to entice homeless people to better comply with the law by arbitrary and discriminatory deterrence.

What forms of indeterminacy can have such effects? It was not semantic vagueness that caused the Jacksonville vagrancy ordinance to be unconstitutionally indeterminate. Semantic vagueness is undeniably a problem for the *rule of law* due to the existence of borderline cases, higher-order vagueness, and Sorites susceptibility. However, these are primarily theoretical problems. In practice, semantic vagueness is rarely an issue. In this book, I showed this in a number of ways.

In the first chapter, I clarified that semantic vagueness is but one of many forms of indeterminacy. There is not only ambiguity and generality with which semantic vagueness is commonly contrasted but also conversational vagueness and pragmatic indeterminacy such as standard-relativity. These forms of indeterminacy are structurally confused with semantic vagueness or ignored altogether.

In the second chapter, I argued that especially in the law, semantic vagueness is likely to be (even) less relevant than in ordinary conversation because it is not linguistic content that ultimately matters. The content of the law can be indeterminate in a number of ways, some of which are entirely non-linguistic. Conversely, the law can be determinate even in actual borderline cases due to considerations of intent, purpose, or other interpretive techniques.

In the third chapter, I demonstrated that many of the supposed examples of semantic vagueness in the law are in fact instances of other forms of indeterminacy. In fictitious cases such as the vehicle in the park statute, a segway is ex hypothesi a borderline case of "vehicle." In actual legal cases, however, no such stipulation can be made. The relevant aspects of context are often precisely the matter of dispute. Most terms are not only vague but also general, polysemous, or standard-relative. Before one can determine whether a case is borderline, one has to determine the context, namely to disambiguate and rule out other forms of indeterminacy. Particularly in law, this is often a normative matter and complicated by theoretical disagreement about legal methodology and meta-interpretation.

In the fourth chapter, I refuted a series of arguments so far made for the value of semantic vagueness. Most of them show merely that it is preferable to use vague terms in contrast to not using any language at all or that some property of vague terms is functional. But they consistently fail to show that borderline cases or Soriticality have a positive function. While it cannot be ruled out that semantic vagueness has some hitherto unknown or hidden function, all arguments made so far either fail to uncover it or inadvertently show that some other form of indeterminacy such as standard-relativity, conversational vagueness, or misunderstood irony has one.

In the fifth chapter, I gave a positive account of the functions of indeterminacy in law that confirmed that the forms of indeterminacy that do fulfill some function are primarily polysemy, conversational vagueness, and pragmatic indeterminacy. Semantic vagueness, on the other hand, is, if anything, problematic. Borderline cases cannot be anticipated as easily as indeterminate cases due to polysemy or standard-relativity. By definition they occur at the fringes of a term's extension. This makes them distinctly less suited for any potential strategic use.

It is also easier to resolve cases of ambiguity or pragmatic indeterminacy than semantic vagueness. It is not possible to rationally question a vague term's applicability in borderline cases. At best a line can be drawn for pragmatic reasons. In contrast, in cases of ambiguity or pragmatic indeterminacy, it is generally possible to find (new) arguments for one or the other interpretation. Most other forms of linguistic indeterminacy cannot only be used with reasonably fair foresight, but they are also a remedy for the negative effects of semantic vagueness. We (often unconsciously) determine the sense of a vague and polysemous expression or the contextually valued standard of a vague and standard-relative expression in such a way as to avoid the borderline area and ensure clear application.

In sum, I found answers to the three questions asked in the introduction. I identified the (1) sources, (2) effects, and (3) strategic uses of indeterminacy in the law, including the source of the "much needed flexibility" of legal language. It mainly consists in the discretion given by polysemy and pragmatic indeterminacy. The resulting delegation of power or deferral allows to build "play into the joints" and adapt the content of law to reduce overinclusion and underinclusion.

The findings in this book also have further implications for language, law, and philosophy. First, they additionally provide insight into the role of semantic vagueness in natural language. Analogously to the legal realm, if an utterance in real life conversation is indeterminate, it is, in all likelihood, unclear due to some other form of indeterminacy than semantic vagueness. We might thus have overestimated the importance of semantic vagueness also with respect to its function in everyday life.

Second, while indeterminacy may not be generally an evil, many of its functions are not for the greater good. Indeterminacy is a means to an end. Its use can be rather selfish, such as the exploitation of unawareness or the deniability of face threatening commitments. Particularly, legal practitioners should know about the different forms of indeterminacy and remind themselves that indeterminacy in law is not necessarily an accident. It might very well be deliberately introduced. The use of indeterminacy can also be benign, however, as the formal resolution of conflict in controversial matters of society or the delegation of power to better informed institutions. In either case, legal practitioners should not worry too much about borderline cases since neither the "much needed flexibility" of legal language nor the "curse of fluidity" stem from semantic vagueness.

Fourth, the findings in this book may also have repercussions for the analysis and resolution of disagreement in law more generally. Some disagreements are hard to resolve because they are matters of ideology. They might be reflected in different senses or conceptions of multi-dimensionally polysemous and evaluative terms. Other disagreements are hard to resolve because there is some other form of linguistic indeterminacy involved, such as standard-relativity or conversational vagueness. However, since it hardly ever is the case that deep disagreements revolve around borderline cases, they can generally be furthered by rational argument.

Fifth, and most importantly, the findings in this book imply that the philosophical debate on vagueness in law is to some degree misguided. Semantic vagueness is not the most relevant form of indeterminacy in law. The preoccupation of philosophers with the Sorites and other problems of semantic vagueness are certainly important theoretical challenges for logic and philosophy. They are not, however, important sources of unclarity in the law. The participants in the debate on vagueness in law should take seriously the fact that laws, verdicts, and contracts have not only linguistic but also legal content. But even context and pragmatic indeterminacy often override precision on the semantic level. As Benjamin N. Cardozo (1921, 161) famously said, "We draw our little lines, and they are hardly down before we blur them." We should thus concentrate more on other forms of indeterminacy such as polysemy, conversational vagueness, and pragmatic indeterminacy—in particular, if we are interested in the potential value or strategic use of indeterminacy in the law.

The Key Theses

1. Semantic vagueness is less relevant than commonly assumed in the debate on vagueness in law for three basic reasons.

    (a) The communication theory of law, which is commonly presupposed by many participants in the debate on vagueness in law, is incorrect. Because legal content is not (solely) determined by linguistic content, linguistic indeterminacy does not directly translate into legal indeterminacy.

    (b) The role of context and other forms of linguistic indeterminacy are systematically underestimated or confused. As a consequence, most examples given for semantic vagueness in the law turn out to be instances of other forms of indeterminacy when more closely scrutinized.

    (c) There is no evidence that semantic vagueness has a value. All arguments for the (strategic) use of semantic vagueness fail, once properly differentiated from other phenomena.

2. Other forms of linguistic indeterminacy can be used strategically in the law in at least five basic ways.

    (a) Indeterminacy can facilitate compromise.

    (b) Indeterminacy can decrease overinclusiveness and underinclusiveness.

    (c) Indeterminacy can reduce information and drafting costs.

    (d) Indeterminacy can be used as double-talk.

    (e) Indeterminacy can improve compliance.

APPENDIX

A.1 Strategies of Semantic Vagueness

We will formally prove the claim that semantic vagueness understood as *noise* is beneficial in a particular signaling game. Consider the signaling game in which the sender S knows when the deal is closed (ω_2) or not (ω_1) and the receiver R holds (a_1), cancels (a_2), or postpones (a_3) the meeting. Each state occurs with the same probability, that is, $\pi(\omega_1) = \pi(\omega_2) = 1/2$. Let us further assume that the interests between S and R diverge in the way depicted in Table 2.

TABLE 2

Signaling Game 2

$u(\omega, a)$	a_1	a_2	a_3
ω_1	3,3	1,0	0,2
ω_2	6,0	5,3	0,2

In this game, R likes the meeting to be held (a_1) when the deal is not closed yet (ω_1), and he likes it to be canceled (a_2) when it already is (ω_2). Moreover, R prefers postponing the meeting (a_3) in cases of doubt. In contrast, S has a private agenda—she prefers the meeting to be held always to its being canceled or postponed. While R benefits somewhat from postponing the meeting, S strictly opposes it now.

If only precise messages are available, there are two Nash-equilibria. They are the combined strategies in which S either always sends m_1 or m_2 and R always chooses a_3. S's expected utility is $u_S^* = 0$, and R's expected utility is $u_R^* = 2$, which is the maximal expected utility that S and R can achieve by using precise messages.

Let us now consider the possibility of *noisy* (i.e., semantically vague) messages by assuming that R interprets message m_1 half of the time correctly as m_1, sometimes mistakenly as m_2, and is the rest of the time uncertain about its content (interpreting it as m_Δ) such that the probabilities are the following:

$$\mu(m_1|m_1) = 1/2 \quad \mu(m_2|m_1) = 1/10 \quad \mu(m_\Delta|m_1) = 2/5$$

Let us also assume that R interprets m_2 half of the time as m_2 but is the other half of the time uncertain about its content: that is, $\mu(m_2|m_2) = \mu(m_\Delta|m_2) = 1/2$. Then, R's expected utility is greatest for the combined strategies of (a_1, m_1), (a_2, m_2), and (a_3, m_Δ).

We can show this by considering the expected utility for each individual combination in turn. R's expected utility for taking action a_1 when perceiving message m_1 is

$$EU_R(a_1, m_1) = 5/6 \cdot 3 + 1/6 \cdot 0 = 2 1/2.$$

The expected utility of taking action a_2 is

$$EU_R(a_2, m_1) = 5/6 \cdot 0 + 1/6 \cdot 3 = 1/2.$$

The expected utility of taking action a_3 is

$$EU_R(a_3, m_1) = 5/6 \cdot 2 + 1/6 \cdot 2 = 2.$$

Hence, R strictly prefers to take action a_1 when perceiving message m_1, that is, R holds the meeting when the deal is not closed yet.

R's expected utility of taking action a_1 when perceiving message m_2, on the other hand, is

$$EU_R(a_1, m_2) = 0 \cdot 3 + 1 \cdot 0 = 0.$$

The expected utility of taking action a_2 is

$$EU_R(a_2, m_2) = 0 \cdot 0 + 1 \cdot 3 = 3.$$

The expected utility of taking action a_3 is

$$EU_R(a_3, m_2) = 2.$$

Hence, R strictly prefers to take action a_2 when perceiving message m_2, that is, R cancels the meeting when the deal is already closed.

R's expected utility of taking action a_1 when perceiving no message (i.e., m_Δ) is finally

$$EU_R(a_1, m_\Delta) = 5/9 \cdot 3 + 4/9 \cdot 0 = 1 2/3.$$

The expected utility of taking action a_2 is

$$EU_R(a_2, m_\Delta) = 5/9 \cdot 0 + 4/9 \cdot 3 = 1 1/3.$$

The expected utility of taking action a_3 is as usual

$$EU_R(a_3, m_\Delta) = 2.$$

In this case, R strictly prefers to take action a_3, that is, R postpones the meeting when he is uncertain about whether the deal is closed or not. Thus, for all messages, R performs the appropriate action when perceiving it. We showed that

$$EU_R(a_2, m_1) < EU_R(a_3, m_1) < EU_R(a_1, m_1),$$

$$EU_R(a_1, m_2) < EU_R(a_3, m_2) < EU_R(a_2, m_2) \text{ and}$$

$$EU_R(a_2, m_\Delta) < EU_R(a_1, m_\Delta) < EU_R(a_3, m_\Delta).$$

S has no incentive to deviate from her strategy either. This can be shown by analogously considering S's expected utility for each individual combination. When knowing that ω_1 occurs, S's payoff of sending message m_1 is

$$EU_S(m_1, \omega_1) = 1/2 \cdot 3 + 0 \cdot 1 + 1/2 \cdot 0 = 1 1/2.$$

S's expected utility of sending message m_2 is

$$EU_S(m_2, \omega_1) = 1/10 \cdot 3 + 1/2 \cdot 1 + 2/5 \cdot 0 = 4/5.$$

Thus, it is the case that $EU_S(m_2, \omega_1) < EU_S(m_1, \omega_1)$. When knowing that ω_2 occurs, on the other hand, her expected utility of sending message m_1 is

$$EU_S(m_1, \omega_2) = 1/2 \cdot 6 + 0 \cdot 5 + 1/2 \cdot 0 = 3.$$

S's expected utility of sending message m_2 is

$$EU_S(m_2, \omega_2) = 1/10 \cdot 6 + 1/2 \cdot 5 + 2/5 \cdot 0 = 3 1/10.$$

Thus, it is the case that $EU_S(m_1, \omega_2) < EU_S(m_2, \omega_2)$.

In summary, S always reports truthfully the state that she experiences: that is, S tells R that the deal is closed iff the deal is closed and she tells him that the deal is not closed iff the deal is not closed. Just as R performs the appropriate action when perceiving it, S sends the appropriate message when observing the state of the world.

Because both S and R have no incentive to deviate from their strategies, this combination is a Nash equilibrium. But is it also an equilibrium that gives higher payoffs than the one with precise messages? To determine this, we compare the total expected payoffs for vague messages with the ones for precise messages.

The total expected utility of S when messages are vague is

$$EU_S(m, \omega) = 1/2 \cdot 1 1/2 + 1/2 \cdot 3 1/10 = 2 1/3.$$

The total expected utility of R when messages are vague is

$$EU_R(a, \omega) = 1/2(1/2 \cdot 3 + 1/10 \cdot 0 + 2/5 \cdot 2) + 1/2 \cdot (1/2 \cdot 3 + 1/2 \cdot 2) = 2 4/10.$$

Both S and R's expected utility is strictly greater than the respective utility in the best equilibrium with precise messages. Thus, we have shown that vague messages can be useful in cases of conflicting interests. S states truthfully when the deal is closed, even though she does vaguely so. The vagueness allows R to trust S and hold the meeting when the deal is not closed, cancel it when the deal is closed, and postpone it when he is uncertain.

A.2 Strategies of Conversational Vagueness

We will formally prove the claim that conversational vagueness can be beneficial in a particular signaling game. Consider the signaling game in which the sender S observes one of three states—the deal is not closed (ω_1), the deal is closed (ω_2), or the Executive Board opposes the meeting (ω_3)—and the receiver R holds (a_1), cancels (a_2), or postpones the meeting (a_3). Each state occurs with the same probability, that is, $\pi(\omega_1) = \pi(\omega_2) = \pi(\omega_3) = 1/3$. Let us further assume that the interests between S and R diverge in the way depicted in Table 3.

TABLE 3
Signaling Game 3

$u(\omega, a)$	a_1	a_2	a_3
ω_1	3,3	6,2	2,2
ω_2	2,0	2,6	2,2
ω_3	0,0	0,0	2,2

In states ω_1 and ω_2, interests conflict because S prefers action a_2 in ω_1, while R will choose action a_3; and S prefers action a_3 in ω_2, while R will go for action a_2. As long as S can send specific messages only, R will not believe messages sent by S in ω_1 and ω_2 because S does not report them truthfully.

This results in R choosing always a_3 since this maximizes his utility. The combined strategies where S sends any message m and R chooses a_3 independently from m are the only Nash-equilibria in this game with specific messages, yielding a maximal expected utility of $EU_S^* = EU_R^* = 2$. Thus, no matter what S tells R, R always postpones the meeting, which is clearly sub-optimal for both S and R.

Now consider the possibility in which S can send the general message that the Executive Board does not oppose the meeting, namely, S can send the general message $m_{1\vee2}$, which unspecifically reports ω_1 and ω_2. The message effectively partitions Ω by differentiating between the combined state $\omega_1 \cup \omega_2$, on one hand, and the single state ω_3, on the other, but not between the individual states ω_1 and ω_2. The expected utility of S and R is then maximized for a_2 if the "general" state $\omega_{1\cup2}$ persists. It will be

$$EU_S(m_{1\vee2}, \omega_{1\cup2}) = EU_R(a_2, \omega_{1\cup2}) = 4.$$

In ω_3, the expected utility is maximized for a_3, which is

$$EU_S(m_3,\omega_3) = EU_R(a_3,\omega_3) = 2.$$

Generality thus facilitates credible communication. S sends $m_{1\vee 2}$ in both ω_1 and ω_2, such that R performs a_2; and m_3 in ω_3, such that R performs a_3. This is the only Nash-equilibrium in this game with general messages. The total expected utility for both agents will be

$$EU_S = EU_R = 1/3 \cdot 4 + 1/3 \cdot 4 + 1/3 \cdot 2 = 3 1/3.$$

It is strictly greater than any Nash-equilibrium achievable for specific messages. This shows that it can be advantageous for both S and R to withhold some information by communicating with conversationally vague messages.

A.3 Strategies of Ambiguity

We will formally prove the claim that ambiguity can be beneficial in a particular signaling game. The proof is based on an example by de Jaegher and van Rooij (2010). Let us first consider a signaling game with unambiguous messages in which the sender S observes one of two states and the receiver R can hold (a_1), cancel (a_2), or postpone the meeting (a_3). The two states occur with the same frequency such that $\pi(\omega_1) = \pi(\omega_2) = 1/2$: either the Supervisory Board approves of the meeting (ω_1) or the Executive Board approves of it (ω_2).

The payoffs of sender S and receiver R depend on the state of the world $\omega \in \Omega$ and R's action according to the utility function given in Table 4.

TABLE 4

Signaling Game 4

$u(\omega,a)$	a_1	a_2	a_3
ω_1	3,3	1,0	0,2
ω_2	1,0	0,3	−1,2

In words, both S and R want to hold the meeting (a_1) iff the Supervisory Board wants it too (ω_1). However, if the Executive Board wants it to take place (ω_2), only S still wants to hold the meeting (a_1), while R would rather cancel it (a_2). Again, R prefers to postpone the meeting (a_3) if uncertain about whether the Supervisory or Executive Board want it to take place.

Evidently, there is no effective communication because S prefers R to choose action a_1 in every state, that is, S prefers R to hold the meeting under any circumstances. Because of that, R cannot trust S and will thus always choose action a_3. The best Nash-equilibrium for precise messages is the combined strategy in which S either sends always m_1 or m_2 and R always performs a_3. S's utility is $u_S^* = -1/2$ and R's is $u_S^* = 2$.

Assume now that S can send an ambiguous message m_1 ("The Board supports the meeting."). It is ambiguous because it can be used to refer to the state that the Supervisory Board wants the meeting to take place (ω_1) or the state that the Executive Board wants it (ω_2). S can send either this ambiguous message or the unambiguous m_2 ("The Executive Board supports the meeting.").

We use the concept of *correlated equilibria* to incorporate the ambiguity of m_1 in the game. Assume that S sends and R receives m in a particular context c that they perceive slightly differently. Context c_S and context c_R are correlated, but not perfectly so. S is either in context c_{S1} or c_{S2}, and R is in either c_{R1} or c_{R2}. Even though contexts c_{S1} and c_{R1} as well as contexts c_{S2} and c_{R2} do not always match, they give some clue about the other agent's perception. As a consequence, S sends message m depending on state ω and context c_S, while R chooses action a depending on message m and context c_R. Ambiguous messages can thus be interpreted differently in different contexts.

Let us assume that the probabilities for both contexts that S can perceive are the same, namely, $\pi(c_{S1}) = \pi(c_{S2}) = 1/2$. Let us further assume that the probability that S and R perceive the context differently is $\pi(c_{R1}|c_{S2}) = \pi(c_{R2}|c_{S1}) = 1/2$. In other words, the probability that S and R are in the same context is 50%. They might have different opinions about what the relevant aspects of context are or different knowledge about some relevant aspect: and, as a result, they interpret m differently. We might say that in contexts c_{S1} and c_{R1}, the Supervisory Board is more salient; while in c_{S2} and c_{R2}, it is the Executive Board.

Consider the case when S sends the ambiguous m_1 in case of ω_1 under any context as well as in case of ω_2 under context c_{S1}. If S observes ω_2 in context c_{S2}, she sends the unambiguous m_2. In other words, S thinks that the meeting should take place even when the Executive Board does not want it. R will then perform a_1 when receiving m_1 under context c_{R2} and a_3 when receiving m_1 under context c_{R1}. If R receives m_2, R prefers a_2 independently from the context that R perceives.

R's expected utility for action a_1, when message m_1 and context c_{R1} are observed, is then

$$EU_R = 2/3 \cdot 3 + 1/3 \cdot 0 = 2.$$

For action a_2, it is $EU_R = 2/3 \cdot 0 + 1/3 \cdot 3 = 1$; and for action a_3, it is $EU_R = 2/3 \cdot 2 + 1/3 \cdot 2 = 2$. Hence, R weakly prefers to perform action a_1, that is, he holds the meeting.

When message m_1 and context c_{R2} are observed, his expected utility for action a_1 is $EU_R = 2/3 \cdot 3 + 1/3 \cdot 0 = 2$. While for action a_2, it is $EU_R = 2/3 \cdot 0 + 1/3 \cdot 3 = 1$, for action a_3, it is fixed at $EU_R = 2$. Hence, R weakly prefers to perform action a_3, that is, he postpones the meeting.

The expected utility for action a_1 when message m_2 and context c_{R1} or c_{R2} are observed is $EU_R = 0 \cdot 3 + 1 \cdot 0 = 0$. For action a_2, it is $EU_R = 0 \cdot 0 + 1 \cdot 3 = 3$; and for action a_3, finally, $EU_R = 0 \cdot 2 + 1 \cdot 2 = 2$. Hence, R strictly prefers to perform action a_2, that is, he cancels the meeting.

The expected utility for R in the individual cases are thus

$$EU_R(a_1, m_1, c_{R1}) \geq EU_R(a_3, m_1, c_{R1}) > EU_R(a_2, m_1, c_{R1}),$$

$$EU_R(a_3, m_1, c_{R2}) \geq EU_R(a_1, m_1, c_{R2}) > EU_R(a_2, m_1, c_{R2}),$$

$$EU_R(a_2, m_2, c_{R1}) > EU_R(a_3, m_2, c_{R1}) > EU_R(a_1, m_2, c_{R1}), \text{ and}$$

$$EU_R(a_2, m_2, c_{R2}) > EU_R(a_3, m_2, c_{R2}) > EU_R(a_1, m_2, c_{R2}).$$

S's expected utility for sending message m_1 when in state ω_1 and under context c_{S1} or c_{S2} is $EU_S = 1/2 \cdot 3 + 0 \cdot 1 + 1/2 \cdot 0 = 1 1/2$. Her expected utility for sending message m_2 when in state ω_1 and under context c_{S1} or c_{S2}, is $EU_S = 0 \cdot 3 + 1 \cdot 1 + 0 \cdot 0 = 1$. For sending message m_1 when in state ω_2 and under context c_{S1} or c_{S2} it is $EU_S = 1/2 \cdot 1 + 0 \cdot 0 + 1/2 \cdot -1 = 0$; and for sending message m_2 when in state ω_2 and under either context c_{S1} or c_{S2}, it is $EU_S = 0 \cdot 1 + 1 \cdot 0 + 0 \cdot -1 = 0$. Thus, S strictly prefers to send message m_1 when in state ω_1 under any context. Moreover, she prefers weakly to send message m_1 when in state ω_2 under context c_{S1} and to send message m_2 when in state ω_2 under context c_{S2}. Hence, S reports truthfully what she observes, while R acts according to her messages.

S has now no incentive to deviate from her strategy because

$$EU_S(m_1, \omega_1, c_{S1}) > EU_S(m_2, \omega_1, c_{S1}),$$

$$EU_S(m_1, \omega_1, c_{S2}) > EU_S(m_2, \omega_1, c_{S2}),$$

$$EU_S(m_1, \omega_2, c_{S1}) \geq EU_S(m_2, \omega_2, c_{S1}), \text{ and}$$

$$EU_S(m_2, \omega_2, c_{S2}) \geq EU_S(m_1, \omega_2, c_{S2}).$$

Hence, this combination of strategies is a Nash-equilibrium. The agents successfully communicate with ambiguous messages because neither of them has any incentive to deviate from their strategies. But is it also a better equilibrium than the one with unambiguous messages?

The total expected utility of S when the messages are ambiguous is

$$EU_S(m, \omega) = 1/2 \cdot 1 1/2 + 1/2 \cdot 0 = 3/4.$$

The total utility of R when the messages are ambiguous is:

$$EU_R(a, \omega) = 1/2 \cdot 2 + 1/4 \cdot (1/2 \cdot 3 + 1/2 \cdot 2) + 1/4 \cdot 3 = 2 3/8.$$

Both S and R thus realize a higher utility than any equilibrium with unambiguous messages where only $EU_S = -1/2$ and $EU_R = 2$, respectively, are achievable. Since the expected utility for both agents in this Nash-equilibrium with ambiguous messages is greater than in the best equilibrium with unambiguous messages, we showed that ambiguity has a positive function.

A.4 The Strategy of Saving Face in Verdicts

We will formally prove the claim that indeterminacy increases non-compliance and makes it at the same time harder to prove when someone does not comply with a (legal) instruction, based on a model by Staton and Vanberg (2008). Assume that a court reviews a law and renders a verdict. The verdict demands that the law be applied according to the court's policy preferences. The verdict can, however, vary in how clearly it articulates this demand. In response to the court's verdict, the legislature implements a certain policy.

Formally, there is a sender S (the court) and a receiver R (the legislature). S can be interpreted as giving instructions m (the verdict) to R. Doing this, S uses a language that is more or less determinate about its implications for R. This degree of determinacy will be represented by parameter $\zeta \in [0, 1]$. Based on S's message, R performs action $a \in A$.

The consequence of R's action is $x = a - \eta$, where $\eta \in [-\gamma, \gamma]$ measures the unforeseeability of the consequences of R's actions. The greater the interval $[-\gamma, \gamma]$ is, the harder it is for S and R to foresee the consequences of R's actions. We will assume that η is uniformly distributed on $[-\gamma, \gamma]$. The unforeseeability of consequences η can be interpreted as an exogenous shock. It thus represents the agents' uncertainty about contingencies.

A quadratic loss function is assumed to represent the agents' payoff. R's payoff is given by

$$U_R(a) = -(r - (a - \eta))^2 - \zeta \cdot b \cdot a^2,$$

where r is R's ideal point, and $(r - (a - \eta))^2$ is R's payoff when performing action a. From this, the term $\zeta \cdot b \cdot a^2$, representing the cost of deviating from S's instructions, is subtracted. It consists of a fixed amount of potential costs b, the severity of deviation a, and the determinacy of message ζ.

When $\zeta = 1$, S sends completely determinate instructions that R might have to follow to the letter, thereby incurring maximal costs. When $\zeta = 0$, m is completely indeterminate, and R can do whatever he wants without any costs whatsoever.

S's payoff is given by

$$U_S(\zeta) = -(a - \eta)^2 - \zeta \cdot s \cdot a^2.$$

The term $-(a - \eta)^2$ is S's payoff when R performs action a. From this, the term $\zeta \cdot s \cdot a^2$ is subtracted, which represents the costs when R deviates from S's instructions. It consists of the severity of deviation a, the determinacy of message ζ, and S's concern s about R's compliance with her instructions.

S is more concerned, that is, s is greater, when either (1) there is less public support for S's decision, or (2) the public is less aware of R's possible defiance. Whether the legislature openly opposes a judicial decision depends thus on how popular the court's verdict is and how transparent defiance would be to the public. If S is not concerned at all about compliance, that is, if $s = 0$, her payoff is given by $-(a - \eta)^2$ alone, and the degree of determinacy ζ in her instructions m is irrelevant.

R's best response to verdict m is given by

$$a^* = \arg\max_a - (r - a - \eta)^2 - \zeta \cdot b \cdot a^2 = \frac{r + \eta}{1 + \zeta \cdot b}.$$

In words, the legislature's optimal response to the court's verdict is to maximize the outcome based on action a. R chooses a such that S's ex post payoff for R's action a^* is then

$$U_S^*(\zeta) = -(\frac{r + \eta}{1 + \zeta \cdot b})^2 - \frac{\zeta \cdot s \cdot (r + \eta)^2}{(1 + \zeta \cdot b)^2}.$$

S's ex ante expected utility is

$$EU_S(\zeta) = \int_{-\gamma}^{\gamma} (-(\frac{r + \eta}{1 + \zeta \cdot b})^2 - \frac{\zeta \cdot s \cdot (r + \eta)^2}{(1 + \zeta \cdot b)^2}) \cdot (\frac{1}{2\gamma}) d\eta.$$

S will choose a degree of determinacy such that her ex ante expected utility $EU_S(\zeta)$ is maximal. On one hand, when R's potential cost is $b < 1$, and S's concern is $s \leq b$, there are cases where the optimal degree of determinacy is $0 < \zeta^* < 1$: that is, neither completely indeterminate nor completely determinate. This holds, at least as long as S and R's preferences diverge sufficiently, that is, when $r > \gamma/\sqrt{3}$. In those cases, m becomes less determinate when the court's concern for compliance s increases and more determinate when the legislature's ideal point r increases.

On the other hand, when R's potential cost is $b > 1$, S's concern is $s \leq b$, and their preferences diverge sufficiently, there are cases where the optimal degree of determinacy is $0 < \zeta^* < 1$ such that ζ^* decreases with s when $r > \gamma/\sqrt{3}$ and increases with s when $\gamma/\sqrt{3} < r < \sqrt{b} \cdot \gamma/\sqrt{3}$. However, for any potential cost b, when S's concern s increases and preferences sufficiently diverge, m goes from completely determinate to completely indeterminate, as s reaches a certain level.

Hence, S can use an indeterminate m to mask potential resistance by R, even though it also encourages R to further diverge from S's instructions. Depending on potential costs b, S's concern for compliance s, and the divergence between S and R's preferences, S will try to find a different balance between both options. If potential costs b are relatively small, on one hand, a greater concern for compliance s will generally make indeterminacy more desirable because S prefers R to diverge to some degree from her instructions m to him fully and openly opposing them. Thus, a concerned S should employ indeterminate language when she expects R to defy her instructions if they were phrased in more determinate terms.

If S has leverage over R (potential costs b being relatively great), on the other hand, and preferences only moderately diverge, m should be more determinate the greater s is. As long as the agents' preferences do not diverge too greatly, S should force R to fully comply with her determinate instructions m—phrasing them less determinately, however, the more S's concern for compliance s rises. When preferences diverge more, she should first phrase m determinately, but once s surpasses a certain point, mask possible non-compliance by issuing a completely indeterminate m. If preferences diverge greatly, m should be completely determinate for small s and completely indeterminate for greater s.

In short, the court should try to make the legislature comply with its instructions by phrasing them in determinate terms when preferences diverge to a degree neither too high nor too low. If the court's concern for compliance is too great, however, it should at some point always try to save face by masking its inability to ensure compliance. Indeterminacy is thus a tool for courts to exercise control over the degree to which non-compliance will be detected.

A.5 The Strategy of Exploiting Unawareness in Contracts

We will formally show the utility of conversational vagueness in an insurance contract under unforeseen contingencies, based on a model by Zhao (2011). Let us call the insurer S and the insuree R. There is the real state space Ω of all possible contingencies ω and the subjective state space Θ of foreseen contingencies θ. Θ is a subset of Ω and relative to an agent. It comprises the states of the world of which the agent is aware. The three possible states of the world are the events in which R suffers no damage, damage due to fire, or damage due to vehicles:

State	Interpretation
ω_1	No damage
ω_2	Damage due to fire
ω_3	Damage due to vehicles

Assume that R only foresees two states such that $\Theta = \{\omega_1, \omega_2\}$. R foresees the contingencies of there being no damage and there being damage due to fire but is unaware of the possibility that there may be damage due to vehicles.

All events foreseen by R can be directly referred to in R's language. In the model, the language of R with subjective state space Θ is the smallest algebra $\mathcal{L}(\Theta)$ over Ω such that $X \in \mathcal{L}(\Theta)$; and, for all $\omega \in \Theta$, it holds that $\{\omega\} \in \mathcal{L}(\Theta)$. Thus, foreseeability determines the richness of R's language, that is, R's language depends on Θ. It is assumed that $\mathcal{L}(\Theta)$ is closed under complement, union, and intersection.

Assume further that there are two general, non-empty events X and Y such that $X \subset \Omega$ and $Y = \Omega \backslash X$. In other words, X and Y divide the possible states in two exclusive sets. Even though an event might not be expressible in R's language because R does not foresee such a contingency, R is still able to refer to it by the general term "X."

If there are three states of the world such that $\Omega = \{\omega_1, \omega_2, \omega_3,\}$, R foresees two states such that $\Theta = \{\omega_1, \omega_2\}$, and there is the general term $X = \{\omega_2, \omega_3,\}$, R's language will be

$$\mathcal{L}(\Theta) = \{\emptyset, \{\omega_1\}, \{\omega_2\}, \{\omega_1, \omega_2\}, \{\omega_2, \omega_3\}, \Omega\}.$$

R's language is limited to expressions such as "there will be damage due to fire," "there will be no damage," "there will be damage," and "there will be no damage or damage due to fire." What R cannot specify in the contract is, for instance, that "there will be damage due to vehicles." In other words, event ω_3 is not directly expressible in R's language.

The states of the world occur with probabilities. Formally, there is an objective probability space defined by $(\Omega, 2^\Omega, \mu)$ such that μ is a measure on 2^Ω, which is the collection of all subsets of Ω. S judges the probabilities of all states of the world correctly.

R, however, does not. R knows $\mu(\{\theta\})$ for all states $\theta \in \Theta$. For all other states $\omega \in \Omega \backslash \Theta$, he will be more or less aware of his unawareness. This awareness of unawareness is measured by the subjective weight $\epsilon_X(\Theta)$ on the unforeseen general event $X \backslash \Theta$. The smaller $\epsilon_X(\Theta)$ is, the less aware R is about his unawareness. Thus, $\epsilon_X(\Theta)$ may be said to represent the degree to which R does not know that he does not know.

R's subjective probability space is then different from S's one, which is identical to the objective probability space. R's subjective probability measure is π_R^Θ : $\mathcal{L}(\Theta) \mapsto \mathbb{R}_+$ such that

$$\pi_R^\Theta(\{\omega\}) = \frac{\pi(\{\omega\})}{\sum_{\omega \in \Theta} \pi(\{\omega\}) + \sum_X \epsilon_X(\Theta)} \text{ for all } \omega \in \Theta, \text{ and}$$

$$\pi_R^\Theta(X \backslash \Theta) = \frac{\epsilon_X(\Theta)}{\sum_{\omega \in \Theta} \pi(\{\omega\}) + \sum_X \epsilon_X(\Theta)} \text{ for all } X.$$

R is unaware of some contingencies. But despite this unawareness, he can use a heuristic to determine the probability of each event expressible in her language. For all foreseen events ω, R's subjective probability of ω is the ratio of its weight to the sum of the weights of all foreseen events and the general event that comprises the residual unforeseen contingencies. In contrast, R determines the probability of the general event by the ratio of its weight to the sum of all weights.

In principle, it may be possible that if event $X \cup \Theta$ is not foreseen, and R judges the probability of X, ϵ_X could become negative. This is due to the common fallacy of conjunction (cf. Kahneman and Tversky, 1983). However, in this model, R is fully aware of all contingencies in Θ, so by inclusion, she is also fully aware of all contingencies in $X \cup \Theta$. Thus, it is always the case that $\epsilon_X \geq 0$.

Let us now consider other, more interesting, degrees of R's awareness of unawareness. If $\epsilon_X(\Theta) = 0$, $X \backslash \Theta$ is completely unforeseen. R believes that ω_1 and ω_2 are the only possible contingencies and that he would be fully aware of any others if there were any. In other words, he does not know that he does not know about some events.

If $\epsilon_X(\Theta) = \sum_{\omega \in X \backslash \Theta} \pi(\{\omega\})$, R correctly anticipates the probability of any unforeseen contingency. R gives the correct weight to the general event, which precisely corresponds to the probability of the sum of all unforeseen contingencies. He is perfectly aware of her unawareness by correctly estimating their probability. In other words, he perfectly knows that he does not know about some events. Note that this also provides an answer to the critique on the connection between incomplete contracts and unforeseen contingencies by Maskin and Tirole (1999). In this case, the contingency is foreseeable in principle but for whatever reasons unforeseen or indescribable by R. As a consequence, the contract would count as (formally) complete.

If $\epsilon_X(\Theta) < \sum_{\omega \in X \backslash \Theta} \pi(\{\omega\})$, R is aware that there are other contingencies in $X \backslash \Theta$, but he underestimates their existence. This interpretation conforms to the sub-additivity assumption for implicit disjunction of support theory, which describes how people actually deal with probabilities in such cases (cf. Tversky and Koehler, 1994). If $\epsilon_X(\Theta) > \sum_{\omega \in X \backslash \Theta} \pi(\{\omega\})$, R is aware that there are other contingencies in $X \backslash \Theta$, but he overestimates their existence. In both cases, R knows that he does not know about some events but misjudges their probability.

A contract based on the foreseen contingencies Θ is a mapping $C^\Theta : \mathcal{P}(\Theta) \mapsto F$, where $\mathcal{P}(\Theta)$ is the finest possible partition of Θ, and F is the choice set. A partition $\mathcal{P}(\Theta)$ is the finest possible one iff $\mathcal{P}(\Theta) = \{\{\omega\} : \omega \in \Theta\} \cup \{X \backslash \Theta\} \cup \{Y \backslash \Theta\}\}$. Thus, a contract maps from the finest expressible event to the agents' choice.

As the contract has been proposed, R can become aware of more contingencies. He might then update his subjective state space from Θ to Θ^1. This also affects R's subjective weight $\epsilon_X(\Theta)$, which becomes $\epsilon_X(\Theta^1)$.

A contract C^{Θ^1} is then conversationally vague in X if $X \nsubseteq \Theta^1$. In other words, it is vague with respect to the general term X if the agent is still unaware of some contingencies in X after C^{Θ^1} has been proposed.

R's subjective expected utility is given by

$$EU_R(C^{\Theta^1}) = \sum_{E \in \mathcal{P}(\Theta^1)} \mu^{\Theta^1}(E) \sum_X I_{E \subseteq X} \cdot u_R^X(C^{\Theta^1}(E)).$$

$I_{E \subseteq X}$ is an index function such that $I_{E \subseteq X} = 1$, if $E \subseteq X$, and $I_{E \subseteq X} = 0$ otherwise. The utility $u_R^X(C^{\Theta^1}(E))$ depends on the general event X and the contractual clauses for event E. It is assumed to be a continuous, strictly increasing, and strictly concave von Neumann-Morgenstern utility function $u_R : \Omega \times F \mapsto \mathbb{R}$.

S's subjective expected utility is completely contingency independent and given by

$$EU_S(C^{\Theta^1}) = \sum_{E \in \mathcal{P}(\Theta^1)} \mu(E) \cdot u_S(C^{\Theta^1}(E)).$$

When will S prefer a conversationally vague contract? S offers insurance contract C to R. R knows about the risks of fires and wants to be insured against them. We assume that R's orphanage can suffer no damage, damage due to fire, and damage due to vehicles and that all three events are equally likely, that is

$$\mu(\{\omega_1\}) = \mu(\{\omega_2\}) = \mu(\{\omega_3\}) = 1/3.$$

The utility function of R is $u_R(\omega, t) = u(g - t)$, where g is the monetary gain for running the orphanage in the light of possible damage and t is the insurance fee. The gain g is reduced when some damage is suffered. If there is no damage, it is strictly positive, that is, $g_1 > 0$. If there is some damage, the gain is strictly smaller than it would have been without damage, that is, $g_0 < g_1$. The utility function of S is $u_S(t) = t$, so that S can choose whatever insurance premium she likes.

If the contract is determinate, then all contingencies are listed:

$$C^{\{\omega_1, \omega_2, \omega_3\}} = \begin{pmatrix} \omega_1, & t_{\omega_1} & \text{no damage} \\ \omega_2, & t_{\omega_2} & \text{damage due to fire} \\ \omega_3, & t_{\omega_3} & \text{damage due to vehicles} \end{pmatrix}$$

S's expected utility is then $1/3 \cdot t_{\omega_1} + 1/3 \cdot t_{\omega_2} + 1/3 \cdot t_{\omega_3}$. R's expected utility, on the other hand, is $1/3 \cdot u(g_1 - t_{\omega_1}) + 1/3 \cdot u(g_0 - t_{\omega_2}) + 1/3 \cdot u(g_0 - t_{\omega_3})$. R can reject the contract such that $t(\omega) = 0$ for all $\omega \in \Omega$ and his final utility becomes $1/3 \cdot u(g_1) + 2/3 \cdot u(g_0)$.

S will maximize her final payoff such that

$$1/3 \cdot u(g_1 - t_{\omega_1}) + 1/3 \cdot u(g_0 - t_{\omega_2}) + 1/3 \cdot u(g_0 - t_{\omega_3}) \geq$$

$$1/3 \cdot u(g_1) + 2/3 \cdot u(g_0).$$

Let us consider an example. Assume that $u(\cdot) = ln(\cdot)$, $g_1 = 2$, and $g_0 = 1$. Then, $1/3 \cdot ln(2 - t_{\omega_1}) + 1/3 \cdot ln(1 - t_{\omega_2}) + 1/3 \cdot ln(1 - t_{\omega_3}) \geq 1/3 \cdot ln(2) + 2/3 \cdot ln(1) = 0.23$. The solution supposes that $g_1 - t_{\omega_1} = g_0 - t_{\omega_2} = g_0 - t_{\omega_3}$. Hence, it must be the case that $ln(2 - t_{\omega_1}) \geq 0.23$. Then, the payoff is maximal if $t_{\omega_1} = 0.74$ and $t_{\omega_2} = t_{\omega_3} = -0.26$.

Hence, R will pay to S an insurance premium of 0.74 when there is no damage, and S will pay R an insurance benefit of 0.26 when there is damage. S's payoff is then $1/3 \cdot 0.74 + 1/3 \cdot (-0.26) + 1/3 \cdot (-0.26) = 0.073$. At the same time, R's payoff is $1/3 \cdot ln(2 - 0.74) + 2/3 \cdot ln(1 + 0.26) = 0.23$.

If the contract is conversationally vague, on the other hand, then some contingencies are not listed:

$$C^{\{\omega_1,\omega_2\}} = \begin{pmatrix} \omega_1, & t_{\omega_1} & \text{no damage} \\ \omega_2, & t_{\omega_2} & \text{damage due to fire} \\ \omega_3, & t_{\omega_3} & \text{other damage} \end{pmatrix}$$

The conversationally vague contract has the same mapping as the determinate one, but it is framed differently. Event ω_3 is framed generally as "other damage." R's expected utility depends thus on his subjective weights for the general event of other damage, that is, it is $EU_R(C^{\{\omega_1,\omega_2\}}) =$

$$\frac{1/3}{2/3 + \epsilon} \cdot u(g_1 - t_{\omega_1}) + \frac{1/3}{2/3 + \epsilon} \cdot u(g_0 - t_{\omega_2}) + \frac{\epsilon}{2/3 + \epsilon} \cdot u(g_0 - t_{\omega_3}).$$

R can reject the contract such that his final utility is $EU_R(-) =$

$$\frac{1/3}{2/3 + \epsilon} \cdot u(g_1) + \frac{1/3 + \epsilon}{2/3 + \epsilon} \cdot u(g_0).$$

Again, S will maximize her final payoff $1/3 \cdot t_{\omega_1} + 1/3 \cdot t_{\omega_2} + 1/3 \cdot t_{\omega_3}$ such that

$$1/3 \cdot u(g_1 - t_{\omega_1}) + 1/3 \cdot u(g_0 - t_{\omega_2}) + \epsilon \cdot u(g_0 - t_{\omega_3}) \geq$$

$$1/3 \cdot u(g_1) + (1/3 + \epsilon) \cdot u(g_0).$$

Let us consider the same scenario as before where $u(\cdot) = ln(\cdot)$, $g_1 = 2$, and $g_0 = 1$. Again, it has to be the case that $1/3 \cdot ln(2 - t_{\omega_1}) + 1/3 \cdot ln(1 - t_{\omega_2}) + \epsilon \cdot ln(1 - t_{\omega_3}) \geq 1/3 \cdot ln(2) + (1/3 + \epsilon) \cdot ln(1) = 0.23$. It follows that S will prefer to propose the vague contract to the precise one when R's degree of awareness of unawareness is either $\epsilon > 1/3$ or $\epsilon < 0.16$.

If $\epsilon = 1/4$, for example, then R is sufficiently aware of his unawareness such that S cannot profit from the vague contract. If R's degree is $\epsilon = 1/10$, however, then he is not and conversational vagueness pays off because the insurance benefit in case of damage due to vehicles will be sufficiently low. R underestimates the probability of damage due to vehicles, which allows S to offer relatively lower insurance benefits for this contingency. The same is true for a degree of $\epsilon = 1/2$, where R overestimates the likelihood of unforeseen contingencies. S profits then from charging for a relatively more expensive insurance premium for the contingency of damage due to vehicles. In either case, insurer S exploits the insuree R's unawareness by using general terms to cover unforeseen contingencies.

BIBLIOGRAPHY

Åkerman, J. and P. Greenough (2010). Hold the Context Fixed, Vagueness Still Remains. In R. Dietz and S. Moruzzi (Eds.), *Cuts and Clouds*, pp. 275–288. Oxford, New York: Oxford University Press.

Alexy, R. (1980). Logische Analyse juristischer Entscheidungen. *Archiv für Rechts- und Sozialphilosophie 14*, 181–212.

Alexy, R. (1995). *Recht, Vernunft, Diskurs: Studien zur Rechtsphilosophie*. Frankfurt am Main: Suhrkamp.

Allon, G. and A. Bassamboo (2009). Cheap Talk in Operations: Role of Intentional Vagueness. In C. S. Tang and S. Netessine (Eds.), *Consumer-Driven Demand and Operations Management Models*, Volume 131: *International Series in Operations Research & Management Science*, pp. 3–36. Berlin: Springer.

Alston, W. P. (1964). *Philosophy of Language*. Englewood Cliffs, NJ: Prentice-Hall.

Alston, W. P. (1967). Vagueness. In P. Edwards (Ed.), *The Encyclopedia of Philosophy*, pp. 218–221. New York: MacMillan.

Amit, R. (2006). The Paradox of the Law: Between Generality and Particularity—Prohibiting Torture and Practising It in Israel. In O. Perez and G. Teubner (Eds.), *Paradoxes and Inconsistencies in the Law*, pp. 275–300. Oxford: Hart.

Anderlini, L. and L. Felli (2004). Bounded Rationality and Incomplete Contracts. *Research in Economics 58*(1), 3–30.

Anderson, S. A. (2006). *Legal Indeterminacy in Context*. Doctoral dissertation, The Ohio State University, Ohio.

Aquinas, T. (2006). *Summa Theologiæ*. London: Burns Oates & Washbourne. (Original work published 1912)

Aranson, P. H., E. Gellhorn, and G. O. Robinson (1982). A Theory of Legislative Delegation. *Cornell Law Review 68*(1), 1–67.

Arielli, E. (2005). *Unkooperative Kommunikation: Eine handlungstheoretische Untersuchung*, Volume 1: *Grundlagen der Kommunikation und Kognition*. Münster: LIT-Verlag.

Aristotle (1984). Nicomachean Ethics. In J. Barnes (Ed.), *The Complete Works*, pp. 1729–1867. Princeton, NJ: Princeton University Press.

Asch, S. E. (1946). Forming Impressions of Personality. *The Journal of Abnormal and Social Psychology 41*(3), 258–290.

Asgeirsson, H. (2012a). Vagueness and Power-Delegation in Law: A Reply to Sorensen. In M. D. A. Freeman and F. Smith (Eds.), *Current Legal Issues*, pp. 344–355. Oxford: Oxford University Press.

Asgeirsson, H. (2012b). *Vagueness, Legal Content, and Legal Interpretation*. Doctoral dissertation, University of Southern California, Los Angeles.

Asgeirsson, H. (2015). On the Instrumental Value of Vagueness in the Law. *Ethics* 125 (2), 425–448.

Asgeirsson, H. (2016). Can Legal Practice Adjudicate Between Theories of Vagueness? In G. Keil and R. Poscher (Eds.), *Vagueness and the Law*, pp. 95–125. Oxford: Oxford University Press.

Atiyah, P. S. (1986). The Modern Role of Contract Law. In *Essays on Contracts*, pp. 1–9. Oxford: Clarendon Press.

Aumann, R. J. (1974). Subjectivity and Correlation in Randomized Strategies. *Journal of Mathematical Economics 1*, 67–96.

Austin, J. (1999/1832). *The Province of Jurisprudence Determined*. Union, NJ: Lawbook Exchange.

Austin, J. L. (1946). Other Minds. *Proceedings of the Aristotelian Society, Supplementary Volumes 20*, 148–187.

Austin, J. L. (1957). A Plea for Excuses: The Presidential Address. *Proceedings of the Aristotelian Society 57*, 1–30.

Austin, J. L. (1962). *How to Do Things With Words*. Oxford: Clarendon Press.

Austin, J. L., P. F. Strawson, and D. R. Cousin (1950). Symposium: Truth. *Proceedings of the Aristotelian Society, Supplementary Volumes 24*, 111–172.

Austin, J. L. and G. J. Warnock (1962). *Sense and Sensibilia*. London and New York: Oxford University Press.

Ayaß, W. (2012). Demnach ist zum Beispiel asozial …: Zur Sprache sozialer Ausgrenzung im Nationalsozialismus. *Beiträge zur Geschichte des Nationalsozialismus 20*, 69–89.

Ayres, I. and R. Gertner (1989). Filling Gaps in Incomplete Contracts: An Economic Theory of Default Rules. *Yale Law Journal 99*(1), 87–130.

Azar, M. (2007). Transforming Ambiguity into Vagueness in Legal Interpretation. In A. Wagner, W. G. Werner, and D. Cao (Eds.), *Interpretation, Law, and the Construction of Meaning*, pp. 121–137. Dordrecht, Netherlands: Springer.

Bach, K. (1982). Semantic Nonspecificity and Mixed Quantifiers. *Linguistics & Philosophy 4*(4), 593–605.

Bach, K. (1994). Conversational Impliciture. *Mind & Language 9*(2), 124–162.

Bach, K. (2005). Context ex Machina. In Z. Szabó (Ed.), *Semantics versus Pragmatics*, pp. 15–44. Oxford: Oxford University Press.

Bach, K. (2010). Impliciture vs Explicature: What's the Difference? In M. B. Soria Casaverde and E. Romero (Eds.), *Explicit Communication*, pp. 126–137. New York: Palgrave Macmillan.

Bach, K. (2012). Context Dependence. In M. García-Carpintero and M. Kölbel (Eds.), *The Continuum Companion to the Philosophy of Language*, Continuum companions, pp. 153–184. London and New York: Continuum International.

Bach, K. and R. M. Harnish (1979). *Linguistic Communication and Speech Acts*. Cambridge, MA: MIT Press.

Baddeley, A. (2007). *Working Memory, Thought, and Action*. Oxford: Oxford University Press.

Balkin, J. M. (2011). *Living Originalism*. Cambridge, MA: Belknap Press.

Balkin, J. M. and B. A. Ackerman (2001). *What Brown v. Board of Education Should Have Said: The Nation's Top Legal Experts Rewrite America's Landmark Civil Rights Decision*. New York: New York University Press.

Ballmer, T. T. and W. Brennenstuhl (1981). *Speech Act Classification: A Study in the Lexical Analysis of English Speech Activity Verbs*. Berlin: Springer.

Bartsch, R. (1984). Norms, Tolerance, Lexical Change, and Context-Dependence of Meaning. *Journal of Pragmatics 8*(3), 367–393.

Bassenge, P. and O. Palandt (2013). *Bürgerliches Gesetzbuch* (72nd ed.), Volume 7: *Beck'sche Kurz-Kommentare*. München: Beck.

Batey, R. (1998). Vagueness and the Construction of Criminal Statues: Balancing Acts. *Virginia Journal of Social Policy and Law 5*(1), 1–96.

Bazzanella, C. (2011). Indeterminacy in Dialogue. *Language and Dialogue 1*(1), 21–43.

Bennett, R. W. and L. B. Solum (2011). *Constitutional Originalism*. Ithaca, NY: Cornell University Press.

Bentham, J. (1776). *A Fragment on Government*. Cambridge: Cambridge University Press.

Bernal, C. L. (2007). A Speech Act Analysis of Judicial Decisions. *European Journal of Legal Studies 1*(2), 1–24.

Besson, S. (2005). *The Morality of Conflict: Reasonable Disagreement and the Law*. Oxford: Hart.

Bhatia, V. K. (2005). Specificity and Generality in Legislative Expression: Two Sides of the Coin. In V. K. Bhatia, J. Engberg, M. Gotti, and D. Heller (Eds.), *Vagueness in Normative Texts*, Volume 23: *Linguistic Insights*, pp. 337–356. Bern: Lang.

Bierling, E. R. (1905). *Juristische Prinzipienlehre*. Tübingen: Mohr Siebeck.

Bix, B. (2003). *Law, Language and Legal Determinacy*. Oxford: Clarendon Press.

Bix, B. (2012a). Legal Interpretation and the Philosophy of Language. In L. M. Solan and P. M. Tiersma (Eds.), *Oxford Handbook of Language and Law*, pp. 145–157. Oxford: Oxford University Press.

Bix, B. (2012b). Theories of Contract Law and Enforcing Promissory Morality: Comments on Charles Fried. *Suffolk University Law Review 45*(3), 719–734.

Black, M. (1937). Vagueness: An Exercise in Logical Analysis. *Philosophy of Science 4*(4), 427–455.

Black, M. (1954). Metaphor. *Proceedings of the Aristotelian Society 55*, 273–294.

Board, O. J. and A. Blume (2013). Intentional Vagueness. *Erkenntnis Online*, 1–45.

Board, O. J., A. Blume, and K. Kawamura (2007). Noisy Talk. *Theoretical Economics 2*(4), 395–440.

Bobbitt, P. (1982). *Constitutional Fate: Theory of the Constitution*. Oxford: Oxford University Press.

Bobzien, S. (2010). Higher-order Vagueness, Radical Unclarity, and Absolute Agnosticism. *Philosophers' Imprint 10*(10), 1–30.

Boot, A. W. A., S. I. Greenbaum, and A. V. Thakor (1993). Reputation and Discretion in Financial Contracting. *American Economic Review 83*(5), 1165–1183.

Bosch, P. (1979). Vagueness, Ambiguity, and All the Rest: An explication and an Intuitive Test. In M. v. d. Velde and W. Vandeweghe (Eds.), *Sprachstruktur, Individuum und Gesellschaft*, pp. 9–19. Tübingen: Niemeyer.

Breyer, S. G. (2005). *Active Liberty: Interpreting Our Democratic Constitution*. New York: Knopf.

Brown, P. and S. C. Levinson (1987). *Politeness: Some Universals in Language Usage*. Cambridge: Cambridge University Press.

van der Burg, W. (2009). Essentially Ambiguous Concepts and the Fuller-Hart-Dworkin Debate. *Archiv für Rechts-und Sozialphilosophie 95(3)*, 305–326.

Burk, D. L. (1999). Muddy Rules for Cyberspace. *Cardozo Law Review 21*, 121–179.

Burks, A. W. (1946). Empiricism and Vagueness. *The Journal of Philosophy 43*(18), 477–486.

Burnyeat, M. F. (1982). Gods and Heaps. In M. Schofield and M. C. Nussbaum (Eds.), *Langage and Logos*, pp. 315–338. Cambridge: Cambridge University Press.

Burton, S. J. (2009). *Elements of Contract Interpretation*. Oxford: Oxford University Press.

Busse, D. (1991). Der Bedeutungswandel des Begriffs „Gewalt" im Strafrecht: Über institutionell-pragmatische Faktoren semantischen Wandels. In D. Busse (Ed.), *Diachrone Semantik und Pragmatik*, pp. 259–275. Tübingen: Niemeyer.

Bydlinski, F. (1991). *Juristische Methodenlehre und Rechtsbegriff* (2nd ed.). New York: Springer.

Cappelen, H. and E. Lepore (2005). *Insensitive Semantics: A Defense of Semantic Minimalism and Speech Act Pluralism*. Malden, MA: Wiley-Blackwell.

Cardozo, B. N. (1921). *The Nature of the Judicial Process*. New Haven, CT: Yale University Press.

Cardozo, B. N. (1924). *The Growth of the Law*. New Haven, CT: Yale University Press.

Carlson, G. N. and F. J. Pelletier (1995). *The Generic Book*. Chicago: University of Chicago Press.

Carlson, L. (1985). *Dialogue Games: An Approach to Discourse Analysis*. Dordrecht: Reidel.

Carlsson, H. and S. Dasgupta (1997). Noise-Proof Equilibria in Two-Action Signaling Games. *Journal of Economic Theory 77*(2), 432–460.

Carnap, R. (1955). Meaning and Synonymy in Natural Languages. *Philosophical Studies 6*(3), 33–47.

Carston, R. (2002). *Thoughts and Utterances: The Pragmatics of Explicit Communication*. Oxford: Blackwell.

Carston, R. (2013). Legal Texts and Canons of Construction: A View from Current Pragmatic Theory. In M. D. A. Freeman and F. Smith (Eds.), *Law and Language*, Volume 15: *Current Legal Issues*, pp. 8–33. Oxford: Oxford University Press.

Cho, I.-K. and D. M. Kreps (1987). Signaling Games and Stable Equilibria. *Quarterly Journal of Economics 102*, 179–221.

Choi, A. H. and G. G. Triantis (2010). Strategic Vagueness in Contract Design: The Case of Corporate Acquisitions. *Yale Law Journal 119*, 848–924.

Chomsky, N. (1965). *Aspects of the Theory of Syntax*. Cambridge, MA: MIT Press.

Christensen, R. (1989). *Was heißt Gesetzesbindung? Eine rechtslinguistische Untersuchung*, Volume 140: *Schriften zur Rechtstheorie*. Berlin: Duncker & Humblot.

Christensen, R. and H. Kudlich (2008). *Gesetzesbindung: Vom vertikalen zum horizontalen Verständnis*. Schriften zur Rechtstheorie. Berlin: Duncker & Humblot.

Christie, G. C. (1964). Vagueness and Legal Language. *Minnesota Law Review 48*, 885–911.

Clare, T. A. (1994). Smith v. United States and the Modern Interpretation of 18 U.S.C. 924(c): A Proposal to Amend the Federal Armed Offender Statute. *Notre Dame Law Review 69*, 815–855.

Cohen, F. S. (1959). *Ethical Systems and Legal Ideals: An Essay on the Foundations of Legal Criticism*. Ithaca, NY: Great Seal Books.

Coleman, J. L. (2001). *The Practice of Principle*. Oxford: Oxford University Press.

Constable, M. (2011). Law as Claim to Justice: Legal History and Legal Speech Acts. *UC Irvine Law Review 1*(3), 631–640.

Cooper, J. M. (2007). *Cognitive Dissonance: Fifty Years of a Classic Theory*. Los Angeles: Sage.

Corbin, A. L. (1965). The Interpretation of Words and the Parol Evidence Rule. *Cornell Law Quarterly 50*, 161–190.

Cotterill, J. (2007). "I Think He Was Kind of Shouting or Something": Uses and Abuses of Vagueness in the British Courtroom. In J. Cutting (Ed.), *Vague Language Explored*, pp. 97–114. Basingstoke: Palgrave.

Craswell, R. (2005). The "Incomplete Contracts" Literature and Efficient Precautions. *Case Western Reserve Law Review 56*(1), 151–186.

Craswell, R. and J. E. Calfee (1986). Deterrence and Uncertain Legal Standards. *Journal of Law, Economics, and Organization 2*(2), 279–303.

Crawford, V. P. and J. Sobel (1982). Strategic Information Transmission. *Econometrica 50*(6), 1431–1451.

Cray, E. (1997). *Chief Justice: A Biography of Earl Warren*. New York: Simon & Schuster.

Cresswell, M. J. (1979). The World Is Everything That Is the Case. In M. J. Loux (Ed.), *The Possible and the Acutal*, pp. 129–145. Ithaca, NY: Cornell University Press.

Crocker, K. J. and K. J. Reynolds (1993). The Efficiency of Incomplete Contracts: An Empirical Analysis of Air Force Engine Procurement. *RAND Journal of Economics 24*(1), 126–146.

Croft, W. (1994). Sentence Typology and the Taxonomy of Speech Acts. In S. L. Tsohatzidis (Ed.), *Foundations of Speech Act Theory*, pp. 460–477. London: Routledge.

Cruz, M., J. Foster, B. Quillin, and P. Schellekens (2015). Ending Extreme Poverty and Sharing Prosperity: Progress and Policies. Available at http://pubdocs.worldbank.org/pubdocs/pu bdocs/publicdoc/2015/10/109701443800596288/PRN03-Oct2015-TwinGoals.pdf. Last checked on 16 June 2016.

Culver, K. C. (2004). Review: Varieties of Vagueness. *The University of Toronto Law Journal 54*(1), 109–127.

Cunningham, C. D., J. N. Levi, G. M. Green, and J. P. Kaplan (1994). Plain Meaning and Hard Cases. *The Yale Law Journal 103*(6), 1561–1625.

Dahlman, C. J. (1979). The Problem of Externality. *The Journal of Law and Economics 22*(1), 141–162.

Dan-Cohen, M. (1983). Decision Rules and Conduct Rules: On Acoustic Separation in Criminal Law. *Harvard Law Review 97*, 625–677.

Danet, B. (1980). Language in the Legal Process. *Law and Society Review 14*, 445–564.

Decker, J. F. (2002). Addressing Vagueness, Ambiguity, and Other Uncertainty in American Criminal Laws. *Denver University Law Review 80*, 241–343.

van Deemter, K. (2010). *Not Exactly: In Praise of Vagueness*. Oxford: Oxford University Press.

Dickerson, R. (1975). *The Interpretation and Application of Statutes*. Boston, MA: Little, Brown & Co.

Dickerson, R. (1983). Statutory Interpretation: Dipping into Legislative History. *Hofstra Law Review 11*(4), 1125–1162.

Dickey, E. J. (1999). *Milk in My Coffee*. New York: Signet.

Diver, C. S. (1983). The Optimal Precision of Administrative Rules. *The Yale Law Journal 93*(1), 65–109.

Donnellan, K. S. (1966). Reference and Definite Descriptions. *The Philosophical Review 75*(3), 281–304.

Driedger, E. A. (1983). *The Construction of Statutes*. Toronto: Butterworths.

Dubroff, H. (2012). The Implied Covenant of Good Faith in Contract Interpretation and Gap-Filling: Reviling a Revered Relic. *St. John's Law Review 80*(2), 559–619.

Dworkin, R. M. (1975). Hard Cases. *Harvard Law Review 88*(6), 1057–1109.

Dworkin, R. M. (1977). No Right Answer? In H. L. A. Hart, P. M. S. Hacker, and J. Raz (Eds.), *Law, Morality, and Society*, pp. 58–84. Oxford: Clarendon Press.

Dworkin, R. M. (1978). *Taking Rights Seriously*. Cambridge, MA: Harvard University Press.

Dworkin, R. M. (1982). Law as Interpretation. *Texas Law Review 60*(2), 527–550.

Dworkin, R. M. (1986). *Law's Empire*. Cambridge, MA: Belknap Press.

Dworkin, R. M. (2006). *Justice in Robes*. Cambridge, MA: Belknap Press.

Dworkin, R. M. (2011). *Justice for Hedgehogs*. Cambridge, MA: Belknap Press.

van Eemeren, F. H. and R. Grootendorst (1992). *Argumentation, Communication, and Fallacies: A Pragma-Dialectical Perspective*. Hillsdale, NJ: Lawrence Erlbaum Associates.

Égré, P. and D. Bonnay (2010). Vagueness, Uncertainty and Degrees of Clarity. *Synthese 174*(1), 47–78.

Ehrlich, I. and R. A. Posner (1974). An Economic Analysis of Legal Rulemaking. *The Journal of Legal Studies 3*(1), 257–286.

Eikmeyer, H.-J. and H. Rieser (1983). A Formal Theory of Context Dependence and Context Change. In M. Pinkal and T. T. Ballmer (Eds.), *Approaching Vagueness*, pp. 131–188. Amsterdam: Elsevier.

Eklund, M. (2011). What Are Thick Concepts? *Canadian Journal of Philosophy 41*(1), 25–49.

Ellsberg, D. (1961). Risk, Ambiguity, and the Savage Axioms. *Quarterly Journal of Economics 75*(4), 643–669.

Endicott, T. A. O. (1996). Linguistic Indeterminacy. *Oxford Journal of Legal Studies 16*(4), 667–697.

Endicott, T. A. O. (1998). Questions of Law. *Law Quarterly Review 114*, 292–321.

Endicott, T. A. O. (2000). *Vagueness in Law*. Oxford: Oxford University Press.

Endicott, T. A. O. (2001). Law Is Necessarily Vague. *Legal Theory 7*(4), 379–385.

Endicott, T. A. O. (2005). The Value of Vagueness. In V. K. Bhatia, J. Engberg, M. Gotti, and D. Heller (Eds.), *Vagueness in Normative Texts*, Volume 23, *Linguistic Insights*, pp. 27–48. Bern: Lang.

Endicott, T. A. O. (2011a). Vagueness and Law. In G. Ronzitti (Ed.), *Vagueness*. Dordrecht, Netherlands: Springer.

Endicott, T. A. O. (2011b). The Value of Vagueness. In A. Marmor and S. Soames (Eds.), *Philosophical Foundations of Language in the Law*, pp. 14–30. Oxford: Oxford University Press.

Endicott, T. A. O. (2012). Legal Interpretation. In A. Marmor (Ed.), *The Routledge Companion to Philosophy of Law*, pp. 109–122. New York: Routledge.

Endicott, T. A. O. (2014). Interpretation and Indeterminacy: Comments on Andrei Marmor's Philosophy of Law. *Jerusalem Review of Legal Studies 10*, 46–56.

Engberg, J. and D. Heller (2007). Vagueness and Indeterminacy in Law. In V. K. Bhatia, C. Candlin, and J. Engberg (Eds.), *Legal Discourse Across Cultures and Systems*, pp. 145–168. Hong Kong: Hong Kong University Press.

Engisch, K. (1943). *Logische Studien zur Gesetzesanwendung*. Heidelberg: C. Winter.

Enquist, A. and L. C. Oates (2013). *Just Writing: Grammar, Punctuation, and Style for the Legal Writer*. New York: Wolters Kluwer Law & Business.

Epstein, D. and S. O'Halloran (1998). The Nondelegation Doctrine and the Separation of Powers: A Political Science Approach. *Cardozo Law Review 20*, 947–987.

Epstein, D. and S. O'Halloran (1999). *Delegating Powers: A Transactions Cost Politics Approach to Policy Making under Separate Powers*. Cambridge: Cambridge University Press.

Ernst, P. (2002). *Pragmalinguistik: Grundlagen, Anwendungen, Probleme*. De-Gruyter-Studienbuch. Berlin: de Gruyter.

Farnsworth, E. A. (1967). "Meaning" in the Law of Contracts. *Yale Law Journal 76*(5), 939–965.

Farrell, J. (1987). Cheap Talk, Coordination, and Entry. *RAND Journal of Economics 18*(1), 34–39.

Farrell, J. (1993). Meaning and Credibility in Cheap-Talk Games. *Games and Economic Behavior 5*(4), 514–531.

Fine, K. (1975). Vagueness, Truth and Logic. *Synthese 30*(3/4), 265–300.

Fine, K. (2015). The Possibility of Vagueness. Published online and available at http://dx.doi.org/10.1007/s11229-014-0625-9 (Synthese).

Finkbeiner, R., J. Meibauer, and P. B. Schumacher (2012). *What Is a Context? Linguistic Approaches and Challenges*. Philadelphia: John Benjamins Publishing Company.

Finnis, J. (1980). *Natural Law and Natural Rights*. Clarendon Law Series. Oxford: Clarendon Press.

Finnis, J. (1987). On Reason and Authority in Law's Empire. *Law and Philosophy 6*, 357–380.

Fiorito, L. (2006). On Performatives in Legal Discourse. *Metalogicon 19*(2), 101–112.

Fish, S. E. (1980). *Is There a Text in This Class?* Cambridge, MA: Harvard University Press.

Fish, S. E. (1989). *Doing What Comes Naturally: Change, Rhetoric, and the Practice of Theory in Literary and Legal Studies*. Durham, NC: Duke University Press.

Fish, S. E. (2005). There Is No Textualist Position. *San Diego Law Review 42*, 629–650.

Fotion, N. (1971). Master Speech Acts. *The Philosophical Quarterly 21*(84), 232–243.

Frances, A. (2013). *Saving Normal: An Insider's Revolt Against Out-of-Control Psychiatric Diagnosis, DSM-5, Big Pharma, and the Medicalization of Ordinary Life*. New York: HarperCollins.

Frank, J. and R. Gray (1930). *Law and the Modern Mind*. New York: Brentano's.

Frankfurter, F. and N. Green (1930). *The Labor Injunction*. New York: MacMillan.

Fraser, B. (1974). An Analysis of Vernacular Performative Verbs. In C.-J. Bailey and R. W. Shuy (Eds.), *Towards Tomorrow's Linguistics*, pp. 139–158. Washington, DC: Georgetown University Press.

Frege, G. (1882). Über die wissenschaftliche Berechtigung einer Begriffsschrift. *Zeitschrift für Philosophie und philosophische Kritik 81*, 48–56.

Fried, C. (1981). *Contract as Promise*. Cambridge, MA: Harvard University Press.

Fuller, L. L. (1958). Positivism and Fidelity to Law—A Reply to Professor Hart. *Harvard Law Review 71*(4), 630–672.

Fuller, L. L. (1969). *The Morality of Law*. New Haven, CT: Yale University Press.

Gallie, W. B. (1956). Essentially Contested Concepts. *Proceedings of the Aristotelian Society 56*, 167–198.

Gärdenfors, P. (2004). *Conceptual Spaces*. Cambridge, MA: MIT Press.

Garstka, H. (1976). Generalklauseln. In H.-J. Koch (Ed.), *Juristische Methodenlehre und analytische Philosophie*, pp. 96–122. Kronberg: Athenäum Verlag.

Gazdar, G. (1979). *Pragmatics: Implicature, Presupposition and Logical Form*. New York: Academic Press.

Geeraerts, D. (1993). Vagueness's Puzzles, Polysemy's Vagaries. *Cognitive Linguistics 4*(3), 223–272.

Geraats, P. M. (2007). The Mystique of Central Bank Speak. *International Journal of Central Banking 3*(1), 37–80.

Gilbert, A. M. (1997). Defining Use of a Firearm. *Journal of Criminal Law and Criminology 87*(3), 842–863.

Gilbert, D. T. (1991). How Mental Systems Believe. *American Psychologist 46*(2), 107–119.

Gillon, B. S. (1990). Ambiguity, Generality, and Indeterminacy: Tests and Definitions. *Synthese 85*(3), 391–416.

Glenn, J. (2007). May Judges Sometimes Lie? Remarks on Sorensen's Views of Vagueness and Law. *Sorites 18*, 10–16.

Gluck, A. R. (2010). The States as Laboratories of Statutory Interpretation: Methodological Consensus and the New Modified Textualism. *Yale Law Journal 119*, 1750–1862.

Glucksberg, S., P. M. Gildea, and H. B. Bookin (1982). On Understanding Non-Literal Speech: Can People Ignore Metaphor. *Journal of Verbal Learning and Verbal Behavior 21*, 85–98.

Gneezy, U. and A. Rustichini (2000). Pay Enough or Don't Pay at All. *Quarterly Journal of Economics 15*(3), 791–810.

Goetz, C. J. and R. E. Scott (1981). Principles of Relational Contracts. *Virginia Law Review 67*(6), 1089–1150.

Golanski, A. (2002). Linguistics in Law. *Albany Law Review 66*(1), 61–121.

Gotti, M. (2005). Vagueness in the Model Law on International Commercial Arbitration. In V. K. Bhatia, J. Engberg, M. Gotti, and D. Heller (Eds.), *Vagueness in Normative Texts*, Volume 23: *Linguistic Insights*, pp. 227–254. Bern: Lang.

Graber, M. A. (1993). The Nonmajoritarian Difficulty: Legilative Deference to the Judiciary. *Studies in American Political Development 7*, 35–73.

Graff Fara, D. R. (2000). Shifting Sands: An Interest-Relative Theory of Vagueness. *Philosophical Topics 28*(1), 45–81.

Graff Fara, D. R. and T. Williamson (2002). *Vagueness*, Volume 27. Aldershot: Ashgate Dartmouth.

Green, M. J. and K. van Deemter (2011). Vagueness as Cost Reduction: An Empirical Test. *Proceedings of the CogSci Workshop on the Production of Referring Expressions 33*, 1–6.

Green, M. J. and K. van Deemter (2013). The Utility of Vagueness: Does It Lie Elsewhere? *Proceedings of the CogSci Workshop on the Production of Referring Expressions 35*, 1–5.

Greenawalt, K. (2001). Vagueness and Judicial Responses to Legal Indeterminacy. *Legal Theory 7*(4), 433–445.

Greenawalt, K. (2011). *Legal Interpretation: Broader Perspectives and Private Texts*. New York: Oxford University Press.

Greenberg, M. (2010). The Communication Theory of Legal Interpretation and Objective Notions of Communicative Content. *UCLA School of Law Research Paper 10*(35), 1–8.

Greenberg, M. (2011a). Legislation as Communication? Legal Interpretation and the Study of Linguistic Communication. In A. Marmor and S. Soames (Eds.), *Philosophical Foundations of Language in the Law*, pp. 217–256. Oxford: Oxford University Press.

Greenberg, M. (2011b). The Standard Picture and Its Discontents. In L. Green and B. Leiter (Eds.), *Oxford Studies in Philosophy of Law*, pp. 39–106. Oxford: Oxford University Press.

Grice, H. P. (1968). Utterer's Meaning, Sentence-Meaning and Word-Meaning. *Foundations of Language 4*, 225–242.

Grice, H. P. (1989a). Logic and Conversation. In *Studies in the Way of Words*, pp. 22–40. Cambridge, MA: Harvard University Press.

Grice, H. P. (1989b). *Studies in the Way of Words*. Cambridge, MA: Harvard University Press.

Gruber, H. (1993). Political Language and Textual Vagueness. *Pragmatics 3*(1), 1–28.

Gruschke, D. (2014). *Vagheit im Recht: Grenzfälle und fließende Übergänge im Horizont des Rechtsstaats*, Volume 269: *Schriften zur Rechtstheorie*. Berlin: Duncker & Humblot.

Guest, S. (2009). How to Criticize Ronald Dworkin's Theory of Law. *Analysis 69*(2), 352–364.

Günther, K. (2006). *Politik des Kompromisses: Dissensmanagement in pluralistischen Demokratien*. Westdeutscher Verlag.

Haack, S. (1996). *Deviant Logic, Fuzzy Logic: Beyond the Formalism*. Chicago: University of Chicago Press.

Habermas, J. (1995). *Theorie des kommunikativen Handelns*. Frankfurt am Main: Suhrkamp.

Hadfield, G. K. (1994a). Judicial Competence and the Interpretation of Incomplete Contracts. *Journal of Legal Studies 23*, 159–184.

Hadfield, G. K. (1994b). Weighing the Value of Vagueness: An Economic Perspective on Precision in the Law. *California Law Review 82*(3, Symposium: Void for Vagueness), 541–554.

Haldeman, H. R. (1995). *The Haldeman Diaries: Inside the Nixon White House*. New York: Berkley Books.

Hampton, J. A., B. Aina, J. M. Andersson, H. Z. Mirza, and S. Parmar (2012). The Rumsfeld Effect: The Unknown Unknown. *Journal of Experimental Psychology: Learning Memory & Cognition 38*, 340–355.

Hardin, G. J. (1968). The Tragedy of the Commons. *Science 162*(3859), 1243–1248.

Hart, H. L. A. (1955). Definition and Theory in Jurisprudence. *Proceedings of the Aristotelian Society, Supplementary Volumes 29*, 213–264.

Hart, H. L. A. (1958). Positivism and the Separation of Law and Morals. *Harvard Law Review 71*(4), 593–629.

Hart, H. L. A. (1994). *The Concept of Law* (2nd ed.). Clarendon Law Series. Oxford: Clarendon Press. (Original work published 1961)

Hart, O. D. (1995). *Firms, Constracts, and Financial Structure*. Clarendon Lectures in Economics. Oxford: Clarendon Press.

Haubrich, J. (1995). Vagueness, Credibility, and Government Policy. *Economic Review 31*(1), 13–19.

Hauswald, R. (2014). *Soziale Pluralitäten: Zur Ontologie, Wissenschaftstheorie und Semantik des Klassifizierens und Gruppierens von Menschen in Gesellschaft und Humanwissenschaft*. Münster: mentis.

Hayek, F. A. v. and A. Bosch (2001). *Gesammelte Schriften in deutscher Sprache*. Tübingen: Mohr Siebeck.

Heck, P. (1914). Gesetzesauslegung und Interessenjurisprudenz. *Archiv für die civilistische Praxis 112*(2), 1–365.

Heck, P. (1933). *Interessensjurisprudenz*. Tübingen: Mohr Siebeck.

Held-Daab, U. (1996). *Das freie Ermessen: Von den vorkonstitutionellen Wurzeln zur positivistischen Auflösung der Ermessenslehre*. Berlin: Duncker & Humblot.

Hempel, C. G. (1939). Vagueness and Logic. *Philosophy of Science 6*(2), 163–180.

Herberger, M. (1976). Die deskriptiven und normative Tatbestandsmerkmale im Strafrecht. In H.-J. Koch (Ed.), *Juristische Methodenlehre und analytische Philosophie*, pp. 124–154. Kronberg: Athenäum Verlag.

Herbert, A. P. (1977). *Uncommon Law: Being 66 Misleading Cases Revised and Collected in One Volume*. London: Eyre Methuen.

Herdegen, M. (1991). Beurteilungsspielraum und Ermessen im strukturellen Vergleich. *JuristenZeitung 46*(15/16), 747–751.

Hirschl, R. (2000). The Political Origins of Judicial Empowerment Through Constitutionalization: Lessons from Four Constitutional Revolutions. *Law & Social Inquiry 25*, 91–149.

Ho, H. L. (2006). What Does a Verdict Do? A Speech Act Analysis of Giving a Verdict. *International Commentary on Evidence 4*(2), 1–26.

Holmes, O. W. (1897). The Path of the Law. *Harvard Law Review 10*, 457–478.

Holmes, O. W. (2009). *The Common Law*. Cambridge, MA: Belknap Press. (Original work published 1882)

Horn, L. R. (1984). Towards a New Taxonomy for Pragmatic Inference: Q-based and R-based Implicature. In D. Schiffrin (Ed.), *Georgetown University Round Table on Languages and Linguistics*, pp. 11–42. Washington, DC: Georgetown University Press.

Horn, L. R. (1985). Metalinguistic Negation and Pragmatic Ambiguity. *Language 61*(1), 121–174.

Horwitz, M. (1992). *The Transformation of American Law, 1870-1960: The Crisis of Legal Orthodoxy*. Oxford: Oxford University Press.

Hovenkamp, H. J. (1985). *Economics and Federal Antitrust Law*. St. Paul, MN: West Publishing Co.

Huber, J. and C. Shipan (2002). *Deliberate Discretion: The Institutional Foundations of Bureaucratic Autonomy*. Cambridge: Cambridge University Press.

Hurd, H. M. (1990). Sovereignty in Silence. *The Yale Law Journal 99*(5), 945–1028.

Hurley, S. L. (1989). *Natural Reasons: Personality and Polity*. New York: Oxford University Press.

Hutchinson, D. J. (1980). Unanimity and Desegregation: Decisionmaking in the Supreme Court 1948-1958. *Georgetown Law Journal 68*, 1–96.

Hyde, D. (2008). *Vagueness, Logic and Ontology*. Aldershot: Ashgate.

de Jaegher, K. (2003). A Game-Theoretic Rationale for Vagueness. *Linguistics & Philosophy 26*, 637–659.

de Jaegher, K. and R. van Rooij (2010). Strategic Vagueness, and Appropriate Contexts. In A. Benz, E. Christian, G. Jäger, and R. van Rooij (Eds.), *Meaning and Game Theory*, pp. 40–59. Berlin: Springer.

de Jaegher, K. and R. van Rooij (2013). Game-Theoretic Pragmatics Under Conflicting and Common Interests. *Erkenntnis Online*, 1–52.

Janney, R. W. (2002). Cotext as Context: Vague Answers in Court. *Language & Communication 22*, 457–475.

Jhering, R. v. (1872). *Der Kampf ums Recht*. Wien: Wiener Juristische Gesellschaft.

Johnson, E. J. and J. Hershey (1993). Framing, Probability Distortions, and Insurance Decisions. *Journal of Risk and Uncertainty 7*, 35–51.

Jones, D. (1957). The Enigma of the Clayton Act. *Industrial and Labor Relations Review 10*, 201–221.

Jucker, A. H., S. W. Smith, and T. Lüdge (2003). Interactive Aspects of Vagueness in Conversation. *Journal of Pragmatics 35*, 1737–1769.

Kahn, A. E. (1966). The Tyranny of Small Decisions: Market Failures, Imperfections, and the Limits of Economics. *Kyklos 19*(1), 23–47.

Kahneman, D. (2012). *Thinking, Fast and Slow*. London: Penguin Books.

Kahneman, D. and A. Tversky (1983). Extensional versus Intuitive Reasoning: The Conjunction Fallacy in Probability Judgment. *Psychological Review 90*, 293–315.

Kamp, H. (2013). The Paradox of the Heap. In K. von Heusinger and A. ter Meulen (Eds.), *Meaning and the Dynamics of Interpretation: Selected Papers of Hans Kamp*, pp. 263–323. Leiden: Brill. (Original work published 1981)

Kaplan, D. B. (1978). Dthat. *Syntax and Semantics 9*, 221–243.

Kaplan, J. P., G. M. Green, C. D. Cunningham, and J. N. Levi (1995). Bringing Linguistics into Judicial Decision-Making: Semantic Analysis Submitted to the US Supreme Court. *Forensic Linguistics 2*, 81–98.

Kaplow, L. (1992). Rules Versus Standards: An Economic Analysis. *Duke Law Review 42*, 557–629.

Katz, A. W. (2005). Contractual Incompleteness: A Transactional Perspective. *Case Western Reserve Law Review 56*(1), 169–186.

Katz, J. J. (1977). *Propositional Structure and Illocutionary Force: A Study of the Contribution of Sentence Meaning to Speech Acts*. Cambridge, MA: Harvard University Press.

Kaufmann, A. (1973). Die ipsa res iusta: Gedanken zu einer hermeneutischen Rechtsontologie. In G. Paulus, U. Diederichsen, and C.-W. Canaris (Eds.), *Festschrift für Karl Larenz zum 70. Geburtstag*, pp. 27ff. München: C. H. Beck.

Kavka, G. S. (1990). Some Social Benefits of Uncertainty. *Midwest Studies in Philosophy 15*, 311–326.

Keefe, R. (2000). *Theories of Vagueness*. Cambridge: Cambridge University Press.

Keil, G. (2006). Über die deskriptive Unerschöpflichkeit der Einzeldinge. In G. Keil and U. Tietz (Eds.), *Phänomenologie und Sprachanalyse*, pp. 83–125. Paderborn: mentis.

Keil, G. (2010). Halbglatzen statt Halbwahrheiten: Über Vagheit, Wahrheits- und Auflösungs-grade. In A. Rami and M. Grajner (Eds.), *Realismus, Wahrheit und Existenz*, pp. 81–99. Hausenstamm: Ontos.

Kelsen, H. (1934). *Reine Rechtslehre: Einleitung in die rechtswissenschaftliche Problematik*. Leipzig: Franz Deuticke.

Kelsen, H. (2007). *General Theory of Law and State*. Clark, NJ: Lawbook Exchange. (Original work published 1945)

Kennedy, C. (2011). Vagueness and Comparison. In P. Égré and N. Klinedinst (Eds.), *Vagueness and Language Use*, pp. 73–97. Basingstoke, Hampshire: Palgrave Macmillan.

Kennedy, D. (1986). Freedom and Constraint in Adjudication: A Critical Phenomenology. *Journal of Legal Education 36*, 518.

Kesavan, V. and M. S. Paulsen (2003). The Interpretive Force of the Constitution's Secret Drafting History. *Georgia Law Review 91*, 1113.

Kiesselbach, M. (2012). Was sagt das Gesetz? Zur Rede von »wörtlicher Bedeutung« in Bezug auf Rechtstexte. In C. Bäcker, M. Klatt, and S. Zucca-Soest (Eds.), *Sprache - Recht - Gesellschaft*. Tübingen: Mohr Siebeck.

Kilian, W. (1976). Zur Auslegung zivilrechtlicher Verträge. In H.-J. Koch (Ed.), *Juristische Methodenlehre und analytische Philosophie*, pp. 271–286. Kronberg: Athenäum Verlag.

Klatt, M. (2005). Die Wortlautgrenze. In K. D. Lerch (Ed.), *Recht Verhandeln*, Volume 2: *Die Sprache des Rechts*, pp. 343–368. Berlin: de Gruyter.

Kluck, N. (2014). *Der Wert der Vagheit*. Berlin: de Gruyter.

Knight, F. H. (1921). *Risk, Ucertainty and Profit*, Volume 31: *Hart, Schaffner, and Marx Prize Essays*. New York: Houghton Mifflin.

Koch, H.-J. (1979). *Unbestimmte Rechtsbegriffe und Ermessensermächtigungen im Verwaltungsrecht*. Frankfurt am Main: Alfred Metzner Verlag.

Koch, H.-J. and H. Rüßmann (1982). *Juristische Begründungslehre: Eine Einführung in die Grundprobleme der Rechtswissenschaft*. München: Beck.

Köhler, H. (2010). *BGB: Allgemeiner Teil: Ein Studienbuch* (34th ed.). München: Beck.

Köpcke Tinturé, M. (2010). Law Does Things Differently. *The American Journal of Jurisprudence 55*(1), 201–224.

Korobkin, R. B. (2000). Behavioral Analysis and Legal Form: Rules vs. Standards Revisited. *Oregon Law Review 79*, 23–59.

Kostritsky, J. P. (2005). Incomplete Contracts: Judicial Responses, Transactional Planning, and Litigation Strategies. *Case Western Reserve Law Review 56*(1), 135–150.

Kramer, M. H. (1999). *In Defense of Legal Positivism: Law Without Trimmings*. Oxford: Oxford University Press.

Kress, K. J. (1989). Legal Indeterminacy. *California Law Review 77*(2), 283.

Kriele, M. (1976). *Theorie der Rechtsgewinnung entwickelt am Problem der Verfassungsinterpretation* (2nd ed.), Volume 41: *Schriften zum Öffentlichen Recht*. Berlin: Duncker & Humblot.

Krifka, M. (2009). Approximate Interpretations of Number Words: Case for Strategic Communication. In E. W. Hinrichs and J. Nerbonne (Eds.), *Theory and Evidence in Semantics*, pp. 109–132. Stanford, CA: CSLI Publications.

Kripke, S. A. (1977). Speaker's Reference and Semantic Reference. *Midwest Studies in Philosophy 2*(1), 255–276.

Kurzon, D. (1986). *It Is Hereby Performed: Explorations in Legal Speech Acts*. Pragmatics & Beyond. Amsterdam: John Benjamins Publishing Company.

Kurzon, D. (1997). Legal Language: Varieties, Genres, Registers, Discourses. *International Journal of Applied Linguistics 7*(2), 119–139.

LaFrance, T. C. (2011). Targeting Discretion: An Exploration of Organisational Communication between Rank Levels in a Medium-Sized Southern US Police Department. *International Journal of Police Science and Management 13*(2), 158–171.

Landis, J. M. (1938). *The Administrative Process*. New Haven, CT: Yale University Press.

Langton, R. (1993). Speech Acts and Unspeakable Acts. *Philosophy and Public Affairs 22*(4), 305–330.

Lanius, D. (2011). *Vagueness and Unforeseeability*. Logic Year Thesis: Universiteit van Amsterdam.

Lanius, D. (2013). Has Vagueness Really No Function in Law? In M. Hoeltje, T. Spitzley, and W. Spohn (Eds.), *Was dürfen wir glauben? Was sollen wir tun?*, pp. 60–69. Duisburg-Essen: DuEPublico.

Larenz, K. (1973). Die Bindung des Richters an das Gesetz als hermeneutisches Problem. In E. Forsthoff (Ed.), *Festschrift für Ernst Rudolf Huber zum 70 Geburtstag am 8. Juni 1973*, pp. 291–309. Göttingen: Schwartz.

Larenz, K. (1991). *Methodenlehre der Rechtswissenschaft* (6th ed.). Berlin: Springer.

Larenz, K. and C.-W. Canaris (1995). *Methodenlehre der Rechtswissenschaft* (3rd ed.). Berlin: Springer.

Leib, E. J. and M. Serota (2010). The Costs of Consensus in Statutory Interpretation. *Yale Law Journal 120*, 47–63.

Leiter, B. (2009). Explaining Theoretical Disagreement. *University of Chicago Law Review 76*, 1215–1250.

Lemos, M. H. (2008). The Other Delegate: Judicially Administered Statutes and the Nondelegation Doctrine. *Southern California Law Review 81*, 405–476.

Lemos, M. H. (2015). Interpretive Methodology and Delegations to Courts: Are "Common-Law Statutes" Different? In S. Balganesh (Ed.), *Intellectual Property and the Common Law*, pp. 89–106. Cambridge: Cambridge University Press.

Levenbook, B. B. (2015). Dworkin's Theoretical Disagreement Argument. *Philosophy Compass 10*(1), 1–9.

Levinson, S. C. (2000). *Presumptive Meanings: The Theory of Generalized Conversational Implicature*. Cambridge, MA: MIT Press.

Lewis, D. K. (1969). *Convention: A Philososophical Study*. Cambridge, MA: Harvard University Press.

Lewis, D. K. (1986). *On the Plurality of Worlds*. Malden, MA: Blackwell.

Lindley, D. V. (2006). *Understanding Uncertainty*. Hoboken, NJ: Wiley-Interscience.

Lipman, B. L. (2009). Why Is Language Vague? Current Draft. http://people.bu.edu/blipman/Pap ers/vague5.pdf.

Llewellyn, K. N. (1962). *Jurisprudence: Realism in Theory and Practice*. Chicago: University of Chicago Press.

Lovell, G. I. (2010). *Legislative Deferrals: Statutory Ambiguity, Judicial Power, and American Democracy*. Cambridge: Cambridge University Press.

Lowe, W. (2001). Towards a Theory of Semantic Space. *Proceedings of the Annual Conference of the Cognitive Science Society 23*, 576–581.

Ludlow, P. (1989). Implicit Comparison Classes. *Linguistics & Philosophy 12*, 519–533.

Lyons, J. (2005). *Linguistic Semantics: An Introduction* (2nd ed.). Cambridge: Cambridge University Press.

Manning, J. F. (2003). The Absurdity Doctrine. *Harvard Law Review 116*(8), 2387–2486.

Marmor, A. (2005). *Interpretation and Legal Theory* (2nd ed.). Oxford: Hart.

Marmor, A. (2008). The Pragmatics of Legal Language. *Ratio Juris 21*, 423–452.

Marmor, A. (2011a). Can the Law Imply More than It Says? On Some Pragmatic Aspects of Strategic Speech. In A. Marmor and S. Soames (Eds.), *Philosophical Foundations of Language in the Law*, pp. 83–104. Oxford: Oxford University Press.

Marmor, A. (2011b). *Philosophy of Law*. Princeton, NJ: Princeton University Press.

Marmor, A. (2014). *The Language of Law*. Oxford: Oxford University Press.

Maskin, E. and J. Tirole (1999). Unforeseen Contingencies and Incomplete Contracts. *Review of Economic Studies 66*(1), 83–114.

Matthews, S. A. and L. J. Mirman (1983). Equilibrium Limit Pricing: The Effects of Private Information and Stochastic Demand. *Econometrica 51*(4), 981–996.

Maurer, H. (2011). *Allgemeines Verwaltungsrecht* (18th ed.). München: Beck.

McCarthy, J. and P. J. Hayes (1969). Some Philosophical Problems from the Standpoint of Artificial Intelligence. *Machine Intelligence 4*, 463–502.

McCloskey, M. E. and S. Glucksberg (1978). Natural Categories: Well Defined or Fuzzy Sets? *Memory and Cognition 6*(4), 462–472.

McNeill, D. and P. Freiberger (1993). *Fuzzy Logic*. New York: Simon & Schuster.

Meibauer, J. (2009). Implicature. In J. L. Mey (Ed.), *Concise Encyclopedia of Pragmatics*, pp. 365–378. Oxford: Elsevier.

Merrill, T. W. (2000). The Landscape of Constitutional Property. *Virginia Law Review 86*(5), 885–999.

Milgrom, P. and J. Roberts (1982). Limit Pricing and Entry under Incomplete Information: An Equilibrium Analysis. *Econometrica 50*, 443–460.

Moline, J. (1969). Aristotle, Eubulides and the Sorites. *Mind 78*(311), 393–407.

Moore, M. S. (1981). The Semantics of Judging. *Cardozo Law Review 54*, 151–294.

Moore, M. S. (2002). Legal Reality: A Naturalist Approach to Legal Ontology. *Law and Philosophy 21*(6), 619–705.

Moore, M. S. (2012). Targeted Killings and the Morality of Hard Choices. In C. O. Finkelstein, J. D. Ohlin, and A. Altman (Eds.), *Targeted Killings*, pp. 434–466. Oxford: Oxford University Press.

Moreso, J. J. (1998). *Legal Indeterminacy and Constitutional Interpretation*. Dordrecht, Netherlands: Kluwer Academic Publishers.

Müller, F. and R. Christensen (2004). *Juristische Methodik* (9th ed.). Berlin: Duncker & Humblot.

Müller-Mall, S. (2012). *Performative Rechtserzeugung: Eine theoretische Annäherung*. Weilerswist: Velbrück.

Neale, S. (2005). Pragmatism and Binding. In Z. Szabó (Ed.), *Semantics versus Pragmatics*, pp. 165–285. Oxford: Oxford University Press.

Neumann, U. (1986). *Juristische Argumentationslehre*. Darmstadt: Wissenschaftliche Buchgesellschaft.

Nietzsche, F. (1883). *Also sprach Zarathustra*. Chemnitz: Schmeitzner.

Nourse, V. A. and J. Schacter (2002). The Politics of Legislative Drafting: A Congressional Case Study. *New York University Law Review 77*, 575–624.

Nussbaumer, M. (2005). Zwischen Rechtsgrundsätzen und Formularsammlung: Gesetze brauchen (gute) Vagheit zum Atmen. In V. K. Bhatia, J. Engberg, M. Gotti, and D. Heller (Eds.), *Vagueness in Normative Texts*, Volume 23: *Linguistic Insights*. Bern: Lang.

Ogletree, C. J. (2005). *All Deliberate Speed: Reflections on the First Half Century of Brown v. Board of Education*. New York: W.W. Norton & Co.

Oliphant, H. (1928). A Return to Stare Decisis. *American Bar Association Journal 14*, 71.

Orwell, G. (1968). Politics and the English Language. In S. Orwell and I. Angos (Eds.), *Collected Essays*, pp. 127–140. New York: Harcourt, Brace and Javanovich. (Original work published 1946)

Parikh, P. (1991). Communication and Strategic Inference. *Linguistics and Philosophy 14*, 473–513.

Parikh, R. (1994). Vagueness and Utility: The Semantics of Common Nouns. *Linguistics & Philosophy 17*(6), 521–535.

Partee, B. (1984). Compositionality. In F. Landman and F. Veltman (Eds.), *Varieties of Formal Semantics*, pp. 281–311. Dordrecht, Netherlands: Foris Publications.

Patterson, D. M. (1990). Law's Pragmatism: Law as Practice & Narrative. *Virginia Law Review 76*, 937–996.

Patterson, D. M. (2005). Interpretation in Law. *San Diego Law Review 42*, 685–709.

Patterson, J. T. (2001). *Brown v. Board of Education: A Civil Rights Milestone and Its Troubled Legacy*. New York: Oxford University Press.

Pawlowski, H.-M. (1991). *Methodenlehre für Juristen: Theorie der Norm und des Gesetzes* (2nd ed.). Heidelberg: Müller.

Pei, M. (1978). *Weasel Words: The Art of Saying What You Don't Mean*. New York: Harper & Row.

Peirce, C. S. (1902). Vague. In J. M. Baldwin (Ed.), *Dictionary of Philosophy and Psychology*, p. 748. New York: MacMillan.

Peirce, C. S. (1960). Pragmatism and Pragmaticism. In C. Hartshorne, P. Weiss, and A. W. Burks (Eds.), *Collected Papers*. Cambridge, MA: Harvard University Press.

Peller, G. (1985). The Metaphysics of American Law. *California Law Review 73*, 1151–1290.

Peller, G. and M. V. Tushnet (2004). State Action and a New Birth of Freedom. *Georgia Law Review 92*, 779–817.

Peltason, J. W. (1961). *Fifty-Eight Lonely Men: Southern Federal Fudges and School Desegregation*. Illini books, IB 74. New York: Harcourt, Brace and World.

Perelman, C. and L. Olbrechts-Tyteca (1969). *The New Rhetoric: A Treatise on Argumentation*. Notre Dame: University of Notre Dame Press.

Pinkal, M. (1995). *Logic and Lexicon: The Semantics of the Indefinite*. Dordrecht, Netherlands: Springer.

Pinker, S., M. A. Nowak, and J. J. Lee (2008). The Logic of Indirect Speech. *Proceedings of the National Academy of Sciences 105*(3), 833–838.

Pino, G. (2013). "What's the Plan?": On Interpretation and Meta-interpretation in Scott Shapiro's Legality. In D. Canale and G. Tuzet (Eds.), *The Planning Theory of Law*, Volume 100, pp. 187–205. New York: Springer.

Plunkett, D. and T. Sundell (2013a). Disagreement and the Semantics of Normative and Evaluative Terms. *Philosophers' Imprint 13*(23), 1–37.

Plunkett, D. and T. Sundell (2013b). Dworkin's Interpretivism and The Pragmatics of Legal Disputes. *Legal Theory 19*, 242–281.

Podlech, A. (1976). Die juristische Fachsprache und die Umgangssprache. In H.-J. Koch (Ed.), *Juristische Methodenlehre und analytische Philosophie*, pp. 31–52. Kronberg: Athenäum Verlag.

Pogarsky, G. and L. Babcock (2001). Damage Caps, Motivated Anchoring, and Bargaining Impasse. *The Journal of Legal Studies 30*(1), 143–159.

Poggi, F. (2010). Law and Conversational Implicatures. *International Journal for the Semiotics of Law 24*(1), 21–40.

Poirier, M. R. (2002). The Virtue of Vagueness in Takings Doctrine. *Cardozo Law Review 24*(1), 93–191.

Polich, J. (1994). The Ambiguity of Plain Meaning: Smith v. United States and the New Textualism. *Southern California Law Review 68*, 259–282.

Poscher, R. (2009). The Hand of Midas: When Concepts Turn Legal. In J. C. Hage and D. v. d. Pfordten (Eds.), *Concepts in Law*, Volume 88: *Law and Philosophy Library*, pp. 99–115. Dordrecht, Netherlands: Springer.

Poscher, R. (2012). Ambiguity and Vagueness in Legal Interpretation. In L. M. Solan and P. M. Tiersma (Eds.), *Oxford Handbook of Language and Law*, pp. 128–144. Oxford: Oxford University Press.

Poscher, R. (2013). Wozu Juristen streiten. *JuristenZeitung 68*(1), 1–11.

Posner, R. A. (1973). An Economic Approach to Legal Procedure and Judicial Administration. *Journal of Legal Studies 2*, 399–458.

Posner, R. A. (1983). Statutory Interpretation: In the Classroom and in the Courtroom. *University of Chicago Law Review 50*, 800–822.

Posner, R. A. (1993). *The Problems of Jurisprudence*. Cambridge, MA: Harvard University Press.

Posner, R. A. (2005). The Law and Economics of Contract Interpretation. *Texas Law Review 83*(6), 1581–1614.

Posner, R. A. (2012). The Incoherence of Antonin Scalia. Available online at https://newrepublic.co m/article/106441/scalia-garner-reading-the-law-textual-originalism.

Powe, L. A. (2000). *The Warren Court and American Politics*. Cambridge, MA: Belknap Press.

Quine, W. V. O. (1960). *Word and Object* (24th ed.). Cambridge, MA: MIT Press.

Radin, M. (2000). *Law as Logic and Experience*. Union, NJ: Lawbook Exchange. (Original work published 1940)

Raffman, D. (1994). Vagueness Without Paradox. *The Philosophical Review 103*(1), 41–74.

Raffman, D. (1996). Vagueness and Context-Relativity. *Philosophical Studies 81*(2/3), 175–192.

Raffman, D. (2014). *Unruly Words: A Study of Vague Language*. Cary, NC: Oxford University Press.

Raskin, V. (1984). *Semantic Mechanisms of Humor*, Volume 24: *Synthese Language Library*. Dordrecht: D. Reidel Pub. Co.

Rawls, J. (2005). *Political Liberalism* (2nd ed.). New York: Columbia University Press.

Raz, J. (1990). *Practical Reason and Norms* (2nd ed.). Oxford: Clarendon Press.

Raz, J. (1994). Authority, Law, and Morality. In *Ethics in the Public Domain*. Oxford and New York: Clarendon Press and Oxford University Press.

Raz, J. (2001). Sorensen: Vagueness Has No Function in Law. *Legal Theory 7*(4), 417–419.

Raz, J. (2009a). *The Authority of Law: Essays on Law and Morality* (2nd ed.). Oxford: Oxford University Press.

Raz, J. (2009b). *Between Authority and Interpretation: On the Theory of Law and Practical Reason*. New York: Oxford University Press.

Recanati, F. (1989). The Pragmatics of What Is Said. *Mind & Language 4*(4), 295–329.

Recanati, F. (2001). What Is Said. *Synthese 128*(1–2), 75–91.

Recanati, F. (2004). *Literal Meaning*. Cambridge: Cambridge University Press.

Recanati, F. (2014). Pragmatic Enrichment and Conversational Implicature. In G. Russell and D. R. Graff Fara (Eds.), *The Routledge Companion to Philosophy of Language*, pp. 67–78. New York: Routledge.

Rett, J. (2014). *The Semantics of Evaluativity*, Volume 54: *Oxford Studies in Theoretical Linguistics*. Oxford: Oxford University Press.

Rhodes, R. M., J. W. White, and R. S. Goldman (1978). The Search for Intent: Aids to Statutory Construction in Florida. *Florida State University Law Review 6*, 383.

Ribeiro, M. (2004). *Limiting Arbitrary Power: The Vagueness Doctrine in Canadian Constitutional Law*. Vancouver: UBC Press.

Richter, T. S. (2009). *Vertragsrecht: Die Grundlagen des Wirtschaftsrechts*. München: Vahlen.

Ripley, D. (2011). Contradictions at the Borders. In R. Nouwen, R. van Rooij, U. Sauerland, and H.-C. Schmitz (Eds.), *Vagueness in Communication*, pp. 169–188. Berlin: Springer.

Rodgers, D. T. (1998). *Contested Truths: Keywords in American Politics Since Independence*. Cambridge, MA: Harvard University Press.

Rogers, J. R. (2001). Information and Judicial Review: A Signaling Game of Legislative-Judicial Interaction. *American Journal of Political Science 45*(1), 84–99.

Rolf, B. (1980). A Theory of Vagueness. *Journal of Philosophical Logic 9*(3), 315–325.

van Rooij, R. (2011). Vagueness and Linguistics. In G. Ronzitti (Ed.), *Vagueness*, pp. 123–170. Dordrecht, Netherlands: Springer.

Rosch, E. H. (1973). Natural Categories. *Cognitive Psychology 4*(3), 328–350.

Rosch, E. H., C. B. Mervis, W. D. Gray, D. M. Johnson, and P. Boyes-Braem (1976). Basic Objects in Natural Categories. *Cognitive Psychology 8*(3), 382–439.

Rosen, G. (2011). Textualism, Intentionalism and the Law of the Contract. In A. Marmor and S. Soames (Eds.), *Philosophical Foundations of Language in the Law*, pp. 130–164. Oxford: Oxford University Press.

Rubin, E. L. (1992). On Beyond Truth: A Theory for Evaluating Legal Scholarship. *California Law Review 80*, 889–963.

Rubin, E. L. (2010). Legal Scholarship. In D. M. Patterson (Ed.), *A Companion to Philosophy of Law and Legal Theory*, Volume 8: *Blackwell Companions to Philosophy*, pp. 548–558. Malden, MA: Wiley-Blackwell.

Ruiter, D. W. P. (1993). *Institutional Legal Facts: Legal Powers and Their Effects*. Law and Philosophy Library. Boston , MA: Kluwer Academic Publishers.

Rumsfeld, D. (2011). *Known and Unknown: A Memoir*. New York: Sentinel.

Russell, B. (1905). On Denoting. *Mind 14*(56), 479–493.

Russell, B. (1923). Vagueness. *The Australasian Journal of Psychology and Philosophy 1*(2), 84–92.

Rüthers, B. (2008). *Rechtstheorie: Begriff, Geltung und Anwendung des Rechts* (4th ed.). München: C. H. Beck.

Sainsbury, R. M. (1997). Concepts without Boundaries. In R. Keefe and P. Smith (Eds.), *Vagueness*, pp. 251–264. Cambridge, MA: MIT Press.

Saphire, R. B. (1978). Specifying Due Process Values: Toward a More Responsive Approach to Procedural Protection. *University of Pennsylvania Law Review 127*, 111–195.

Saul, J. M. (2002). Speaker Meaning, What Is Said, and What Is Implicated. *Nous 36*(2), 228–248.

Saul, J. M. (2012). *Lying, Misleading, and What Is Said: An Exploration in Philosophy of Language and in Ethics*. Oxford: Oxford University Press.

von Savigny, E. (1991). Passive Disobedience as Violence: Reflections on German High Court Decisions. In J. B. Brady and N. Garver (Eds.), *Justice, Law, and Violence*, pp. 53–64. Philadelphia: Temple University Press.

von Savigny, E., U. Neumann, and J. Rahlf (1976). *Juristische Dogmatik und Wissenschaftstheorie*. München: Beck.

Scalia, A. (1997). *A Matter of Interpretation: Federal Courts and the Law*. Princeton, NJ: Princeton University Press.

Scalia, A. and B. A. Garner (2012). *Reading Law: The Interpretation of Legal Texts*. St. Paul, MN: West.

Schane, S. (2012). Contract Formation as Speech Act. In L. M. Solan and P. M. Tiersma (Eds.), *Oxford Handbook of Language and Law*, pp. 100–113. Oxford: Oxford University Press.

Schauer, F. F. (1985). Easy Cases. *Southern California Law Review 58*, 399–440.

Schauer, F. F. (1988). Formalism. *The Yale Law Journal 97*(4), 509–548.

Schauer, F. F. (2008). A Critical Guide to Vehicles in the Park. *New York University Law Review 83*, 1109–1134.

Schauer, F. F. (2009). *Thinking Like a Lawyer*. Cambridge, MA: Harvard University Press.

Scheiber, H. N. (2007). *Earl Warren and the Warren Court: The Legacy in American and Foreign Law*. Lanham, MD: Rowman & Littlefield.

Schiffer, S. (2001). A Little Help From Your Friends? *Legal Theory 7*(4), 421–431.

Schlag, P. J. (1985). Rules and Standards. *UCLA Law Review 33*, 379.

Schmitt, C. (1993). *Verfassungslehre* (8th ed.). Berlin: Duncker & Humblot. (Original work published 1928)

Schmitt, C. (2008). *Constitutional Theory*. Durham, NC: Duke University Press.

Schumann, E. (1968). Das Rechtsverweigerungsverbot. *Zeitschrift für Zivilprozess 81*, 79–102.

Schwartz, A. and R. E. Scott (2003). Contract Theory and the Limits of Contract Law. *Yale Law Journal 113*, 541–619.

Schwartz, B. (1983). *Super Chief: Earl Warren and His Supreme Court—A Judicial Biography*. New York: New York University Press.

Schweizer, U. (1999). *Vertragstheorie*. Tübingen: Mohr Siebeck.

Scott, R. E. and G. G. Triantis (2005). Incomplete Contracts and the Theory of Contract Design. *Case Western Reserve Law Review 56*(1), 187–201.

Searle, J. R. (1976). The Classification of Illocutionary Acts. *Language in Society 5*(1), 1–24.

Searle, J. R. (1983). *Intentionality*. Cambridge: Cambridge University Press.

Searle, J. R. (2002). Collective Intentions and Actions. In *Consciousness and Language*, pp. 90–105. New York: Cambridge University Press.

Searle, J. R. and D. Vanderveke (1985). *Foundations of Illocutionary Logic*. Cambridge: Cambridge University Press.

Shapiro, S. (2006). *Vagueness in Context*. Oxford: Clarendon Press.

Shapiro, S. (2007). The Hart-Dworkin Debate: A Short Guide for the Perplexed. In A. Ripstein (Ed.), *Ronald Dworkin*, Volume Contemporary Philosophy in Focus, pp. 22–55. Cambridge: Cambridge University Press.

Shapiro, S. J. (2011). *Legality*. Cambridge, MA: Belknap Press.

Shiffrin, S. (2012). Are Contracts Promises? In A. Marmor (Ed.), *The Routledge Companion to Philosophy of Law*. New York: Routledge.

Simon, H. A. (1959). Theories of Decision Making in Economics and Behavioural Science. *American Economic Review 49*(3), 253–283.

Sinclair, M. B. W. (1997). Statutory Reasoning. *Drake Law Review 46*, 299–382.

Singer, R. (1986). On Classism and Dissonance in the Criminal Law: A Reply to Professor Meir Dan-Cohen. *Journal of Criminal Law and Criminology 77*, 69–100.

Sinko, D. (2015). The Use of "Use": Legislative Intent, Plain Meaning, & Corpus Linguistics. Published online and available at http://dx.doi.org/10.2139/ssrn.2560305 (SSRN).

Skyrms, B. (2010). *Signals: Evolution, Learning and Information*. Oxford: Oxford University Press.

Slocum, B. G. (2010). The Importance of Being Ambiguous: Substantive Canons, Stare Decisis and the Central Role of Ambiguity Determinations in the Administrative State. *Maryland Law Review 69*, 791–848.

Slocum, B. G. (2016). Conversational Implicatures and Legal Texts. *Ratio Juris 29*(1), 23–43.

Smith, D. (2010). Theoretical Disagreement and the Semantic Sting. *Oxford Journal of Legal Studies 30*(4), 635–661.

Soames, S. (2008a). Interpreting Legal Texts: What Is, and What Is Not, Special about the Law. In S. Soames (Ed.), *Philosophical Essays, Volume 1*, pp. 403–424. Princeton, NJ: Princeton University Press.

Soames, S. (2008b). *Philosophical Essays, Volume 1: Natural Language: What It Means and How We Use It*. Princeton, NJ: Princeton University Press.

Soames, S. (2010). *Philosophy of Language*. Princeton, NJ: Princeton University Press.

Soames, S. (2011). What Vagueness and Inconsistency Tell Us about Interpretation. In A. Marmor and S. Soames (Eds.), *Philosophical Foundations of Language in the Law*, pp. 31–57. Oxford: Oxford University Press.

Soames, S. (2012). Vagueness in the Law. In A. Marmor (Ed.), *The Routledge Companion to Philosophy of Law*, pp. 95–108. New York: Routledge.

Solan, L. M. (1993). *The Language of Judges*. Chicago: University of Chicago Press.

Solan, L. M. (1995). Judicial Decisions and Linguistic Analysis: Is There a Linguist in the Court? *Washington University Law Quarterly 73*, 1069–1080.

Solan, L. M. (1998). Law, Language, and Lenity. *William and Mary Law Review 40*(1), 57–144.

Solan, L. M. (2001). Why Laws Work Pretty Well, but Not Great: Words and Rules in Legal Interpretation. *Law & Social Inquiry 26*(1), 243–270.

Solan, L. M. (2004). Pernicious Ambiguity in Contracts and Statutes. *Chicago-Kent Law Review 79*, 859–888.

Solan, L. M. (2005). Vagueness and Ambiguity in Legal Interpretation. In V. K. Bhatia, J. Engberg, M. Gotti, and D. Heller (Eds.), *Vagueness in Normative Texts*, Volume 23: *Linguistic Insights*, pp. 73–96. Bern: Lang.

Solan, L. M. (2010). *The Language of Statutes: Laws and Their Interpretation*. Chicago: University of Chicago Press.

Solum, L. B. (1987). On the Indeterminacy Crisis: Critiquing Critical Dogma. *University of Chicago Law Review 54*, 462–503.

Solum, L. B. (2006). The Supreme Court in Bondage: Constitutional Stare Decisis, Legal Formalism, and the Future of Unenumerated Rights. *University of Pennsylvania Journal of Constitutional Law 9*, 155–208.

Solum, L. B. (2010a). Indeterminacy. In D. M. Patterson (Ed.), *A Companion to Philosophy of Law and Legal Theory*, Volume 8: *Blackwell Companions to Philosophy*, pp. 479–492. Malden, MA: Wiley-Blackwell.

Solum, L. B. (2010b). The Interpretation-Construction Distinction. *Constitutional Commentary 27*(95), 95–118.

Solum, L. B. (2013). Communicative Content and Legal Content. *Notre Dame Law Review 89*, 479–520.

Sorensen, R. A. (2001). Vagueness Has No Function in Law. *Legal Theory 7*(4), 387–417.

Sorensen, R. A. (2004). *Vagueness and Contradiction*. Oxford: Clarendon Press.

Spence, A. M. (1973). Job Market Signaling. *Quarterly Journal of Economics 87*(3), 355–374.

Spence, D. B. and F. Cross (2000). A Public Choice Case for the Administrative State. *Georgetown Law Journal 89*, 97–142.

Sperber, D. (2010). The Guru Effect. *Review of Philosophy and Psychology 1*(4), 583–592.

Sperber, D. and D. Wilson (2001). *Relevance: Communication and Cognition* (2nd ed.). Oxford: Blackwell.

Spier, K. E. (1992). Incomplete Contracts and Signalling. *The RAND Journal of Economics 23*(3), 432–443.

Stainton, R. J. (2006). *Words and Thoughts*. Oxford: Oxford University Press.

Stalnaker, R. C. (1970). Pragmatics. *Synthese 22*(1/2), 272–289.

Stalnaker, R. C. (2006). Saying and Meaning, Cheap Talk and Credibility. In A. Benz, G. Jäger, and R. van Rooij (Eds.), *Game Theory and Pragmatics*, pp. 83–100. Basingstoke: Palgrave Macmillan.

Stanley, J. and Z. G. Szabó (2000). On Quantifier Domain Restriction. *Mind and Language 15*, 219–261.

Starr, K. W. (2004). *Starr Report: Narrative*. Washington, DC: US Government Printing Office.

Staton, J. K. (2006). Constitutional Review and the Selective Promotion of Case Results. *American Journal of Political Science 50*(1), 98–112.

Staton, J. K. and G. Vanberg (2008). The Value of Vagueness: Delegation, Defiance, and Judicial Opinions. *American Journal of Political Science 52*(3), 504–519.

Stenström, A.-B., G. Andersen, and I. K. Hasund (2002). *Trends in Teenage Talk: Corpus Compilation, Analysis, and Findings*, Volume 8: *Studies in Corpus Linguistics*. Philadelphia: John Benjamins Publishing Company.

Stiglitz, J. E. and A. Weiss (1990). Sorting out the Differences Between Screening and Signalling Models. In M. O. L. Dempster, M. A. H. Bacharach, and J. L. Enos (Eds.), *Mathematical Models in Economics*, pp. 1–34. Oxford: Oxford University Press.

Stoljar, N. (2001). Vagueness, Counterfactual Intentions, and Legal Interpretation. *Legal Theory 7*(4), 447–465.

Strawson, P. F. (1964). Intention and Convention in Speech Acts. *The Philosophical Review 73*, 439–460.

Stumpff, A. M. (2013). The Law is a Fractal: The Attempt to Anticipate Everything. *Loyola University Chicago Law Journal 44*, 649–681.

Sunstein, C. R. (1995). Incompletely Theorized Agreements. *Harvard Law Review 108*, 1733–1772.

Sunstein, C. R. (1996). Foreword: Leaving Things Undecided. *Harvard Law Review 110*(1), 4–101.

Sunstein, C. R. (2014). The Supreme Court Will Always Split 5-4. Available at https://www.bloomberg.com/view/articles/2014-06-16/the-supreme-court-will-always-split-5-4.

Swinburne, R. G. (1969). Vagueness, Inexactness, and Imprecision. *The British Journal for the Philosophy of Science 19*(4), 281–299.

Tappenden, J. (1994). Some Remarks on Vagueness and a Dynamic Conception of Language. *The Southern Journal of Philosophy 33*, 193–201.

Teubner, G. (1995). Zur Argumentation im Recht: Entscheidungsfolgen als Rechtsgründe? In G. Teubner (Ed.), *Entscheidungsfolgen als Rechtsgründe*, pp. 89–120. Baden-Baden: Nomos.

Tezner, F. (1892). Über das freie Ermessen der Verwaltungsbehörden als Grund der Unzuständigkeit der Verwaltungsgerichte. *GrünhutsZ 19*, S. 327ff.

Thomale, C. (2013). Sprache und Recht. *Archiv für Rechts- und Sozialphilosophie 99*(3), 420–432.

Thorelli, H. B. (1954). *The Federalist Antitrust Policy: Organization of an American Tradition.* Baltimore: Johns Hopkins Press.

Tiersma, P. M. (1986). The Language of Offer and Acceptance: Speech Acts and the Question of Intent. *California Law Review 74*, 189–232.

Tiersma, P. M. (1999). *Legal Language.* Chicago: University of Chicago Press.

Tiersma, P. M. (2004). Did Clinton Lie? *Chicago-Kent Law Review 79*, 927–958.

Tiersma, P. M. (2015). Some Myths about Legal Language. In Lawrence Solan, Janet Ainsworth, Roger W. Shuy, and Peter M. Tiersma (Eds.), *Speaking of Language and Law. Conversations on the Work of Peter Tiersma*, Oxford Studies in Language and Law, 27–34. Oxford: Oxford University Press.

Tiffany, H. T. (1900). Interpretation and Contruction. In D. S. Garland and L. P. McGehee (Eds.), *The American and English Encyclopedia of Law*, Volume 17, pp. 1–26. Northport, NY: Edward Thompson Company.

Tirole, J. (1999). Incomplete Contracts: Where Do We Stand? *Econometrica 67*(4), 741–781.

Tirole, J. (2009). Cognition and Incomplete Contracts. *American Economic Review 99*(1), 265–294.

Triantis, G. G. (2001). The Efficency of Vague Contract Terms: A Response to the Schwartz-Scott Theory of U.C.C. Article 2. *Louisiana Law Review 62*, 1065–1079.

Trosborg, A. (1995). Statutes and Contracts: An Analysis of Legal Speech Acts in the English Language of the Law. *Journal of Pragmatics 23*(1), 31–53.

Tuggy, D. (1993). Ambiguity, Polysemy, and Vagueness. *Cognitive Linguistics 4*(3), 273–290.

Tushnet, M. V. (1993). Defending the Indeterminacy Thesis. *University of Pennsylvania Law Review 142*, 339–356.

Tversky, A. and D. J. Koehler (1994). Support Theory: A Nonextensional Representation of Subjective Probability. *Psychological Review 101*(4), 547–567.

Tye, M. (1997). Sorites Paradoxes and the Semantics of Vagueness. In R. Keefe and P. Smith (Eds.), *Vagueness*, pp. 281–293. Cambridge, MA: MIT Press.

Ulmer, S. S. (1971). Earl Warren and the Brown Decision. *Journal of Politics 33*, 689–702.

Urbanová, L. (1999). On Vagueness in Authentic English Conversation. *Brno Studies in English 25*, 99–107.

USDA (2005). Food Standards and Labeling Policy Book. Available online: http://www.fsis.usda. gov/OPPDE/larc/Policies/Labeling_Policy_Book_082005.pdf.

Vanberg, G. (2005). *The Politics of Constitutional Review in Germany.* Cambridge, UK: Cambridge University Press.

Väyrynen, P. (2013). Thick Concepts and Underdetermination. In S. Kirchin (Ed.), *Thick Concepts*, pp. 136–160. Oxford: Oxford University Press.

Veltman, F. (2002). Het Verschil tussen "Vaag" en "Niet Precies" (The Difference between "Vague" and "Not Precise"). Speech at the University of Amsterdam. Amsterdam: Vossiuspers.

Venzke, I. (2012). *How Interpretation Makes International Law*. On Semantic Change and Normative Twists. Oxford: Oxford University Press.

Vermeule, A. (2000). Interpretive Choice. *New York University Law Review 74*(1), 74–149.

Vermeule, A. (2006). The Delegation Lottery: Replying to Matthew C. Stephenson. *Harvard Law Review Forum 119*, 105–111.

Vesting, T. (2007). *Rechtstheorie*. München: Beck.

Volokh, E. (2003). Mechanisms of the Slippery Slope. *Harvard Law Review 116*(4), 1026–1137.

Waismann, F. (1945). Open Texture. *Proceedings of the Aristotelian Society, Supplementary Volumes 19*, 119–150.

Waismann, F. (1965). *The Principles of Linguistic Philosophy*. London: Macmillan und St. Martin's Press.

Waismann, F. (1978). Language Strata. In A. Flew (Ed.), *Logic and Language*, First Series. Oxford: Basil Blackwell.

Waldron, J. (1994). Vagueness in Law and Language: Some Philosophical Issues. *California Law Review 82*(3), 509–540.

Waldron, J. (1999). *Law and Disagreement*. Oxford: Clarendon Press.

Waldron, J. (2002). Is the Rule of Law an Essentially Contested Concept (in Florida)? *Law and Philosophy 21*(2), 137–164.

Waldron, J. (2011). Vagueness and the Guidance of Action. In A. Marmor and S. Soames (Eds.), *Philosophical Foundations of Language in the Law*, pp. 58–82. Oxford: Oxford University Press.

Walton, D. N. (1992). *Slippery Slope Arguments*. Oxford: Clarendon Press.

Walton, D. N. (1996). *Fallacies Arising from Ambiguity*, Volume 1: *Applied Logic Series*. Dordrecht: Kluwer Academic.

Wambach, E. (1894). *The Study of Cases: A Course of Instruction in Reading and Stating Reported Cases, Composing Head-Notes and Briefs, Criticising and Comparing Authorities, and Compiling Digests*. Boston: Little, Brown & Co.

Wank, R. (2011). *Die Auslegung von Gesetzen* (5th ed.). München: Vahlen.

Weber, M. (1967). *Rechtssoziologie* (2nd ed.). Darmstadt and Neuwied: Luchterhand.

Williams, B. (1985). *Ethics and the Limits of Philosophy*. Cambridge: Harvard University Press.

Williams, B. (2002). *Truth and Truthfulness: An Essay in Genealogy*. Princeton, NJ: Princeton University Press.

Williamson, O. E. (1979). Transaction-Cost Economics: The Governance of Contractual Relations. *The Journal of Law and Economics 22*, 233–262.

Williamson, T. (1994). *Vagueness*. London: Routledge.

Williamson, T. (1999). On the Structure of Higher-Order Vagueness. *Mind 108*(429), 127–143.

Williamson, T. (2001). Vagueness, Indeterminacy and Social Meaning. In C. B. Grant and D. McLaughlin (Eds.), *Critical Studies*, pp. 61–76. Amsterdam, New York: Rodopi.

Wittgenstein, L. (2009/1953). *Philosophical Investigations* (4th ed.). Chichester: Wiley-Blackwell.

Wright, C. (1997). Language-Mastery and the Sorites Paradox. In R. Keefe and P. Smith (Eds.), *Vagueness*, pp. 151–173. Cambridge, MA: MIT Press.

Wright, C. (2010). The Illusion of Higher-Order Vagueness. In R. Dietz and S. Moruzzi (Eds.), *Cuts and Clouds*. Oxford: Oxford University Press.

Wydick, R. C. (2005). *Plain English for Lawyers*. Durham, NC: Carolina Academic Press.

Zhao, X. (2011). Framing Contingencies in Contracts. *Mathematical Social Sciences 61*, 31–40.

Zipf, G. K. (1949). *Human Behavior and the Principle of Least Effort: An Introduction to Human Ecology*. Cambridge, MA: Addison-Wesley Press.

Zippelius, R. (2006). *Juristische Methodenlehre* (10th ed.). München: Beck.

Zwicky, A. M. and J. M. Sadock (1975). Ambiguity Tests and How to Fail Them. In J. P. Kimball (Ed.), *Syntax and Semantics*, Volume 4, pp. 1–36. New York: Academic Press.

INDEX